# PERSPECTIVISM IN SOCIAL PSYCHOLOGY

# PERSPECTIVISM IN SOCIAL PSYCHOLOGY

## THE YIN AND YANG
### OF SCIENTIFIC PROGRESS

**EDITED BY**

**JOHN T. JOST,**

**MAHZARIN R. BANAJI,**

**AND DEBORAH A. PRENTICE**

DECADE
*of* BEHAVIOR

AMERICAN PSYCHOLOGICAL ASSOCIATION
WASHINGTON, DC

Copyright © 2004 by the American Psychological Association. All rights reserved. Except as permitted under the United States Copyright Act of 1976, no part of this publication may be reproduced or distributed in any form or by any means, or stored in a database or retrieval system, without the prior written permission of the publisher.

Published by
American Psychological Association
750 First Street, NE
Washington, DC 20002
www.apa.org

To order
APA Order Department
P.O. Box 92984
Washington, DC 20090-2984

Tel: (800) 374-2721, Direct: (202) 336-5510
Fax: (202) 336-5502, TDD/TTY: (202) 336-6123
Online: www.apa.org/books/
E-mail: order@apa.org

In the U.K., Europe, Africa, and the Middle East, copies may be ordered from
American Psychological Association
3 Henrietta Street
Covent Garden, London
WC2E 8LU England

Typeset in Century Schoolbook by NOVA Graphic Services, Jamison, PA

Printer: Book-Mart Press, North Bergen, NJ

Cover Designer: Anne Masters, Washington, DC
Project Manager: NOVA Graphic Services, Jamison, PA

The opinions and statements published are the responsibility of the authors, and such opinions and statements do not necessarily represent the policies of the American Psychological Association.

**Library of Congress Cataloging-in-Publication Data**
Perspectivism in social psychology : the yin and yang of scientific
progress / edited by John T. Jost, Mahzarin R. Banaji, and Deborah A. Prentice.
    p. cm.— (APA science series. APA decade of behavior series)
Proceedings of a festschrift conference held in Apr. 2001 at Yale University in honor of William J. McGuire.
Includes bibliographical references and index.
  ISBN 1-59147-022-6
  1. Social perception. 2. Social psychology. I. Jost, John T. II. Banaji, Mahzarin R. III. Prentice, Deborah A. IV. McGuire, William James, 1925- V. Title. VI. Series.
  HM1041.P465 2004
  302—dc22

2003020888

**British Library Cataloguing-in-Publication Data**
A CIP record is available from the British Library.

*Printed in the United States of America*
*First Edition*

We dedicate this book to Claire V. McGuire.

## APA Science Volumes

*Attribution and Social Interaction: The Legacy of Edward E. Jones*
*Best Methods for the Analysis of Change: Recent Advances, Unanswered Questions, Future Directions*
*Cardiovascular Reactivity to Psychological Stress and Disease*
*The Challenge in Mathematics and Science Education: Psychology's Response*
*Changing Employment Relations: Behavioral and Social Perspectives*
*Children Exposed to Marital Violence: Theory, Research, and Applied Issues*
*Cognition: Conceptual and Methodological Issues*
*Cognitive Bases of Musical Communication*
*Cognitive Dissonance: Progress on a Pivotal Theory in Social Psychology*
*Conceptualization and Measurement of Organism–Environment Interaction*
*Converging Operations in the Study of Visual Selective Attention*
*Creative Thought: An Investigation of Conceptual Structures and Processes*
*Developmental Psychoacoustics*
*Diversity in Work Teams: Research Paradigms for a Changing Workplace*
*Emotion and Culture: Empirical Studies of Mutual Influence*
*Emotion, Disclosure, and Health*
*Evolving Explanations of Development: Ecological Approaches to Organism–Environment Systems*
*Examining Lives in Context: Perspectives on the Ecology of Human Development*
*Global Prospects for Education: Development, Culture, and Schooling*
*Hostility, Coping, and Health*
*Measuring Patient Changes in Mood, Anxiety, and Personality Disorders: Toward a Core Battery*
*Occasion Setting: Associative Learning and Cognition in Animals*
*Organ Donation and Transplantation: Psychological and Behavioral Factors*
*Origins and Development of Schizophrenia: Advances in Experimental Psychopathology*
*The Perception of Structure*
*Perspectives on Socially Shared Cognition*
*Psychological Testing of Hispanics*
*Psychology of Women's Health: Progress and Challenges in Research and Application*
*Researching Community Psychology: Issues of Theory and Methods*
*The Rising Curve: Long-Term Gains in IQ and Related Measures*
*Sexism and Stereotypes in Modern Society: The Gender Science of Janet Taylor Spence*
*Sleep and Cognition*
*Sleep Onset: Normal and Abnormal Processes*
*Stereotype Accuracy: Toward Appreciating Group Differences*

## APA Decade of Behavior Volumes

# Contents

# Contributors

**Norman H. Anderson,** Department of Psychology, University of California, San Diego, La Jolla, CA

**Mahzarin R. Banaji,** Department of Psychology, Harvard University, Cambridge, MA

**John T. Cacioppo,** Department of Psychology, University of Chicago, Chicago, IL

**Amanda B. Diekman,** Department of Psychology, Miami University, Oxford, OH

**Willem Doise,** Department of Psychology, Université de Genève, Geneva, Switzerland

**Alice H. Eagly,** Department of Psychology, Northwestern University, Evanston, IL

**Phoebe C. Ellsworth,** Department of Psychology, University of Michigan, Ann Arbor

**Anthony G. Greenwald,** Department of Psychology, University of Washington, Seattle

**Curtis D. Hardin,** Department of Psychology, University of California, Los Angeles

**Reid Hastie,** Center for Decision Research, Graduate School of Business, University of Chicago, Chicago, IL

**E. Tory Higgins,** Department of Psychology, Columbia University, New York

**György Hunyady,** Department of Social and Educational Psychology, Eötvös Lorand University, Budapest, Hungary

**Shanto Iyengar,** Department of Communication, Stanford University, Stanford, CA

**John T. Jost,** Department of Psychology, New York University, New York

**Shulamith Kreitler,** Department of Psychology, Tel Aviv University, Tel Aviv, Israel

**William J. McGuire,** Department of Psychology, Yale University, New Haven, CT

**Richard E. Petty,** Department of Psychology, Ohio State University, Columbus

**Deborah A. Prentice,** Department of Psychology, Princeton University, Princeton, NJ

**Katherine A. Rawson,** Department of Psychology, University of Colorado, Boulder

**Derek D. Rucker,** Department of Psychology, Ohio State University, Columbus

**David O. Sears,** Department of Psychology, University of California, Los Angeles

**Gün R. Semin,** Department of Social Psychology, Free University of Amsterdam, Amsterdam, The Netherlands

**Zakary L. Tormala,** Department of Psychology, Indiana University, Bloomington

**Robert S. Wyer, Jr.,** Department of Marketing, Hong Kong University of Science and Technology, Kowloon, Hong Kong, China

*Front row (kneeling, sitting, left to right)*: Deborah Prentice, Anne McGuire, Claire McGuire, William McGuire, James McGuire, and John Jost. *Middle row (standing, left to right):* E. Tory Higgins, Mahzarin Banaji, Shulamith Kreitler, Anthony Greenwald, John Cacioppo, Norman Anderson, and Phoebe Ellsworth. *Back row (left to right):* David Sears, Richard Petty, Willem Doise, Shanto Iyengar, Gun Semin, Robert Wyer, Alice Eagly, and Curtis Hardin. *Not shown:* Reid Hastie and György Hunyady.

# Foreword

In early 1988, the American Psychological Association (APA) Science Directorate began its sponsorship of what would become an exceptionally successful activity in support of psychological science—the APA Scientific Conferences program. This program has showcased some of the most important topics in psychological science and has provided a forum for collaboration among many leading figures in the field.

The program has inspired a series of books that have presented cutting-edge work in all areas of psychology. At the turn of the millennium, the series was renamed the Decade of Behavior Series to help advance the goals of this important initiative. The Decade of Behavior is a major interdisciplinary campaign designed to promote the contributions of the behavioral and social sciences to our most important societal challenges in the decade leading up to 2010. Although a key goal has been to inform the public about these scientific contributions, other activities have been designed to encourage and further collaboration among scientists. Hence, the series that was the "APA Science Series" has continued as the "Decade of Behavior Series." This represents one element in APA's efforts to promote the Decade of Behavior initiative as one of its endorsing organizations. For additional information about the Decade of Behavior, please visit http://www.decadeofbehavior.org.

Over the course of the past years, the Science Conference and Decade of Behavior Series has allowed psychological scientists to share and explore cutting-edge findings in psychology. The APA Science Directorate looks forward to continuing this successful program and to sponsoring other conferences and books in the years ahead. This series has been so successful that we have chosen to extend it to include books that, although they do not arise from conferences, report with the same high quality of scholarship on the latest research.

We are pleased that this important contribution to the literature was supported in part by the Decade of Behavior program. Congratulations to the editors and contributors of this volume on their sterling effort.

Kurt Salzinger, PhD
*Executive Director for Science*

Virginia E. Holt
*Assistant Executive Director for Science*

# Acknowledgments

This book grew out of a Festschrift conference held at Yale University April 19–22, 2001, in honor of William J. McGuire. Because neither conferences nor books happen by themselves, there are several parties that deserve special thanks for contributing to the success of the conference and to the publication of this volume.

Our first and strongest debt is to Bill and Claire McGuire, who have long inspired us personally and professionally in immeasurable ways. The fact that so many of the world's most talented social psychologists eagerly made the trip to New Haven and submitted rich, thoughtful chapters to this book testifies to the magnitude of the McGuires' influence. We are grateful to Jim, Steve, and Anne McGuire for being with us at the conference and for their invaluable contributions to the proceedings.

This project was made possible only because of scientific and financial commitments made by the American Psychological Association (APA). Funding came from the APA Science Directorate, for which we are extremely grateful. We would especially like to acknowledge the help and support of Sangeeta Panicker.

A number of people at Yale University worked especially hard to coordinate onsite conference activities. Brian Nosek was instrumental in posting the conference Web site and organizing the cooperative efforts of many Yale graduate students, including Wil Cunningham, Tony Freitas, Nicole Gleason, Kristen Lane, David Pizarro, Susan Rivers, Bethany Teachman, Eric Uhlmann, and Sarah Wert. We thank the chair of the Department of Psychology, Peter Salovey, as well as Judy Falcigno, Ann Guarino, and Amanda Parsons.

We are also grateful to the Graduate School of Business at Stanford University, the Department of Psychology at Princeton University, and the Radcliffe Institute for Advanced Study at Harvard University for their support of this work at various stages. The development editor for APA Books, Phuong Huynh, was extremely diligent in preparing the manuscript for publication. Her work (and the work of two anonymous reviewers) improved the quality and coherence of this book.

Finally, we thank the many attendees of the conference and the readers of this volume who will continue the difficult, rewarding work of perspectivism in social psychology.

William J. McGuire

# *Part I*

## Introductory Material

# 1

# Perspectivist Social Psychology: A Work in Progress

*John T. Jost, Mahzarin R. Banaji, and Deborah A. Prentice*

This book presents an edited collection of new essays inspired by William J. McGuire's work on perspectivist social psychology on the occasion of his retirement from Yale University. The essays contained herein address the past, present, and especially the future of theory and research on social psychology. The authors are friends, colleagues, students, and admirers of Bill McGuire, and all have undertaken to illustrate the benefits of applying perspectivist social psychological methods to their own problem areas.

Drawing our subtitle from McGuire's classic (1973) article, the focus of this book is on *Perspectivism in Social Psychology: The Yin and Yang of Scientific Progress*. McGuire, who is justly regarded as one of the pioneers of cognitively oriented social psychology, has contributed enormously to unifying the scientific study of social cognition. His dynamic theory of thought systems, for instance, integrates areas of attitude change, language, social cognition, stereotyping, ideology, and political psychology (see McGuire, 1999). His perspectivist metatheory, which provides dozens of heuristics and guiding principles for the creative generation and rigorous assessment of hypotheses, is similarly applicable to social cognition and all of its subfields (see McGuire, 1997). The "working premise" of the perspectivist is that "all knowledge representations are imperfect but all catch some aspect of the known" (McGuire, 1999, p. 400). If one accepts that all knowledge—including scientific knowledge—is contextualized or situated, that is, it is knowledge *from some perspective*, then the task of the researcher is to creatively generate and critically assess multiple hypotheses, each of which presumably has some domain of truthful application. What results is an expansive search for the enabling and boundary conditions of as many worthwhile hypotheses as possible. The unifying theme of the book, accordingly, is that of a perspectivist approach to the study of thought systems, which reflects McGuire's practical, systematic approach to social cognition broadly defined.

It is a rare psychology book that gives equal billing to theory, methodology, and empirical data, but McGuire's work has consistently balanced these scientific ideals, and all of the contributors to this volume subscribe to these same ideals. Because it is such a significant (and McGuirean) challenge to cover the past, present, and future of any social psychological theme in a single chapter, we invited a select group of top social psychological researchers from around the world. They were asked to write theoretical and empirical chapters that will serve as important orienting stimuli for future research in the interrelated subfields of social cognition. They were also asked to provide personal reflections on their own ways of doing social psychology. These reflections serve as prologues for each chapter that follows the introductory section of the book. The author prologues are, in many ways, the most fitting tribute to McGuire, who has written extensively on conceptual, methodological, and practical issues in the conduct of psychological research.

The book is organized according to the following topical themes, which reflect substantive research programs initiated by McGuire and further advanced by the accomplished researchers who have contributed chapters:

1.  Attitudes, persuasion, and social influence
2.  Information processing, affect, and behavior
3.  Language and the self-concept
4.  Stereotyping, prejudice, and intergroup relations in society
5.  Political communication and mass media
6.  Theory and metatheory in social psychological science

The timeliness and uniqueness of this project derive from the fact that, at a time when social cognition research is becoming ever more specialized and geographically dispersed, this book (a) brings together psychologists from Europe, Israel, and North America; (b) balances and integrates issues of theory, method, and data; (c) highlights commonalities and shared assumptions of relatively diverse subfields of social cognition; and (d) points the way toward a future agenda for research. The volume should be particularly valuable for graduate students and young scholars, because it is planned at a time when historical perspective, theory–method integration, and the "big picture" are in danger of losing out to professional specialization, concentration, and pressures for publication.

The primary audience for this work consists of psychologists and those in related fields (cognitive science, sociology, political science, communications, marketing, and organizational behavior) who share interests in social cognition and the dynamic operation of thought systems. The chapters include topics of interest for anyone who relishes theoretical and methodological innovations in social cognition. Because the contributors are commenting on the past, present, and future of social cognition, the essays will be of great interest to contemporary colleagues and friends of Bill McGuire as well as to graduate students and young scholars.

## Attitudes, Persuasion, and Social Influence

McGuire's work has probably had its most profound impact in the study of persuasion and attitude change, including his groundbreaking empirical work on cognitive responses, belief systems, and resistance to persuasion (McGuire, 1964) and the remarkably ambitious, integrative handbook chapters that served to reorient the study of attitude change around concepts of input and output steps and their mediating cognitive processes (McGuire, 1968, 1985). The influence of this work on subsequent social psychological treatments can scarcely be exaggerated (e.g., Cialdini, Petty, & Cacioppo, 1981; Eagly & Chaiken, 1993; Petty & Cacioppo, 1986; Petty, Ostrom, & Brock, 1981; Pratkanis, Breckler, & Greenwald, 1989). Thus, our first substantive section addresses theoretical and empirical progress that has been made in understanding attitude change, persuasion, and social influence.

Petty, Tormala, and Rucker explore the utility of McGuire's contextualist (later referred to as perspectivist) framework for understanding the literature on attitude change, especially the topic of resistance to persuasion, in chapter 4. In chapter 5, Hastie and Rawson address an issue that is central to McGuire and McGuire's (1991) dynamic theory of thought systems, namely, the remote ramifications of belief change in thought systems. Original empirical studies, inspired by the McGuires' theory, are reported to illustrate some of the statics and dynamics of these thought systems. In chapter 6, Prentice applies McGuire's theorizing about attitude systems to the study of values and their relations to other aspects of the person. She reviews two lines of research, one that examines the relation of values to choices and evaluations of well-being and a second that examines their relation to material possessions and sociopolitical attitudes.

## Information Processing, Affect, and Behavior

McGuire has been referred to as the "father of social cognition" (Wyer, 1991, p. vii), so it is fitting that our second section addresses issues of information processing, especially insofar as cognition (or information processing) relates to the other two components of attitudes, namely affect (or evaluation) and behavior (e.g., Breckler, 1984; McGuire, 1985). McGuire's studies of information processing began with his "probabilogical model" and its accompanying "syllogistic analysis" of relations among beliefs (McGuire, 1960); his contributions were fruitfully advanced by, among others, Anderson (1971) and Wyer (1970, 1972, 1975). Later research on the dynamic theory of thought systems (McGuire, 1990; McGuire & McGuire, 1991) and on positive–negative asymmetries in thinking about the self-concept (McGuire & McGuire, 1992, 1996) further strengthened our understanding of social cognition, and these themes are taken up by contributors to this volume.

The seventh chapter, by Cacioppo, addresses asymmetries in affect-laden information processing. Specifically, he reviews recent work on the autonomic differentiation of emotion, which indicates that negative emotions are associated with greater visceral activation in comparison with positive emotions. In chapter 8, Wyer integrates traditional research on belief and attitude change and recent work on social comprehension and verification processes, as well as research on communication, persuasion, and the spontaneous activation of thoughts about oneself and others in social contexts. Kreitler, in chapter 9, explores theoretical and empirical bases of the cognitive guidance of health-related behavior, identifying the major problems that have remained unresolved and spelling out directions for future research. In chapter 10, Banaji argues that oppositional thinking as prescribed by perspectivism would have enabled researchers of implicit social cognition to anticipate two surprising conclusions: (a) implicit and explicit attitudes are often dissociated from one another, but there are specifiable conditions under which clear associations are observable, and (b) implicit attitudes often appear to be relatively stable, but they can be highly malleable in response to social situations.

## Language and the Self-Concept

McGuire's contributions to social cognition led organically to interests in the use of natural language, especially the use of state versus action verbs (McGuire & McGuire, 1986), and changes in the spontaneous self-concept (McGuire & McGuire, 1988; McGuire, McGuire, & Cheever, 1986; McGuire & Padawer-Singer, 1976). These convergent research programs have influenced a number of researchers, including Greenwald and Pratkanis (1984), Hardin and Banaji (1993), Markus and Nurius (1986), Prentice (1990), and Semin and Fiedler (1989). Current perspectives on language and the self-concept (and their reciprocal influences) are offered in this volume by Semin in chapter 11 and Hardin in chapter 12.

Semin reviews different facets of the language that people use when they are describing themselves and others in varying contexts (e.g., home, school, and work). He provides a comprehensive review of the linguistic category model and argues persuasively for the diagnostic value of analyzing features of language to uncover general social psychological processes in the description of self and others. Hardin adopts a thoroughly perspectivist approach—which he interprets in the context of pragmatist philosophy of science—to the study of the self. Specifically, he argues that self-conceptions not only arise from important social relationships, but they also serve to affirm those relationships.

## Stereotyping, Prejudice, and Intergroup Relations in Society

Although McGuire's own work has seldom, if ever, focused on issues of stereotyping, prejudice, and intergroup relations, his impact can be felt in these areas as well. Research on the numerical distinctiveness of the self-concept, including effects of gender (McGuire, McGuire, & Winton, 1979) and ethnicity (McGuire, McGuire, Child, & Fujioka, 1978), has been used to understand social identification among minority groups in society (e.g., Deaux & Major, 1987; Lord & Saenz, 1985; Turner, 1987). McGuire's perspectivist methodology has generally proved useful to researchers of stereotyping and intergroup relations, and so has his approach to ideological belief systems in particular (e.g., Converse, 1964; Doise, 1986; Hunyady, 1998; Kay, Jimenez, & Jost, 2002).

In chapter 13, Doise adopts a historical perspective, linking the work of McGuire and his generation of social psychologists to the history of the last hundred years on multiple levels, including the personal, interpersonal, group, and system levels of analysis. In chapter 14, Hunyady uses McGuirean qualitative methods to explore longitudinal changes in the structure of stereotypes in European society, revealing that stereotypical categories fit mosaic-like into a comprehensive view of society. In chapter 15, Eagly builds on McGuire's (1990) dynamic theory of thought systems to argue that in the examination of prejudice, it is useful to distinguish between the perceived likelihood that group members will have particular characteristics and the perceived desirability of their having these characteristics. Jost, in chapter 16, illustrates the use of several of McGuire's (1997) perspectivist strategies in the study of intergroup relations, including accounting for deviations from the general trend, pursuing the contrary of a banal hypothesis, reconciling conflicting outcomes, considering nonmonotonic relations, and "quixotically defending a theory."

## Political Communication and Mass Media

McGuire's influence on the field of political psychology has grown more direct over the years. His work on attitude change—especially his partitioning of independent variables into source, message, channel, receiver, and target factors (see McGuire, 1968, 1985)—has had an enormous impact on the study of public opinion, political perception, leader communication, and political advertising. Although a persistent theme in McGuire's work is that television and other mass media are not as successful at influencing people as is often assumed (see McGuire, 1986), he has been as clear as anyone at delineating the circumstances under which social influence may be expected. McGuire's most direct contribution to political psychology is the (1993) volume that he edited with Iyengar entitled *Explorations in Political Psychology*.

In chapter 17, Sears reviews several decades of research on racial politics from the perspective of symbolic racism theory. He argues that, recent changes notwithstanding, the fundamental pattern in intergroup relations has been one of continuity in which Black–White conflict has been the dominant theme. Iyengar writes in chapter 18 that to an extent not previously seen, the use—and even manipulation—of the mass media to promote political objectives is now not only standard practice but is in fact essential to political survival. Consequently, as Iyengar points out, McGuire's work on communication and persuasion has become central to the study of American politics.

## Theory and Metatheory in Social Psychological Science

McGuire is unique, even in the context of his most eminent contemporaries, for having made major contributions not only to theory and research in social psychology but also to metatheory and the philosophy of social psychological science (see McGuire, 1999). In this respect, he inspires comparisons to both Kurt Lewin and Donald Campbell (see Jost & Kruglanski, 2002, concerning the latter comparison). McGuire (1983) at first referred to the complete set of epistemological tenets and methodological tactics as "contextualism," but over time he settled on the preferred term "perspectivism" (McGuire, 1989, 1999). This is a book about perspectivism, insofar as most or all of the chapters describe empirical research programs that have been approached or consolidated through perspectivist means. In the final section, the focus is even more squarely on the contributions of perspectivist metatheory.

In chapter 19, Ellsworth meditates on the first of McGuire's (1973) methodological koan, "The Sound of One Hand Clapping . . . and the Wrong Hand," arguing that since 1973, social psychology has moved away from narrow hypothesis-testing approaches. Ellsworth worries that the new, descriptive, qualitative research is often not designed in such a way that it will ever generate hypotheses and that the old hypothesis-testing mode has increasingly moved toward the strategy of confirmation rather than disconfirmation of hypotheses. In chapter 20, Greenwald argues provocatively that illusory competition among theories causes wasted effort in scientific psychology. Specifically, he claims that lengthy episodes of intertheory competition in cognitive psychology have resulted in (a) no decisive choice among competing theories and (b) little product in the form of intellectual advances or useful applications.

In chapter 21, Anderson lays out the tenets of his "unified theory," which rests on the axiom of purposiveness and is implemented through cognitive algebra. Extensive experimental work on his information integration theory demonstrates that approach–avoidance tendencies obey exact algebraic models in social psychology and in several other fields, including developmental psychology, psychophysics, and judgment and decision-making. Higgins, in chapter 22, proposes an eighth methodological koan to be added to McGuire's (1973) list of seven. Higgins' observation is that a variable anointed as "special" tends to demand special treatment; he argues that this tendency is often functional but can impede progress in social psychology by leading researchers to overlook general principles that underlie many different phenomena.

## The Future of Perspectivism

With the two exceptions of Wyer and Srull's (1991) volume in the *Advances in Social Cognition* series and McGuire's own (1999) collection of papers entitled *Constructing Social Psychology: Creative and Critical Processes*, there has been no previous comprehensive, book-length treatment of perspectivism and its application to core topics in social psychology. Our hope is that this book will help to inspire others to follow perspectivist methods in social science. McGuire's own views have been summarized extremely well in his (1989) chapter, his (1997) *Annual Review of Psychology* chapter, and his (1999) volume of collected essays. In the appendix of this book, we have reproduced a set of McGuire's famous "perspectivist worksheets," which should be useful for students (at any level) who are seeking to inject their own research programs with the kind of creativity and precision that has characterized 40 years of work by William J. McGuire and the scores of collaborators, students, and scientists who have been heavily influenced by him. The remaining chapters in this book, written by some of the most illustrious social psychologists still working, should provide proof enough of the promise of perspectivism. It is the job of future generations to fulfill that promise and to push our science forward in our own individual ways, as McGuire (1999) invites us to do, with "glances at paths made by travelers who have gone before" (p. 432).

# References

Anderson, N. H. (1971). Integration theory and attitude change. *Psychological Review, 78*, 171–206.

Breckler, S. J. (1984). Empirical validation of affect, behavior, and cognition as distinct components of attitude. *Journal of Personality and Social Psychology, 47*, 1191–1205.

Cialdini, R. B., Petty, R. E., & Cacioppo, J. T. (1981). Attitude and attitude change. *Annual Review of Psychology, 32*, 357–404.

Converse, P. (1964). The nature of belief systems in mass publics. In D. E. Apter (Ed.), *Ideology and discontent* (pp. 206–261). London: Collier-MacMillan.

Deaux, K., & Major, B. (1987). Putting gender into context: An interactive model of gender-related behavior. *Psychological Review, 94*, 369–389.

Doise, W. (1986). *Levels of explanation in social psychology*. Cambridge: Cambridge University Press.

Eagly, A. H., & Chaiken, S. (1993). *The psychology of attitudes*. Philadelphia: Harcourt, Brace, Jovanovich.

Greenwald, A. G., & Pratkanis, A. R. (1984). The self. In R. S. Wyer, Jr. & T. K. Srull (Eds.), *Handbook of social cognition* (Vol. 3, pp. 3–26). Hillsdale, NJ: Erlbaum.

Hardin, C., & Banaji, M. R. (1993). The influence of language on thought. *Social Cognition, 11*, 277–308.

Hunyady, Gy. (1998). *Stereotypes during the decline and fall of Communism*. New York: Routledge.

Iyengar, S., & McGuire, W. J. (Eds.) (1993). *Explorations in political psychology*. Durham, NC: Duke University Press.

Jost, J. T., & Kruglanski, A. W. (2002). The estrangement of social constructionism and experimental social psychology: History of the rift and prospects for reconciliation. *Personality and Social Psychology Review, 6*, 168–187.

Kay, A. C., Jimenez, M. C., & Jost, J. T. (2002). Sour grapes, sweet lemons, and the anticipatory rationalization of the status quo. *Personality and Social Psychology Bulletin, 28*, 1300–1312.

Lord, C. G., & Saenz, D. S. (1985). Memory deficits and memory surfeits: Differential cognitive consequences of tokenism for tokens and observers. *Journal of Personality and Social Psychology, 49*, 918–926.

Markus, H. R., & Nurius, P. (1986). Possible selves. *American Psychologist, 41*, 954–969.

McGuire, W. J. (1960). A syllogistic analysis of cognitive relationships. In M. J. Rosenberg & C. I. Hovland (Eds.), *Attitude organization and change* (pp. 140–162). New Haven: Yale University Press.

McGuire, W. J. (1964). Inducing resistance to persuasion. In L. Berkowitz (Ed.), *Advances in experimental social psychology* (Vol. 1, pp. 191–229). New York: Academic Press.

McGuire, W. J. (1968). Personality and susceptibility to social influence. In E. F. Borgatta & W. W. Lambert (Eds.), *Handbook of personality theory and research* (pp. 1130–1187). Chicago: Rand McNally.

McGuire, W. J. (1973). The yin and yang of progress in social psychology: Seven koan. *Journal of Personality and Social Psychology, 26*, 446–456.

McGuire, W. J. (1983). A contextualist theory of knowledge: Its implications for innovation and reform in psychological research. *Advances in Experimental Social Psychology, 16*, 1–47.

McGuire, W. J. (1985). The nature of attitudes and attitude change. In G. Lindzey & E. Aronson (Eds.), *Handbook of social psychology* (3rd ed., Vol. 2, pp. 233–346). New York: Random House.

McGuire, W. J. (1986). The myth of massive media impact: Savagings and salvagings. In G. Comstock (Ed.), *Public communication and behavior, Vol. 1* (pp.173–257). New York: Academic Press.

McGuire, W. J. (1989). A perspectivist approach to the strategic planning of programmatic scientific research. In B. Gholson, W. R. Shadish, Jr., R. A. Niemeyer, & A. C. Houts (Eds.), *The psychology of science: Contributions to metascience* (pp. 214–245). New York: Cambridge University Press.

McGuire, W. J. (1990). Dynamic operations of thought systems. *American Psychologist, 45*, 504–512.

McGuire, W. J. (1997). Creative hypothesis generating in psychology: Some useful heuristics. *Annual Review of Psychology, 48,* 1–30. Palo Alto, CA: Annual Reviews.

McGuire, W. J. (1999). *Constructing social psychology: Creative and critical processes.* Cambridge: Cambridge University Press.

McGuire, W. J., & McGuire, C. V. (1986). Differences in conceptualizing self versus conceptualizing other people as manifested in contrasting verb types in natural speech. *Journal of Personality and Social Psychology, 51,* 1135–1143.

McGuire, W. J., & McGuire, C. V. (1988). Content and process in the experience of self. *Advances in Experimental Social Psychology, 21,* 97–144.

McGuire, W. J., & McGuire, C. V. (1991). The content, structure and operation of thought systems. In R. S. Wyer & T. K. Srull (Eds.), *Advances in social cognition* (Vol. 4, pp. 1–78). Hillsdale, NJ: Erlbaum.

McGuire, W. J., & McGuire, C. V. (1992). Cognitive-versus-affective positivity asymmetries in thought systems. *European Journal of Social Psychology, 22,* 571–591.

McGuire, W. J., & McGuire, C. V. (1996). Enhancing self-esteem by directed-thinking tasks: Cognitive and affective positivity asymmetries. *Journal of Personality and Social Psychology, 70,* 1117–1124.

McGuire, W. J., McGuire, C. V., & Cheever, J. (1986). The self and society: Effects of social contexts on the sense of self. *British Journal of Social Psychology, 25,* 259–270.

McGuire, W. J., McGuire, C. V., Child, P., & Fujioka, T. (1978). Salience of ethnicity in the spontaneous self-concept as a function of one's ethnic distinctiveness in the social environment. *Journal of Personality and Social Psychology, 36,* 511–520.

McGuire, W. J., McGuire, C. V., & Winton, W. (1979). Effects of household sex composition on the salience of one's gender in the spontaneous self-concept. *Journal of Experimental Social Psychology, 15,* 77–90.

McGuire, W. J. & Padawer-Singer, A. (1976). Trait salience in the spontaneous self-concept. *Journal of Personality and Social Psychology, 33,* 743–754.

Petty, R. E., & Cacioppo, J. T. (1986). *Communication and persuasion: Central and peripheral routes to attitude change.* New York: Springer-Verlag.

Petty, R. E., Ostrom, T. M., & Brock, T. C. (Eds.). (1981). *Cognitive responses in persuasion.* Hillsdale, NJ: Erlbaum.

Pratkanis, A. R., Breckler, S. J., & Greenwald, A.G. (Eds.). (1989). *Attitude structure and function.* Hillsdale, NJ: Erlbaum.

Prentice, D. A. (1990). Familiarity and differences in self- and other-representations. *Journal of Personality and Social Psychology, 59,* 369–383.

Semin, G. R., & Fiedler, K. (1989). Relocating attributional phenomena within the language-cognition interface: The case of actor-observer perspectives. *European Journal of Social Psychology, 19,* 491–508.

Turner, J. C. (1987). *Rediscovering the social group. A self-categorization theory.* Oxford, England: Blackwell.

Wyer, R. S. (1970). The quantitative prediction of belief and opinion change: A further test of a subjective probability model. *Journal of Personality and Social Psychology, 16,* 559–571.

Wyer, R. S. (1972). Test of a subjective probability model of social evaluation processes. *Journal of Personality and Social Psychology, 22,* 279–286.

Wyer, R. S. (1975). Functional measurement analysis of a subjective probability model of cognitive functioning. *Journal of Personality and Social Psychology, 31,* 94–100.

Wyer, R. S. (1991). Preface. In R. S. Wyer & T. K. Srull (Eds.), *Advances in social cognition* (Vol. 4). Hillsdale, NJ: Erlbaum.

Wyer, R. S., & Srull, T. K. (Eds.) (1991). *Advances in social cognition* (Vol. 4). Hillsdale, NJ: Erlbaum.

# 2

# The Perspectivist in Historical and Scientific Perspective: McGuire's Role in Twentieth-Century Social Psychology

*György Hunyady and John T. Jost*

It is safe to say that social psychology has never seen anyone else like William J. McGuire and probably never will again. He is notorious for being brilliant, fastidious, generous, humble, grandiose, short-tempered, iconoclastic, and hilarious, and he has set almost unattainable standards for the field in at least three ways. First, he started as one of the field's most painstaking and precise experimental pioneers in social cognition (e.g., McGuire, 1960, 1964). Later, he became one of its most ambitious and integrative historians of cumulative knowledge (e.g., McGuire, 1968a, 1985). By now, his reputation is secure as one of the most creative, witty, and erudite writers ever to ponder the social mind (e.g., McGuire, 1973, 1989, 1999). He once mused, for example, that, "the thinker I have depicted here has every right to look as puzzled as Rodin represented him. He is juggling many balls in many dimensions" (McGuire, 1968b, p. 147).

On the subject of the ethics of persuasion, McGuire wrote, adapting Churchill, that "a few aberrant young who see visions and old who dream dreams may discern that persuasion is the worst possible mode of social mobilization and conflict resolution—except for all the others" (McGuire, 1985, p. 235). At a time of great scientific and political crisis for the field of experimental social psychology, he commented, "In our father's house there are many rooms. . . . there is a place for the philosopher of mind and the social philosopher, as well as for the scientific psychologist" (1973, p. 452). He went on to defend his own professional choices in language that somehow managed to resolve rather than aggravate ideological differences:

> But the scientific psychologist can offer something beside and beyond these armchair thinkers in that we not only generate delusional systems, but we go further and test our delusional systems against objective data as well as for their subjective plausibility. (p. 452)

His writing is poignant, humorous, and unswervingly truthful.

Although the vast oeuvre that followed from McGuire's "delusional systems" has been as influential as any other in determining the course of

20th century research on attitudes, social cognition, and countless other social psychological topics, McGuire himself is fond of joking that the magnitude of his professional reputation is squared with every mile he travels away from Yale University. It is absolutely true that his impact is palpable in social psychological circles throughout England, France, Italy, Germany, Canada, Switzerland, Holland, Belgium, Hungary, Poland, Australia, Japan, Israel, and many other places. At the same time, it would be nothing more than playful naughtiness to suggest that he is unappreciated at home, as the New Haven Festschrift conference in 2001 and this resulting volume should attest once and for all. In this chapter, we seek to place the perspectivist in perspective, that is, to offer an appraisal of McGuire's thinking in relation to major historical developments in the 20th century that were occurring both inside and outside of social psychology.[1]

## Attitudes as the Unifying Theme of Social Psychology

From a McGuirean perspective, there is no social psychology without the study of attitudes. More precisely, any psychological investigation of social relations requires that one brings to light the dynamic relations among thoughts, feelings, and behavior occurring within the individual (e.g., McGuire, 1968a, 1985). The propaganda needs of World War II brought about essential changes in the study of persuasive communication and attitude change, including a shift from content to process (see McGuire, 1999). In the international context, the study of attitude change gained real urgency, and it became the dominant subfield in social psychology for decades. McGuire, of course, was a direct witness and a full-fledged participant in this epoch-making transformation.

The intellectual life of Bill McGuire thus coincided with the birth of attitude dynamics in social psychology. The stirring experiences and unique opportunities arising from World War II, it is fair to say, are what put him on an academic path. More than most other scientific psychologists, McGuire has always appreciated the role of history and context in determining individual attitudes and behaviors, and this is one reason his voice was a steady one throughout the "crisis" in social psychology (e.g., McGuire, 1973, 1983, 1999). His life and work provide as good an example as any of how specific social and historical events determine the course of scientific progress even as scientists themselves strive for universalism.

## The Life and Times of Bill McGuire

Bill McGuire was born to a poor, Catholic family. Social disadvantage and the unfavorable position of belonging to a religious minority are touched on in his autobiographical memories (McGuire, 1999). He was born in New York City in 1925, and the specter of the Great Depression lurks in the background of child-

---

[1]For other biographical and autobiographical treatments, see Evans, 1980, chapter 15; Banaji and Hastie, 1999; McGuire, 1999, chapter 1; and McGuire, 2002.

hood memories in which he accompanied his father, a milkman, on delivery routes to 125th Street stores at dawn. By McGuire's own account, the children of Catholic laborers at that time sought primarily to make a living, and if they were successful in their studies, the highest achievers became priests or lawyers in civil service.

McGuire's early educational experiences revealed no particular talent. It was a complete surprise to him when the school director, scolding him for some minor disciplinary offense, mentioned that he had achieved an outstanding score on an intelligence test (already administered on a regular basis there). He laughed away this embarrassing news, explaining that many of his classmates were creative, whereas he possessed a very good memory.

His mysterious and initially latent abilities would not have come to the surface—or at least not in the way that they did—had the government not offered a university scholarship equal to time served in the military during World War II. The horrors of war and the suffering of others left indelible marks on Bill McGuire. It is a powerful consequence of his experiences that McGuire, who drove a tank into Nazi-occupied territories, has refrained from automobile driving for the past 50 years.

In his first year at Fordham College, McGuire experienced an academic metamorphosis. Suddenly, he excelled in everything and grew concerned if he fell behind the achievable maximum score by a few percentage points. As a result of his successes, he was invited to teach courses in Rational Psychology and Natural Theology at his alma mater and was admitted to do postgraduate work in experimental psychology.

For McGuire, the year of 1949–1950 was, as he would put it, a period of "Stakhanovite labor." In addition to receiving his MA, McGuire showed more than a theoretical interest in political science, doing active organizational work for the Democratic Party. A completely different sphere of activities awaited him in 1950–1951, when he returned to a relatively peaceful Europe on a Fulbright scholarship to share in the intellectual life at the University of Louvain in Belgium. There he encountered the Husserl Archives and Simone de Beauvoir (playing billiards!) and the famous Gestalt psychologist A. E. Michotte, whose courses he attended and whose laboratory he visited. During the course of this year, experimental psychology finally won out over philosophy as his dominant career interest, although epistemological and metaphysical interests continue to inform both his perspectivist method (including the "tragic theory of knowledge") and his empirical work on the self-concept (especially distinctiveness theory).

McGuire (1999) described the first few tentative steps of his professional career as full of misunderstanding and chance. When applying to doctoral programs, he was faced with a fateful choice between B. F. Skinner's Harvard and Clark Hull's Yale, a difference that he calls a "trifle" from the outside but a fundamental one in the insular world of the behaviorists. A volume by Hull and colleagues (1940) on the *Mathematico-Deductive Theory of Rote Learning*, in which the authors applied symbolic logic to the processes of learning and memory, had captivated the young McGuire's imagination, and that book was the reason he decided on Yale. McGuire (1965) later joked that just as the poet Robert Browning believed that the word "Italy" must have been engraved on his heart and on Mary, Queen of Scots's, the word "Calais," a postmortem would eventually reveal that his own heart was marked with "Hull" (p. 136).

## The Yale School of Persuasive Communication

The psychology department at Yale, however, had already moved on from learning theory to the study of communication and persuasion under the direction of Carl Hovland, a former student of Hull and, ultimately, McGuire's mentor. Hovland began his career with the study of verbal learning in the spirit of behaviorism but was also famous for having studied the frustration–aggression hypothesis by examining relations between economic indicators and lynching in the old South (Hovland & Sears, 1940). By the time he reached the age of 30, Hovland was already considered to be a leading figure in psychology. During World War II, Hovland served as Head of the Section of Experiment in the Division of Information and Education in the U.S. War Department, under the leadership of S. A. Stouffer. During the war, he initiated a systematic experimental program on persuasive communication, resulting in studies published in volume 3 of the important series *The American Soldier* (Hovland, Lumsdaine, & Sheffield, 1949). Persuasion had been a bold change of topic for Hovland, but he managed to preserve his attachment to behaviorist learning theory while working prodigiously on attitude change. With the financial support of Yale and the Rockefeller Foundation, he continued this program of research after the war, editing several volumes under the series title *Yale Studies on Communication and Attitudes.*

Hovland said nothing when McGuire chose the topic of verbal learning (rather than persuasion) for his graduate work, and so McGuire avoided—for the time being, at least—his professional destiny as heir apparent of the scientific movement to study the dynamics of attitude change. McGuire began his career as a behaviorist and was initially reserved about the study of attitudes.[1] His dissertation expounded a model of paired associate learning that anticipated social learning theory, including an enrichment of behaviorist theory by incorporating cognitive elements.

In most historical surveys in psychology, a rigid distinction is made between behaviorist and cognitive approaches, and the disciplinary transition from one paradigm to the other during the 1950s is often represented as radical and absolute. In point of fact, however, behaviorist learning theory led rather smoothly into the study of cognitive factors in persuasion, at least at Yale. The connections between the two traditions are quite explicit, for example, in Hovland's work on source factors in persuasion and in work by another of McGuire's teachers, Leonard Doob, who contributed to the study of propaganda during and after World War II and wrote an influential (1947)

---

[1]It is perhaps worth a historical footnote, especially in light of McGuire's eventual career interests, that after ten full years of investigating persuasive communication, Hovland changed the focus of his research again, this time to the microanalysis of thought processes, especially the topic of positive–negative asymmetry, which was taken up again many years later by McGuire and McGuire (1992). Hovland also became a pioneer in the computer simulation of cognition until his premature death in 1961.

article entitled "The Behavior of Attitudes." Attitude researchers within the social cognitive movement a few decades later similarly saw themselves as focusing on "cognitive responses" (i.e., internally generated thoughts and arguments) elicited by persuasive stimuli (e.g., Greenwald, 1968; Petty, Ostrom, & Brock, 1981), and this blending of cognitive and behavioral metaphors dominates experimental social psychology even today.

McGuire's earlier philosophical forays into epistemology and phenomenology prepared him well for the infusion of cognitivism that took place in psychology during the 1950s. In another example of what McGuire (1999) described as being in the right place for the wrong reasons, he moved to the University of Minnesota in 1954 as a postdoctoral researcher in the laboratory of Leon Festinger and Stanley Schachter. Although he had hoped to work with Festinger on interpersonal relationships and group dynamics, by the time he arrived, Festinger was already nursing the theory of cognitive dissonance, which dealt famously with *intrapersonal* aspects of attitude dynamics. Just as the adolescence of a strong, maturing personality is not an easy period—this much can be accepted from psychoanalytic theories of human development even by those who have reservations about depth psychology in general—the time it takes for a talented and ambitious youth to adapt to the intellectual and institutional environment is not smooth. McGuire (1999) repeatedly mentioned in his autobiographical memoirs that he was not in the inner circle of Hovland's group at Yale, and he says little more about his time in Minnesota than that "it was exciting to participate . . . in the early dissonance research" (p. 10). Festinger and his group during the period in which the theory of cognitive dissonance was developed (e.g., Festinger, 1957). Nevertheless, any contextualist must admit that the scientific environments at Yale and Minnesota, which turned out to be so historically significant, influenced McGuire considerably and paved the way for his groundbreaking contributions to the theory and practice of cognitive social psychology.

## Contrasting Styles of Research: Hovland, Festinger, and McGuire

Throughout his career, McGuire drew strong, polarized comparisons between two of his mentors, Hovland and Festinger (e.g., McGuire, 1985, 1999). He was, of course, in the exceptional position of having closely observed both of these epoch-making individuals and their professional environments. Moreover, McGuire was literally "there" when the center of research on attitude dynamics moved from Hovland's laboratory at Yale to that of Festinger at the University of Minnesota. In keeping with his character, McGuire's impressions are far from anecdotal or fragmented. Rather, on the basis of his personal experience with Hovland and Festinger, McGuire formulated a systematic analysis of contrasting research styles (convergent vs. divergent), focusing especially on the assumed relation between theorizing and empirical data collection and on the foundations and consequences of this theory–data relation. McGuire's (1985, 1999) analysis of the differences between Hovland and Festinger provides a useful framework for understanding his own subsequent contributions in proper context.

According to McGuire, Hovland's style was a convergent one, in that he would first fix his sights on a single effect (or a single dependent variable) and then use multiple theories (and multiple independent variables) to try to explain as much of the statistical variance as possible. Theorizing, with this model, is an eclectic endeavor that revolves around the phenomenon to be explained. In contrast, Festinger's divergent style led him to start off with a theoretical or explanatory principle and then to apply it to as many domains as possible, accounting for small amounts of variance in a wide range of phenomena. McGuire (1985) contrasted both convergent and divergent styles with his own preferred "systems" style of research, according to which the scientist "attempts to trace the alternative, often bidirectional, pathways of causality by using an inclusive research design" (p. 238).

McGuire is generally more critical of Festinger than of Hovland. From a systems perspective, McGuire (1985, 1999) concluded that cognitive dissonance theory is not a proper theory but rather a "guiding idea." He objected also to the indifference with which the divergent researcher selects the local contexts for his or her studies of the general theory, and he despaired of Festinger's methodological weaknesses in measuring and analyzing the dependent variables that seemed so arbitrarily chosen. Nor did McGuire much appreciate the ingenuity of the "Festingerians" in developing experimental situations, and he implied that this was a questionable way of hunting professional glory. McGuire frequently remarked that it is unfortunate to mistake the role of researcher for that of stage director (see also Ellsworth, chapter 19 of this volume).

McGuire's criticism of Hovland carries much less tension. From McGuire's point of view, Hovland's studies of persuasive communication did not rely on conspicuous tests of inflexible theories; rather, Hovland is given credit for systematically scrutinizing phenomena from many different sides. Nevertheless, Hovland's hypotheses are occasionally dismissed for their "banality," and the convergent approach is seen as relatively primitive and "unidirectional," at least in comparison with the systems style of research (McGuire, 1985).

## "The Father of Social Cognition"

Following his postdoctoral training with Festinger, McGuire returned to Yale as an assistant professor, from 1955–1958, for his second of three stints there. He recalled that he "worked away without completely unpacking" (McGuire, 1999, p. 45), and within three years he had moved to the University of Illinois at Urbana–Champaign. There he joined the Communication Research Institute under the "fertile dictatorship" of Charles Osgood. Part of the McGuire legend is that he made a pledge not to publish *any* articles before receiving tenure. Supportive evidence comes from his vita, in which a glut of publications appeared in 1960 and 1961, immediately after his tenured appointment. By 1961, McGuire had returned to his hometown of New York City to teach at Columbia University.

McGuire's first major scholarly contributions addressed theories of "cognitive consistency" (see Wyer, chapter 8 of this volume), and this fact alone might provide some background for understanding his sharp criticism of Festinger.

Following Hull's lead, McGuire started by clarifying his concepts precisely and then deducing from them a few postulates concerning the structural organization of ideas and beliefs. He proposed that a fundamental organizing principle of cognition would be the system of formal logic. Thus, he linked probabilogical thinking (including estimates of likelihood) to the structure of logical syllogisms (McGuire, 1960). McGuire was justly proud of his contributions to theories of cognitive consistency (see Abelson et al., 1968), and he felt that his "probabilogical model" was more "cognitive" than any other consistency theory, including the celebrated theory of cognitive dissonance (Festinger, 1957). Nevertheless, the significance of his work was not immediately recognized (e.g., Insko, 1967), and it was only later, following subsequent work by Wyer (1970, 1972, 1975), that the value of McGuire's probabilogical model was appreciated.

It was instead the topic of resistance to persuasion that brought McGuire widespread success and recognition in social psychology. Drawing on an analogy from medical science, McGuire (1964) offered "inoculation theory" to explain why people's beliefs are susceptible to persuasion in ideological domains that are seldom exposed to attack. Cultural truisms, he reasoned, are considered by everyone to be obvious, and so the underlying beliefs are never strengthened. As a result, they should be defenseless against unanticipated persuasive attacks. McGuire demonstrated not only that this vulnerability to persuasion existed but also that it could be overcome by prior "immunization" of the person by exposing him or her to a relatively weak attack on the beliefs, which he or she could then counterargue. This theory-driven empirical contribution effectively started the ball rolling on "cognitive response" theories of persuasion (e.g., Greenwald, 1968; Petty, Ostrom, & Brock, 1981), and it guaranteed McGuire a place in the annals of attitude change research (see also Petty, Tormala, & Rucker, chapter 4 of this volume).

Not too surprisingly, the impact of McGuire's work on inoculation theory brought public criticism as well as recognition. The most banal of these criticisms questioned the generalizeability of the results and bickered about gaps in experimental evidence, but the more painful attacks questioned the originality of the theory, suggesting that it was merely derivative of previous findings from the Hovland group concerning the effectiveness of two-sided argumentation (support and the provision of counterarguments) in persuasive communication (e.g., Kiesler, Collins, & Miller, 1969; Sahakian, 1982). Such criticism was undeserved not only because the act of persuasion is substantially different from the defense of one's beliefs but also because it failed to appreciate the novelty of perspective in the whole theory. It is original to McGuire's conception that (a) the individual's beliefs form a coherent thought system that has emergent properties, (b) changes in one belief are capable of affecting other beliefs in the system, and (c) the individual receiver of a persuasive communication is an active participant in that situation. All of these points represent major advances over the Hovland approach, and they are central to what would become known as the "dynamic theory of thought systems" (McGuire & McGuire, 1991; see also Hastie & Rawson, chapter 5 of this volume).

Looking back on his career, McGuire (1986) recollected that he "had the delight of entering psychology in an epistemological age" and adapted

Wordsworth's *Prelude* in the follow terms: "Bliss it was in that dawn to be [a psychologist] but to be [a cognitive social psychologist] was very heaven" (p. 271). The time was indeed right for social cognition, but McGuire's work, first on the probabilogical model of attitude change (McGuire, 1960), then on belief inoculation and resistance to persuasion (McGuire, 1964), and then on cognitive and personality factors in processes of attention, comprehension, yielding, and memory (McGuire, 1968a), almost single-handedly brought about the change. In summarizing his impact on the field, Wyer (1991) aptly characterized McGuire as "the father of social cognition" (p. vii). This appellation prompted Bill to begin referring to his wife and longtime collaborator, Claire McGuire, as "the mother of social cognition."

## The Crisis in Society and Social Psychology

The McGuires spent society's conflict-ridden years of 1967–1970 at the University of California in San Diego, on the campus where Herbert Marcuse and Angela Davis were stirring up student revolt. Once again, historical events left an indelible mark on social psychology in general and on McGuire's thought in particular. Opposition to the Vietnam War and to the "Establishment" led young people to question received wisdom in matters of society and science, creating direct consequences for academic departments of sociology and psychology. As editor of the flagship *Journal of Personality and Social Psychology,* McGuire was a trustee of the field at one of its most challenging times.

The turmoil of the 1960s and 1970s manifested itself in what came to be known as the "crisis of social psychology." Critics attacked the ahistorical aims and political aloofness of social psychology, arguing that societal relevance deserved to be a core value of the discipline and that experimental precision had been overemphasized relative to other criteria (e.g., Gergen, 1973). Debates over these issues frequently appeared in professional journals and at conferences for a number of years in North America and Europe. Above the cacophony, the voices of French-inspired New Leftists reached the ears of those who were sensitive to it: "Indeed! The cultivators of bourgeois pseudoscience have finally come into contradiction with themselves and must give up their misconceptions about how to map social reality!"

From a distance, one can see that the avalanche was caused not only by the times but also by the weight of tensions that had built up within the field of social psychology. One source of tension arose from the recognition of certain limitations of the experimental method that had been used almost exclusively to produce knowledge in social psychology. Interest in qualitative methods and field studies increased as new generations demanded ecological realism and real-world applicability. There was by now relatively widespread dissatisfaction with dissonance theory, which had filled journal pages for many years, and neither attribution theory nor pure information-processing approaches were poised to satisfy escalating expectations concerning social and political significance. Thus, questions concerning the respective and appropriate roles of theory, methodology, and societal relevance came to the fore, and McGuire played a key role in responding to these questions as a result of his situation, authority, interests, and motivation (see also Jost & Kruglanski, 2002).

In some ways, McGuire sympathized with the critics and their frustration. He agreed, for example, that the professional dominance of dissonance theory was not well justified, and he disparaged the conjurors' tricks relied on by experimentalists. He believed that scientific psychology should be conducted ethically, and he agreed that experimenters had not always satisfied basic ethical standards. It also seems that he recognized some of the limits of the information-processing approach, although he had been instrumental in developing it, and he yearned for the fertile combination of high-level theory and increasingly complex and reliable empiricism. His feelings of responsibility for the health of social psychology led him to respond in a way that was both critical and constructive, as demonstrated by his famous (1973) "Yin and Yang" article, which became an important document of the times. His almost elastic patience with social psychology's critics was not accompanied by a loss of faith in empirical methods. The aim of research, according to McGuire, is not to render a verdict concerning the truth of a general theorem but rather to clarify the particular conditions under which any statement of a theorem comes true. McGuire's primary goal, therefore, was to improve the scientific quality of social psychology, and by most accounts this goal has been successfully attained. The "crisis of social psychology" turned out to be a peculiar one in that rather than contributing to a withering of institutions, departments, books, students, and social psychological experts, it brought about a rapid growth in their numbers (Hunyady, 1984).

Throughout the "crisis" period (and afterward), McGuire remained faithful to his scientific and moral ideals, which matured in the course of battle. A spectacular example comes from his research program on the "spontaneous self-concept" (McGuire & McGuire, 1988), including a series of studies that elegantly demonstrate processes whereby the self is socially constructed according to features of the immediate situation (see also Hardin, chapter 12 of this volume). The methodologies that were adopted for this program of research made use of the agentic self-characterizations of research participants, minimized the interventions of the researcher, and followed a subtle analysis of qualitative data. With this work, there is an obvious break from the scaling methodologies of traditional attitude-measurement studies and an attempt to allow respondents "to express themselves in their own terms rather than by restricting them to making check marks on semantic differential polar opposites of the researcher's (or C. E. Osgood's) choosing" (McGuire, 1999, p. 292). A descriptive, multivariate approach to understanding the psychological meaning of participant responses on open-ended, nonreactive measures also characterizes subsequent work on the dynamic theory of thought systems (McGuire & McGuire, 1991).

## Later Years

It was during the midst of the "crisis" that McGuire returned to Yale University for the third and longest time. He had been a doctoral student at Yale and then an "up-or-out" assistant professor, and in 1971, he became chair of the

Department of Psychology, a position that he held until 1973. For the next 25 years, McGuire would enjoy the most productive period of his career. A large part of his published work, including many of his most profound syntheses, appeared after he turned 50. From this point on, McGuire left behind most of his editorial and other high-visibility professional duties and focused instead on working quietly and steadily on the operation of thought systems in stimulating intellectual environments around the world (especially London and Paris) in collaboration with his wife, Claire.

When in New Haven, the McGuires often hosted home-cooked dinners for scores of faculty and students at departmental happenings. Their house is spacious, well-worn, and within easy walking distance of the department, ideal for gatherings large and small. The living room preserves the memory of their once-lively social life, including the formerly rambunctious activities of three children who are now in their 30s and 40s. Visitors are drawn immediately to the sofa pillows that present a fading line of portraits of Marx, Lenin, Zhou Enlai, and others; these were sewn years ago by Claire from cloth propaganda posters acquired in New York. Books flood almost every corner of the house. It is virtually impossible to keep up with Bill McGuire's breadth and depth of knowledge, not only in psychology, but also in history, politics, and even natural sciences. One cannot escape the feeling that no meaningful intellectual recess exists where he has not been well ahead of us in gaining knowledge and in mental initiative.

The opportunity to assemble, edit, and publish (complete with personal commentary) the rich products of a long and fruitful professional life is one that is granted only to a few lucky intellectual personages. McGuire received this grace of fate when, at the age of 74, in 1999, Cambridge University Press published his personal synthesis entitled *Constructing Social Psychology: Creative and Critical Processes*. This Festschrift volume, too, demonstrates the power and enduring influence of his ideas. It represents a living, breathing dialogue that exists between McGuire and two dozen of his closest followers, including friends, colleagues, and students (for overviews, see Jost, Banaji, & Prentice, chapter 1 of this volume; McGuire, chapter 3 of this volume).

## The Yin and Yang of Bill McGuire

There is perhaps something of a distortion in portraying McGuire as the prototype of a scientific psychologist, that is, as the attitudes *expert*. It would be more accurate to say that he is an *ambassador* or a *representative*: He knows the attitude literature in its full cross section and historical depth, and he is a master of its cultivation from practical opinion formation to the most comprehensive theory of thought systems. At the same time, he is more than and different from that: His life work goes beyond the limits of the most broadly understood problems of attitude research, it does not tolerate restrictions arising from traditional methodologies, and it unequivocally pushes the study of attitudes well beyond the conventional dimension of evaluation to other, more subtle, complex, and aesthetically pleasing dimensions of thought (see also Eagly & Diekman, chapter 15 of this volume). McGuire has revealed a deep appreciation of historical predecessors from Duns Scotus to Merleau-Ponty to Clark Hull, but he has also demonstrated a willingness to break with dominant trends and to maintain a visionary commitment to the future. He is, in addition, a convinced and tolerant believer in the richness and diversity of intellectual and ideological pluralism. In many, many ways, he defies classification.

In the final analysis, should we say that his perspective is that of a behaviorist, or just the opposite, that he is a faithful disciple of the cognitive approach? Is he a distinctively American thinker or is he a classic intellectual in the European tradition? Is he a religious Catholic or a keenly rational post-Enlightenment thinker? Is he an abstract philosopher of idealism or the champion of multivariate experimental investigations? Is he devotedly attached to his professional past or is he a reformer of restless mind? Is he an inexhaustibly diligent servant or a passionate tyrant of labor? Does he turn with caring kindness to the needy or is he an ironically reserved intellectual aristocrat? Is he a great, esoteric scientist or a sensitive thinker who is ready to use all of his knowledge in order to solve the world's social problems? For all of these antinomies, both extremes seem to characterize (and mischaracterize) him equally. Fittingly, McGuire himself proves the utter inadequacy of one-dimensional judgment, demonstrating the need to consider interrelated systems of thought. These observations reveal what is probably the main dimension in which McGuire differs from almost all other social psychologists: complexity.

The complexity of McGuire's intellectual and personal virtues has no doubt provided him with a useful foundation for facing the most complicated phenomena and seeking to express their simplest essence. This is true of the central theme of his life work, of the subject matter that continues to fill libraries all over the world, namely the psychological study of attitudes. What is an attitude? McGuire provides a famous answer: the location of an object of thought on a dimension of judgment. This lucid, inclusive operational definition can be applied to any attitudinal object; it can even be applied to the creator of the definition. This chapter, we hope, has provided converging (and contextualized) evidence for the judgment, shared by all of the contributors to this volume, that on the vertical dimension of attitudinal evaluation, the work of William J. McGuire is at the very peak.

# References

Abelson, R. P., Aronson, E., McGuire, W. J., Newcomb, T. M., Rosenberg, M. J., & Tannenbaum, P. H. (Eds.). (1968). *Theories of cognitive consistency: A sourcebook.* Chicago: Rand McNally.

Banaji, M. R., & Hastie, R. (1999). Foreword. In W. J. McGuire (Ed.), *Constructing social psychology: Creative and critical processes* (pp. xiii–xv). Cambridge: Cambridge University Press.

Doob, L. W. (1947). The behavior of attitudes. *Psychological Review, 54,* 135–156.

Evans, R. I. (1980). William McGuire [Interview]. In R. I. Evans (Ed.), *The making of social psychology: Discussions with creative contributors* (pp. 171–186). New York: Gardner Press.

Festinger, L. (1957). *A theory of cognitive dissonance.* Stanford, CA: Stanford University.

Gergen, K. J. (1973). Social psychology as history. *Journal of Personality and Social Psychology, 26,* 309–320.

Greenwald, A. G. (1968). Cognitive learning, cognitive response to persuasion, and attitude change. In A. G. Greenwald, T. C. Brock, & T. M. Ostrom (Eds.), *Psychological foundations of attitudes* (pp. 47–170). San Diego, CA: Academic Press.

Hovland, C. I., Lumsdaine, A. A., & Sheffield, F. D. (1949). *Experiments on mass communication* (Studies in social psychology in World War II, Vol. 3.). Princeton, NJ: Princeton University Press.

Hovland, C. I., & Sears, R. R. (1940). Minor studies of aggression: VI. Correlation of lynchings with economic indices. *Journal of Psychology, 9*, 301–310.

Hull, C., Hovland, C. I., Ross, R. T., Hall, M., Perkins, D. T., & Fitch, F. B. (1940). *Mathematico-deductive theory of rote learning: A study in scientific methodology.* New Haven, CT: Yale University Press.

Hunyady, Gy. (1984). A kísérleti szociálpszichológia amerikai válságirodalma és amit kiolvasunk belőle. *Pszichológia, 1*, 147–158.

Insko, C. A. (1967). *Theories of attitude change.* New York: Appleton-Century-Crofts.

Jost, J. T., & Kruglanski, A. W. (2002). The estrangement of social constructionism and experimental social psychology: History of the rift and prospects for reconciliation. *Personality and Social Psychology Review, 6*, 168–187.

Kiesler, C., Collins, B. E., & Miller, N. (1969). *Attitude change: A critical analysis of theoretical approaches.* New York: Wiley.

McGuire, W. J. (1960). A syllogistic analysis of cognitive relationships. In M. J. Rosenberg & C. I. Hovland (Eds.), *Attitude organization and change* (pp. 140–162). New Haven: Yale University Press.

McGuire, W. J. (1964). Inducing resistance to persuasion. In L. Berkowitz (Ed.), *Advances in experimental social psychology* (Vol. 1, pp. 191–229). New York: Academic Press.

McGuire, W. J. (1965). Learning theory and social psychology: Discussion of W. N. Schoenfeld's paper. In O. Klineberg & R. Christie (Eds.), *Perspectives in social psychology* (pp. 135–140). New York: Holt, Rinehart, & Winston.

McGuire, W. J. (1968a). Personality and susceptibility to social influence. In E. F. Borgatta & W. W. Lambert (Eds.), *Handbook of personality theory and research* (pp. 1130–1187). Chicago: Rand McNally.

McGuire, W. J. (1968b). Theory of the structure of human thought. In R. P. Abelson, E. Aronson, W. J. McGuire, T. M. Newcomb, M. J. Rosenberg, & P. H. Tannenbaum (Eds.), *Theories of cognitive consistency: A sourcebook* (pp. 140–162). Chicago: Rand McNally.

McGuire, W. J. (1973). The yin and yang of progress in social psychology: Seven koan. *Journal of Personality and Social Psychology, 26*, 446–456.

McGuire, W. J. (1983). A contextualist theory of knowledge: Its implications for innovation and reform in psychological research. *Advances in Experimental Social Psychology, 16*, 1–47.

McGuire, W. J. (1985). The nature of attitudes and attitude change. In G. Lindzey & E. Aronson (Eds.), *Handbook of social psychology* (3rd ed., Vol. 2, pp. 233–346). New York: Random House.

McGuire, W. J. (1986). A perspectivist looks at contextualism and the future of behavioral science. In R. L. Rosnow & M. Georgoudi (Eds.), *Contextualism and understanding in behavioral science: Implications for research and theory* (pp. 271–301). New York: Praeger.

McGuire, W. J. (1989). A perspectivist approach to the strategic planning of programmatic scientific research. In B. Gholson, W. R. Shadish, Jr., R. A. Niemeyer, & A. C. Houts (Eds.), *The psychology of science: Contributions to metascience* (pp. 214–245). New York: Cambridge University Press.

McGuire, W. J. (1999). *Constructing social psychology: Creative and critical processes.* Cambridge: Cambridge University Press.

McGuire, W. J. (2002). Doing psychology my way. In R. J. Sternberg (Ed.), *Psychologists defying the crowd: Stories of those who battled the establishment and won.* Washington, DC: APA Books.

McGuire, W. J., & McGuire, C. V. (1988). Content and process in the experience of self. *Advances in Experimental Social Psychology, 21*, 97–144.

McGuire, W. J., & McGuire, C. V. (1991). The content, structure and operation of thought systems. In R. S. Wyer & T. K. Srull (Eds.), *Advances in social cognition* (Vol. 4, pp.1–78). Hillsdale, NJ: Erlbaum.

McGuire, W. J., & McGuire, C. V. (1992). Cognitive-versus-affective positivity asymmetries in thought systems. *European Journal of Social Psychology, 22*, 571–591.

Petty, R. E., Ostrom, T. M., & Brock, T. C. (Eds.). (1981). *Cognitive responses in persuasion.* Hillsdale, NJ: Erlbaum.

Sahakian, W. S. (1982). *History and systems of social psychology* (2nd ed.). Washington, DC: Hemisphere.

Wyer, R. S. (1970). The quantitative prediction of belief and opinion change: A further test of a subjective probability model. *Journal of Personality and Social Psychology, 16,* 559–571.

Wyer, R. S. (1972). Test of a subjective probability model of social evaluation processes. *Journal of Personality and Social Psychology, 22,* 279–286.

Wyer, R. S. (1975) Functional measurement analysis of a subjective probability model of cognitive functioning. *Journal of Personality and Social Psychology, 31,* 94–100.

Wyer, R. S. (1991). Preface. In R. S. Wyer & T. K. Srull (Eds.), *Advances in social cognition* (Vol. 4). Hillsdale, NJ: Erlbaum.

# 3 ──────────────────────────────

# A Life in Psychology:
# The Human Element

## *William J. McGuire*

How delighted I am that John Jost, Mahzarin Banaji, and Deborah Prentice organized this Festschrift and recruited as chapter writers a galaxy of superstars who are personally and intellectually meaningful in my life. I shall mention here factors that brought me and the chapter authors into beautiful and fertile friendships and have enriched my life in research.

## Attitude Change and Social Influence (Chapters 4, 5, 6)

The first substantive section's three chapters are on persuasion, the third topic on which I worked heavily (following my earlier wrestlings with human learning and with thought systems). Richard Petty's chapter deals with immunization against persuasion, Reid Hastie's with remote persuasive impacts, and Deborah Prentice's with the persuasive impact of values.

### *Richard E. Petty, Chapter 4*

That Rich Petty and I should have connected was inevitable, considering that he and I each served a term of being regarded as numero uno, the big enchilada, of attitude change research. We first met in late 1975 when Rich was a graduate student at Ohio State University (OSU). Wasn't everyone? He invited me to contribute to the *Cognitive Responses* (1981) book, the second volume in the OSU attitudes trilogy. I had already contributed to the first volume and would later contribute to the third.

Petty's 1981 OSU *Cognitive Responses* may be the most important attitude-change book since the 1950s Hovland/Yale series, but getting it out became a perils-of-Pauline farce. It suffered such growing pains as a change of publisher, renegotiation of contracts, illness of participants, and a reduction of page allotments. When work on the book started, Rich Petty was a third-year graduate student; when the book finally appeared, he was a tenured associate professor, illustrating how long it can take a good book to reach your newsstand and how quickly Rich achieved tenure. Here he deals with my earliest attitude-change focus, inducing resistance to persuasion. I took an inoculation theory approach; here Rich Petty takes a new attitude-strength approach.

### *Reid Hastie, Chapter 5*

If my meeting with Richard Petty was inevitable, my meeting with Reid Hastie was an unlikely stroke of good luck. When Reid and his friend Dan Bernstein graduated from Stanford in 1968, Dan joined me at the University of California, San Diego (UCSD) to earn a PhD in social psychology and Reid went to Harvard seeking a PhD in cultural anthropology. Reid wasn't enthralled with Harvard, 3000 miles from the Pacific Ocean. Dan, liking UCSD, sent [him] the word, "Come on in, the water's fine," drawing Reid to UCSD to work with me.

After Reid Hastie's first year at UCSD, I decided to return to Yale for the third time, stopping en route at the London School of Economics (LSE) for the 1970-1971 year. I invited Reid to come to LSE for that year and then to transfer with me to Yale for his PhD. However, some personal responsibilities (don't ask!) prevented his spending a year in London, so he went immediately to Yale. By the time I got back to Yale after my LSE sabbatical, Reid had switched from social to cognitive psychology and was working with Endel Tulving. Still, we have remained close personally and professionally. Reid and I have both done much work on his topic here, namely, thought structures that channel the remote ramifications of persuasive communications.

### *Deborah A. Prentice, Chapter 6*

During Deborah Prentice's four years in Yale's social psychology doctoral program, we interacted in many ways: She took my courses, and served as my teaching assistant, I chaired her doctoral dissertation committee (although with her independence this was hardly a mentor-protégée relationship). Three days in May at the end of her first year of graduate study illustrate our interactions. On May 12, 1985, I sent her a multipage critique of her first-year self-evaluation and second-year plans. (I argued that her printer needed a blood transfusion or even a heart transplant, that her next year's statistics studies should drop assessment and add causal models, that she misused "hopefully," and so on). The next day Debbie wrote me a long memo on how to improve my teaching of the social psychology proseminar. The next day I wrote her a long commentary on her work in my attitude change course. My critiques were long because her originals were so good that one wanted them perfect.

In her chapter here on values, by assigning me a new topic on which to work, she implies that this old dog can learn some new tricks. Hopefully.

## Cognitive Organization and Information Processing
### (Chapters 7, 8, 9, 10)

This book's second section, on cognitive organization, includes John Cacioppo's chapter on asymmetries, Robert Wyer's on organization of general knowledge,

Shulamith Kreitler's on relation of cognition to behavior, and Mahzarin Banaji's on implicit cognitions.

## John T. Cacioppo, Chapter 7

John Cacioppo became so prolific so early that I was already familiar with his research as an OSU graduate student carrying out attitude change research that brought him early recognition as an evolving supernova. We first met in 1981 when I was visiting the University of Iowa, which had recently had the wisdom to promote him early to a tenured associate professorship. That visit added friendship to admiration in my relationship with John. Another lovely memory is that during his 1986 sabbatical at Yale, he gifted me with two of his then recent productions: (a) a prepublication signed copy of his 1986 book *Communication and Persuasion* and (b) chances to dance around the living room with his months-old daughter Christina.

His work on positive-negative affective asymmetries, described here, enriches my own work on cognitive, affective, and favorability asymmetries, but what I cherish most is his footnote acknowledging that the precocious Christina has contributed helpful comments on his chapter. Will you, won't you . . . will you join the dance?

## Robert S. Wyer, Jr., Chapter 8

Who can read Bob Wyer's chapter without envying me for having such a colleague? He and I, being of the old writing generation, went head-to-head on paper for 20 years before we first met face-to-face. We criticized each other's manuscripts as journal editor and author, our roles frequently reversing. Rather than being corrupted into a "New York Review of Each Other's Books" reciprocity, we pushed one another to make good manuscripts better. For example, in 1969, he sent a manuscript to me as editor of the *Journal of Personality and Social Psychology (JPSP),* which I accepted with enthusiasm and with nine single-spaced pages of critique and suggestions. He returned a greatly revised manuscript plus seven single-spaced pages of comments on my comments. I accepted the revision with five single-spaced pages of replies to his responses. Since then Bob has published more articles in *JPSP* than anyone else, indeed, twice as many as the runner-up.

Years ago my boast that Bob and I became good friends by criticizing each other's work without ever having met induced a grad student of mine to ask Bob what he imagined I looked like. Bob guessed that I was bald, with a full white beard, taller than average but heavy even for my height. That is not me, Bob, that's Alfred Lord Tennyson, but if I so described you, I'd be picturing you as Santa Claus because of all the intellectual stimulation you gave me.

## Shulamith Kreitler, Chapter 9

My interaction with Shulamith Kreitler is a tale of two cities, Tel Aviv and New Haven (and occasional neutral third places such as Cardiff). I first met the Kreitlers (Shulamith, Hans, and Ron) around 1980, when they were engaged in a tour de force involving spending fellowship years successively at Harvard, Princeton, and Yale. I already admired their book *Psychology of Art* (1973), my last best hope for keeping psychology of art courses pervasively in the curricula. We often discussed relations between attitudes and actions, Shulamith's topic here.

Among the pleasures that make it delightful to be with Shulamith at Yale or at Tel Aviv University are her commitment to advance both basic theory and practical applications, her immense scholarship in seeming to know and use creatively every study ever done on her topic, and her ability to get vast amounts of high-quality work done elegantly with very modest funding. She is indeed a rara avis, not to be caged but encouraged to fly by her own internal compass. If only, if only. Good night, Hans. Good morning, grandson Jonathan.

## *Mahzarin R. Banaji, Chapter 10*

Another chapter author whom I met first at Ohio State University (OSU) is Mahzarin Banaji. After my 1980s colloquium at OSU, I went with a small band of entranced or hungry graduate students, including Mahzarin, to a Chinese restaurant to continue post-colloquium discussions. Mahzarin's criticisms and suggestions were so impressive that when a Yale job opened, I urged going after her. The rest is history. (An alternative account is that at that post-colloquium Chinese dinner Marzu took much of the cashews and chicken dish and I had to take her to a New Haven restaurant to get my revenge.)

During her triumphant years at Yale, Mahzarin made formidable contributions to implicit cognition as described here, and I have had the pleasure of her company that allowed our respect and affection to grow while we created new meanings to colleagueship.

## Language and the Self-Concept (Chapters 11, 12)

The next section, on language and the self-concept, contains a chapter by Gün Semin on the language of self and another by Curtis Hardin on self-contradictions.

## *Gün R. Semin, Chapter 11*

If my relationship with Shulamith Kreitler is a tale of two cities, that with Gün Semin involves a gazetteer of locations: London, New Haven, Brighton/Sussex, Amsterdam, Paris, Bologna, Budapest, Giessen/Rauschholzhausen, and elsewhere. We were first brought together by a special 1986 issue of the *British Journal of Social Psychology*. Even better was our week-long conference on language and cognition at Giessen. Best of all was our coteaching in the 1986 (Bologna) Summer School of the European Association (EAESP). Over the years we helped one another with journal articles, research programs, funding proposals, and career moves. We share numerous interests, including self and language, on which Gün focuses here.

These hot cognition exchanges between Gün and me often occured in hot affective situations while we showed each other touristic sites grand or grotesque; while we rolled on the floor and inflated balloons for laughing children; and while eating gourmet meals in splendid restaurants or, better still, from our own kitchens. I am a loner in work style, but Gün helped me appreciate also the joys of collaboration.

## Curtis D. Hardin, Chapter 12

In any social psychology doctoral program there occur golden ages best appreciated in retrospect, when hindsight distinguishes the good from the great. At these ages the program lucks out as unusually brilliant entering students develop a chemistry that strikes fire in one another. This occurred in the Yale doctoral program around 1990, when Curtis Hardin graced the program. Curtis makes terms like "grace," "gentleman," and "happy warrior" come trippingly to the tongue. He enriches our relationships personally and professionally. Here he deals with self, a topic of mutual interest, but Curtis is as eager to discuss his colleagues' research as his own.

An era ended in the Yale program when Curtis completed his doctoral studies. The day he left was a day when one senses something slightly unusual happened. "Don't let it be forgot that once there was a spot, for one brief shining moment, that was known as Camelot. . . ."

## Stereotypes and Intergroup Relations (Chapters 13, 14, 15, 16)

The next four interpersonal chapters are Willem Doise's on societal psychology, György Hunyady's on stereotypes, Alice Eagly's on social groups, and John Jost's on system justification.

## Willem Doise, Chapter 13

Willem and I first met glancingly in the late 1960s at a London conference. By the 1970s, we were following each other's overlapping work, both empirical (e.g., on effects of social contexts on identity) and metatheoretical (e.g., his on levels of psychological explanation and mine on perspectivism). Willem honors me here by relating some of his grand ideas to notions of my own. We met most royally in 1986, when the Summer School of the European Association (EAESP) was hosted by the University of Bologna on its 900th anniversary. There, I was proud to coteach with Willem the section on intergroup conflict and social identity. What pleasure it was to hear Willem's lectures that made sense of enormous bodies of scattered findings, integrating them into intellectual cathedrals for the benefit of gifted students from Eastern, Western, and Central Europe.

Two of my personal debts to Willem deserve mention. First, he has many times lent Claire and me his pied-à-terre in Paris for months at a time. The 14th Arrondissement is worth an acknowledgment. Second, when at age 75 I walked the 700-km Camino de Santiago, I met by chance some Doise brothers also walking el Camino. Without their help, I might not have earned my Compostela. Hardly able to walk, weighed down by cruel packs, we yet found strength to express our affection and admiration for Willem, our brother.

### György Hunyady, Chapter 14

For decades, well before the Berlin Wall came down, György Hunyady and I were exchanging hospitality and ideas. At first there was still a war on, the Cold War, but he and I were fighting a more important war to promote understanding. I admired György's work for its high quality (despite his being somewhat isolated) and for its courage (he dared do politically sensitive research on national stereotypes). Despite György's Stakhanovite work level while visiting Yale and while home at Eötvös Lorand University, he always found time to extend a helping hand. I do not know if György Hunyady is genealogically related to the formidable Janos Hunyadi, elected King of Hungary in 1446, but years of interacting with him have taught me that György is a prince among people.

Recently, when my then-student, John Jost (see chapter 16) participated in a European meeting, I urged him to visit Budapest and exchange ideas with György. Some years later, at beautiful Lake Balaton, a romance blossomed and in 2001 John (my last doctoral student) and Orsolya (György's daughter) were wed. May their story give pleasure for a thousand years.

### Alice H. Eagly, Chapter 15

My relations with all the chapter authors have been preponderantly pleasant, but some of our exchanges have had usefully contentious aspects. New PhD Alice Eagly and I started off by disagreeing on a manuscript in 1968, but within a year we were zealous colleagues in research, giving one another feedback and suggestions. Rich Petty (chapter 4), Alice, and I each served a term of being regarded as numero uno in attitude change research, but each of us has moved to other subjects such as the prediction and explanation of future events, the topic that Alice discusses here. All three of us have profited from and appreciated the other's work, although seldom have we met face-to-face. Indeed, I have had as much face time with Willem Doise at Genève and György Hunyady at Budapest as I have had with Rich Petty and Alice Eagly, fellow travelers in the Lower 48. This cosmopolitanism becomes our field, even if it violates Zipf's law.

Of course, Alice and I have met at colloquia and conventions and occasionally at exotic venues. One night I met Alice on the shoulder of a Venezuelan road along which we were trudging to a meeting in Caracas after we bailed out of a stalled bus. Easy for me to do, who, like Fred Astaire, didn't have to dance backward in high heels.

### John T. Jost, Chapter 16

From Dimitri Papageorgis (dead before his time) to John Jost, my Dan to Beersheba, my first to last PhD students, from these two and the ones in between (including Debbie Prentice, chapter 6) I have had the good fortune of having splendid graduate students. My last best service to these gifted students has been to stay out of their way and to delight in their progress. When John was admitted to the Yale psychology doctoral program more than a decade ago, I encouraged him first to spend a year completing his Wittgenstein research at the University of Cincinnati philosophy department. Later, back at Yale, he educated us all regarding Wittgenstein and Marx and other heavy hitters, and he made their grand notions relevant to his and our empirical work. His ideological inclusiveness and interdisciplinary broadness made all of us more sophisticated.

How appropriate that in 1994 he was the first North American student invited to enter an EAESP Summer School (at Warsaw). There he not only shared his ideas on system justification (see chapter 16) but also scored both goals in the Summer School's 2-0 victory over the Warsaw football team. That got social psychology some respect. I have received much from John; to John I have given something exceptional. Most mentors give good advice, but how many mentors play *shadchen,* occasioning their student's meeting of a brilliant and beautiful spouse?

## Politics and the Mass Media (Chapters 17, 18)

The next section, on communication and politics, includes David Sears's chapter on racial politics and Shanto Iyengar's on political communication.

### David O. Sears, Chapter 17

Dave and I met in 1958, a vintage year in a great era of social psychology at Yale. The founding giants still walked the earth (e.g., Carl Hovland, Irv Janis, Irv Child, Leonard Doob) and an astonishing number of Young Turks were running wild in the streets (Bob Cohen, Milt Rosenberg, Irv Sarnoff, Jack Brehm, myself, etc.). This exciting year was Dave Sears's first as a Yale grad student and my last as an up-or-out assistant professor. On the basis of our interactions during this one-year overlap, Dave does me the honor of calling me his first mentor. We talked about attitude change and political psychology but also about weekend adventures under the clock at the Biltmore Hotel. Did this make me his mentor? Wouldn't it be nice for me to think so?

When Claire and I and our Jim (then 10 months old) left Yale for the University of Illinois at the end of the 1958 academic year, Dave took over our New Haven apartment. Perhaps he found that we hadn't cleaned the oven adequately, but that was then and this is now, when Dave will evaluate generously the staying power of my seven koan.

### Shanto Iyengar, Chapter 18

Two decades later, back at Yale, I was teaching a graduate attitude-change course when the little band of heroes who showed up for the meetings was augmented by a handsome, suave stranger, not on my class list, who tended to take over the class meetings. He was Shanto Iyengar, who had resigned from a tenured political science associate professorship at Kansas State University in exchange for some informal status at Yale like "spouse of a law student," whose tenuousness worried him less than it did me. His self-confidence proved well founded, because in his next five years of flying around Yale without a parachute, he became director of Yale's Psychology and Politics doctoral program, revived the agenda-setting hypothesis, bridged communications and political science, and introduced laboratory manipulational experiments into political science before going on to even greater triumphs elsewhere. Shanto and I took pleasure in one another's company, even bringing out a book together despite our disagreement on issues such as the efficacy of the mass media, which he discusses here.

Let me ask Shanto (and Mahzarin Banaji, chapter 10) how it happens when a Festschrift is organized for this old guy, born of poor but honest parents on the East Side of New York, that among the superstars contributing chapters no fewer than two are degree holders from Osmania University? Do they put something in the Hyderabad water that fosters greatness?

## Social Psychological Theory (Chapters 19, 20, 21, 22)

The final "theory" section of this book includes Phoebe Ellsworth's chapter on simultaneous hypotheses, Tony Greenwald's on defensibility of theories, Norman Anderson's on unified theory, and E. Tory Higgins's on anointed variables.

### Phoebe C. Ellsworth, Chapter 19

My life in psychology has been greatly enriched by an awareness that Phoebe is somewhere out there, able and willing to take on the tough tasks that call for a heavy lifter with a big brain and a heart of gold. She was still a mere undergraduate when I, as *JPSP* editor, asked her to send me her 1966 Radcliffe senior essay, which ingeniously tested dissonance theory predictions phenomenologically. Soon after, as a grad student, she submitted a fine manuscript that I accepted subject to some minor revisions. Phoebe thereupon withdrew the manuscript until she collected further data to resolve some minor ambiguities that she found and then she resubmitted. Of the 1500 manuscripts that I handled as *JPSP* editor, this was the only case in which I as editor accepted a manuscript and the author rejected it.

What a privilege and pleasure it was to serve with Phoebe on the Yale faculty during the 1970s as she grew from new PhD to full professor. What withdrawal symptoms I had to endure when she left. A university without Phoebe is a lesser place.

### Anthony G. Greenwald, Chapter 20

Like Phoebe Ellsworth, Tony Greenwald was known to me when he was still an undergraduate, at Yale College. In the late 1950s he was one of those smart undergraduate students one remembers for decades. After he survived doctoral studies at Harvard in the early 1960s, Tony and I renewed our reversible interactions as author and editor of books and journals. How proud I am to have contributed to and profited from his editing of all three OSU volumes on attitude change. A decade after my term as *JPSP* editor, Tony became an innovative editor of that journal; I wish I had dared to be as creative and courageous an editor as he.

One of the pleasures of being on the Yale faculty is getting to teach brilliant undergraduates. During my second, up-or-out assistant professor term at Yale in the late 1950s, in one year I had in my classes no fewer than four social psychologists-to-be, Tony Greenwald, Bob Helmreich, Bibb Latané, and Ken Gergen. All were "A" students in the age of the gentleman "C," before grade inflation. Now, a half-century later, I still remember their individual research papers. Tony Greenwald's revealed no interest in parrots or desserts, so what's with the funny title?

## Norman H. Anderson, Chapter 21

It is my good fortune to have been a colleague of Norman Anderson twice, once in the late 1950s when we were both assistant professors at Yale and again in the late 1960s when we were both professors at the University of California, San Diego (UCSD), profiting from each other's findings and advice. For a half-century, we have shared a common approach to research (rigorous, elegant, and programmatic) and a deep meaning for friendship.

How impressive it was to watch Norman in the late 1960s political turmoil at UCSD continue his research on topics such as information integration theory, functional measurement, cognitive algebra, parallel and fan cases, and unified theory. Bliss it was in those heroic years to be studying social cognition; to be studying it with Norman Anderson was very heaven. His chapter here on unified theory shows that his purpose holds; Norman Anderson has stayed the course.

## E. Tory Higgins, Chapter 22

Close, but no cigar. Tory Higgins and I played hopscotch beginning in his graduate student years, carrying out related research in the same venue but not in the same years. He was a student at the London School of Economics in 1967–1968, just before I arrived there as visiting faculty, and just after I ended my years as professor at Columbia University, Tory spent his 1968–1972 doctoral studies years there. I was aware of him as a rising star and followed his work assiduously, both because of its high quality and because we had the good taste of often working on similar topics, such as persuasive communication, multiple selves, and metamethod concepts such as the one he discusses here, the effects of anointing certain variables as "special."

Had my knowledge of Tory been accompanied by more propinquity, who knows, I might have been a contender. All of us are dependent on the kindness of strangers, and I have been blessed by many kindnesses from Tory that I have discovered, hide them though he modestly tried. There are probably still other favors I have received from this scholar and gentleman of which I have not yet learned.

## A Summing Up

I am fortunate to enjoy as friends all these chapter authors and so many others. As I read these chapters and reminisce about their authors, I resonate with Yeats's lines from *The Municipal Gallery Revisited*:

> You that would judge me, do not judge alone
> This book or that; come to this hallowed place
> Where my friends' portraits hang and look thereon; . . .
> Think where man's glory most begins and ends,
> And say my glory was I had such friends. (lines 50–55)

# Part II

## Attitudes, Persuasion, and Social Influence

# 4

# Resisting Persuasion by Counterarguing: An Attitude Strength Perspective

*Richard E. Petty, Zakary L. Tormala,*
*and Derek D. Rucker*

## Prologue[1]

My approach to the topic in this chapter, and to social psychology more generally, is compatible with Bill McGuire's contextualist/perspectivist framework. According to this view, almost every finding in social psychology depends on some contextual factors that moderate when the finding occurs, when it does not, and when it reverses. Because a contextualist already knows that nearly anything is possible, it becomes particularly important to understand *when* various phenomena occur. In order to understand when something will occur, one often has to understand *why* it occurs—and to understand why something occurs, it is often useful to understand when it occurs. Thus, my work has focused on the moderation and mediation of social phenomena—especially in the area of attitudes.

Exhibit 1 in this regard is the Elaboration Likelihood model of persuasion—a theory of moderated mediation (Petty & Cacioppo, 1986; Petty & Wegener, 1999). That is, the theory specifies how social psychological variables (e.g., source credibility, mood) can produce different outcomes via different mediating mechanisms depending on the context. When introduced, this contextualist theory stood in contrast to what was perhaps the more natural and appealing inclination of attitude theorists: to postulate that variables had one true effect and one true process by which the effect was achieved (Petty, 1997). However, the contextualist approach was necessary to understand the diversity of research findings obtained.

A danger of contextualist frameworks is that they can become meaningless by simply postulating that anything can happen. With this philosophy, one can never be wrong! Thus, the most useful contextualist studies and theories are careful to specify which contexts produce which effects and for which reasons. When this is accomplished, contextualism provides a powerful

---

[1]The prologue to this chapter was written by Richard E. Petty.

framework for understanding the complexities that are inherent in social behavior.

\* \* \*

This chapter is about people's attempts to resist persuasion by counterarguing and the consequences of that attempted resistance for the strength of the resulting attitudes. Counterarguing is not the only way in which people try to resist, of course, but it is the most commonly studied. Thus, it is useful to understand the implications of trying to counterargue as a starting point for understanding the implications of trying to resist persuasion more generally. Our approach to this topic is a contextualist one: We hold that a diversity of outcomes is possible depending on the particular contextual factors present.

Our framework can be stated simply in three propositions. First, when people attempt to counterargue a message, sometimes they resist the message and attitudes do not change, but at other times, despite the attempted counterarguing, attitudes are changed in the direction of the advocacy. Second, when people do not change attitudes following counterarguing, sometimes their confidence in their old attitudes is increased, but sometimes confidence in their old attitudes is decreased. Third, when people change their attitudes despite attempted counterarguing, sometimes confidence in the new attitudes is increased compared with situations in which the attitudes are changed the same amount but without attempted counterarguing, but sometimes confidence in the new attitudes is decreased compared with situations in which counterarguing was not attempted.[2] Because numerous outcomes are possible, our objective in this chapter is to outline the conditions under which each of these effects is likely to occur and to present some preliminary research on the topic. In the first phase of our research program, we have focused on cases in which confidence in one's old or new attitude is likely to be increased as a result of attempted counterarguing.

Understanding the consequences of attempted counterarguing for attitudinal confidence is potentially important because the more confidence people have in their attitudes, the stronger those attitudes are. During the 1990s, attitudes researchers clearly showed that the valence of an attitude is not the only important factor in persuasion situations. This is because attitudes of the same valence (e.g., +2) can also vary in their strength (Petty & Krosnick, 1995). The concept of attitude strength recognizes that all attitudes of the same valence are not equally consequential. In general, the stronger the attitude is, the more resistant it is to subsequent attacks, the longer it endures over time, and the greater the impact it has on judgments and behavior (Krosnick & Petty, 1995). An attitude's overall strength is determined by a number of features such as how accessible the attitude is (Fazio, 1995), how much prior thought was devoted to it (Petty, Haugtvedt, & Smith, 1995), how much confidence one has in it (Gross, Holtz, & Miller, 1995), and so forth. In

---

[2]It is also possible for people to show attitude change in the direction opposite to the advocacy (i.e., a boomerang effect). We suspect that the level of confidence in these attitudes would be quite high and that variations in confidence would follow from the same principles that we outline for attitudes that are unchanged following attempted counterarguing.

our work, we focus on the confidence or certainty with which people hold their attitudes, because this is a reliable determinant of attitude strength and is something people are likely to reflect upon following attempted resistance.

Before turning to our recent work, it is useful to review some background information on resistance research. Early on in the study of attitude change, investigators were concerned primarily with making persuasion work. It was not until the early 1960s that researchers began to systematically investigate *resistance* to persuasive communications. Indeed, in his 1964 paper, Bill McGuire noted that "little was being done on ways of producing resistance to persuasion" (p.192). Sparked by McGuire's inoculation theory (McGuire, 1964; McGuire & Papageorgis, 1961), however, a new interest grew in the exploration of resistance, and this interest continues today (e.g., see Knowles & Linn, 2004). Attitude researchers have used the term "resistance" in a variety of ways over the years. We address these next.

## The Multiple Meanings of Resistance

Perhaps the dominant use of the term resistance is as an *outcome*. As an outcome, resistance refers to the absence or attenuation of attitude change. That is, resistance can imply zero attitude change, reduced attitude change in one condition relative to another, or even reversed attitude change (i.e., boomerang). Although zero attitude change is often construed as resistance, it is important to note that this outcome can be obtained for reasons that have little to do with resistance processes or resistance motivation. For example, zero attitude change can stem from simple failure to attend to or understand a message (Hovland, Janis, & Kelley, 1953).

As a *motivation*, resistance refers to having the goal of resisting attitude change or the desire to keep one's current attitude. Such motivation may or may not result in the outcome of resistance. Several specific motives that can instill a desire to resist persuasion or defend one's attitude from attack have been identified. For example, *reactance* involves the motivation to restore freedom (Brehm, 1966). Thus, when people believe someone is attempting to influence or persuade them, they may react against that attempt and stubbornly refuse to change (Petty & Cacioppo, 1979a). *Consistency* motives have also been implicated in this regard. According to cognitive dissonance theory (Festinger, 1957), for example, people are motivated to resist changing their attitudes when doing so will result in inconsistent beliefs or attitudes that are inconsistent with prior behavior. It is perhaps surprising that increasing *accuracy motives* might also make people more defensive of their current attitudes if they are highly confident that those attitudes are correct (Petty & Wegener, 1999). Indeed, our subjectively correct attitudes are presumably most worthy of defense.

Resistance *processes* refer to the specific mechanisms by which resistance outcomes can be obtained (e.g., counterarguing). Sometimes these resistance processes stem directly from resistance motives, but at other times, resistance processes can occur naturally in the course of thinking about a message objectively (e.g., when a person motivated to be objective finds that the message arguments are weak and therefore counterargues them; Petty & Cacioppo,

1986). When studying resistance as a process, researchers move beyond trying to understand whether a variable (e.g., low source credibility) ultimately reduces persuasion and focus on *how* that variable reduces persuasion. Researchers have identified a number of mechanisms through which resistance occurs. For example, generating *counterarguments* or *unfavorable thoughts* has typically been found to reduce or prevent attitude change (e.g., Brock, 1967; Killeya & Johnson, 1998; see Petty, Ostrom, & Brock, 1981). This mechanism is the focus of the current research and is especially likely to operate when processing motivation (e.g., Petty & Cacioppo, 1979a) and ability (e.g., Wood, Rhodes, & Biek, 1995) are high, such as when the topic is one that is important to the person. In addition, people have been shown to resist through *attitude bolstering*, meaning that they selectively generate or recall information or beliefs that support their attitudes (Lydon, Zanna, & Ross, 1988). Resistance can also occur by *derogating the source* of a persuasive message (e.g., Tannenbaum, Macauley, & Norris, 1966). Furthermore, resistance can occur through *selective attention* to or *avoidance* of attitude-congruent information (Frey, 1986; Gilbert, 1993). Also, *negative affect*, or irritation, has been found to enhance resistance outcomes (e.g., Cacioppo & Petty, 1979; Zuwerink & Devine, 1996).

Finally, research on resistance as a *quality* examines the types of people or attitudes that are resistant to change. Certain types of people (e.g., those high in authoritarianism; Rokeach, 1960) are more difficult to persuade than others. They are resistant individuals (see Briñol et al., 2004). Similarly, certain types of attitudes are more resistant to persuasion than others (Petty & Krosnick, 1995). For example, attitudes that are accessible (Fazio, 1995) or formed with much thought (Petty et al., 1995) are more resistant than those that are inaccessible or formed without much thought. Most germane for the current research is the idea that attitudes held with high confidence are more resistant to change than are attitudes held with low confidence (e.g., Bassili, 1996).

## McGuire's Inoculation Theory

Inoculation theory (McGuire, 1964) is an outstanding example of research on resistance because it exemplifies all four of the meanings of resistance we have outlined. To review briefly, inoculation theory draws on the common medical practice of immunizing people against disease by exposing them to an initial weak dose of the disease. Exposure to the weak disease inoculates the body by causing the formation of antibodies that help people resist more serious exposures to the disease later on. McGuire (1964; McGuire & Papageorgis, 1961) argued that just as the body can be inoculated against diseases, attitudes can be inoculated against persuasive messages, that is, exposure to a *mild* persuasive attack that could be refuted would help people resist a stronger persuasive attack in the future.

In the original test of inoculation theory, McGuire and Papageorgis (1961) gave people persuasive messages attacking cultural truisms—beliefs that are widely shared in a society and rarely, if ever, attacked (e.g., "It's a good idea to brush your teeth after every meal."). Such truisms should be highly vulnerable to persuasive attacks because people have little or no experience defending them: These attitudes have no "antibodies." In their study, McGuire and Papageorgis (1961) first assessed participants' endorsement of several cultural truisms. In one condition, participants then read several paragraphs containing arguments supporting the truisms (support condition). In another condition, participants were exposed to several arguments against the truisms and then read paragraphs refuting each of the arguments raised (inoculation condition). In a third condition, participants were given no information at all (no defense condition). Two days after participants had been exposed to the treatment conditions, they were presented with persuasive messages attacking each truism. McGuire found that the attitudes of participants in the no-defense and support conditions evinced substantial change toward the position of the persuasive message. Participants in the inoculation condition, however, showed significantly less change (i.e., attitudes were more resistant). It is important to note that in the inoculation approach, the initial arguments refuted do not have to match the arguments presented in the follow-up persuasive messages, that is, exposing participants to an initial weak attack confers increased resistance even if the second attack contains completely different arguments (see Papageorgis & McGuire, 1961).

Inoculation theory addresses each of the four aforementioned aspects of resistance. First, McGuire's objective with inoculation theory was to demonstrate a powerful way to reduce attitude change (i.e., to produce a resistance outcome). He accomplished this goal by providing and eliciting counterargumentation to an initial mild attack (i.e., resistance as a process). The initial mild attack was intended to instill a desire to resist a later message by showing people that an important attitude was vulnerable (i.e., resistance as a motivation). In addition to instilling some resistance motivation, the initial attack gave people some preliminary practice in defending their attitudes. Finally, the inoculation treatment rendered the initial attitude more resistant to subsequent attempts to change it (resistance as a quality).

## Implications of Attempted Counterarguing
## for Attitude Strength

In McGuire's work on inoculation, the resistance quality of an attitude was changed by providing people with an inoculation treatment. In his research, the inoculation treatment was designed to be relatively weak so that it would not undermine people's initial attitudes but would simply make them more resistant to future attacks. As noted previously, the mechanism by which the attitudes became more resistant was presumed to be that the inoculation treatment enhanced the motivation and ability of recipients to counterargue future attacks.

In this chapter, we describe an alternative mechanism by which attitudes can become more resistant to future attacks as a result of attempting to resist an initial message. The research is presented in two parts. First, we describe a program of research in which people attempt to resist a message and are successful—that is, their attitudes are unchanged (Tormala & Petty, 2002). Next, we describe a program of research in which people attempt to resist a message but are unsuccessful—that is, their attitudes are changed (Rucker & Petty, in press). In each line of research, we are interested in how the resistance attempt, whether successful or not, can lead to enhanced attitude confidence. Finally, we outline a model of when successful and failed resistance might lead to reduced as well as enhanced attitude confidence.

## Successful Resistance

The first program of research, on successful resistance (Tormala & Petty, 2002), expands on some possibilities first raised in McGuire's inoculation theory. First, consistent with McGuire's findings, we believe that resistance to initial persuasive attacks may sometimes confer greater resistance to later attacks as well. We depart from the specific mechanism proposed by inoculation theory, however. Most important, we argue that an attack on one's attitude has potential consequences for the strength of the attitude attacked. We postulate that the increased resistance induced by inoculation treatments and other persuasive messages need not stem exclusively from increasing a person's motivation and ability to counterargue. Rather, such resistance could arise from fundamental changes in the underlying confidence with which the person holds the initial attitude. If there is a change in attitude confidence, it follows that there should be a change not only in terms of the extent to which the attitude is resistant to subsequent persuasion attempts but also in other consequences, such as the ability of the attitude to predict behavior. Finally, we postulate that changes in attitude strength come about through a metacognitive mechanism whereby people perceive their own resistance and form inferences about their attitudes.

To illustrate the metacognitive process we propose, consider a person who is strongly opposed to animal testing and is presented with a pro-testing advocacy. He or she might want to resist persuasion and thus actively counterargue the message and avoid any attitude change. Given the importance of the topic and the active nature of this resistance, it is likely that the individual is aware of his or her counterarguing and recognizes that this effort was effective in preventing persuasion. We posit that when people try to resist a message and perceive that they were successful in resisting the message, the confidence with which the person holds the attitude can increase because successful resistance implies attitude validity. This newly acquired sense of validity or confidence should lead the individual to be more resistant to future persuasion and more likely to behave in accord with the attitude in the future (Fazio & Zanna, 1978).

Our metacognitive analysis allows for a unique prediction about the nature of the message a person resists. Specifically, the stronger the person perceives the resisted message to be, the more confidence that person should develop in his or her attitude. Perhaps it was not salient before the successful resistance that one's position was so good that it could withstand a strong attack; if the attitude can withstand a strong attack, however, it is reasonable to infer that the attitude must be valid. On the other hand, if people successfully defend their attitudes against a weak attack, confidence in the attitude should not increase. When resisting a weak attack, one cannot be certain that the attitude would have survived a strong challenge. Under these circumstances, one's successful resistance is less diagnostic regarding the validity of the target attitude. Thus, varying the perceived quality of the arguments that people resist provides one way of testing whether the metacognitive processes we propose are operating. We next describe a series of studies designed to explore these possibilities.

STUDY 1. To examine whether our metacognitive framework held any promise, we conducted an initial study in which students were presented with a proposal from their university's board of trustees to institute a policy requiring college seniors to pass a comprehensive exam in their major area in order to graduate (see Petty & Cacioppo, 1979b). All participants received a message that contained two strong and two weak arguments on the issue. An example of a strong argument was that implementing the exam policy would increase the starting salary for graduates. An example of a weak argument was that implementing the exam policy would allow students to compare their scores with students at other universities (see Petty & Cacioppo, 1986). The students were also told that in order to get reactions to all kinds of arguments in favor of the exam policy, we were presenting some students with strong arguments and some with weak arguments. In the *perceived strong arguments* condition, the students were told that the experimenters included only the strongest of all the arguments raised in favor of the exam policy. In the *perceived weak arguments* conditions, they were told that the experimenters included only the weakest of all the arguments in favor of the exam policy.

To encourage resistance to change, all students were told to try to counterargue the message. They then read the message, listed their counterarguments, and completed the key measures—attitudes toward the issue and confidence in their attitudes. A control group consisting of students who did not receive a message was included so that we could determine the direction of any confidence effects that emerged.

The results of this study revealed that the counterargument instructions were successful in getting students to resist persuasion. Neither the group that received the arguments labeled strong nor the group that received the arguments labeled weak differed in attitudes from the no-message control group. However, the confidence measure showed a different pattern. When people resisted what they thought was a strong message, their attitude confidence increased compared with that of the perceived weak message and control groups; that is, when people successfully resisted strong arguments, their attitude confidence increased. When these people successfully resisted weak arguments, attitude confidence did not increase. This finding is consistent with our metacognitive framework: People only gained confidence when their resistance was diagnostic.

STUDY 2. Study 1 demonstrated that confidence in one's initial attitude can be increased by metacognitive processes that follow successful resistance—but is this enhanced confidence in one's initial attitude meaningful? For example, does it render the attitude more resistant to subsequent attacks? Such an effect would parallel what McGuire (1964) was able to show with his inoculation treatments. We examined this possibility in our second experiment.

After participants counterargued an ostensibly strong or weak message and reported their attitudes (as in Study 1), we had them engage in a 15-min filler task and then exposed them to a second, stronger message containing new arguments in favor of the same issue (comprehensive exams). Participants were told to try and counterargue the first message but were not told to counterargue the second. As in Study 1, there were no differences in attitudes after the first message. As expected, though, participants who had initially resisted a message believed to be strong showed significantly *less* change in response to the second message than did participants who had initially resisted a message believed to be weak. Thus, it appears that resistance to future attacks is enhanced when people initially resist an attack that is believed to be strong. In other words, the group that presumably developed the most confidence in the initial attitude was most resistant to a future attack. Because the perceived strong and weak groups actually received the same initial attack on their initial attitudes and resisted it to the same degree, the inoculation approach would predict the same level of subsequent resistance from these groups. Because we found differences in subsequent resistance, however, our metacognitive perspective increases understanding of when inoculation-type effects are most likely to occur.

STUDY 3. In a third study, we sought to test whether the new attitude strength that results from resisting a message perceived as strong could have implications beyond future resistance. We tested the possibility that the increased attitude confidence we observed would strengthen attitude–behavior consistency. To examine this notion, at the end of an experiment that was essentially identical to Study 1, we told participants that the university would be holding a student vote on the issue raised in the message (comprehensive exams), and we asked them how they planned to vote. The key new result was that compared with a control group, attitudes were more highly correlated with voting intentions after participants had resisted a message they believed to be strong than after they had resisted a message believed to be weak. These findings illustrate that our attitude strength perspective permits predictions unanticipated by inoculation theory. In addition to increasing resistance to subsequent attacks, initial successful resistance can enhance the relationship between attitudes and intended behavior.

SUMMARY. In our first series of studies (Tormala & Petty, 2002), we showed that getting people to resist an initial attacking message can cause an increase in attitude confidence. This only occurs, however, to the extent that people believe they resisted a message that was reasonably cogent. People who successfully resisted a message perceived as weak did not show an increase in attitude confidence even though their initial resistance was in fact the same. Furthermore, analysis of the counterarguments listed by participants in the strong and weak conditions of each study demonstrated that the counterarguments generated were equivalent in number, quality, and focus (i.e., which arguments in the messages they addressed). The only difference appeared to be the inference they drew about their attitudes based on their resistance.[3]

## Unsuccessful Resistance

In the studies described so far, counterarguing produced successful resistance. This was ensured because the initial messages participants confronted contained a mix of strong and weak arguments. But what if people were trying to resist by counterarguing and were not successful? What would happen if the arguments in the message were so strong that despite people's best efforts, they could not generate counterarguments? Under these conditions, attitudes would be expected to change in the direction of the message advocacy. In this section, we describe a program of research by Rucker and Petty (in press) that examines cases in which people try to counterargue a message but are unsuccessful in doing so. These individuals are compared with people who change their attitudes to the same degree but who are not trying explicitly to resist.

Much prior work in the attitude change literature shows that if you can get people to think carefully about strong message arguments, attitude change will follow from the favorable thoughts that they generate toward these arguments (see Petty & Cacioppo, 1986; Petty, Ostrom & Brock, 1981). Is there any possible advantage to persuading people by encouraging them to try to counterargue a strong message rather than to simply think about it? Our metacognitive framework makes a unique prediction in this respect. First, recall from our first series of studies (Tormala & Petty, 2002) that if people are trying to counterargue a message and feel successful, they have greater confidence in the attitude they just defended. If people are trying to counterargue and fail, however, we expect them to have more confidence in their *new* attitudes than if their attitudes changed *the same degree* as a result of more objective (undirected) thinking about the topic.

Why would this be? The reason for this is that if people are just thinking naturally about strong arguments, they will presumably be generating favorable thoughts toward the message and attitudes will change because of the favorable thoughts generated. If people specifically are trying to counterargue but can only come up with favorable thoughts, however, they will realize both that there are favorable thoughts *and* that there are no viable counterarguments against the position. This additional inference should enhance confidence in the new (changed) attitude.

STUDY 1. In our first study on this topic, we instructed some college students to try to counterargue an advertisement and others to simply think about it carefully. All participants were told that they would be receiving some facts about a familiar brand of aspirin. After receiving the "counterargue" or "think" instructions, participants received a message about the aspirin that contained some very compelling facts (e.g., "clinically proven to outlast all

---

[3]Additional studies in this paradigm further suggested that the same effects occur when participants are presented with messages that are actually strong or weak rather than merely labeled strong or weak. This suggests that people will naturally make inferences about the strength of the message they resisted and helps rule out various alternative explanations for the data.

other brands of aspirin by 4 hours"). Following the message, each of the persuasive arguments was presented to the participants separately on a computer screen and the participants were told to use the keyboard to enter a "thought" or a *negative* thought" (i.e., counterargument) depending on condition. If no appropriate thoughts came to mind, participants were told that they could type the word "none." The latter instruction was included so that participants in the counterargue condition were "allowed" to fail if they really could not generate any negative thoughts. A group that did not receive any message or any thought instruction was included as a control.

On the attitude measure that followed the message and thought listing task, both the thought and the counterargue groups showed the same favorable attitudes toward the new aspirin. As expected, these groups were both more favorable than the control group, indicating that attitude change had occurred. However, the ratings of attitude confidence showed that participants who tried to generate negative thoughts had more confidence in their favorable attitudes than did individuals who simply thought about the strong arguments.

STUDY 2. Our hypothesis is that trying to counterargue and failing is critical to producing increased confidence in one's new attitude, but we have only compared trying to counterargue with trying to think. Counterarguing is an attempt to generate a particular kind of valenced thought, whereas thinking allows free reign. Perhaps trying to generate any kind of valenced thought leads to more confidence than freely thinking does. If so, then instructing people to generate favorable thoughts should produce the same results as instructing people to counterargue. In addition, in this study we wanted to determine if the enhanced certainty we have obtained was consequential. Thus, in addition to measuring attitudes, we assessed behavioral intentions regarding the product (i.e., purchase likelihood).

The procedure for this study was basically the same as for Study 1, though we used a new and unfamiliar aspirin product so that behavioral intentions would not be based on habitual patterns. Participants were told that they should try to think about, try to generate negative thoughts about, or try to generate positive thoughts in response to an advertisement about a new brand of aspirin. A control group that received no message was also included. As in Study 1, the strong arguments were successful in producing the same amount of attitude change relative to the control for all groups. However, only the group trying to counterargue showed enhanced confidence in their new attitudes. Furthermore, the attitudes of individuals trying to counterargue were more predictive of their behavioral intentions ($r = .80$) than were the attitudes of those simply thinking ($r = .39$) or generating favorable thoughts ($r = .31$) to the message.

STUDY 3. In a third study, we wanted to examine mediation of the confidence effect. Our postulated mediator is a metaperception that there are few counterarguments that can be generated against the advocated product. People who counterargue and fail should have this metaperception, whereas the other thinking groups should not. The groups are not expected to differ in their perception regarding the number of favorable thoughts that were provoked by the message. The procedure of this study was close to that of Study 1, with the key addition of a measure of people's perceptions of how many counterarguments were available against the advocated position as well as a measure of how many favorable thoughts were available in support of the advocacy.

As in our prior studies, the thought group and the counterargue group showed the same favorable attitudes toward the aspirin relative to the control group. However, the counterargue group held these favorable attitudes with more confidence than did the group instructed just to think. In addition, the two groups did not differ in the actual number of counterarguments they generated (each group generated very few counterarguments). The group that was attempting to counterargue, however, had the *perception* that there were fewer counterarguments available. Important to note, subsequent analyses revealed that the effect of the manipulation on attitude confidence was mediated by people's perception of the number of counterarguments available. It was not mediated by the actual number of counterarguments or favorable thoughts generated or by the perception of the number of favorable thoughts available.

SUMMARY. In our second series of studies (Rucker & Petty, in press), we showed that people who attempted to counterargue a message but failed changed their attitudes to the same extent as people simply thinking or trying to be favorable, but we showed that they had more confidence in their new attitudes. In these studies, people who tried to counterargue had the perception that fewer counterarguments could be made against the message. Because these individuals are surer that there are no flaws in the advocacy, they can be more confident in their new attitudes.

These studies show that the act of counterarguing an initial message can have an important impact on people's attitudes even when the counterarguing fails. Just as successful resistance can increase confidence in one's old attitude (Tormala & Petty, 2002), unsuccessful resistance can enhance confidence in one's *new* attitude. This confidence can increase the overall strength of the new attitude, as is evident in the enhanced correlation between attitudes and behavioral intentions.

## Being Unimpressed With One's Resistance or Lack of Resistance: Future Directions

In this chapter, we briefly reviewed two lines of research in which people were asked to try to counterargue a persuasive message. In the first line of research, by Tormala and Petty (2002), we examined cases in which people were able to counterargue the message successfully. These individuals resisted, and when they were impressed with their resistance, such as when they resisted arguments believed to be strong, confidence in their initial attitudes increased. In the second line of research, by Rucker and Petty (in press), we examined cases in which people had difficulty counterarguing when attempting to do so. These individuals succumbed to the persuasive message. When they were impressed with how hard it was to counterargue and how few counterarguments they could generate, they became more confident in their new attitudes than did people who were undirected in their processing of the message. What these two lines of research have in common is that people were impressed either with their ability or their inability to counterargue the message. Being impressed with one's resistance led to increased confidence in one's initial attitude, but being impressed with one's failure to resist led to increased confidence in one's new attitude. But what if people were not so impressed with either their resistance or their lack of resistance? Under these conditions, we might expect a very different pattern of effects.

## Being Unimpressed With One's Resistance

Consider first the case in which a person is able to counterargue and resists the message but believes that his or her resistance was ineffective or lacking in some way. That is, even though resistance may have been successful in the sense of preventing attitude change, an individual might still perceive that the resistance was flawed or very difficult (e.g., "Whew! I resisted by the skin of my teeth."). We postulate that even when resistance is successful, if people feel that their resistance was in some way flawed or very difficult, the strength of their initial attitude will not increase. On the contrary, it will stay the same or could even decrease. A decrease in attitude strength would suggest that although the persuasive message did not produce attitude change per se (in terms of outcome), it was partially successful in that it weakened the targeted attitude. Such an attitude would then be rendered more susceptible to future attempts to change it and less predictive of behavior than it was previously (see Petty & Krosnick, 1995).

## Being Unimpressed With One's Failure to Resist

Just as people might be unimpressed with their resistance, they might sometimes be unimpressed with their failure to resist: Rather than being impressed with how hard they tried to resist but failed, they may have the feeling that they did not try very hard to resist, that there were distractions present preventing effective resistance, or that the few counterarguments they generated were quite good. In such cases, confidence in the new attitude might be reduced below what more objective thinking would foster.

## A Model of Attempted Resistance

Figure 4.1 presents a summary of the key ideas presented in this chapter. We recognize in our model that when attempting to counterargue a message, people can either succeed or fail in their attempt and they can either be impressed or unimpressed with their success or failure. The model outlines how one's metacognitions about one's resistance or failure to resist can either enhance or undermine confidence in one's initial (unchanged) attitude or can enhance or undermine confidence in one's newly changed attitude. The model is clearly a contextualist one in that all things are possible. Important to note,

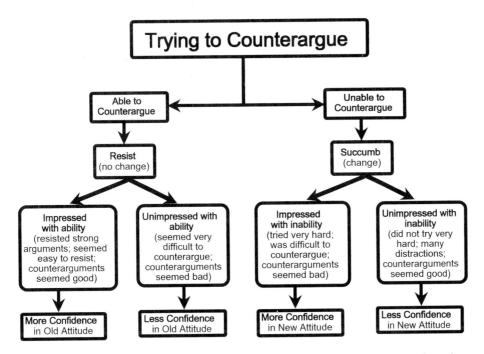

**Figure 4.1.** Implications for attitude confidence of attempted counterarguing of persuasive messages.

however, we attempt to specify in the model the general conditions under which the various outcomes occur.

Our model indicates that the process of trying to resist by counterarguing can enhance the strength of an existing attitude if the person feels that the counterarguing was effective against a strong attack. This enhanced confidence will not only help the attitude in future resistance but will also help the attitude to guide behavior immediately. This process is potentially important for any attitude that is already optimal in valence but not in confidence. This outcome is bad news, however, for would-be persuaders who had assumed that a failed attempt at persuasion at least did no harm to their cause. Second, attempting to counterargue may also enhance the strength of a changed attitude over the same persuasion produced by more objective thinking. Thus, when arguments are very strong, recipients might be challenged to counterargue rather than think about the message. The amount of change produced will be the same, but the directed counterarguing technique may produce stronger new attitudes.

As we noted previously, our strength model of attempted resistance addresses issues similar to those in McGuire's classic work on inoculation theory. The work on inoculation theory dealt largely with cultural truisms. Confidence in these attitudes was presumably very high prior to the presentation of an attacking message. Inoculation treatments showed individuals that their cherished beliefs were susceptible to attack, thereby motivating them to marshal defenses against future attacks. In the language of attitude strength, the inoculation treatment might first undermine confidence but then restore it to a high level along with the tools to defend the attitude. For attitudes that are nontruisms, such as those used in the discussed research, it is presumably rare to be at a state of maximum confidence initially. Therefore to instill future resistance for these attitudes, it might make sense to give treatments that enhance confidence, thereby motivating people to resist in the future. It is important to note that enhancing attitude confidence should also produce consequences beyond increased resistance—such as enhanced attitude–behavior consistency.

# References

Bassili, J. N. (1996). Meta-judgmental versus operative indexes of psychological attributes: The case of measures of attitude strength. *Journal of Personality and Social Psychology, 71,* 637–653.

Brehm, J. W. (1966). *A theory of psychological reactance.* San Diego, CA: Academic Press.

Briñol, P., Rucker, D. D., Tormala, Z. L., & Petty, R. E. (2004). Individual differences in resistance to persuasion: Outcomes and mechanisms. In E. S. Knowles & J. A. Linn (Eds.), *Resistance and persuasion.* Mahwah, NJ: Erlbaum.

Brock, T. C. (1967). Communication discrepancy and intent to persuade as determinants of counterargument production. *Journal of Experimental Social Psychology, 3,* 296–309.

Cacioppo, J. T., & Petty, R. E. (1979). The effects of message repetition and position on cognitive responses, recall, and persuasion. *Journal of Personality and Social Psychology, 37,* 97–109.

Fazio, R. H. (1995). Attitudes as object-evaluation associations: Determinants, consequences, and correlates of attitude accessibility. In R. E. Petty & J. A. Krosnick (Eds.), *Attitude strength: Antecedents and consequences* (pp. 247–282). Mahwah, NJ: Erlbaum.

Fazio, R. H., & Zanna, M. P. (1978). Attitudinal qualities relating to the strength of the attitude-behavior relationship. *Journal of Experimental Social Psychology, 14,* 398–408.

Festinger, L. (1957). *A theory of cognitive dissonance.* Evanston, IL: Row, Peterson.

Frey, D. (1986). Recent research on selective exposure to information. *Advances in Experimental Social Psychology, 19,* 41–80.

Gilbert, D. T. (1993). The assent of man: Mental representation and the control of belief. In D. M. Wegner & J. W. Pennebaker (Eds.), *Handbook of mental control* (pp. 57–87). Englewood Cliffs, NJ: Prentice Hall.

Gross, S. R., Holtz, R., & Miller, N. (1995). Attitude certainty. In R. E. Petty & J. A. Krosnick (Eds.), *Attitude strength: Antecedents and consequences* (pp. 215–246). Mahwah, NJ: Erlbaum.

Hovland, C. I., Janis, I. L., & Kelley, J. J. (1953). *Communication and persuasion.* New Haven: Yale University Press.

Killeya, L. A., & Johnson, B. T. (1998). Experimental induction of biased systematic processing: The directed-thought technique. *Personality and Social Psychology Bulletin, 24,* 17–33.

Knowles, E. S., & Linn, J. S. (Eds.). (2004). *Resistance and persuasion.* Mahwah, NJ: Erlbaum.

Krosnick, J. A., & Petty, R. E. (1995). Attitude strength: An overview. In R. E. Petty & J. A. Krosnick (Eds.), *Attitude strength: Antecedents and consequences* (pp. 1–24). Mahwah, NJ: Erlbaum.

Lydon, J., Zanna, M. P., & Ross, M. (1988). Bolstering attitudes by autobiographical recall: Attitude persistence and selective memory. *Personality and Social Psychology Bulletin, 14,* 78–86.

McGuire, W. J. (1964). Inducing resistance to persuasion: Some contemporary approaches. In L. Berkowitz (Ed.), *Advances in experimental social psychology* (Vol. 1, pp. 191–229). New York: Academic Press.

McGuire, W. J., & Papageorgis, D. (1961). The relative efficacy of various types of prior belief-defense in producing immunity against persuasion. *Journal of Abnormal and Social Psychology, 62,* 327–337.

Papageorgis, D., & McGuire, W. J. (1961). The generality of immunity to persuasion produced by pre-exposure to weakened counterarguments. *Journal of Abnormal and Social Psychology, 62,* 475–481.

Petty, R. E. (1997). The evolution of theory and research in social psychology: From single to multiple effect and process models. In C. McGarty & S. A. Haslam (Eds.), *The message of social psychology: Perspectives on mind in society* (pp. 268–290). Oxford, England: Blackwell Publishers, Ltd.

Petty, R. E., & Cacioppo, J. T. (1979a). Effects of forewarning of persuasive intent and involvement on cognitive responses. *Personality and Social Psychology Bulletin, 5,* 173–176.

Petty, R. E., & Cacioppo, J. T. (1979b). Issue involvement can increase or decrease persuasion by enhancing message-relevant cognitive responses. *Journal of Personality and Social Psychology, 37,* 1915–1926.

Petty, R. E., & Cacioppo, J. T. (1986). *Communication and persuasion: Central and peripheral routs to attitude change.* New York: Springer-Verlag.

Petty, R. E., Haugtvedt, C. P., & Smith, S. M. (1995). Elaboration as a determinant of attitude strength: Creating attitudes that are persistent, resistant, and predictive of behavior. In R. E. Petty & J. A. Krosnick (Eds.), *Attitude strength: Antecedents and consequences* (pp. 93–130). Mahwah, NJ: Erlbaum.

Petty, R. E. & Krosnick, J. A. (Eds.). (1995). *Attitude strength: Antecedents and consequences.* Mahwah, NJ: Erlbaum.

Petty, R. E., Ostrom, T. M., & Brock, T. C. (Eds.). (1981). *Cognitive responses in persuasion.* Hillsdale, NJ: Erlbaum.

Petty, R. E., & Wegener, D. T. (1999). The Elaboration Likelihood Model: Current status and controversies. In S. Chaiken & Y. Trope (Eds.), *Dual process theories in social psychology* (pp. 41–72). New York: Guilford Press.

Rokeach, M. (1960). *The open and closed mind.* New York: Basic Books.

Rucker, D. D., & Petty, R. E. (in press). When resistance is futile: The effects of failed counterarguing on attitude certainty. *Journal of Personality and Social Psychology.*

Tannenbaum, P. H., Macauley, J. R., & Norris, E. L. (1966). Principle of congruity and reduction of persuasion. *Journal of Personality and Social Psychology, 3,* 233–238.

Tormala, Z. L., & Petty, R. E. (2002). What doesn't kill me makes me stronger: The effects of resisting persuasion on attitude certainty. *Journal of Personality and Social Psychology, 83,* 1298–1313.

Wood, W., Rhodes, N., & Biek, M. (1995). Working knowledge and attitude strength: An information-processing analysis. In. R. E. Petty & J. A. Krosnick (Eds.), *Attitude strength: Antecedents and consequences* (pp. 283–313). Mahwah, NJ: Erlbaum.

Zuwerink, J. R., & Devine, P. G. (1996). Attitude importance and resistance to persuasion: It's not just the thought that counts. *Journal of Personality and Social Psychology, 70,* 931–944.

# 5

# Dynamic Networks and Other Thought Systems: Remote Ramifications of a Focused Persuasive Communication

## Reid Hastie and Katherine A. Rawson

What a piece of work is man! How noble in reason! how infinite in faculty! in form, in moving, how express and admirable! in action how like an angel! in apprehension how like a god! (*Hamlet,* II. ii., 316)

## Prologue[1]

The study reported in this chapter was the first author's maiden voyage in behavioral research. I was fortunate to have Bill McGuire as my captain, and that year of discovery in psychology, across the desk from one of the field's greatest minds, was an exciting beginning to my professional life. Bill introduced me to psychology in his challenging, intense, and generous way. Let me provide a sample of four insights that I first learned from Bill and that have proved exceptionally useful during my happy life as an experimental psychologist. (I am still far from the level of intellectual satori that Bill probably achieved when he was in grammar school, so the best I can do is summarize these insights in the form of hokey bumper stickers rather than the elegant koan that Bill would have composed.)

1.  *Just do it!* After you've designed and implemented your experimental procedure, sit down and perform the task as if you were a participant. Of course, you cannot adopt the perspective of a naïve participant, but by performing your own experimental task you will reap a surprisingly rich harvest of insights into procedural artifacts of the task: confusing instructions, missing information, misdirected dependent variable questions, and so on. Most important, you will learn more about the cognitive strategies invoked by the task than you could glean from a hundred think-aloud self-reports from actual participants. If you want to know what your participants are doing in your experiment, "walk that experimental mile in their shoes."

---

[1]The prologue to this chapter was written by Reid Hastie.

2. *Some people are rational some of the time.* Bill taught me that often the best route to a process model of cognition and behavior is the high road of a rational analysis (cf. Anderson, 1990; Edwards, 1967; Gigerenzer, 2000). Even if the normative model is not descriptive of participants' behavior, it provides profound insights into the experimental task, tells you what is important about the task, and gives you a standard for best performance (cf. Garner, 1974). Furthermore, we need to remind ourselves that our descriptive models should not preclude the possibility that some of the participants are performing at optimally adaptive or rational levels. This is especially important in this age of "heuristics and biases" and "bounded rationality."

3. *It is better to have loved and lost (your theory), than never to have lost at all.* Every great scientist must have the capacity for naïve, unconditional acceptance of theoretical assumptions. You're not going to get far with the inferential process of deriving interesting predictions from a theory, unless you can "embrace it." Bill exemplifies this essential capacity to accept theoretical assumptions and then to think far ahead to infer subtle implications of those assumptions. The crucial second clause of this aphorism reminds us that after the enchanting theory has been embraced, you must be willing to reconsider your relationship when brutal data rear their ugly heads. So, in science (as in the rest of life) it is essential to "love" your theory, but also to "lose it" when facts tell you it is time to give up. To quote another of Bill's twisted aphorisms: "A thing of beauty is a joy . . . for a while."

4. *Inside every big fat thesis there is a small elegant thesis struggling to escape.* Fortunately, I do not have any copies of the early drafts I wrote of the master's thesis that was the tangible product of my first year as Bill's student. It was a vast, motley collection of assertions, hypotheses, and messy conclusions in the midst of puddles of half-baked data summaries. What I have in hand today is a neat, succinct summary of the essential theoretical claims with one table and three relevant data analyses. I would never have gotten to that useful, even elegant document without Bill's constructive, good-humored, and copious revisions. If you're a student, give yourself time and the courage to step back from that bloated mess of a first draft, to figure out what the real point of the study was, and then to revise, revise, revise, until the supple, handsome thesis is visible. If you're an advisor or collaborator, make sure you have the time and energy available at the end of the project to help that hidden thesis escape from its gross first draft form.

It is impossible to summarize all of the wise precepts and attitudes that I learned from Bill that year as we discussed topics ranging from the New York subway system to Paul Ricoeur's essays on the phenomenology of evil. Those were golden days, when Bill steered me toward enlightenment as a professional psychologist, and my life was changed forever . . . thank you, Bill.

* * *

## Belief Systems and Belief Revision

Higher-order cognitive processes are an extension of the powerful perceptual processes that evolved as an adaptive specialty of primates navigating through a three-dimensional, arboreal world. The distinctive human capacity for complex judgments and inferences is an evolutionary successor to our remarkable abilities to perceive and mentally represent three-dimensional scenes given two-and-a-half-dimensional information (Pinker, 1997, chapter 4). What we call higher-order cognition is the successor of the "unconscious inferences" that underlie our native perceptual capacities (Helmholtz, 1910/1925; Hochberg, 1988). These inferential processes developed so that a person could see what was hidden behind other physical objects, but also to "see" into the future, "to anticipate significant core events that might befall him or her" (McGuire & McGuire, 1991, p. 1).

Empirical research has demonstrated that humans are capable of accomplishing complicated inferential tasks (e.g., J. R. Anderson & Hastie, 1974; Collins & Quillian, 1969; Hayes-Roth & Hayes-Roth, 1975; Moeser & Tarrant, 1977; Newell & Simon, 1972; Rips, 1994; Sternberg, 1980). For example, Moeser and Tarrant (1977) constructed a complex network consisting of nodes representing 12 people and 11 direct connections based on the relations of their ages (e.g., "John is older than Carl"). Participants first learned these 11 basic premise relations. After training, a speeded verification test, in which participants were presented with a relational statement (e.g., "John is older than Carl") and were asked to indicate as quickly as possible whether the relation was true or false, was administered. Tested relations included both the direct relations presented during training and indirect relations that were not presented during training but could be inferred from the direct relations. The proportion of correct verifications overall was greater for direct relations than for indirect relations (.97 and .90, respectively). Overall, response times were slower for verification of indirect relations than for direct relations (4.2 s and 5.6 s, respectively), implying that inferential processes were needed in addition to retrieval processes for the verification of indirect relations. The rate of correct verification for indirect relations was well above chance, an impressive achievement given that some of the indirect relations required traversing three or four direct relations to verify.

Another complex inferential achievement occurs when a person has to reason from a collection of premises with the knowledge that some of these assumptions may be false. The reasoner must be prepared to add or delete some beliefs from the original "database" and then change the conclusions to maintain logical consistency with the new information. This belief revision process raises many fascinating problems and paradoxes for everyday and technical reasoning (Quine & Ullian, 1970). Some of the most interesting theoretical research in artificial intelligence has been directed at these puzzles of nonmonotonic inference and truth-maintenance in logical reasoning systems (Genesereth & Nilsson, 1987; see entries for "Reasoning, Non-monotonic" and "Belief Revision" in Shapiro, 1990).

The philosopher Gilbert Harman (1986, 1996) provides an apt illustration of everyday belief revision: Suppose you initially believe a friend to be a vegetarian but then notice that she orders a steak when you go out to dinner with her. How should you revise your beliefs about that person? You would certainly change the central belief that she is a vegetarian, but which other related beliefs would you change in your belief system? For example, you may also reduce your confidence in the belief that she is an animal-rights activist and you may add the belief that she was recently diagnosed as iron-deficient.

Similar processes of belief revision also underlie the intellectual work of scientists. A researcher may believe a set of assumptions that support her belief in a theoretical framework, which supports her belief in specific hypotheses, which support her belief in an empirical prediction. But when the prediction is not borne out by data, which of the many relevant beliefs must also be changed? Harman (1986) noted that processes of belief revision should serve two goals: to preserve *coherence* among a system of beliefs and to be *conservative* in changing as few related beliefs as possible when revision is necessary. However, belief revision in the service of these goals may lead to some irrational outcomes, including making inferences that are not logically justified, maintaining two beliefs that are logically contradictory, and breaking the chains of premises and derivations that originally supported current beliefs.

Harman (1986) relied primarily on conjectures and intuitively compelling examples to support his conclusions, but he might have cited empirical research by psychologists to make his points. (Harman did cite one experiment conducted by Ross, Lepper, & Hubbard, 1975, on belief perseverance, although his interpretation of that study is moot; cf. Rips, 1987). Bill McGuire conducted pioneering empirical research to study these belief revision processes forty years ago (e.g., Watts & McGuire, 1964). The culmination of McGuire's research program is his dauntingly comprehensive and detailed Theory of Thought Systems, developed in collaboration with Claire McGuire (McGuire, 1990; McGuire & McGuire, 1991). Although McGuire and McGuire address the same phenomena as Harman, they present a more specific, rationally inspired model of the dynamics of these thought processes. The original inspirations for McGuire and McGuire's system were deductive logic and probability theory, including Bayes' Theorem (McGuire, 1960a, 1968, 1981; cf. Edwards, 1967). The central precept in the McGuire and McGuire proposal was that people are intuitive logicians and probability theorists but with numerous corrections of a nonlogical nature, including a weakness for wishful thinking, temporal inertia in the revision process, and thresholds for change that make the revision process conservative and occasionally erratic.

Given the assumption articulated by Harman (1986) that individuals pursue the dual goals of belief coherence and conservative revision, if a person is presented with a statement that introduces inconsistency into a belief system, that person should change beliefs that are implicationally related to the statement in the system. McGuire (1960a, 1960b) provided some of the earliest evidence for the operation of such goals in belief revision tasks. In one early experiment, college students rated the probability of 24 propositions that composed eight syllogisms (1960b). A week later, the same participants read four persuasive messages targeting one premise in each of four syllogisms (the other four syllogisms were used as no-message controls). Each message included arguments for an increase in the likelihood of the premise. Participants then made probability judgments for all 24 propositions again. McGuire found that after reading persuasive messages, people increased their judgments of the probability of the premise that was explicitly mentioned in the persuasive messages relative to their first set of judgments and relative to a set of judgments made by people who read no messages. More important, after reading the message about the premise, people also increased their judgments of probability for the logically related conclusions that were not mentioned directly in the messages.

Dillehay, Insko, and Smith (1966) replicated and extended McGuire's findings by showing that both direct and remote effects of persuasive communication did not depend on making specific rated propositions salient. Specifically, in some experimental conditions, Dillehay et al. eliminated initial exposure to the premises and conclusions and only collected judgments after persuasive messages had been presented. Persuasive messages still influenced the judged probability of both explicitly mentioned premises and unmentioned conclusions (relative to no-message controls) when judgments were only collected after message presentation (see also McFarland & Thistlethwaite, 1970; Watts & Holt, 1970).

Holt and Watts (1969) explored the effects of the salience of the interrelations between propositions on direct and remote belief changes in response to persuasion. They hypothesized that making the relationships between beliefs more salient would result in less change in beliefs directly targeted by persuasive messages because it would be more obvious that changes would need to be made elsewhere in the system to maintain consistency. However, if a targeted belief was changed, there would be more changes in other related beliefs if the relationships were salient. Holt and Watts manipulated salience by varying the order of presentation of propositions during a premessage session in which initial probability judgments were collected. Propositions from all the syllogisms were either presented in a scrambled format (as in previous research) or were presented as intact syllogisms to increase the salience of the relationships between propositions. As predicted, compared with a scrambled presentation format, people were less likely to change their beliefs on the targeted premise when propositions were presented as intact syllogisms. But, they also found that people who exhibited greater change on the premises targeted by the persuasive messages exhibited more change in their judgments for related conclusions (see also Watts & Holt, 1970).

Other research has also implicated the operation of logical processes in belief revision tasks. McFarland and Thistlethwaite (1970; Watts & Holt, 1970) found no "illogical" effects of persuasive messages targeting minor premises on the judged probabilities of major premises; they also found no change resulting from persuasive messages targeting major premises on the judged probabilities of minor premises. They did show that persuasive messages targeting either major or minor premises were both effective at influencing the judged probabilities for the conclusions (previous research had only used messages targeting minor premises).

Findings such as these support the notion that people pursue conservatism and coherence goals when revising their beliefs in light of new information. People conservatively resist change in beliefs that imply change, but once a belief is changed, they make changes in related beliefs to restore coherence to their larger system of beliefs.

Note that all of these studies demonstrating remote ramifications in probabilistic judgments have exploited thought systems based on *logical* relationships (e.g., three-proposition syllogisms). Do these demonstrations of remote ramifications generalize to more complex belief systems based on *causal* relationships, which are more common in our beliefs about many real-world situations? McGuire (1990) conducted research suggesting that individuals do maintain relatively complex thought systems based on causal relations. He presented research participants with core events (e.g., the United States converts to the metric system), asked people to perform a thought listing task, and found that more than 80% of the generated thoughts are either *causal* antecedents or consequences of the core event. However, McGuire did *not* find evidence for remote effects on subjective probability judgments within these causal systems. In one study, McGuire presented participants with core events and asked them to list either promotion antecedents (i.e., conditions that would make the core event more likely) or prevention antecedents (i.e., conditions that would make the core event less likely). The rated probability of the core events did not differ between the two groups, and neither group differed from control conditions in which no antecedents were generated. In 1970, McGuire encouraged Hastie to conduct additional studies to take a closer look at remote belief revision within causal thought systems.

## An Empirical Study of the Remote Ramifications of Focused Persuasive Communications in Causal Belief Systems (Hastie & McGuire, 1970)

McGuire and Hastie planned an empirical study of belief revision that differed from earlier research on remote ramifications in two important respects. First, the underlying system of ideas was based on causal relationships rather than on logical relationships. Second, the belief system was highly complex, involving interconnections among 21 propositions (compared to prior research on three-proposition syllogisms composed of two premises and a conclusion).

The experimental strategy was to capture the participants' own prior beliefs in a conceptual network, to induce change in one part of the network, and then to measure the remote ramifications of the induced change on beliefs about other related events in the network. In the first stage of the research, a survey was conducted to collect the research participants' beliefs about a sample of public policy issues. These responses were used to construct two belief networks containing events relevant to a medical issue (funding for cancer research) and an education issue (nonresident enrollments in state universities). Specifically, the elicitation procedure asked the participants to generate from imagination the causal antecedents and consequents of two target events selected for use because their average subjective probability ratings were near .50: "A sizeable proportion of medical research will be diverted out of cancer research and into the study of heart disease" and "An increasing proportion of students will attend universities in their own states rather than out-of-state universities."

From the resulting pool of responses, two antecedents and consequents were selected for each core event based on the following criteria: (a) events had mean subjective base rate probability ratings of about .50 (+/− .10), (b) events were generated by at least 50% of participants, and (c) the pairs of antecedent and consequent events were judged by the experimenters to be causally independent of one another. Each of the selected antecedent and consequent events was then presented to a second sample of participants, who were asked to generate antecedents and consequents for each. For each antecedent and consequent event, two antecedents and two consequents were again selected based on the criteria described above. This resulted in a modal, 21-event belief network for each of the two issue domains (see Figure 5.1 for images of 9 of the 21 events in our experimental belief networks).

The next stage of the study involved an experimental manipulation in which a third sample of research participants received persuasive communications designed to change their beliefs about one event in one of the networks of interrelated beliefs. Participants first read about an expert's (medical policy analyst or educational policy analyst) assessment of the probability of the target event occurring within the next ten years. For half of the participants, the expert's message was designed to persuade them that the event was likely to occur with a probability of .93, and for the other half, with a probability of .07. Then participants were asked to make their own estimates of the likelihood of occurrence of (a) the target event, (b) each of the 20 antecedent and consequent events associated with that target, and (c) each of the 21 events associated with the other target issue for which they had received no expert judgment (this last set of judgments would serve as a "no message" control condition). These assessments of the participants' beliefs about the probability of occurrence of all the events in a network provide a measure of belief revision in response to the experimentally induced change in beliefs about the likelihood of occurrence of the central, target event.

The ratings of interest for present purposes are those corresponding to the event nodes depicted in Figure 5.1. The network notation is used to summarize the conditional dependencies between events in the network. For purposes of illustration, we treat each event as a binary variable that has only two levels (we will label them present–absent, but more complex variables and interevent relationships can be expressed in this notation). Direct arrows imply conditional dependencies, and they can be interpreted as participants' beliefs about causal relationships between the occurrence and nonoccurrence of certain events (Glymour, 2001; Kenny, 1979; Pearl, 2000). The exact form of a causal relationship, for example, whether it represents a necessary or a sufficient causal relationship, can be expressed in conditional probability distributions in the tables next to each link (in this example, all the causal relationships are assumed to be independent and "necessary and sufficient").

Across the medical and educational issues, the mean prior probability rating for the target event on which no expert judgment had been provided was .52, very close to the intended .50 level. For participants who were told that an expert judged the target event to be very likely to occur (the expert estimated the probability it would occur at .93), the mean subjective probability rating for that target event was .60. For participants who received an expert judgment of .07 for the target event, the mean subjective probability rating for that target

A

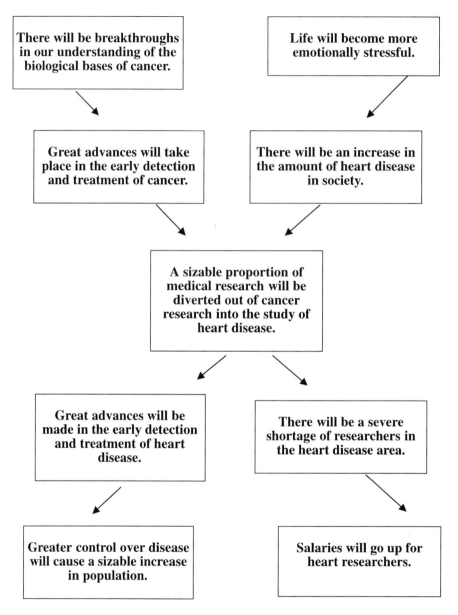

**Figure 5.1.**   Belief networks depicting the probabilistic causal relationships between nine hypothetical events concerning public health (A) and education (B). Each node represents an event (e.g., "There will be breakthroughs in our understanding of the biological bases of cancer"), and the arrows represent causal relationships. In the experiment, participants received messages designed to change their beliefs about the probability of occurrence of the central "target event" in each network and, subsequently, made ratings of the probabilities of occurrence for every event in the networks. The impact of change in belief in the target on directly (one-step) and indirectly (two-step) related events could be inferred from these ratings.

B

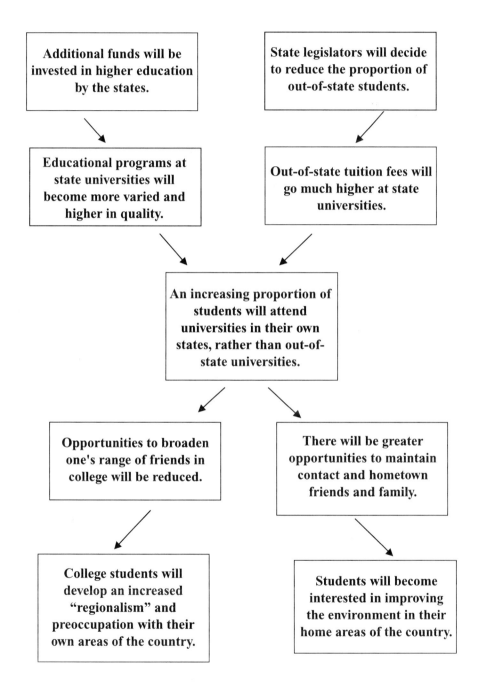

event was .47. These two means differed significantly, $F(1, 44) = 7.39$, $p < .01$. Thus, the persuasive expert judgment did influence participants' judgments of the probability of the target event in the predicted directions, although the effect was not nearly as large as McGuire and Hastie had anticipated.

The major goal of the experiment was to assess changes in beliefs about events that were not mentioned directly in the expert's persuasive messages. The subjective probability ratings for the "remote" antecedents and consequents to the target event showed small but significant changes. The difference between the mean subjective probability ratings of participants given a high expert judgment compared to participants given a low expert judgment was .08 for the antecedent events directly linked to the target event and .07 for the consequent events directly linked to the target event, $F(1, 94) = 4.47$, $p < .05$. For the events indirectly linked to the target event (i.e., the antecedents of each antecedent and the consequents of each consequent), the overall average difference between the ratings by the two groups dropped to a trivial .01. Thus, the .13 difference in beliefs about the occurrence of the target events was translated into a .08 difference for direct antecedents and consequents and to a .01 difference for indirect, remote events.

An additional interesting relationship in the judgments concerned the dependencies between participants' judgments of antecedents and consequents. For example, when one antecedent's (or consequent's) value increased, did other antecedents also increase or did they decrease or remain the same? A small negative correlation between belief changes in antecedents was observed, suggesting that participants reasoned as though the antecedent events were uniquely sufficient ($r = -.07$, n.s.). At the same time, a larger positive correlation between belief changes in the consequents was observed, suggesting that the target "cause" had multiple effects ($r = +.24$, $p < .05$) or was "multiply sufficient." When reasoning backward in time, participants treated antecedents as though they were independent, but when reasoning forward in time, participants reasoned as though both consequents would change.

## A Bayesian Network Model of Ideal Belief Revision in the Hastie and McGuire Experimental Task

Given different kinds of relationships within thought systems, logical versus causal, what are the different models we might use to capture the dynamic processes operating on them? McGuire (1990) and many others have proposed that dynamic networks provide the most useful models of thought processes. One of the earliest manifestations of this theoretical metaphor in psychology was the proposal of electrical switchboards (literally telephone switchboards) as models of the physical substrate for learned associations (John, 1972; Roediger, 1980). But since the 1970s, abstract mathematical graphs are the source metaphor for many models of thoughts and thinking processes (Anderson & Bower, 1973; Bechtel & Abrahamson, 2002; Schum, 1990; Strogatz, 2001). Briefly stated, there are two primary justifications for network representations and formal operations that update or revise the states represented by values of the variables embedded in a network. First, networks are good analogs to neural pathways in the human brain and body that must be the ultimate substrate in which thought is "implemented" (e.g., Grossberg, 1980; Hebb, 1949; Hopfield, 1982; O'Reilly & Munakata, 2000; Rosenblatt, 1958; Rumelhart, McClelland, & the PDP Research Group, 1986). Second, networks provide a means to represent the calculations implied by normative principles of inferential coherence and rationality (e.g., Corfield & Williamson, 2001; Lauritzen & Spiegelhalter, 1988; Pearl, 2000; Schum, 1994: Wigmore, 1937).

The most useful networks to model belief systems composed of causal relationships are Bayesian Networks for belief revision and propagation (e.g., Pearl, 2000; historically, the Bayesian Networks we focus on here were a product of efforts in computer science to build deductive "expert systems," e.g., Castillo, Gutiérrez, & Hadi, 1997). It turns out that these Bayesian Networks are exactly what McGuire had in mind in 1960, when he wrote his first paper on human thought systems. Only since the 1980s have useful computational algorithms been developed to implement this formalism (e.g., Cowell, Dawid, Lauritzen, & Spiegelhalter, 1999; Lauritzen & Spiegelhalter, 1988; Pearl, 1988), allowing the dreams of theorists like McGuire to be realized in a practical computational system.

We implemented a mental model of causal relationships in the medical and educational policy domains from our experiment in the form of a Bayesian Network incorporating the relationships in Figure 5.1. Our simulation of the results of the remote ramifications experiment is qualitative. We did not attempt to reproduce or fit the exact numerical values from the research participants' ratings. We simply wanted to test if the qualitative patterns in our research participants' judgments could be reproduced in a simple Bayesian Network. We report the global results from one simulation in which we assumed that participants reasoned about cause–effect relationships as though they were necessary and sufficient. More specifically, we assumed the base rate $p(\text{cause}) = p(\text{effect}) = .50$, and the $p(\text{effect} | \text{cause}) = .90$, and $p(\text{cause} | \text{effect}) = .90$. In other words, we put necessary and sufficient causal relationships into the model. The experimental participants' average ratings of the base rate corresponding to the events referenced in the causal structure depicted in Figure 5.1 corresponded closely to the .50 base rate used in this simulation. However, the .90 values in the simulation were selected to produce a good statistical fit overall across all postrevision ratings. (The participants' actual ratings of the conditional probabilities were more moderate than those in the simulation, averaging $p(\text{effect} | \text{cause}) = .65$. Furthermore, these conditional probability ratings were highly variable, partly because they were averages of different participants' estimates and partly because the participants were not given training in the difficult probability estimation tasks.)

The qualitative fit to human judgments was good. First, there was a sharp decline in impact of the message on related beliefs, less impact with greater distance in the causal network. In the simulation, we forced the change in the target event, at the center of the network, to be +/– .10, approximating the weak direct attitude change produced by our experts' persuasive communications. With this small change in the target belief, the belief revision for the nearest antecedents, one step "up" in the network, was +/– .05 and for the indirect, two steps "up" antecedents, was +/– .003. For nearest consequents, one step "down," the change was +/– .08, and for indirect consequents, two steps "down," the change was +/– .03.

Like the model, participants showed a pattern of lesser impact of target belief change on more distant events, but there are qualitative patterns in the model that differ from those in human judgments. For example, for necessary and sufficient causal relationships, the impact of a change in the probability of a cause has a larger impact on its consequent effects than on its antecedent causes. However, the human participants showed equal changes in beliefs about antecedents and consequents (perhaps demonstrating an averaging adjustment process; e.g., N. H. Anderson, 1981, 1996). Furthermore, human participants exhibited less belief revision than predicted by the probabilities generated by the model. This departure from the rational model's predictions is consistent with McGuire's principles of "cognitive inertia" and "loose linkage" in belief systems (e.g., McGuire's "spatial inertia threshold hypotheses," 1960a, p. 3; and his "loose linkage" postulate, McGuire & McGuire, 1991, p. 8). There also may be practical, adaptive reasons for conservatism in belief revision (e.g., Harman, 1986; McGuire, 1968, 1969, 1981; Quine & Ullian, 1970; Winkler & Murphy, 1973). In a world in which the evidence for change in a "target" belief is always uncertain, a conservative inference process would be more adaptive than the liberal inferential responses dictated by the Bayesian Network model. However, we should emphasize again, that the present model analysis is illustrative and should not be taken as a definitive test of the general class of all plausible Bayesian models.

## Conclusions and Conjectures: The Future of Bayesian Network Models of Thought Systems

People have a remarkable capacity to create mental models of their environments; their values and goals; people, including themselves; and even the relationships among all three. No other living creature is close to humans in this cognitive achievement. However, it is unlikely that people are capable of updating and revising the beliefs in such a system to maintain a perfect rational coherence among all components of the system when beliefs change. In fact, the technical problem of defining coherence in a realistically complex system is still a challenge to modern philosophical and scientific analysis, and the calculations required within even simple Bayesian Networks were first specified in the late 1980s. The present research explores belief revision in a small model system, it applies a rational model of belief revision to that system, and it compares patterns of human and rational belief revision.

The illustrative Bayesian Network model we present in this chapter only approximately mimics human belief revision judgments. For example, the model predicted asymmetries between revision of causal antecedents and effect consequents when the probability of occurrence of a central event was changed, but people tended to revise symmetrically upward and downward. However, we hope that the present method, including the theoretical analysis, will serve as an example of a useful approach to the study of belief revision and will encourage further studies of this neglected, important, and essentially human higher-order cognitive process. The basic experimental method, invented by Bill McGuire, is distinctly appropriate for such studies. Furthermore, in spite of the descriptive weaknesses of the simple model we present, we believe that the Bayesian framework is a promising basis for cognitive theories of these phenomena.

Could college students consistently be naïve Bayesians? Probably not. Most psychological research on judgment under uncertainty undermines the notion that people are fundamentally Bayesian (e.g., Fischhoff & Lichtenstein, 1978; Lopes, 1985, 1987; Slovic & Lichtenstein, 1971; Tversky & Kahneman, 1974), although some psychologists (e.g., J. R. Anderson, 1990; Gigerenzer, 2000; Luce, 2000; Oaksford & Chater, 1998) and most economists believe that human beings are approximately rational under some conditions (cf., McFadden, 1999; Rabin, 1998). Perhaps, as McGuire hypothesized many years ago, cognitive processes are essentially rational but with some, usually adaptive, qualifications. Certainly, at a minimum, our models should allow some of the people to be rational some of the time.

It is also possible, at this early stage in our theoretical analysis, that we have attributed an incorrect, overly simple belief system to our research participants. The present research raises the interesting and fundamental question of what constitutes a rational cognitive representation of the decision situation. Indeed, one critique of many empirical proofs of human irrationality is that the research participants and the experimenter may not share a common representation of the task posed by the experimental situation (Hastie & Rasinski, 1988; Miller & Cantor, 1982). Larry Samuelson, a prominent game theorist, points out:

> The key point is that people adapt their behavior to their circumstances. Is a model of Bayesian updating the best way to capture this behavior? Perhaps sometimes, but in many cases, Bayesian models divert attention from the important aspects of behavior. A Bayesian analysis requires the agents to begin with a consistent model of their environment, which can then be mechanically adjusted as new information is received. Attention is directed away from the process by which this consistent model is achieved and focused on the subsequent adjustments. However, I think the crucial aspects of the learning process often occur as agents attempt to construct their models of the situation they face. These attempts may often fail to produce consistent models, with agents unknowingly relying on a contradictory specification, until some event exposes the inconsistency and sends them scurrying back to the model construction stage. The models people use may often be so simple as to make Bayesian analysis of the model trivial, but to make the model construction process extremely important. (1997, p. 23)

The Bayesian Networks formalism also offers a serious, practical approach to the study of the manner in which people comprehend and structure their mental models of situations. Applied research by many computer scientists and cognitive scientists provides several alternative computational models for the induction of causal structures (e.g., Cooper & Herskovits, 1992; Glymour, 1998; Glymour & Cooper, 1999; Spirtes, Glymour, & Scheines, 2001), and behavioral researchers have begun to study this structure discovery and creation process (see especially Danks, 2001; Tennenbaum & Griffths, 2001). The use of Bayesian Networks as a model of human thought raises many fundamental questions for future research: Is change in belief about the probability of a target event transmitted differentially to its antecedents compared to its consequents? Is change in belief about an event transmitted less efficiently to beliefs further removed from the target event than to those more closely associated with it? Under what conditions does knowing that one cause occurred have implications for the probability that another cause has occurred?

> . . . There are more things in heaven and earth, Horatio
> Than are dreamt of in your philosophy. (*Hamlet*, I, v., 166)

# References

Anderson, J. R. (1990). *The adaptive character of thought*. Hillsdale, NJ: Erlbaum.

Anderson, J. R., & Bower, G. H. (1973). *Human associative memory*. Washington, DC: V. H. Winston.

Anderson, J. R., & Hastie, R. (1974). Individuation and reference in memory: Proper names and definite descriptions. *Cognitive Psychology, 6,* 495–514.

Anderson, N. H. (1981). *Foundations of Information Integration Theory*. New York: Academic Press.

Anderson, N. H. (1996). *A functional theory of cognition*. Mahwah, NJ: Erlbaum.

Bechtel, W., & Abrahamson, L. (2002). *Connectionism and the mind: Parallel processing dynamics and evolution* (2nd ed.). New York: Blackwell.

Castillo, E., Gutiérrez, J. M., & Hadi, A. S. (1997). *Expert systems and probabilistic network models*. New York: Springer-Verlag.

Collins, A. M., & Quillian, M. R. (1969). Retrieval time from semantic memory. *Journal of Verbal Learning and Verbal Behavior, 8,* 240–248.

Cooper, G. F., & Herskovits, E. (1992). A Bayesian method for the induction of probabilistic networks from data. *Machine Learning, 9,* 309–347.

Corfield, D., & Williamson, J. (Eds.). (2001). *Foundations of Bayesianism*. Dordrecht, The Netherlands: Kluwer.

Cowell, R. G., Dawid, A. P., Lauritzen, S. L., & Spiegelhalter, D. J. (1999). *Probabilistic networks and expert systems*. New York: Springer-Verlag.

Danks, D. (2001). *The psychology of causation*. Unpublished doctoral dissertation, University of California at San Diego, La Jolla.

Dillehay, R. C., Insko, C. A., & Smith, M. B. (1966). Logical consistency and attitude change. *Journal of Personality and Social Psychology, 3,* 646–654.

Edwards, W. (1967). Conservatism in human information processing. In B. Kleinmuntz (Ed.), *Formal representation of human judgment* (pp. 17–52). New York: Wiley.

Fischhoff, B., & Lichtenstein, S. (1978). Don't attribute this to Reverend Bayes. *Psychological Bulletin, 85,* 239–243.

Garner, W. R. (1974). *The processing of information and structure*. Potomac, MD: Erlbaum.

Genesereth, M. R., & Nilsson, N. J. (1987). *Logical foundations of artificial intelligence*. Los Altos, CA: Morgan Kaufmann.

Gigerenzer, G. (2000). *Adaptive thinking: Rationality in the real world*. New York: Oxford University Press.

Glymour, C. (1998). Learning causes: Psychological explanations of causal explanation. *Minds and Machines, 8,* 39–60.

Glymour, C. (2001). *The mind's arrows: Bayes nets and graphical models in psychology*. Cambridge: MIT Press.

Glymour, C., & Cooper, G. F. (Eds.). (1999). *Computation, causation, and discovery*. Cambridge: MIT Press.

Grossberg, S. (1980). How does the brain build a cognitive code? *Psychological Review, 87,* 1–51.

Harman, G. (1986). *Change in view*. Cambridge, MA: MIT Press.

Harman, G. (1996). Rationality. In E. E. Smith and D. N. Osherson (Eds.), *An invitation to cognitive science: Vol. 3. Thinking* (pp. 175–211). Cambridge, MA: MIT Press.

Hastie, R., & McGuire, W. J. (1970). *Remote ramifications of focused persuasive communications*. Unpublished masters thesis, University of California at San Diego, La Jolla.

Hastie, R., & Rasinski, K. A. (1988). The concept of accuracy in social judgment. In D. Bar-Tal and A. W. Kruglanski (Eds.), *The social psychology of knowledge* (pp. 193–208). Cambridge, UK: Cambridge University Press.

Hayes-Roth, B., & Hayes-Roth, F. (1975). Plasticity in memorial networks. *Journal of Verbal Learning and Verbal Behavior, 14,* 506–522.

Hebb, D. O. (1949). *The organization of behavior.* New York: Wiley.

Helmholtz, H. L. F. von (1925). *A treatise on physiological optics* (J. P. Southall, Trans.). New York: Dover. (Original work published 1910)

Hochberg, J. (1988). Visual perception. In R. C. Atkinson, R. J. Herrnstein, G. Lindzey, & R. D. Luce (Eds.), *Stevens' handbook of experimental psychology* (2nd ed., pp. 195–276). New York: Wiley.

Holt, L. E., & Watts, W. A. (1969). Salience of logical relationships among beliefs as a factor in persuasion. *Journal of Personality and Social Psychology, 11,* 193–203.

Hopfield, J. J. (1982). Neural networks and physical systems with emergent collective computational abilities. *Proceedings of the National Academy of Sciences, 79,* 2554–2558.

John, E. R. (1972). Switchboard versus statistical theories of learning and memory. *Science, 177,* 849–864.

Kenny, D. A. (1979). *Correlation and causation.* New York: Wiley.

Lauritzen, S. L., & Spiegelhalter, D. J. (1988). Local computations with probabilities on graphical structures and their application to expert systems (with discussion). *Journal of the Royal Statistical Society, Series B, 50,* 157–224.

Lopes, L. L. (1985). Averaging rules and adjustment processes in Bayesian inference. *Bulletin of the Psychonomic Society, 23,* 509–512.

Lopes, L. L. (1987). Procedural debiasing. *Acta Psychologica, 64,* 167–185.

Luce, R. D. (2000). *Utility of gains and losses: Measurement-theoretical and experimental approaches.* Mahwah, NJ: Erlbaum.

McFadden, D. (1999). Rationality for economists? *Journal of Risk and Uncertainty, 19,* 73–105.

McFarland, S. G., & Thistlethwaite, D. L. (1970). An analysis of a logical consistency model of belief change. *Journal of Personality and Social Psychology, 15,* 133–143.

McGuire, W. J. (1960a). Cognitive consistency and attitude change. *Journal of Abnormal and Social Psychology, 60,* 345–353.

McGuire, W. J. (1960b). Direct and indirect persuasive effects of dissonance-producing messages. *Journal of Abnormal and Social Psychology, 60,* 354–358.

McGuire, W. J. (1968). Theory of the structure of human thought. In R. P. Abelson, E. Aronson, W. J. McGuire, T. M. Newcomb, M. J. Rosenberg, & P. H. Tannenbaum (Eds.), *Theories of cognitive consistency: A sourcebook* (pp. 140–162). Chicago: Rand McNally.

McGuire, W. J. (1969). The nature of attitudes and attitude change. In G. Lindzey & E. Aronson (Eds.), *Handbook of social psychology* (Vol. 3, pp. 136–314). Reading, MA: Addison-Wesley.

McGuire, W. J. (1981). The probabilogical model of cognitive structure and attitude change. In R. E. Petty, T. M. Ostrom, & T. C. Brock (Eds.), *Cognitive responses in persuasion* (pp. 291–307). Hillsdale, NJ: Erlbaum.

McGuire, W. J. (1990). Dynamic operations of thought systems. *American Psychologist, 45,* 504–512.

McGuire, W. J., & McGuire, C. V. (1991). The content, structure, and operation of thought systems. In R. S. Wyer, Jr., & T. K. Srull (Eds.), Advances in social cognition (Vol. 4, pp. 1–78). Mahwah NJ: Erlbaum.

Miller, G. A., & Cantor, N. (1982). Review of *Human inference: Strategies and shortcomings of social judgment. Social Cognition, 1,* 83–93.

Moeser, S. D., & Tarrant, B. L. (1977). Learning a network of comparisons. *Journal of Experimental Psychology: Human Learning and Memory, 3,* 643–659.

Newell, A., & Simon, H. A. (1972). *Human problem solving.* Englewood Cliffs, NJ: Prentice-Hall.

Oaksford, M., & Chater, N. (1998). *Rationality in an uncertain world: Essays on the cognitive science of human reasoning.* Philadelphia: Taylor and Francis.

O'Reilly, R. C., & Munakata, Y. (2000). *Computational explorations in cognitive neuroscience: Understanding the mind by simulating the brain.* Cambridge, MA: MIT Press.

Pearl, J. (1988). Fusion, propagation, and structuring in belief networks. *Artificial Intelligence, 29,* 241–288.

Pearl, J. (2000). *Causality: Models, reasoning, and inference.* New York: Cambridge University Press.

Pinker, S. (1997). *How the mind works.* New York: Norton.

Quine, W. V. O., & Ullian, J. S. (1970). *The web of belief.* New York: Random House.

Rabin, M. (1998, March). Psychology and economics. *Journal of Economic Literature, 36,* 11–46.

Rips, L. J. (1987). On second thought. *Contemporary Psychology, 32,* 245–246.

Rips, L. J. (1994). *The psychology of proof: Deductive reasoning in human thinking.* Cambridge, MA: MIT Press.

Roediger, H. L., III (1980). Memory metaphors in cognitive psychology. *Memory & Cognition, 8,* 231–246.

Rosenblatt, F. (1958). The perceptron: A probabilistic model for information storage and organization in the brain. *Psychological Review, 65,* 386–408.

Ross, L., Lepper, M. R., & Hubbard, M. (1975). Perseverance in self perception and social perception: Biased attributional processes in the debriefing paradigm. *Journal of Personality and Social Psychology, 32,* 880–892.

Rumelhart, D. E., McClelland, J. L., & the PDP Research Group (1986). *Parallel distributed processing: Exploration in the microstructure of cognition* (2 volumes). Cambridge, MA: MIT Press.

Samuelson, L. (1997). *Evolutionary games and equilibrium selection.* Cambridge, MA: MIT Press.

Schum, D. A. (1990) Inference networks and their many subtle properties. *Information and Decision Technologies, 16,* 69–98.

Schum, D. A. (1994). *Evidential foundations of probabilistic reasoning.* New York: Wiley.

Shapiro, S. C. (Ed.). (1990). *Encyclopedia of artificial intelligence.* New York: Wiley.

Slovic, P., & Lichtenstein, S. (1971). A comparison of Bayesian and regression approaches to the study of information processing in judgment. *Organizational Behavior and Human Performance, 6,* 649–744.

Spirtes, P., Glymour, C., & Scheines, R. (2001). *Causation, prediction, and search.* Cambridge, MA: MIT Press.

Sternberg, R. J. (1980). Representation and process in linear syllogistic reasoning. *Journal of Experimental Psychology: General, 109,* 119–159.

Strogatz, S. H. (2001). Exploring complex networks. *Nature, 410,* 268–276.

Tennenbaum, J. B., & Griffiths, T. L. (2001). Structure learning in human causal induction. *Advances in Neural Information Processing Systems, 13,* 323–328.

Tversky, A., Kahneman, D. (1974). Judgment under uncertainty: Heuristics and biases. *Science, 185,* 1124–1131.

Watts, W. A., & Holt, L. E. (1970). Logical relationships among beliefs and timing as factors in persuasion. *Journal of Personality and Social Psychology, 16,* 571–582.

Watts, W. A., & McGuire, W. J. (1964). Persistence of induced opinion change and retention of inducing content. *Journal of Abnormal and Social Psychology, 68,* 233–241.

Wigmore, J. H. (1937). *The science of judicial proof: As given by logic, psychology, and general experience and illustrated in judicial trials* (3rd ed.). Boston: Little, Brown.

Winkler, R. L., & Murphy, A. H. (1973). Experiments in the laboratory and the real world. *Organizational Behavior and Human Performance, 10,* 252–270.

# 6

# Values and Evaluations

*Deborah A. Prentice*

## Prologue

I have never been comfortable with the distinction, so familiar to social psychologists, between content and process. For me, it is very difficult to conceive of a psychological process without reference to the substance of what is being processed, and usually that substance seems to matter critically to the way the process unfolds. As a consequence, my investigations of psychological processes are always content-bound. For example, I do not study beliefs but rather the antecedents and consequences of particular beliefs: beliefs about the attitudes and opinions of peers, beliefs about social difference, beliefs about what women and men are and should be like. I do not study values but rather the correlates of particular values: values that emphasize symbolic ideals versus those that emphasize instrumentality, values that emphasize conservation versus those that emphasize openness to change. I study the processing of *fictional* information, the use of *gendered* language, and the internal dynamics of *campus* groups. I also study college students—quite explicitly and extensively. I often argue that this research reveals something more general about the underlying psychological processes; I make such an argument in this chapter. For me, however, the work is fundamentally about the particular beliefs, values, groups, and populations under investigation.

In addition, I have never been entirely confident in the importance of a process—its relevance for understanding the way people actually lead their lives—unless I could find some evidence of it in their ordinary thoughts and actions. Thus, I steer away from complicated laboratory procedures in favor of those that closely simulate real-life experiences. I avoid asking participants to answer complex questions or to do mind-bending tasks in favor of simple rating scales and open-ended measures. Although I am most at home in the laboratory, I also conduct surveys and field experiments outside the lab. These methodological predilections often frustrate my love of clever, elegant experimentation and clean, parsimonious results. On occasion, I manage to have it both ways, and those are my most rewarding experiences as a researcher.

Bill McGuire was my graduate advisor, but you would never know it from what I study. Bill never gave me (or anybody else) a project, nor did he even suggest that one project would be better than another; he simply advised me on the projects I chose. You would also never know he was my advisor from my tendency toward particularism, for Bill is a universalist par excellence. I am sure that if I told him my latest hypothesis, he would be able to rattle off a half-dozen more, many of them seeming to contradict my own but all of them following from the operation of the same psychological mechanism. If you saw how I do social psychology, though—if you perused my notes on a research project, for example, the materials from my latest study, my plans for subsequent studies, or the many, many drafts of a manuscript that I go through— you would know I was a student of Bill's: What I learned from Bill is not so much what to do as how to do it—how to design studies and research programs, how to measure things, how to interpret data, and how to think and write clearly. Working with Bill was like receiving a private tutorial in perspectivism from the master. It was an extraordinary experience, one for which I am very grateful.

* * *

When a person says that she values equality more than achievement or security more than self-direction, what does this tell us about her? What do a person's values signify? This question has been a passing preoccupation of mine since I was in graduate school at Yale some 15 years ago. The opportunity to participate in this celebration of Bill McGuire's career prompts me to reconsider it, not because it is a particularly McGuirean question, but rather because Bill has always evinced complete respect for preoccupations of all sorts. Indeed, he helped me considerably in my initial thinking about this one.

Values have always seemed to me an important psychological linchpin— the glue that makes individuals and collectives cohere. For example, values are what members of a culture share; they are a source of consistency within social groups and differentiation between them. Values also characterize individuals and bind them to the people, objects, and issues in their environment. What has interested me most about values is their role within individuals. Specifically, I have been intrigued by the idea that what is common to an individual's beliefs, attitudes, possessions, actions, sociometric choices, and evaluations more generally is somehow reflected in the values she holds. Values, then, would function for individuals in very much the same way they function for cultures and other social groups. They would be a source of coherence and consistency within individuals as well as of differentiation between them.

Guided by this interest in values and personality, I, along with several colleagues, have examined the significance of values in the lives of college students (Prentice, Trail, & Cantor, 2001). Our research has focused on one particular dimension of values that, at its extremes, contrasts students who value being open to change (i.e., those who place a high priority on self-direction and freedom from constraints) with students who value conservation (e.g., those who place a high priority on security, conformity, and tradition). Students whose values fall to the openness side of the continuum come to college with an open mind, ready to explore new activities and interests, evaluate their experiences, and ultimately settle on a set of future goals that promise to be rewarding. Students whose values tend to the conservation side come to college with clear goals already established and treat their four years on campus as a means of achieving, or at least making progress toward, those goals. Our research has examined the day-to-day lives of students in light of their standing on this dimension, the choices they make in college, and their evaluations of how their lives are going, both day-to-day and more generally.

A central goal of this research has been to test the claim that values have their influence by determining the criteria people use to evaluate issues, options, and experiences. The idea that values serve as criteria for evaluation has been around for quite some time. It was articulated several decades ago by theorists in the social sciences (see Williams, 1968, for a review). It has been an important, though sometimes unarticulated, assumption on which researchers have based claims for the relation of values to attitudes, choices, and behaviors (e.g., Feather, 1995; Maio & Olson, 2000; Rokeach, 1973; Schwartz, 1992). Moreover, it is broadly consistent with expectancy value models of the relation between values and behaviors, which have proven empirically successful and quite influential in this field (see, e.g., Feather, 1990). The theoretical framework for our research draws on these various traditions.

## Theoretical Framework

### Values and Value Systems

Values are beliefs about which outcomes and courses of action are desirable or good. They are organized hierarchically into a set of beliefs that express preferences among different modes of conduct and end states of existence (Rokeach, 1973). These preferences derive in part from individual needs and desires and in part from societal demands. Thus, values are individual needs represented in a socially acceptable form. Because values map onto biological and social needs, they are limited in number. Because they are central beliefs, values are linked to a wide variety of attitudes, goals, and behaviors. Although value systems are fairly stable, they can and do undergo change; in particular, because values are organized into hierarchies, they are continually in conflict. Acting to promote one value often means sacrificing another. As a result, a person is routinely forced to choose among values when setting goals, expressing attitudes, or engaging in behaviors, and this process can lead to reorganization of values (see Rokeach, 1973, 1979).

The structure of value systems reflects commonalities and compatibilities among different types of values. In an effort to elucidate this structure, Schwartz (1992, 1996) developed a taxonomy of ten types of values that differ in the motivational goals they express. These ten types of values (with examples of each) are power (e.g., authority, wealth), achievement (e.g., successful, ambitious), hedonism (e.g., pleasure, enjoying life), stimulation (e.g., daring, an exciting life), self-direction (e.g., creativity, freedom), universalism (e.g., broadminded, social justice), benevolence (e.g., helpful, forgiving), tradition (e.g., humble, devout), conformity (e.g., politeness, self-discipline), and security (e.g., family security, social order). Schwartz derived this typology by reasoning that values represent three universal requirements of human existence: biological needs, requisites of coordinated social interaction, and demands of group survival and functioning. People represent these requirements cognitively in the form of specific values, which they use to explain and coordinate behavior.

A central claim of Schwartz's (1992) theory is that these ten types of values are interrelated in a structure that is invariant across cultures. The logic of this claim is that the actions people take in pursuit of their values have psychological, practical, and social consequences; these consequences may either conflict or be compatible with the pursuit of other values. For example, the pursuits of power and achievement are quite compatible in that both emphasize social superiority and esteem. Similarly, the pursuits of universalism and benevolence are compatible in that both entail concern for enhancement of others and transcendence of selfish interests. However, power and universalism conflict with each other and therefore cannot easily be pursued at the same time. These tensions produce a natural organization of value systems, which can be represented as a circular structure defined by two dimensions, with competing value types on opposing sides of the center and complementary types adjacent or in close proximity. One dimension contrasts values that emphasize openness to change (e.g., self-direction and stimulation) with those that emphasize conservation (e.g., conformity, security, tradition). The other dimension contrasts values that emphasize self-enhancement (e.g., achievement, power) with those that emphasize self-transcendence (e.g., universalism, benevolence). This organization should characterize the value systems of all groups in all cultures.

The empirical evidence available to date has supported this claim for a universal structure. Analyses of values ratings provided by multiple samples of participants in 41 countries have found support for the two proposed dimensions of organization in 95% of the samples (see Schwartz, 1992).

*Value Relevance*

Although everybody holds values—and indeed, responses to value surveys suggest that most people place at least some importance on just about any value one can name—not all of these values come into play every time an individual makes a judgment, choice, or evaluation. Instead, only relevant values have an impact. There are two components of relevance that matter. First, if values are to exert an impact on evaluation, they must be a relevant concern for the individual at the time of the evaluation, that is, they must be salient, either chronically or temporarily. Second, they must be relevant to the object of evaluation, that is, the object must have value-relevant properties. Put simply, for values to serve as a link between the person and the object of evaluation, they must be relevant to both.

The logic of value relevance is illustrated by our choice of the open-to-change/conservation value dimension in our research on the day-to-day lives of college students. We focused on this dimension in particular because of its strong relevance for students' ongoing concerns. Schwartz (1996) described this dimension as one that "reflects a conflict between emphases on own independent thought and action and favoring change versus submissive self-restriction, preservation of traditional practices, and protection of stability" (p. 5). We maintained that this dimension should offer particular insight into the behavior and experiences of college students because it embodies contrasting solutions to the central problem of adolescence: acquiring a sense of identity (Erikson, 1968). As with most late adolescents, college students are actively engaged in a process of fashioning an identity, using both intrapsychic experience and external standards and reinforcements as inputs (Marcia, 1966). Values determine which of these sources of information is the more powerful. Students who place a high priority on open-to-change values seek a sense of identity through adherence to the dictates of their own thoughts and feelings. Students who place a high priority on conservation values seek a sense of identity through adherence to established norms and roles. Because identity seeking is the central task of this developmental stage, it is a strong motivator of behavior. Therefore, the values students hold in this regard are likely to be salient in their minds most of the time. Moreover, the environment of college life is organized in ways that foster opportunities to make value-congruent choices and to engage in activities that serve to define a student via his or her groups and friends. These are precisely the conditions under which we would expect values to play an important role.

## Values as Criteria

The nature of that role is captured by the notion of values as criteria. The idea here is that values select which aspects of a stimulus are important for the evaluation of it. The sociologist Robin Williams (1968) offered this account for the impact of values on evaluations more than 30 years ago:

> Values serve as criteria for selection in action. When most explicit and fully conceptualized, values become criteria for judgment, preference, and choice. When implicit and unreflective, values nevertheless perform *as if* they constituted grounds for decisions in behavior. Men do prefer some things to others; they do select one course of action rather than another out of a range of possibilities; they do judge the conduct of other men. (p. 283)

More recently, this idea has been incorporated into expectancy-value models (or, as McGuire [1985] calls them, attribution X evaluation models) of attitudes and behaviors. According to these models, evaluations (attitudes, valences, etc.) are the sum (or average) of the perceived probability that an object (issue, alternative) has each of a set of attributes multiplied by the perceived desirability of each attribute. Values enter the equation by supplying the desirability information. Thus, when the attributes of a stimulus are known (and therefore expectancies are either 1 or 0), values determine how the various attributes are weighted in the overall evaluation. They influence which attributes of the stimulus matter and how they matter.

Consider, for example, the relation of values to choices. According to this analysis, values should influence choices by determining the criteria on which the choice alternatives are evaluated or, in Feather's (1990) terms, through their capacity to induce valences on alternative options. Values determine what people find attractive about particular objects and situations and thereby influence the objects and situations those people choose. Feather (1988, 1995) has amassed considerable data in support of this idea.

Consider also the relation of values to subjective well-being. Given the overabundance of information people have about their lives, on what criteria do they base their evaluation of how things are going? We would argue that values supply those criteria. Indeed, subjective evaluations of well-being should offer considerable scope for the operation of values in that one's life is so rich and multifaceted a stimulus that the resulting evaluation is highly dependent on which properties of it are selected as relevant (see Schwarz & Strack, 1999). Some initial evidence for this moderating role of values on subjective well-being has been reported (Oishi, Diener, Suh, & Lucas, 1999).

## Values, Choices, and Evaluations of Well-Being

My colleagues and I have collected a considerable amount of data on the relation of values to the activities, choices, and well-being of college students (Prentice, Trail, & Cantor, 2001). The central question of this research is whether students' values—their standing on the openness/conservation value dimension—provide the criteria they use to assess their day-to-day experiences, choice alternatives, and quality of life more generally.

In one study, more than 3000 second-year students at four different academic institutions on the East Coast completed the sophomore student life survey, a written questionnaire that assessed their daily life activities, academic concentration, self-conceptions, extracurricular activities, self-esteem, values, well-being, and personal accomplishments in their first three semesters at college. The inclusion of the Rokeach Values Survey (Rokeach, 1973) provided us with a measure of the extent to which each student's values emphasized openness to change versus conservation. We examined the relation of their score on this dimension to their activities and choices as well as to their well-being.

As we anticipated, values were related in predictable ways to how students spent their nonacademic time. The more conserving the students' values the more time they spent in extracurricular group activities, the greater the percentage of their social time they spent with their extracurricular groupmates, and the greater the percentage of their close friends and roommates who were also members of their main extracurricular group. Moreover, the types of activities students chose varied with values: Students whose values were near the conservation pole were heavily concentrated in varsity sports and religious groups, whereas students whose values were near the openness-to-change pole participated in a wide range of activities. In addition, the more open the students' values, the more frequently they attended cultural events and the more time they spent socializing, especially just relaxing with others.

Values were also related to the criteria students used to choose an academic major. The more conserving the students' values, the more weight they placed on the advice of family members and members of extracurricular groups. Conserving values were also associated with a greater weight placed on pragmatic considerations, including the number and rigidity of requirements for the major, the amount of time it would take, whether they had done well in classes in the area, and, especially, the opportunities it would provide after graduation. The more open the students' values, the more they were compelled by the intellectual challenge an academic major would present.

Similarly, values were related to the criteria students used when deciding to join their main extracurricular group. The more conserving the students' values, the more weight they placed on the advice of family members, on wanting to be part of a group, and on pragmatic considerations about the future. In contrast, the more open the students' values, the more weight they placed on the opportunity to learn a new skill, the level of interest they had in the activity, and the desire to have fun.

These results support the claim that values serve as criteria for evaluation. The more students' values emphasized the importance of being open to change, the more they tended to choose situations in which their experience and behavior would be guided by their own thoughts and feelings. Moreover, when asked directly to indicate the reasons underlying their major academic and extracurricular choices, students who valued openness cited thoughts and feelings in their responses. In contrast, the more students' values emphasized the importance of conservation, the more they tended to choose situations that would consolidate existing relationships and promote positive long-term outcomes. Again, these themes were more likely to appear in the explicit accounts these students gave of their choice of major and extracurricular activity. In all cases, values were reflected in the properties of extracurricular groups, social situations, and academic majors that students found attractive.

We also examined the values-as-criteria hypothesis in the context of students' subjective evaluations of their own well-being. Again, we anticipated that values would moderate which aspects of one's life were factored into this evaluation. Our central prediction was that the more students valued openness to change, the more their levels of stress and satisfaction would depend on the ups and downs of daily life—that is, the stronger the relation between subjective experience and well-being. The logic of this prediction was as follows: Students whose values place them at different points on the openness/conservation dimension are trying to accomplish very different things in their lives. Students with more open values are trying to identify a set of goals and activities that they will find intrinsically satisfying; students with more conserving values are trying to make progress toward the externally defined goals they have adopted as their own. These tasks differ sharply in the importance they accord to short-term subjective experience. Specifically, the experience of engaging in an activity—how interesting and enjoyable one finds it, how well one does at it, how much it facilitates or interferes with other things one wants to do—provides critical feedback regarding progress on the task of identifying rewarding pursuits but is much less relevant for assessing progress on the task of achieving long-term security by following traditions, norms, and expectations set by others. In other words, experiential information is relevant to open but not conserving values. Thus, we expected subjective experience to be more closely linked to well-being the more open a student's values.

The results were consistent with this prediction across multiple measures of experience and well-being. The more open the students' values, the more their reports of academic difficulties were associated with lower academic satisfaction and higher perceived stress; the more their reports of social difficulties were associated with lower social satisfaction, lower satisfaction with life as a whole, and higher perceived stress; and the more their reports of time difficulties were associated with lower life satisfaction and higher perceived stress. It appears that students with more open values were more inclined to base their evaluations of their lives on the difficulties and opportunities they were encountering day-to-day. Students with more open values also showed a stronger relation between extracurricular activities and extracurricular satisfaction, which, again, is consistent with the view that they were basing their evaluations of well-being in a domain on their subjective experiences in that domain.

What of conservation values? What criteria do they suggest should be important in the evaluation of one's life? In theory, these values should highlight the importance of having stable and secure relations with family members, fitting in well with social groups, and making progress toward long-term goals. Our survey included questions that enabled us to measure the second of these criteria: the extent to which one possessed the attributes that were important for fitting into one's most important extracurricular group. Indeed, the more conserving the students' values, the stronger the negative association between their degree of fit to the norm of this group and their level of perceived stress. Taken together, these results support the notion that values determine the criteria used to evaluate well-being. Open values dictate that the evaluation be based on day-to-day experiences, whereas conservation values dictate that it be based on the security of significant relationships.

We have replicated and extended these findings in a second study, using a very different methodology (Prentice, Trail, & Cantor, 2001, Study 2). In this study, 86 Princeton sophomores completed a version of the sophomore student life survey and then, each evening for the next 21 days, completed a questionnaire that assessed their experiences that day. The daily questionnaire included questions about the hassles and uplifts they experienced, the people with whom they interacted socially, and the amount of stress they were feeling that day.

We examined the relations among values, hassles and uplifts, and perceived stress with the prediction that positive and negative daily experiences would be more closely related to well-being the more open a student's values were. The results confirmed the predicted relationships. Across the 21 days, students with more open values showed a stronger positive correlation between daily hassles and perceived stress and a stronger negative correlation between daily uplifts and perceived stress. Thus, day-to-day experiences again related more strongly to evaluations for students with more open values.

We also examined the relation between daily social experiences and perceived stress as a function of students' values. Students were asked to list, by name, all of the people with whom they socialized during breakfast, lunch, and dinner; at organized social activities; while hanging out or relaxing; and while studying. They also indicated whether each of the individuals they listed was a roommate, classmate, extracurricular groupmate, close friend, casual friend, or boyfriend or girlfriend. We analyzed the extent to which values moderated the relation between the percentage of time spent with each of these categories of people and perceived stress. The results were consistent with those of our first study in emphasizing the importance of significant relationships for students with stronger conservation values. The more conserving the students' values, the stronger the negative correlation between time spent with close friends and perceived stress. In contrast, the opposite relation held for casual friends: The more conserving the students' values, the stronger the positive correlation between time spent with casual friends and perceived stress. Again, we see that conservation values highlight the importance of significant (and, with opposite valence, nonsignificant) relationships in evaluations of well-being.

One issue raised by this latter set of findings is whether the apparent insensitivity of students high in conservation values to the ups and downs of daily life has something to do with the benefits they derive from spending time with close friends. Perhaps these individuals simply enjoy more social support than do their open peers and therefore are less buffeted about by their day-to-day experiences. This explanation suggests a slightly different mechanism underlying the relations among values, day-to-day experiences, and well-being: Specifically, it suggests that students across the open/conservation value dimension may be equally sensitive to daily hassles and uplifts but that these effects may be overridden by social support for students who have more conserving values. To test this possibility, we examined the extent to which the relation we found among values, hassles, and perceived stress was moderated by time spent with close friends. Indeed, it was: For students higher in conservation values, the correlation between hassles and perceived stress was lower the more time they spent with close friends. Conserving values were thus associated with deriving benefits (in the form of lower stress) from social support. However, this social support effect was independent of the relation among values, hassles, and perceived stress. That is, conservation values were still associated with a weaker correlation between hassles and perceived stress, even after the moderating effects of time with close friends were taken into account. Moreover, time with close friends did not moderate the relation among values, uplifts, and perceived stress. Therefore, we can be reasonably confident that the effects we found really do reflect a difference in the criteria students are using to assess their well-being rather than simply a difference in the benefits they derive from social support.

## Values, Attitudes, and Possessions

Our studies of the lives of college students (see Prentice, Trail, & Cantor, 2001) have provided considerable evidence consistent with the notion that values serve as criteria for the evaluation of personal decision alternatives and the quality of one's life as a whole. But do those values play a similar role in other kinds of evaluations? For example, do values determine the criteria people use to form their attitudes? Do they provide criteria for the evaluation of material objects? These are some of the questions I explored in research on values that I conducted, with sage advice from Bill McGuire, in graduate school. My impulse to review this research may be, in part, Festschrift-inspired nostalgia; nevertheless, the work is germane to this discussion in that it provides an additional test of the values-as-criteria hypothesis in a very different substantive context.

The goal of this earlier research was to demonstrate some measure of correspondence among an individual's values, attitudes, and material possessions (Prentice, 1987). The argument for a link between values and attitudes was certainly nothing new: Numerous studies had already demonstrated a modest, though reasonably consistent, relation between the two (see Eagly & Chaiken, 1993, for a review). What was new to my formulation was the addition of material possessions to the picture and a functional analysis of precisely how mental and physical possessions should relate. My hypothesis was that a given individual's values, attitudes, and favorite possessions should be similar in the psychological functions they serve. If one's most important values emphasize symbolic ideals (e.g., valuing a world of beauty, mature love, and true friendship), then one will tend to hold attitudes and value objects for what they symbolize. On the other hand, if one's most important values emphasize instrumentality (e.g., valuing ambition, being intellectual, and being capable), then one will take a similarly instrumental approach to social issues and material possessions. In this view, values should reflect the orientations people adopt—the criteria they use—when evaluating issues and objects of all kinds.

In the studies, college students listed their five favorite material possessions and described why each was a favorite. Several weeks later, they responded to a series of persuasive communications that varied in the type of reasons—symbolic or instrumental—given for each proposed course of action. They also completed the Rokeach Values Survey (Rokeach, 1973). I classified each student's favorite possessions as predominantly symbolic or instrumental and then looked for correspondence among the type of possessions that person valued, the type of arguments she found persuasive, and the type of values she rated as most important.

The results revealed significant correspondence among values, attitudes, and possessions but only when they were symbolic. Students who were favorable toward symbolic values were more likely to value material objects for their symbolic significance and were more likely to endorse proposals supported by symbolic reasons. In terms of the concepts we have developed here, symbolic values provided the criteria used to evaluate material possessions and social issues. There was no such correspondence for instrumental values, attitudes, and possessions. For some reason, instrumentality did not consistently characterize evaluations across domains. This asymmetry across the symbolic and instrumental functions came as a surprise, although similar asymmetries have been observed time and time again in research on the relation between values and attitudes (see Maio & Olson, 2000).

What are the implications of these findings for values as criteria in the domain of attitudes? In particular, is it the case, as the literature suggests, that only some values serve as criteria in the evaluation of social issues? I offered two different responses to this question, both of which hinge on the notion of relevance. First, perhaps the failure to find the predicted correspondence between instrumental values and attitudes was a result of our choices of issues and supporting arguments (see Prentice, 1987). In retrospect, it seems clear that these issues and arguments were almost certainly too distant from students' lives to have any truly instrumental properties for them. In other words, instrumental values were simply not relevant to the issues in question. This explanation implies that if one could identify issues that do have direct and instrumental consequences for participants, one should be able to demonstrate that attitudes toward those issues correspond to the strength of instrumental values. Such a demonstration was provided by Maio and Olson (2000, Study 3). They examined students' attitudes toward attending an entertaining festival that would occur immediately before exams. The more value students placed on self-enhancement (including personal achievement and success), the more negative their attitudes toward the festival. This result suggests that instrumental values, like symbolic values, can serve as evaluative criteria when they are genuinely relevant to the issue in question.

Of course, it is not a coincidence that the issues and arguments researchers have used in their studies of attitudes have proven to be more relevant to symbolic than to instrumental values. Attitudes, as social psychology has traditionally conceived them, are strongly social concepts. They are evaluations of social issues, social groups, and social phenomena. They provide a connection between the individual and the world outside of the individual. This focus on attitudes toward social concepts has had two implications for research on value–attitude relations. First, it has sharply limited the relevance of values, especially certain values, to attitudes. In particular, values pertaining to personal goals, such as achievement (successful, capable, ambitious, influential), self-direction (creativity, freedom, independent, curious, choosing own goals), hedonism (pleasure, enjoying life), and stimulation (daring, a varied life, an exciting life), are unlikely to find expression in the typical attitude study. In contrast, values pertaining to goals for the world, such as security (family security, national security, social order, reciprocation of favors) and universalism (social justice, equality, a world at peace, a world of beauty), are much more likely to find expression. Second, this focus has introduced many additional criteria besides values on which attitudes might be based. One of the most important of these criteria is social-adjustive concerns, which arise when an attitude has implications for one's standing in important social groups or relationships. Attitudes toward social objects are very likely to have this property.

## Concluding Comments

The values-as-criteria hypothesis is a simple yet powerful way to conceptualize the relation between values and evaluations of various kinds. It provides an explicit and testable account of precisely how values have an impact on attitudes, choices, and evaluations of well-being. It specifies when values should relate to these evaluations and when they should not. It is consistent with most of the existing literature on values and yet still has the potential to generate novel predictions. In particular, it seems especially promising as a way to understand individual differences in subjective well-being. The comparison between evaluations of well-being and attitudes is instructive in this regard. Compared with attitudes, evaluations of well-being are considerably more personal and less social; therefore, values should be more relevant and other criteria less relevant to the construction of them. As complex and multifaceted as many social issues are, one's life as a whole is almost certainly more complex and multifaceted, at least in one's own mind. Therefore, one's life will have many properties from which to choose when it comes to evaluating its quality. Finally, although many social issues have strong connections with particular values, few, if any, provide the scope for value expression that evaluations of one's life do. Indeed, values are explicitly defined as beliefs that serve as guiding principles in people's lives (Rokeach, 1973). Given this definition, it is difficult to imagine how one could evaluate one's life without at least passing reference to values.

A second area in which further investigation of values may prove fruitful is in the study of personality. Historically, theorists have had some fascinating ideas about how individual differences in values might be expressed in distinctive patterns of attitudes and behaviors (see, Adorno, Frenkel-Brunswik, Levinson, & Sanford, 1950, on authoritarianism; Rokeach, 1960, on dogmatism); empirically, these ideas have received uneven support. With more attention to the processes that connect values with attitudes, behaviors, and evaluations, it may be possible to develop equally fascinating but more empirically sound hypotheses about values and personality. Imagine a theory like the authoritarian personality, with predictions based on the operation of a well-defined and well-documented psychological mechanism. It is an ambitious project, I realize, and not a very McGuirean one in its substantive focus. Nevertheless, I like to think that Bill would heartily endorse the effort.

# References

Adorno, T. W., Frenkel-Brunswik, E., Levinson, D. J., & Sanford, R. N. (1950). *The authoritarian personality.* New York: Harper & Row.

Eagly, A. H., & Chaiken, S. (1993). *The psychology of attitudes.* Orlando, FL: Harcourt Brace Jovanovich.

Erikson, E. (1968). *Identity: Youth and crisis.* New York: Norton.

Feather, N. T. (1988). Values, valences, and course enrollment: Testing the role of personal values within an expectancy-valence framework. *Journal of Educational Psychology, 80,* 381–391.

Feather, N. T. (1990). Bridging the gap between values and actions: Recent applications of the expectancy-value model. In E. T. Higgins & R. M. Sorrentino (Eds.), *Handbook of motivation and cognition: Foundations of social behavior* (Vol. 2, pp. 151–192). New York: Guilford Press.

Feather, N. T. (1995). Values, valences, and choice: The influence of values on the perceived attractiveness and choice of alternatives. *Journal of Personality and Social Psychology, 68,* 1135–1151.

Maio, G. R., & Olson, J. M. (2000). What *is* a "value-expressive" attitude? In G. R. Maio & J. M. Olson (Eds.), *Why we evaluate: Functions of attitudes* (pp. 249–270). Mahwah, NJ: Erlbaum.

Marcia, J. E. (1966). Development and validation of ego identity status. *Journal of Personality and Social Psychology, 3,* 551–558.

McGuire, W. J. (1985). Attitudes and attitude change. In G. Lindzey & E. Aronson (Eds.), *The handbook of social psychology* (3rd ed., Vol. 2, pp. 233–346). NY: Random House.

Oishi, S., Diener, E., Suh, E., & Lucas, R. E. (1999). Value as a moderator in subjective well-being. *Journal of Personality, 67,* 157–184.

Prentice, D. A. (1987). Psychological correspondence of possessions, attitudes, and values. *Journal of Personality and Social Psychology, 53,* 993–1003.

Prentice, D. A., Trail, T. E., & Cantor, N. (2001). *Making choices and living with the consequences: Values, activities, and well-being among college students.* Unpublished manuscript, Princeton University.

Rokeach, M. (1960). *The open and closed mind.* New York: Basic Books.

Rokeach, M. (1973). *The nature of human values.* New York: Free Press.

Rokeach, M. (Ed.). (1979). *Understanding human values.* New York: Free Press.

Schwartz, S. (1992). Universals in the content and structure of values: Theoretical advances and empirical tests in 20 countries. In M. P. Zanna (Ed.), *Advances in experimental social psychology* (Vol. 25, pp. 1–65). New York: Academic Press.

Schwartz, S. (1996). Value priorities and behavior: Applying a theory of integrated value systems. In C. Seligman, J. M. Olson, & M. P. Zanna (Eds.), *The psychology of values: The Ontario symposium Vol. 8* (pp. 1–24). Mahwah, NJ: Erlbaum.

Schwarz, N., & Strack, F. (1999). Reports of subjective well-being: Judgmental processes and their methodological implications. In D. Kahneman, E. Diener, & N. Schwarz (Eds.), *Well-being: The foundations of hedonic psychology* (pp. 61–84). New York: Russell Sage Foundation.

Williams, R. M. (1968). Values. In E. Sills (Ed.), *International encyclopedia of the social sciences* (Vol. 18, pp. 283–287). New York: Macmillan.

# Part III

## Information Processing, Affect, and Behavior

# 7

# Asymmetries in Affect-Laden Information Processing

*John T. Cacioppo*

## Prologue

The disciplinary pale of economics, my undergraduate major, was appealing in terms of its quantitative logic and formal proofs, but its emphasis on forecasting aggregate end products rather than on understanding underlying mechanisms was less so. The assumptions about rationality were demonstrably incorrect at the level of an individual's behavior, but it was possible that such irrationalities cancelled after aggregation or that aggregate behavior was characterized by emergent properties that were not explicable in terms of individual behavior. In any case, economic models were thought to predict aggregate social behavior reasonably well, and there were more important economic factors to study at that juncture. Nevertheless, the role of affect and cognition in rational and irrational social behavior intrigued me, and social psychology afforded an opportunity to study these processes and mechanisms.

At that point in its history, I discovered, the science of social psychology centered on reportable mental contents, even though most cognitive, affective, and social processes occur unconsciously, with only selected aspects reaching awareness. If the thoughts and processes people experience represent only a small subset of the structures and operations that needed to be explored and understood, then it seemed reasonable that principles and measures of the human brain and physiology could offer theoretical concepts and rigid constraints as well as an expanded set of manipulations and measures with which to explicate the mechanisms and processes of social behavior. Rather than a passive, dispassionate recorder and processor of information, the brain is a builder of meaning within a social context in ways sculpted by experience, personal and ancestral. There was an abyss between social and biological levels of analysis that needed to be bridged first, though, so parts of our early work were designed to help bridge this abyss.

Work reported here was supported in part by National Science Foundation Grant No. BCS-0086314 and National Institute of Mental Health Grant No. P50MH52384-01A1. We thank Christina Cacioppo for her helpful comments on an earlier draft of this chapter.

Disciplinary boundaries or favored paradigms never stopped Bill McGuire from seeking answers, and his example served as a beacon during dark times. Interdisciplinary research involving social scientists, cognitive scientists, and neuroscientists is now fairly common and is indeed advancing our understanding of phenomena in all three disciplines. I suspect we have only begun to see the benefits of reaching beyond the disciplinary pale for understanding complex social behavior, including economic behavior.

* * *

Bill McGuire, throughout his illustrious career, has championed the view that the construction of mental contents is influenced by and fundamental to understanding the social as well as the perceptual world in which we live. The self-concept is not a summary statistic of objective features but a construction based on goals and social context (McGuire & Padawer-Singer, 1976). The inferences drawn from beliefs (e.g., syllogisms) are not coldly calculated conditional probabilities but a calculus shaped in part by wishful thinking (McGuire, 1981). In this chapter, I focus on McGuire's pioneering contributions to our understanding of how the human mind constructs a unique reality for each individual at each moment in time, with a special emphasis on asymmetries in affect-laden information processing.

## Cognitive and Affective Asymmetries in Thought Systems

If one is asked to list all the characteristics that describe or do not describe Bill McGuire, most people would list more characteristics with less mental effort in the former case than in the latter even though there are more characteristics that do not than those that do describe Bill. This *cognitive* asymmetry exists because people are better able to think affirmationally than negationally. From an evolutionary biological perspective, the ability to discern what an organism is—whether a newcomer is hostile, a potential partner is solicitous, a potential ally is captious, or a child is dependent—is more important for reproductive success than is the ability to discern the innumerable characteristics that do not describe each. Small wonder that the brain evolved to preferentially process information about what a stimulus is rather than about what it is not.

McGuire and McGuire (1992) provide compelling evidence for this cognitive bias. They demonstrated, for example, that participants generated more thoughts when given the task of describing what a thought topic is than what it is not (Experiments 1–4)—indicating a positivity bias in thinking ability—and they preferred to describe a topic in terms of what it is rather than what it is not (Experiments 5–8)—suggesting a positivity bias in thinking proclivity.

Positive and negative *affective* asymmetries, in McGuire and McGuire's (1992) terminology, "concern whether people think more effectively about the desirable or the undesirable characteristics possessed or lacked by a topic of thought" (pp. 295–296). McGuire demonstrated an affective *negativity* bias in situations in which a person needs to cope with events in the external environment ("realistic thinking situations") and an affective *positivity* bias in situations in which the person is more concerned with hedonic gratification in fantasy ("autistic thinking situations"). This work has contributed to our understanding of the antecedent conditions for the activation of positive and negative information processing and has helped create the foundation for asking broader questions about the architecture and operation of the affect system itself—a topic to which we turn next.

## Affective Asymmetries: The Positivity Offset and the Negativity Bias

Affective discriminations have traditionally been conceptualized as being bipolar (hostile–hospitable) and have been measured using bipolar scales to gauge the net affective predisposition toward a stimulus. Such an approach treats positive and negative evaluative processes (and the resulting affective states) as equivalent, reciprocally activated, and interchangeable (Cacioppo & Berntson, 1994). Even though physical constraints may restrict behavioral manifestations to bivalent actions (approach–withdrawal), early behavioral theorists recognized that approach and withdrawal were behavioral manifestations that could come from distinguishable motivational substrates. Conflict theory was enriched by conceptualizing approach and withdrawal separately, investigating their unique antecedents and consequences, and examining the psychological constraints that typically led to the reciprocal activation of approach and withdrawal tendencies (e.g., Miller, 1961). Our understanding of affective asymmetries may similarly benefit from expanding the principle of reciprocal evaluative activation to accommodate the distinguishable activation of positive and negative evaluative processes, the investigation of their unique antecedents and consequences, and the examination of the psychological and physiological constraints that produce various modes of evaluative (e.g., reciprocal) activation.

We proposed an evolutionary model of affective processes in which a stimulus may vary in terms of the strength of appetitive evaluative activation (i.e., positivity) and the strength of defensive evaluative activation (i.e., negativity) it evokes (Cacioppo et al. 1997, 1999; Cacioppo & Berntson, 1994;). Although the representation of these separable processes along the bivariate plane in Figure 7.1 may look like the statistical dimensions from studies of the structure of affect, the dimensions in Figure 7.1 are entirely theoretical constructs. The model posits that positive and negative evaluative processes generally have antagonistic effects on a predisposition to respond, the net effect of which is mapped on the z-axis in Figure 7.1.

Whereas a bipolar model allows only for reciprocal activation between positivity and negativity (and hence is represented as the "reciprocal" diagonal on the bivariate plane in Figure 7.1), the evaluative space model (ESM) posits multiple modes of activation of these motivational substrates: (a) reciprocal activation occurs when a stimulus has opposing effects on the activation of positivity and negativity, (b) uncoupled activation occurs when a stimulus affects only positive or only negative evaluative activation, and (c) nonreciprocal activation occurs when a stimulus increases (or decreases) the activation

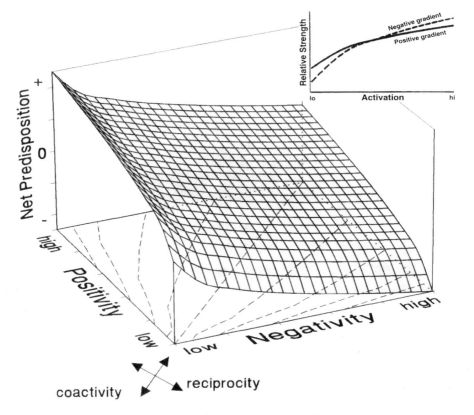

**Figure 7.1.**  The evaluative space model (ESM). Activation functions are quantitative depictions of the output of a processor for zero to maximal levels of input. The ESM posits that two separable affective processors are activated by appetitive (positive) and aversive (negative) information, respectively. All combinations are possible through multiple modes of evaluative activation, so a two-dimensional plane is required to depict these processor states. The distinctive activation functions for positivity and negativity are highlighted in the inset. The outputs of these processors are combined to produce a net predisposition of an individual toward (+) or away from (–) the target stimulus. This is represented by the overlying surface. From "The Affect System Has Parallel and Integrative Processing Components: Form Follows Function," by J. T. Cacioppo, W. L. Gardner, and G. G. Berntson, 1999, *Journal of Personality and Social Psychology, 76,* 842. Copyright 1999 by the American Psychological Association. Reprinted with permission.

of both positivity and negativity (Cacioppo & Berntson, 1994). Accordingly, the ESM model of evaluative space does not reject reciprocal activation but rather subsumes it as one of the three possible modes of activation and explores the antecedents for each mode of evaluative activation *and* as the consequent behavioral predisposition (i.e., *z*-axis).

The model further posits that positivity and negativity are distinguishable (stochastically and functionally independent in specifiable circumstances), are characterized by distinct activation functions (positivity offset and negativity bias principles), are related differentially to ambivalence (corollary of ambivalence asymmetries), have distinguishable antecedents (heteroscedacity principle), and tend to gravitate from a bivariate toward a bipolar structure when the underlying beliefs are the target of deliberation or a guide for behavior (principle of motivational certainty). The aspect of this model most germane here is the differential activation functions for the appetitive and defensive systems underlying affective predispositions and responses, so we turn to this feature in the remainder of this chapter.

## Activation Functions

One consequence of incoming information being processed at least in part separably by appetitive and defensive systems is that evolutionary forces could sculpt different activation functions for these systems (i.e., "positivity" and "negativity"). We have suggested that these activation functions differ in several important ways, two of which are apropos to our understanding of affective asymmetries of the type highlighted by McGuire and McGuire (1992): (a) a *positivity offset,* by which we mean that the output of positivity is higher than the output of negativity at very low levels of affective input, and (b) a *negativity bias,* by which we mean the increase in output per quantum of input is greater for negativity than for positivity.

The *positivity offset* is the tendency for a weak positive (approach) motivational output at zero input, an intercept difference in affective activation. As a consequence of the positivity offset, the motivation to approach is stronger than the motivation to withdraw at low levels of evaluative activation (e.g., at distances far from a goal). The evolutionary significance of the positivity offset is understandable. Without a positivity offset, an organism in a neutral environment may be unmotivated to approach new objects, stimuli, or contexts. Such organisms would learn little about novel or neutral-appearing environments and their potential value or threat. They would also know little about the terrain when predator or prey appeared, decreasing their chances of survival. With a positivity offset, however, an organism facing neutral stimuli or environment would be weakly motivated to engage in exploratory behavior following the habituation of an initial neophobic response. Such a tendency has important survival value, at least at the level of a species.

Exploratory behavior can provide useful information about an organism's environment, but exploration can also place an organism in proximity to hostile stimuli. Because it is more difficult to reverse the consequences of an injurious or fatal assault than to return to an unpursued opportunity, the process of natural selection may also have resulted ceteris paribus in the propensity to react more strongly to negative stimuli than to positive. Termed the *negativity bias* (because it refers to the slope or gain of the activation functions), this heightened sensitivity to negative information is a robust psychological phenomenon. The positivity offset and negativity bias are apparent in the inset in Figure 7.1, which depicts the separate activation functions for positivity and negativity. Note that the intercept for the activation function for positivity is higher than the intercept for the activation function for negativity, whereas the slope for activation of negativity is steeper than the slope for the activation of positivity.

These affective asymmetries may help explain the variations in the negativity and positivity biases noted by McGuire and McGuire (1992). For example, when people rate someone they do not know, they rate the person on the positive side of the scale's neutral point (Anderson, 1981). This is precisely what one would expect if the information presented about the target person was neutral. Such an effect may be based on the diagnosticity of neutral information or the morality or competence of the behaviors ("Don engages in normal behavior so he is probably ok"; cf. Skorwonski & Carlston, 1989). Gardner (1996) examined whether diagnosticity was the critical feature by having participants rate either a hypothetical person (toward whom participants generally felt positive even without any information), an (imaginary) aguaphore fish (toward which participants generally felt neutral without any information), and an (imaginary) entophore insect (toward which participants generally felt negative without any information; see also, Cacioppo et al. 1997). Participants rated each after either receiving no additional information or neutral and nondiagnostic information (e.g., the person is susceptible to the laws of gravity; the entophore has six legs). Results indicated that the person, the aguaphore fish, and the entophore insect were each rated slightly more positively after deliberating about neutral and nondiagnostic information.

Evidence for the positivity offset and negativity bias has also been found in paradigms in which diagnosticity and morality or competence are irrelevant. The rating of triadic (p-o-x) structures consisting of oneself (p), another person (o), and a topic (x) as more pleasant, harmonious, stable, and expected when a positive link (attraction) exists between oneself and the other is consistent with the operation of a positivity bias, as is the finding that this effect emerges earlier than the agreement or balance effect (Cacioppo & Petty, 1981).

Note that the circumstances in which *negative* affective asymmetries were brilliantly observed by McGuire and McGuire (1992) involved significant affective activation, such as the effects of economic progress versus economic decline on electoral support for incumbents and the relative effects of gains versus losses. Inspection of the inset in Figure 7.1 confirms that it is just such circumstances in which an affect system should modulate information processing differently ceteris paribus, producing a greater weighting of negative than positive information.

Miller's (1961) research on rodent behavior provided some of the earliest evidence for a negativity bias and provides some evidence that this is a general behavioral process, as we would expect given the posited evolutionary heritage. Evidence supporting a negativity bias has been found in domains as varied as impression formation, person memory, blood and organ donation, personnel evaluations, and voting behavior and has been found to characterize the judgments of children as well as adults (Cacioppo & Gardner, 1999). Taylor (1991) summarizes a wide range of evidence showing that negative events in a context evoke stronger and more rapid physiological, cognitive, emotional, and social responses than neutral or positive events (see also Skowronski & Carlston, 1989).

Ito, Cacioppo, and Lang (1998) measured the positive and negative feelings evoked by 472 slides selected to represent the full affective space captured by the International Affective Picture System. Arousal ratings were used to index the intensity of the affective stimulus (which was plotted on the abscissa), and the unipolar positivity and unipolar negativity ratings were used to index the magnitude of the affective response (which were plotted on the ordinate). Analyses revealed that the intercept was significantly higher for ratings of positive stimuli than for negative (i.e., a positivity offset). Results also revealed that the slope of the regression line for the ratings of the negative stimuli was significantly steeper than the regression line for the ratings of the positive stimuli (i.e., the negativity bias). Said more simply, positive stimuli have a greater impact than negative stimuli at comparably low levels of activation, but the opposite is the case at equally high levels of activation.

To assess the generalizability of this effect across stimulus items, Ito, Larsen, Smith, and Cacioppo (1998) replicated the regression analyses using 620 words—verbs, nouns, adverbs, and adjectives—from the Affective Norms for English Words database, and we subsequently conducted similar analyses on the 555 trait adjectives from Anderson (1965). As predicted by the ESM, evidence for a positivity offset was found in that the most neutral positive words were judged slightly but significantly more extreme than the most neutral negative words, and evidence for a negativity bias was found such that the slope of the evaluatively negative words was steeper than the slope of the evaluatively positive words. The human mind treats hedonic information differently when constructing a representation of the world within an ecological niche because, at least in the long run, doing so has adaptive advantage over depicting reality objectively.

## Evidence From Social Neuroscience

One of the core predictions of the ESM is that appetitive and aversive information are processed separately at the earliest stages of hedonic information processing and are combined to produce a more integrated guidance in the form of a predisposition to respond positively (or approach) or negatively (or withdraw). Although we have reviewed elsewhere the neural evidence for the separability of positivity and negativity (e.g., Cacioppo & Berntson, 1994, 1999; Cacioppo & Gardner, 1999; Cacioppo et al., 1997, 1999), a report by O'Doherty, Kringelbach, Rolls, Hornak, and Andrews (2001) is illustrative. They conducted a functional magnetic resonance imaging (fMRI) study in which participants performed a gambling task while in a scanner. An increase in the activity of the lateral orbitofrontal cortex (OFC) was related to the participants' receipt of punishment, and the converse pattern was recorded in the medial OFC. O'Doherty et al. concluded that (a) reward and punishment may be processed in distinct subregions of the OFC and (b) the magnitude of activation varied as a function of the magnitude of the reward or punishment. These results add to the increasing evidence that the processing of appetitive and aversive information can be separable at early stages of information processing.

We have further examined whether the negativity bias can operate at the evaluative categorization stage prior to response selection or execution (Ito, Larsen, Smith, & Cacioppo, 1998). Event-related brain potentials (ERPs), which we have shown previously to be more sensitive to evaluative categorization than response stages of information processing (Cacioppo, Crites, Berntson, & Coles, 1993; Cacioppo, Crites, Gardner, & Berntson, 1994; Crites, Cacioppo, Gardner, & Berntson, 1995), were recorded to pleasant, neutral, and unpleasant pictures embedded within sequences of other neutral pictures. Results showed that (a) the evaluative categorization of pleasant or unpleasant stimuli in sequences of neutral stimuli was associated with larger amplitude late positive brain potentials (LPPs) over centroparietal regions that peaked at approximately 550 ms and (b) the evaluative categorization of unpleasant stimuli was associated with a larger amplitude LPP than was the evaluative categorization of equally probable, equally evaluatively extreme, and equally arousing pleasant stimuli. These results provide support for the hypothesis that the negativity bias in affective processing occurs as early as the initial evaluative categorization stage.

In a follow-up, Ito and Cacioppo (2000) used the online measurement of categorization processes provided by ERPs to assess the implicit and explicit categorization of stimuli along evaluative (pleasant, unpleasant) and nonevaluative (people, no-people) dimensions. Participants were exposed to stimuli that simultaneously varied along both dimensions, but half the participants were instructed to count the number of pictures that depicted people (or the absence of people; nonevaluative categorization task) and half were instructed to count the number of pictures that depicted pleasant (or unpleasant) scenes (evaluative categorization task). As in our prior research, the LPP was sensitive to participants' explicit categorization task such that (a) the LPP was larger in the evaluative task when a pleasant picture was presented within a series of unpleasant than in a series of pleasant pictures and when an unpleasant picture was presented within a series of pleasant than in a series of unpleasant pictures and (b) the LPP was larger in the nonevaluative task when a picture depicting people was presented within a series of pictures depicting no people than in a series with people and vice versa. In addition, the LPP was larger in the evaluative task when an unpleasant picture was presented within a series of pleasant pictures than when a pleasant picture was presented within a series of unpleasant pictures (i.e., the negativity bias).

More interesting is that the LPP also revealed implicit categorization along the nontask relevant dimension—with clear evidence of an implicit negativity bias in which rare unpleasant stimuli spontaneously received greater processing than did rare pleasant stimuli. Moreover, the explicit task of categorizing stimuli along a nonevaluative dimension neither diminished nor delayed the LPP to variations in the evaluative dimension. As would be expected at low levels of hedonic activation (see Figure 7.1), the negativity bias and implicit categorization effects have not been observed when using mildly evocative experimental stimuli such as words ("pleasant," "unpleasant"; Cacioppo, Crites, & Gardner, 1996; Crites & Cacioppo, 1996) rather than more evocative emotional pictures (e.g., Ito, Larsen et al., 1998; Ito & Cacioppo, 2000). We interpreted these results as evidence for the operation of adaptively beneficial implicit categorization processes, triggered by significant proximal stimuli, serving broad, cross-situational goals.

Chronometric implicit measures of associations or attitudes have provided provocative evidence for unseen processes underlying thought and judgments. This literature is not sufficient at this juncture to indicate which specific implicit processes each is marking, however. The theoretical constraints from the neurosciences regarding the timing and spatial location of event-related brain potentials may address this limitation in the typical implicit approaches.

The ERP waveform can be represented as a small number of orthogonal underlying components. Component scores index the extent to which each component is present at each moment in time (thereby revealing temporal information about the operation of separable implicit processes), and the scalp region over which the component is maximal may help constrain the nature of each implicit process (e.g., occipital region would suggest altered attention or visual processing, centroparietal region would suggest more associative or polysensory processing; Fabiani, Gratton, & Coles, 2000).

Smith, Cacioppo, Larsen, and Chartrand (2003) manipulated the valence of the target stimuli (pleasant, unpleasant, or neutral) and the probability of the stimuli (frequent vs. rare) in three separate studies. In each study, principal components analysis confirmed that the score for the first positive-going component (P1 amplitude) to all frequent stimuli and to rare negative stimuli was larger than that for P1 amplitude to rare positive stimuli. This component was maximal over the occipital scalp region and peaked at about 140 ms—in the same range of time in which the earliest endogenous attentional components appear. Moreover, this component was only modestly correlated with the LPP, which again was maximal at about 550 ms over the centroparietal areas. Given that the P1 component of the ERP is a proximal index of attention allocation to valenced stimuli, these results suggest an extremely rapid (< 120 ms) differentiation of appetitive and aversive stimuli manifesting as a negativity bias in attention allocation.

These observations are preliminary, and additional research is needed to ensure the generalizability and validity of these interpretations. Two independent sources of evidence, however, suggest a possible pathway for the P1 negativity bias that involves the superior colliculus, posterior pulvinar nucleus, and amygdala. First, patients with striate cortex lesions show preserved abilities to localize and discriminate visual stimuli that are not consciously perceived (blindsight). Second, neuroimaging studies have revealed correlations between amygdala, superior colliculus, and pulvinar cerebral blood flow in masked ("unseen") emotional conditions (e.g., Morris, Ohman, & Dolan, 1999). Thus, whereas the striate cortex visual pathway affords high-resolution visual processing, the superior colliculus and pulvinar pathway afford relatively fast but low-resolution visual processing that can guide (motivate) attention without intention or awareness. Such an affective asymmetry serves to guide attentional and cognitive resources to potential threats in the environment even before they can be recognized.

## Conclusion

Individuals often are revered for cultivated tastes and seemingly dispassionate responses to life's challenges, but the affect system and its output the emotions, archaic in origins, saturate human existence throughout the life span. Emotions guide, enrich, and ennoble life; they provide meaning to everyday existence; they render the valuation placed on life and property. Emotions can promote behaviors that protect life, form the basis for the continuity in life, and compel the termination of life. They can be an essential ingredient in and an overwhelming obstacle to optimizing human potential. Given their evolutionary heritage and daily currency, there is little wonder that emotions have preoccupied humankind throughout recorded history, and there is little doubt that emotions are both biologically rooted and culturally molded.

Negative emotion has been depicted previously as playing a fundamental role in calibrating psychological systems; it serves as a call for mental or behavioral adjustment and problem solving, to perform convergent thinking. Positive emotion, in contrast, serves as a cue to stay the course or as a cue to explore the environment, to perform divergent thinking (see Cacioppo & Gardner, 1999). The separable activation functions provide a complementary, adaptive motivational organization. Species with a positivity offset *and* a negativity bias enjoy the benefits of exploratory behavior and the self-preservative benefits of a predisposition to avoid, scrutinize, and withdraw from threatening events. These features represent only the rudimentary operations of an affect system, however. Work on the relativity of emotion shows that cognitive factors and physiological states affect the extent to which appetitive or defensive motivations are aroused, and recent work suggests that a self-regulatory focus also influences approach and withdrawal gradients (Carver & Scheier, 1990; Higgins 1997). The organization of the affect system, its operating characteristics, and its outputs (e.g., affective asymmetries) warrant further study as a reflection of our evolutionary heritage and a continued force in shaping the mind's construction of the world.

# References

Anderson, N. H. (1965). Adding versus averaging as a stimulus combination rule in impression formation. *Journal of Experimental Social Psychology, 70,* 394–400.

Anderson, N. H. (1981). Integration theory applied to cognitive responses and attitudes. In R. E. Petty, T. M. Ostrom, & T. C. Brock (Eds.), *Cognitive responses in persuasion* (pp. 361–397). Hillsdale, NJ: Erlbaum.

Cacioppo, J. T., & Berntson, G. G. (1994). Relationship between attitudes and evaluative space: A critical review, with emphasis on the separability of positive and negative substrates. *Psychological Bulletin, 115,* 401–423.

Cacioppo, J. T., & Berntson, G. G. (1999). The affect system: Architecture and operating characteristics. *Current Directions in Psychological Science, 8,* 133–137.

Cacioppo, J. T., Crites, S. L., Jr., & Gardner, W. L. (1996). Attitudes to the right: Evaluative processing is associated with lateralized late positive event-related brain potentials. *Personality and Social Psychology Bulletin, 22,* 1205–1219.

Cacioppo, J. T., Crites, S. L., Jr., Berntson, G. G., & Coles, M. G. H. (1993). If attitudes affect how stimuli are processed, should they not affect the event-related brain potential? *Psychological Science, 4,* 108–112.

Cacioppo, J. T., Crites, S. L., Jr., Gardner, W. L., & Berntson, G. G. (1994). Bioelectrical echoes from evaluative categorizations: I. A late positive brain potential that varies as a function of trait negativity and extremity. *Journal of Personality and Social Psychology, 67,* 115–125.

Cacioppo, J. T., & Gardner, W. L. (1999). Emotion. *Annual Review of Psychology, 50,* 191–214.

Cacioppo, J. T., Gardner, W. L., & Berntson, G. G. (1997). Beyond bipolar conceptualizations and measures: The case of attitudes and evaluative space. *Personality and Social Psychology Review, 1,* 3–25.

Cacioppo, J. T., Gardner, W. L., & Berntson, G. G. (1999). The affect system has parallel and integrative processing components: Form follows function. *Journal of Personality and Social Psychology, 76,* 839–855.

Cacioppo, J. T., & Petty, R. E. (1981). Effects of extent of thought on the pleasantness ratings of p-o-x triads: Evidence for three judgmental tendencies in evaluating social situations. *Journal of Personality and Social Psychology, 40,* 1000–1009.

Carver, C. S., & Scheier, M. F. (1990). Origins and functions of positive and negative affect: A control-process view. *Psychological Review, 97,* 19–35.

Crites, S. L., Jr., & Cacioppo, J. T. (1996). Electrocortical differentiation of evaluative and nonevaluative categorizations. *Psychological Science, 7,* 318–321.

Crites, S. L., Jr., Cacioppo, J. T., Gardner, W. L., & Berntson, G. G. (1995). Bioelectrical echoes from evaluative categorization: II. A late positive brain potential that varies as a function of attitude registration rather than attitude report. *Journal of Personality and Social Psychology, 68,* 997–1013.

Fabiani, M., Gratton, G., & Coles, M. G. H. (2000). Event-related brain potentials. In J. T. Cacioppo, L. G. Tassinary, & G. G. Berntson (Eds.), *Handbook of Psychophysiology* (pp. 53–84). New York: Cambridge University Press.

Gardner, W. L. (1996). *Biases in impression formation: A demonstration of a bivariate model of evaluation.* Unpublished doctoral dissertation, The Ohio State University, Columbus.

Higgins, E. T. (1997). Beyond pleasure and pain. *American Psychologist, 52,* 1280–1300.

Ito, T. A., & Cacioppo, J. T. (2000). Electrophysiological evidence of implicit and explicit categorization processes. *Journal of Experimental Social Psychology, 36,* 660–676.

Ito, T. A., Cacioppo, J. T., & Lang, P. J. (1998). Eliciting affect using the International Affective Picture System: Trajectories through evaluative space. *Personality and Social Psychology Bulletin, 24,* 855–879.

Ito, T. A., Larsen, J. T., Smith, N. K., & Cacioppo, J. T. (1998). Negative information weighs more heavily on the brain: The negativity bias in evaluative categorizations. *Journal of Personality and Social Psychology, 75,* 887–900.

McGuire, W. J. (1981). The probabilogical model of cognitive structure and attitude change. In R. E. Petty, T. M. Ostrom, and T. C. Brock (Eds.), *Cognitive responses in persuasion* (pp. 291–307). Hillsdale, NJ: Erlbaum.

McGuire, W. J., & McGuire, C. V. (1992). Cognitive-versus-affective asymmetries in thought systems. *European Journal of Social Psychology, 22,* 571–591.

McGuire, W. J., & Padawer-Singer, A. (1976). Trait salience in the spontaneous self-concept. *Journal of Personality and Social Psychology, 33,* 743–754.

Miller, N. E. (1961). Some recent studies on conflict behavior and drugs. *American Psychologist, 16,* 12–24.

Morris, J. S., Ohman, A., & Dolan, R. J. (1999). A subcortical pathway to the right amygdala mediating "unseen" fear. *Proceedings of the National Academy of Sciences, 96,* 1680–1685.

O'Doherty, J. O., Kringelbach, M. L., Rolls, E. T., Hornak, J., & Andrews, C. (2001). Abstract reward and punishment representations in the human orbitofrontal cortex. *Nature Neuroscience, 4,* 95–102.

Skowronski, J. J., & Carlston, D. E. (1989). Negativity and extremity biases in impression formation: A review of explanations. *Psychological Bulletin, 105,* 131–142.

Smith, N. K., Cacioppo, J. T., Larsen, J. T., & Chartrand, T. L. (2003). May I have your attention, please: Electrocortical responses to positive and negative stimuli. *Neuropsychologia, 41,* 171–183.

Taylor, S. E. (1991). Asymmetrical effects of positive and negative events: The mobilization-minimization hypothesis. *Psychological Bulletin, 110,* 67–85.

# 8

## The Cognitive Organization and Use of General Knowledge

### *Robert S. Wyer, Jr.*

### Prologue

I have always had a desire to develop a comprehensive conceptualization of social phenomena that not only integrates a lot of diverse empirical findings but also is sufficiently rigorous to permit the derivation of new, empirically testable hypotheses. This motive has led me to think both broadly and formally about the cognitive underpinnings of memory, judgment, and behavior. My obsession with formalism as well as with breadth has sometimes led to overly grandiose conceptualizations composed of mind-boggling sets of postulates and assumptions, which few colleagues have had the stamina to digest. But I've found it hard to think in any other way.

Three somewhat diverging comments that I encountered early in my professional life have remained with me over the years and have had a major impact. First, Nan Wertheimer, an epidemiologist, once observed in a seminar that people should attempt to avoid becoming committed to any particular theory for as long as possible, because once that commitment was made, their contribution to psychology was over. That is, they would spend the rest of their lives defending their theory and would blind themselves to new ideas and approaches.

The second comment was made in a book chapter by Bill McGuire. After likening the search for knowledge to that of a boy who is lost in the woods, he continued:

> If the empirical scientist is lost in a complex area, his pursuing the implications of any reasonable paradigm in a steady direction will probably lead him to some ultimate clarification of the area. If instead he drops each theory as soon as the slightest negative evidence crops up, there results the danger that he will wander around in circles and not obtain any clarification. The researcher who keeps the faith and pursues his paradigm to ultimate enlightenment may find that there is a much better theory he could have chosen initially. But his persistence will also have demonstrated the truth of Blake's proverb that "if the fool would persist in his folly, he would become wise." (McGuire, 1972, p. 138)

Finally, while in graduate school, I read an article by Edward Tolman, one of the foremost animal learning theorists of his era, whose views, radical at the time, have since been implicitly vindicated by both cognitive and social psychologists. In reviewing his career, he noted that he, like McGuire's boy in the woods, might not have taken the most direct route to understanding and that if he had it to do over again, he might have taken a different path. However, he had had fun along the way, and that was what mattered.

All three of these comments have had an impact on my philosophy of life, both professionally and personally. Following McGuire, I have tried to develop a conceptual perspective on social phenomena to guide my theoretical and empirical understanding of both new and old information. At the same time, I have tried to follow Nan Wertheimer's advice not to identify too closely with this perspective, not to take myself too seriously, to take my theories with a grain of salt and to challenge them as harshly as I challenge others', and to be receptive to new and better ways of viewing the world. Finally, I, like Tolman, might do things differently if I had them to do over. However, I have also had fun along the way, and I, again like Tolman, think that this is what really matters.

* * *

Having the opportunity to contribute to this volume has stimulated me to reflect more generally on the events that have guided the development of my theoretical and empirical interests over the past 35 years. These reflections have led me to realize that McGuire's influence has been even more pervasive than I had previously assumed. My research over the past 25 years has taken many specific directions, but each avenue of inquiry has focused on one or more stages of information processing, ranging from attention and comprehension to informational organization and storage in memory to its retrieval and integration with new information and past knowledge, to arrive at subjective inferences, judgments, and behavioral decisions. The perspective that McGuire's work gave me in the early 1970s has guided my research and theorizing ever since. In this chapter, I focus on two areas in which McGuire's influence is particularly obvious. They concern (a) the way in which the knowledge on which beliefs and attitudes are based becomes integrated into the cognitive system and (b) the process through which this knowledge influences responses to new information.

## The Content and Structure of Propositional Knowledge

Our knowledge about people, objects, and events can be acquired in a number of sense modalities. It can be represented in memory either linguistically or as mental images (cf. Wyer & Radvansky, 1999). Linguistic representations are often propositional in form. The propositions can be either general (e.g., "Humans' pollution of the environment will lead to their own extinction") or referent specific ("Nixon resigned as President in 1973"). In either event, they can vary in both their likelihood of being true and the desirability of their implications. (Estimates of these properties are usually referred to as *beliefs* and *attitudes*, respectively.) Propositional knowledge is employed in almost every aspect of daily life.

However, relatively little progress has been made in understanding how this sort of knowledge is represented and organized in the cognitive system. Most research and theorizing on the mental representation of social information have focused on much simpler questions, such as the way in which trait and behavioral information about a hypothetical person is organized in memory (Srull & Wyer, 1989). Other lines of research have explored the mental representation of thematically related sequences of events involving unspecified or fictitious individuals (Schank & Abelson, 1977; Wyer & Bodenhausen, 1985; Wyer & Radvansky, 1999). It is unclear whether this work has much to do with the organization of knowledge that provides the basis for beliefs and opinions about events that occur in the real world. (For elaborations of this point, see Wyer, 2003; Wyer & Gruenfeld, 1995.)

Indeed, Bill McGuire (1960b, 1981; McGuire & McGuire, 1991) stands almost alone in his attempt to grapple with these complex issues. In collaboration with Claire McGuire and using techniques stimulated by their earlier work on the spontaneous self-concept (McGuire & McGuire, 1988), he gained insight into the types of knowledge that people spontaneously bring to bear on information about situations that are likely to occur both in their personal lives and in society more generally. Their findings have implications not only for the content and organization of propositional knowledge but also for the specific aspects of this knowledge that people spontaneously retrieve and use to evaluate new belief- and attitude-relevant information. In anticipation of this Herculean effort, however, McGuire (1960b, 1981) developed a model to describe more precisely the manner in which beliefs in specified sets of propositions are interrelated and the impact of one belief on others. Much of my own research and theorizing represent a modest attempt to elaborate the implications of McGuire's more seminal ideas.

Even within a particular content domain, the propositional knowledge we require is quite diverse. My knowledge of World War II, for example, includes propositions that (a) Rommel was involved in a plot to assassinate Hitler, (b) Anne Frank was a victim of the Holocaust, (c) an atomic bomb was dropped on Hiroshima, and (d) $25 war bonds could be purchased for $18.75. These propositions seem almost unrelated. Moreover, if I were writing this chapter tomorrow and were trying to generate examples of my knowledge of World War II, I would probably produce a different set of facts than the ones I have just listed. This observation suggests that the different pieces of knowledge one acquires in a given domain are stored independently of one another and later retrieved from a "memory organization packet" (Schank, 1982) or cognitive "storage bin" (Wyer & Srull, 1989). The accessibility of this knowledge and the likelihood of later retrieving it, can depend on both chronic dispositions and situational factors that influence the recency and frequency of its use (Higgins, 1996; Srull & Wyer, 1979; Wyer & Srull, 1989).

However, people are not passive recipients of information. When they encounter an assertion about a past or future event or state of affairs, they typically comprehend it with reference to their prior knowledge about the same or similar events or states and the conditions in which they occurred. In doing so, they are likely to estimate the assertion's validity and to construe the desirability of its possible consequences. As McGuire and McGuire (1991) note, these estimates could sometimes be based on specific knowledge about antecedents and consequences of the events. Alternatively, they could be the result of a constructive process, reflecting the intersection of several previously acquired concepts and knowledge. In either event, the cognitive activity may produce associations between the assertion and a larger body of knowledge about its referents. As a result, this knowledge is likely to be recalled when the assertion is later thought about.

McGuire and McGuire (1991) assumed that people's cognitive responses to new information are often motivated by the need to maintain both logical and hedonic consistency between the implications of new information and prior knowledge and to cope both realistically and autistically with life experiences. They postulated that when individuals contemplate a real or imagined event or state of affairs, they typically think about either (a) the reasons it might occur (antecedents) or (b) its implications for the future (consequences). In fact, these types of thoughts accounted for more than 65% of participants' spontaneous responses to propositions about the possible occurrence of a target event (e.g., a substantial increase in admission prices of sporting events). The large majority of thoughts pertained to factors that would promote (rather than prevent) the occurrence of the target event and to events that the target event would facilitate rather than inhibit.

In some cases, people's thoughts about the conditions described in a target proposition may reflect previously formed associations between these conditions and their possible causes and effects. Often, however, people might never have contemplated the event described in a proposition before being asked to think about it in the experiment, and so little, if any, previously acquired knowledge may have become associated with it. In these instances, their thoughts may reflect the use of coping strategies similar to those postulated by McGuire and McGuire. That is, people who receive information about a possible (target) event may actively attempt to identify factors that help them predict and perhaps control its occurrence. Alternatively, they may try to construe the consequences of the event in order to become better prepared for it. These cognitive activities could lead to associations between the target event and aspects of their prior knowledge that would not exist if participants had not been motivated to explain the event or construe its implications the time they first encountered it. These possibilities raise two questions. First, when do people search for antecedents of an event and when do they search for consequences? Second, which of several possible antecedents or consequences are they most likely to identify?

## Motivational Determinants of Knowledge Organization

McGuire and McGuire (1991) found that people ponder the antecedents of an event when they consider the likelihood that the event will occur, but they think about the consequences of the event when they consider its desirability. The events that are involved in these cognitive deliberations presumably become associated in memory. That is, an event becomes associated with its antecedents when people engage in the first activity but with its consequences when they engage in the second. Wyer and Hartwick (1984) confirmed this conjecture. Participants first read a list of randomly ordered propositions with instructions to indicate whether they understood them. Thirty-two of these propositions comprised 16 pairs of assertions that occupied the positions of the antecedent (A) and the consequence (C) in a causal statement of the form "If A, then C." Moreover, the normative likelihood that A was true and the clarity of its implications for C were systematically varied. Thus, a pair in which A was likely to be true and had clear implications for C consisted of the statements "Trucks conveying heavy cargo destroy highways" and "The weight limit on truck cargo may be decreased." In contrast, a pair in which A was unlikely to be true and had unclear implications for C was composed of the statements "There will be no national borders by the end of the year 2000" and "War will be a thing of the past by the end of this [the 20th] century." After indicating their understanding of each statement, some participants reported their attitudes toward the situation described in both propositions in a given A–C pair. Others reported their beliefs in both propositions, and still other participants reported their attitude toward one proposition and their belief in the other.

We expected that participants who were asked to make these judgments would base them on the first relevant knowledge that came to mind. Thus, if a relevant proposition had been made salient in the course of performing the initial "comprehension" task, this proposition should be identified and used, and this cognitive activity should establish an association between the two propositions. If this is true, McGuire and McGuire's (1991) findings suggest that A and C should become associated when participants are asked to estimate their belief in C (thus leading them to identify the antecedent A) but not if they are asked to estimate C's desirability. On the other hand, the propositions should become associated if participants are asked to report their attitude toward A (leading them to identify the consequence C) but not if they are asked to report their belief in it.

After reporting their beliefs and attitudes, participants were dismissed. When they returned one week later, they were asked to recall the propositions described in the questionnaires they had been administered 7 days before. For each antecedent–consequence (A–C) pair, we computed the difference between (a) the probability of recalling the antecedent given that the consequence was recalled and (b) the probability of recalling the antecedent given that the consequence was not recalled. Thus, greater differences indicated stronger associations between the two events or states in question. These differences are shown in Table 8.1 as a function of (a) the a priori likelihood of the antecedent, (b) the clarity of its implications for the consequence, and (c) the type of rating that participants had made of these propositions in the first session. When the antecedent's implications for the consequence was clear, it became more strongly associated with the consequence when participants had reported either their belief in the consequence (.589) or their attitude toward the antecedent (.566) than when they had reported either their belief in the antecedent (.358) or their attitude toward the consequence (.331). When the antecedent's implications for the consequence were unclear, however, these

**Table 8.1.** Strength of Association Between Syllogistically Related Propositions as a Function of the Plausibility of the Premise (A), the Clarity of its Implications for the Conclusion (B) and the Type of Ratings Made of A and B

| Characteristics of antecedent (A) | Rating of consequence (C) | | Rating of antecedent (A) | |
|---|---|---|---|---|
| | Likelihood | Desirability | Likelihood | Desirability |
| Clear implications for consequence (C) | | | | |
| Plausible | .734 | .505 | .442 | .798 |
| Implausible | .462 | .156 | .274 | .345 |
| Mean | .598 | .331 | .358 | .572 |
| Unclear implications for consequence (C) | | | | |
| Plausible | .320 | .439 | .366 | .393 |
| Implausible | .375 | .402 | .482 | .295 |
| Mean | .347 | .420 | .424 | .344 |

*Note:* Entries refer to the difference between the probability of recalling A given that C was recalled and the probability of recalling A given that C was not recalled. Adapted from *Journal of Experimental and Social Psychology, 20*, R. S. Wyer, Jr., and J. Hartwick, 76, 1984, with permission from Elsevier.

contingencies were not apparent, suggesting that an association between the propositions was not formed.

## Effects of Knowledge Accessibility on Reported Beliefs and Attitudes

Wyer and Hartwick's (1984) findings have implications for the second question raised previously, that is, which of several possible antecedents or consequences are likely to be used as a basis for judgment? People who are asked to report their belief in a proposition typically rely on only a small subset of knowledge that happens to come to mind at the time (Higgins, 1996; McGuire, 1960a; Taylor & Fiske, 1978; Wyer & Srull, 1989). Therefore, if a particular antecedent (e.g., A) has become associated with a second, target proposition (C), it is likely to be recalled and used to estimate the validity of C at a later point in time. This could be true even though several other equally relevant criteria exist. To this extent, Wyer and Hartwick's findings suggest the cognitive activities that lead different pieces of knowledge to become associated and, therefore, lead a particular piece of knowledge to be used to evaluate the validity of a second one.

However, other factors could influence the recall and use of knowledge as well. For example, propositions that are unlikely to be true (e.g., "Caffeine destroys nerve cells") may be thought about more extensively than propositions about more commonplace situations (e.g., "Drinking coffee can give you insomnia") and may come to mind more easily for this reason alone (Craik & Lockhart, 1972). In fact, data obtained by Wyer and Hartwick (1984; see also Wyer & Hartwick, 1980) confirm this possibility. That is, propositions were generally more likely to be recalled when they were unlikely to be true (.310) than when they were more plausible (.129), independent of their association with the target. In other words, people who are called upon to report their beliefs in a proposition are more disposed to recall judgment-relevant information that they believe to be untrue than information they consider to be true!

The accessibility of knowledge in memory is also influenced by both the *recency* with which it has been acquired and used and the *frequency* with which it has been applied (Higgins, Bargh & Lombardi, 1985; Srull & Wyer, 1979). The effects of recency are exemplified by an unpublished study by Wyer and Hartwick (cited in Wyer & Srull, 1989). Participants were initially given a list of propositions with instructions to read them over and determine if they were comprehensible. In one condition, the proposition "Coffee keeps you alert" was included in the list. In a second condition, however, this proposition was replaced with "Coffee gives you insomnia." Later, as part of an ostensibly different experiment, participants completed a belief questionnaire containing the proposition "Drinking coffee is desirable." Participants reported stronger beliefs in this proposition in the first condition than in the second. Analogously, participants reported stronger beliefs in the proposition "Student use of [the university] health center will increase in the next few years" if the initial comprehension list included the statement "The university health center plans to establish a dental clinic" than if it contained "Some of the doctors at [the university health center] are likely to lose their licenses." Also of interest, participants' beliefs about the use of the university health center persisted over the period of a week, whereas differences in beliefs that drinking coffee was desirable did not. This is presumably because other knowledge about desirability of drinking coffee was activated by participants' experiences during the interim, whereas knowledge bearing on the use of the health center was not.

As McGuire (1991; McGuire & McGuire, 1991) notes, however, an important qualification should be placed on the processes described above. McGuire distinguishes between *latent* and *virtual* knowledge. In particular, the thoughts that people bring to bear on the validity or desirability of an assertion can sometimes be constructed from a number of previously independent bodies of knowledge. McGuire (1991) likens information search to a "mental laser beam" that "passes through thought space" (p. 226) and extracts representations at the intersection of a number of previously independent concepts. Thus, we can generate the image of a tiger walking through Times Square without ever having considered this possibility in the past. Similarly, we might generate reasons why the use of a university health center might increase or decrease without any prior knowledge that bears directly on this possibility. These processes, which may be more the rule than the exception, are unfortunately not captured by the work we have done in the area.

## A Quantitative Description of Belief Formation and Change

The above considerations suggest that people who are called upon to evaluate a proposition about conditions that exist in the real world often restrict their consideration to the implications of a single piece of knowledge that comes to mind most easily. As McGuire (1960b, 1981) postulated, the construal of these implications may involve syllogistic reasoning. In particular, people's use of a particular antecedent *(A)* to infer their belief in a consequence *(C)* might be partly based on the syllogism "*A* is true. If *A* is true, *C* is true. Therefore, *C* is true." McGuire notes that people might also consider the possibility that *C* might be true even if *A* were not true and that their construal of these implications could also be based on the syllogism "*A* is not true. If *A* is not true, *C* is true. Therefore, *C* is true." The two sets of premises that imply that *C* is true are mutually exclusive. Therefore, if people form their beliefs on the basis of syllogistic reasoning, their belief in *C* might be an additive function of their beliefs in these two sets of premises.[1]

Several studies we conducted in the early 1970s provide support for this possibility (for reviews, see Wyer, 1974; Wyer & Hartwick, 1980). If beliefs are measured in units of probability, then the belief that *C* is true, *P(C)*, can theoretically be captured by the equation

$$P(C) = P(A)*P(C/A) + P(\sim A)*P(C/\sim A), \tag{1}$$

where *P(A)* and *P(~A)* [= *1 − P(A)*] are the beliefs that *A* is and is not true, respectively, and *P(C/A)* and *P(C/~A)* are the beliefs that *C* is true *if A* is and is not true, respectively.[2]

In a number of studies in which beliefs in *A* and its implications for *C* were experimentally manipulated (e.g., Wyer, 1970, 1972, 1975), Equation 1 provided a surprisingly accurate quantitative description of the relations among the beliefs involved. If individuals' beliefs are reported along a scale from 0 (not at all likely) to 10 (extremely likely) and then divided by 10 to convert them to units of probability (i.e., values from 0 to 1), the standard error of the difference between predicted and obtained beliefs in *C*, based on this equation, is often less than half a scale unit (.05). Moreover, this accuracy is attained without the use of ad hoc curve-fitting parameters.

## Dynamic Properties of Thought Systems: Inoculation and Socratic Effects

One of the most provocative aspects of McGuire's (1960b, 1981; McGuire & McGuire, 1991) research involves the assumption that individuals are motivated to maintain logical consistency among their beliefs. Because people are unlikely to think about all aspects of their prior knowledge that have implications for the validity of a proposition, some inconsistencies among beliefs are inevitable. However, McGuire (1960b, 1981) hypothesized that if people become aware of these inconsistencies, they try to eliminate them by modifying one or more of the beliefs involved.

Equation 1 describes how people's beliefs in a set of syllogistically related propositions should be related if they are perfectly consistent. Thus, departures

---

[1]Although the analysis in this article is restricted to a particular type of syllogism, McGuire's conceptualization is applicable to other types of syllogisms as well; for a more general analysis of its applicability to barbara syllogisms (i.e., "*A* is *B*; *B* is *C*; therefore, *A* is *C*"), see McGuire (1981).
[2]In fact, the assumption that *P(~A)* = 1 − *P(A)* is not strictly valid; that is, people's estimates of the likelihood that a proposition is true and estimates of the likelihood it is not true sum to approximately 1.1 rather than 1.0, as this equation assumes (Wyer, 1976).

from the relations specified by this equation indicate the subjective inconsistency among the beliefs involved. In fact, Henninger and Wyer (1976) found that, based on this equation, people's estimates of the inconsistency among a set of beliefs of the sort to which Equation 1 pertains were correlated over .90 with the absolute discrepancy between predicted and obtained values of $P(C)$.

If people who become aware of an inconsistency among their beliefs are motivated to reduce it, Equation 1 can be used to evaluate two general types of hypotheses. First, a persuasive communication that bears on beliefs in one proposition should induce a change in beliefs in other propositions to which it is syllogistically related even if the latter propositions are not mentioned in the communication. Second, simply calling people's attention to an inconsistency among their beliefs (e.g., by asking them to report syllogistically related beliefs in temporal proximity) should induce them to change in one or more of these beliefs even in the absence of new information from an outside source.

## Direct Versus Indirect Effects of Persuasive Messages

A persuasive message can influence beliefs not only in the proposition to which it directly pertains but in other, unmentioned propositions as well. Equation 1 can potentially be used to diagnose the conditions in which these effects will occur. The impact of a persuasive communication bearing on one proposition ($A$) on beliefs in a related but unmentioned proposition ($C$) can theoretically be described by the equation

$$\Delta P(C) = \Delta P(A)*[P(C/A - P(C/{\sim}A)], \qquad (2)$$

where $\Delta P(C)$ and $\Delta P(A)$ refer to changes in beliefs in $C$ and $A$, respectively.[3] The quantitative accuracy of the equation in describing changes in people's beliefs about the events that occur in hypothetical situations was demonstrated by Wyer (1970). Additional support for the implications of McGuire's theory was provided by McGuire (1960a,b,c) as well as by Holt and Watts (1969; Holt, 1970; Watts & Holt, 1970).

Equation 2 is more generally useful in conceptualizing the conditions in which a message that focuses on one proposition ($A$) will influence beliefs in a second, unmentioned proposition ($C$). Most obviously, the communication must in fact be effective in changing beliefs in $A$ ($\Delta P(A) > 0$). In addition, $A$ must be considered relevant to $C$; in other words, people must believe that $C$ is more (or less) likely to be true if $A$ is true than if it is not. Finally, even if the two conditional beliefs differ, a change in one's belief in $A$ may not induce a change in one's belief in $C$ unless $A$ is salient at the time $C$ is thought about. Otherwise, beliefs in the two propositions may not be recognized as inconsistent.

## The Socratic Method of Persuasion

Many persuasive messages do not actually convey new information; rather, they call attention to previously acquired knowledge about events and situations that have implications for a proposition that recipients had not been

---

[3]This equation can be derived from Equation 1 by substituting $[P(A) + \Delta P(A)]$ for $P(A)$, substituting $[P(C) + \Delta P(C)]$ for $P(C)$, and solving for $\Delta P(C)$; see Wyer & Goldberg, 1970.

considering at the time. Thus, for example, an attempt to increase people's belief that a member of the American Nazi Party should be allowed to speak on campus ($C$, as denoted in Equation 1) might assert that freedom of speech is guaranteed to all Americans by the U.S. Constitution ($A$). Although recipients are likely to believe this assertion, they may not think about its implications for $C$ unless these implications are called to their attention. Therefore, the communication's effectiveness might not result from any new information it provides. Rather, the communication may simply make recipients aware of an inconsistency between their existing beliefs in Nazis' right to speak in public and their beliefs in other propositions that have implications for it and may induce them to eliminate this inconsistency by modifying their beliefs in these propositions.

This analysis implies that simply calling people's attention to an inconsistency in their logically related beliefs is sufficient to stimulate them to modify one or more of these beliefs. This *Socratic effect*, which was first identified by McGuire (1960b), was also shown by Rosen and Wyer (1972). Specifically, when beliefs in syllogistically related propositions are reported in a questionnaire at two different points in time, the inconsistency of these beliefs (as inferred from the inaccuracy of Equation 1 in describing their relationship) is typically less the second time than it was at first.

Although the Socratic effect is fairly robust, there may be qualifications on its occurrence. Henninger and Wyer (1976) showed that the inconsistency of syllogistically related beliefs only decreased over experimental sessions when participants in the first session had reported their belief in the conclusion of the syllogism before their beliefs in the premise. When participants had evaluated a premise before the conclusion during the first session, their beliefs were consistent at the outset and did not decrease further over time. Perhaps when people become aware of an inconsistency in syllogistically related beliefs, they find it easier to change their belief in the conclusion of the syllogism than to change their belief in a premise. Thus, they may find it relatively easy to change their belief in a conclusion to make it consistent with their belief in a premise they have reported earlier. However, when people recognize that their belief in a premise is inconsistent with their belief in a conclusion they have already considered, they are unable to alter this belief immediately. Alternatively, they may spontaneously modify their belief in the conclusion they had reported earlier, but this change is not reflected in their responses during the first session of the experiment. In either event, the effect of the cognitive activity that was stimulated by the inconsistency may not be apparent until participants report their beliefs a second time, in a later experimental session.

The Socratic effect is worth considering in the context of McGuire's (1964) provocative research on resistance to persuasion. He found that exposing people to arguments against their point of view at one point in time can make them less vulnerable to an attack on their views at a later time and that this is true even though the arguments in the attack differ from those they had encountered earlier. One interpretation of this "inoculation" effect is that the initial message induces an inconsistency in their beliefs that, once salient, they attempt to resolve in ways suggested by the Socratic effect. As a result, they are more resistant to attacks than they might otherwise be. The specific changes that produce this resistance might be conceptualized in terms of the components of Equations 1 and 2.

## Generalizeability

McGuire's model of belief formation and change assumes that people's beliefs are governed in part by syllogistic reasoning. Two qualifications on this assumption are worth noting. First, individual and cultural differences are likely to exist in both the motivation and the ability to reason syllogistically. For example, representatives of Eastern Asian cultures are apparently less inclined to apply analytic reasoning in making inferences about their social world than Westerners are (Nisbett, Peng, Choi, & Norenzayan, 2001; Norenzayan & Nisbett, 2000). If this is so, then the processes described in this chapter may be relatively less evident among Asians than among Americans. Research by Norenzayan and Kim (2000) suggested that this is so. They asked both American and Korean participants to complete a belief questionnaire containing items of the sort to which Equation 1 is applicable. This was done in two experimental sessions 1 week apart. Americans' beliefs became less inconsistent over time. Koreans, however, showed no change whatsoever in the inconsistency of their beliefs. Other general differences in the motivation or ability to engage in syllogistic reasoning are likely to influence the occurrence of the Socratic effect as well.

Second, the processes underlying the Socratic effect are not necessarily mediated by people's conscious awareness of logical inconsistencies in their beliefs per se. In fact, they might think about their beliefs in a way that appears to reduce these inconsistencies without engaging in syllogistic reasoning at all. As Wyer and Hartwick (1980) noted, Equation 1 could alternatively describe a weighted averaging process similar to that proposed by Anderson (1981).[4]

## Hedonic Influences on Beliefs and Attitudes

In concentrating on the role of syllogistic reasoning, I have ignored a very important component of McGuire's general conceptualization of thought processes. That is, this conceptualization assumes that individuals' cognitive activity is guided by the desire not only to establish and maintain logical consistency among their beliefs but also to reconcile these beliefs with their hedonic implications (McGuire, 1960b, 1981; McGuire & McGuire, 1991). For example, a consideration of the possibility that an undesirable event or state of affairs may occur or that a desirable one is unlikely can be cognitively unpleasant. Therefore, individuals may be motivated to adopt beliefs that

---

[4]That is, persons who consider two related beliefs in temporal proximity may first construe the two conditional beliefs composing the equation, $P(C/A)$ and $P(C/\sim A)$, and then average them, weighting them by the relative likelihood that $A$ is and is not true, respectively. These processes, which could occur spontaneously without engaging in syllogistic reasoning per se, are hard to distinguish from the processes assumed by the probabilogical model.

minimize this unpleasantness.[5] Implications of this "wishful thinking" may often conflict with the implications of syllogistic reasoning and consequently may produce logical inconsistencies in the beliefs that people report.

In the paradigm we have used to investigate the Socratic effect, we have found little evidence of systematic differences among beliefs of the sort that could be attributed to wishful thinking (see also McGuire & McGuire, 1991). However, the motivation to engage in wishful thinking may be relatively low when the issues of concern are not particularly important. In more personally involving situations, wishful thinking may be more apparent. It may also be more evident when people are unable to devote cognitive resources to the sort of syllogistic reasoning that is necessary to eliminate logical inconsistencies among their beliefs.

A study by Albarracin and Wyer (2001) is of interest in this context. Participants who felt either happy or unhappy as a result of writing about an emotion-laden personal experience read a communication advocating the introduction of comprehensive examinations. Some recipients were able to concentrate on the content of the message, whereas others were distracted from doing so. Later, participants reported their attitudes toward the institution of comprehensive exams, the desirability of specific consequences of instituting the exams (both those mentioned in the persuasive message and others), and the likelihood that these consequences would occur.

Under low-distraction conditions, participants' estimates of the likelihood and desirability of the possible consequences of comprehensive examinations were primarily influenced by the quality of the arguments contained in the persuasive message, and these outcome-related cognitions combined to influence their attitudes toward the exams in a manner similar to that proposed by Fishbein and Ajzen (1975). Moreover, the extraneous affect they were experiencing had little impact in these conditions. When participants were distracted, however, they based their attitudes on the affect they were experiencing and misattributed them to their feelings about the exams they were considering. Moreover, once this occurred, their attitudes appeared to have reciprocal influences on their beliefs about specific consequences of the exams independent of the content of the message they had received. In other words, participants reported that desirable consequences of the exams were more likely to occur if they were feeling happy (and, therefore, they perceived their attitudes toward the examinations to be favorable) than if they were feeling unhappy (and thus perceived their attitudes to be unfavorable). However, this wishful thinking occurred only when participants were unable to think extensively about the implications of the persuasive message they received and consequently based their attitudes toward the exams on other, message-unrelated criteria.

## Future Directions

The organization of propositional knowledge in memory and the processes that underlie its use in comprehending and evaluating new experiences are essen-

---

[5]Note that wishful thinking motivation could potentially account for individuals' tendencies to maintain beliefs in a just world (Lerner & Miller, 1978).

tial ingredients in a comprehensive theory of communication and persuasion, as well as in the exchange of information more generally. Contemporary theories of communication and persuasion have typically focused on the thoughts that individuals report having had in response to a persuasive message (see Eagly & Chaiken, 1993). Data of this sort can potentially provide insight into the structure and dynamics of human thought systems, as McGuire and McGuire's (1991) efforts testify. Unfortunately, however, few other serious attempts have been made to systematically analyze the specific nature of individuals' spontaneous cognitive responses to new information. More generally, cognitive response methodology has been used only to determine whether recipients of a communication focus on the content of the message itself or on other, peripheral aspects of the communication context. Consequently, an understanding of the interplay of previously acquired knowledge and new information has not evolved from this research paradigm.

In this regard, dual-process models of persuasion (Chaiken, 1987; Petty & Cacioppo, 1986) typically distinguish between the use of the arguments conveyed in a persuasive message as a basis for judgment (as reflected in the impact of the quality of these arguments on persuasion) and the use of more peripheral cues (e.g., the prestige or credibility of the message's source; see Chaiken, 1980). As Kruglanski and Thompson (1999) have pointed out, however, the use of these different criteria may in each case be governed by a syllogistic inference process similar to that postulated by McGuire (1960b) and described in Equation 1. That is, effects of each type of information on beliefs may be the result of applying a syllogism of the form "$A$. If $A$, then $C$. Therefore, $C$" and may differ only in whether the premise, $A$, refers to a proposition that is contained in the persuasive message or to a characteristic of the message's source (e.g., "Person $X$ asserts that $C$ is true"). To this extent, Equations 1 and 2 may potentially capture the processes underlying the use of both sets of criteria.

Several fundamental questions raised by McGuire's research require attention. A particularly central issue concerns the extent to which beliefs and attitudes (i.e., estimates of the likelihood and desirability of an event or state of affairs) are parts of one's world knowledge that are stored in memory along with the propositions to which they pertain or whether they are computed on the basis of prior knowledge at the time one is required to make a judgment or decision. Likelihood estimates, for example, can often be influenced by the subjective ease with which judgment-relevant knowledge bearing on them comes to mind rather than the content of the knowledge itself (Schwarz et al., 1991). Moreover, people's evaluations can be influenced by the affective reactions they experience at the time the evaluations are made, independent of any previously acquired knowledge that might bear on them (Schwarz & Clore, 1996; Wyer, Clore, & Isbell, 1999). In other contexts, Bem (1972) has also argued that individuals do not retrieve previously formed beliefs and opinions from memory but rather compute them at the time of judgment on the basis of whatever relevant knowledge happens to be salient (see also Albarracin & Wyer, 2000). In considering the applicability of Equations 1 and 2 and the processes they presumably capture, these effects must be taken into account.

There are clearly a lot of unresolved questions concerning the structure of real-world knowledge and its use in making judgments and decisions. At the same time, it also seems obvious that McGuire's work will continue to provide a fundamental conceptual framework within which these questions will be asked and answered. The field of social psychology will continue to feel his impact for many years to come.[6]

# References

Albarracin, D., & Wyer, R. S. (2000). The cognitive impact of past behavior: Influences on beliefs, attitudes and future behavioral decisions. *Journal of Personality and Social Psychology, 79,* 5–22.

Albarracin, D., & Wyer, R. S. (2001). Elaborative and nonelaborative processing of a behavior-related communication. *Personality and Social Psychology Bulletin, 27,* 691–705.

Anderson, N. H. (1981). *Foundations of information integration theory.* New York: Academic Press.

Bem, D. J. (1972). Self-perception theory. In L. Berkowitz (Ed.), *Advances in experimental social psychology* (Vol. 6, pp. 1–62). New York: Academic Press.

Chaiken, S. (1980). Heuristic versus systematic information processing and the use of source versus message cues in persuasion. *Journal of Personality and Social Psychology, 39,* 752–766.

Chaiken, S. (1987). The heuristic model of persuasion. In M. P. Zanna, J. M. Olson, & C. P. Herman (Eds.), *Social inference: The Ontario Symposium* (Vol. 5, pp. 3–39). Hillsdale, NJ: Erlbaum.

Craik, F. I. M., & Lockhart, R. S. (1972). Levels of processing: A framework for memory research. *Journal of Verbal Learning and Verbal Behavior, 11,* 671–684.

Eagly, A. H., & Chaiken, S. (1993). *The psychology of attitudes.* Orlando, FL: Harcourt, Brace, Jovanovich.

Fishbein, M., & Ajzen, I. (1975). *Belief, attitude, intention, and behavior: An introduction to theory and research.* Reading, MA: Addison-Wesley.

Henninger, M., & Wyer, R. S. (1976). The recognition and elimination of inconsistencies among syllogistically-related beliefs: Some new light on the "Socratic effect." *Journal of Personality and Social Psychology, 34,* 680–693.

Higgins, E. T. (1996). Knowledge activation: Accessibility, applicability and salience. In E. T. Higgins & A. E. Kruglanski (Eds.), *Social psychology: Handbook of basic principles* (pp. 133–168). New York: Guilford.

Higgins, E. T., Bargh, J. A., & Lombardi, W. (1985). The nature of priming effects on categorization. *Journal of Experimental Psychology: Learning, Memory, and Cognition, 11,* 59–69.

Holt, L. E. (1970). Resistance to persuasion on explicit beliefs as a function of commitment to and desirability of logically related beliefs. *Journal of Personality and Social Psychology, 16,* 583–591.

---

[6]At the beginning of this chapter, I summarized the tangible ways in which Bill McGuire's work has influenced my own, but the most important influence of all is less tangible. I was a very naïve young psychologist back in 1968; almost 6 years after completing my Ph.D., I was still floundering, and wondered whether anyone had even read any of the work I had done, to say nothing of whether they cared about it. During this period of self-doubt, I submitted a paper to the *Journal of Personality and Social Psychology,* which Bill handled as editor. I cannot recall his reactions to the paper itself. However, he undoubtedly called attention to several instances of conceptual and expository sloppiness, because I wrote back a note apologizing to him for putting him through the ordeal of evaluating it. I immediately received a response from Bill that made my day and, ultimately, my career. I cannot recall his exact words, but they were to the effect that he and others had "assumed" that *I* knew I was a good psychologist and that it was only in this context that they bothered to take the time to "carp" about the things he had noted in his review. Leaving aside the fact that his earlier comments were hardly "carps," this was the first time that anyone, let alone someone as eminent as Bill McGuire, had conveyed any interest whatsoever in anything I had done. His encouragement at this critical point in my career gave me the self-confidence to persist. Many years later, it still inspires me during times of disappointment and self-doubt. It is perhaps for this more than anything else that I am indebted to this remarkable psychologist and equally remarkable human being.

Holt, L. E., & Watts, W. A. (1969). Salience of logical relationships among beliefs as a factor in persuasion. *Journal of Personality and Social Psychology, 11,* 193–203.

Kruglanski, A. W., & Thompson, E. K. (1999). Persuasion by a single route: A view from the unimodal. *Psychological Inquiry, 10,* 83–109.

Lerner, M. J, & Miller, D. T. (1978). Just world research and the attribution process: Looking back and ahead. *Psychological Bulletin, 85,* 1030–1051.

McGuire, W. J. (1960a). Cognitive consistency and attitude change. *Journal of Abnormal and Social Psychology, 60,* 345–353.

McGuire, W. J. (1960b). A syllogistic analysis of cognitive relationships. In M. J. Rosenberg & C. I. Hovland (Eds.), *Attitude organization and change* (pp. 140–162). New Haven: Yale University Press.

McGuire, W. J. (1960c). Direct and indirect persuasive effects of dissonance-producing messages. *Journal of Abnormal and Social Psychology, 60,* 354–358.

McGuire, W. J. (1964). Inducing resistance to persuasion. In L. Berkowitz (Ed.), *Advances in experimental social psychology* (Vol. 1, pp. 191–229). New York: Academic Press.

McGuire, W. J. (1972). Attitude change: An information processing paradigm. In C. G. McClintock (Ed.), *Experimental social psychology.* New York: Holt, Rinehart, and Winston.

McGuire, W. J. (1981). The probabilogical model of cognitive structure and attitude change. In R. E. Petty, T. M. Ostrom, & T. C. Brock (Eds.), *Cognitive responses in persuasion* (pp. 291–307). Hillsdale, NJ: Erlbaum.

McGuire, W. J. (1991). Homage to our critics: A dialectical collaboration. In R. S. Wyer & T. K. Srull (Eds.), *Advances in social cognition* (Vol. 4, pp. 215–266). Hillsdale, NJ: Erlbaum.

McGuire, W. J., & McGuire, C. V. (1988). Content and process in the experience of self. In L. Berkowitz (Ed.), *Advances in experimental social psychology* (Vol. 21, pp. 97–144). San Diego, CA: Academic Press.

McGuire, W. J., & McGuire, C. V. (1991). The content, structure and operation of thought systems. In R. S. Wyer & T. K. Srull (Eds.), *Advances in social cognition* (Vol. 4, pp. 1–78). Hillsdale, NJ: Erlbaum.

Nisbett, R. E., Peng, K., Choi, I., & Norenzayan, A. (2001). Culture and systems of thought: Holistic vs. analytic cognition. *Psychological Review, 108,* 291–310.

Norenzayan, A., & Kim, B. (2000). Unpublished data.

Norenzayan, A., & Nisbett, R. E. (2000). Culture and causal cognition. *Current Directions in Psychological Science, 9,* 132–135.

Petty, R. E., & Cacioppo, J. T. (1986) *Communication and persuasion: Central and peripheral routes to attitude change.* New York: Springer-Verlag.

Rosen, N. A., & Wyer, R. S. (1972). Some further evidence for the "Socratic effect" using a subjective probability model of cognitive organization. *Journal of Personality and Social Psychology, 24,* 420–424.

Schank, R. C. (1982). *Dynamic memory.* Hillsdale, NJ: Erlbaum.

Schank, R. C., & Abelson, R. P. (1977). *Scripts, plans, goals, and understanding.* Hillsdale, NJ: Erlbaum.

Schwarz, N., Bless, H., Strack, F., Klumpp, G., Rittenauer-Schatka, H., & Simons, A. (1991). Ease of retrieval as information: Another look at the availability heuristic. *Journal of Personality and Social Psychology, 61,* 195–202.

Schwarz, N., & Clore, G. L. (1996). Feelings and phenomenal experiences. In E. T. Higgins & A. W. Kruglanski (Eds.), *Social psychology: Handbook of basic principles* (pp. 433–465). New York: Guilford.

Srull, T. K., & Wyer, R. S. (1979). The role of category accessibility in the interpretation of information about persons: Some determinants and implications. *Journal of Personality and Social Psychology, 37,* 1660–1672.

Srull, T. K., & Wyer, R. S. (1989). Person memory and judgment. *Psychological Review, 96,* 58–83.

Taylor, S. E., & Fiske, S. T. (1978). Salience, attention and attribution: Top of the head phenomena. In L. Berkowitz (Ed.), *Advances in experimental social psychology* (Vol. 11, pp. 249–288). San Diego, CA: Academic Press.

Watts, W. A., & Holt, L. E. (1970). Logical relationships among beliefs and timing as factors in persuasion. *Journal of Personality and Social Psychology, 16,* 571–582.

Wyer, R. S. (1970). The quantitative prediction of belief and opinion change: A further test of a subjective probability model. *Journal of Personality and Social Psychology, 16,* 559–571.

Wyer, R. S. (1972). Test of a subjective probability model of social evaluation processes. *Journal of Personality and Social Psychology, 22,* 279–286.

Wyer, R. S. (1974). *Cognitive organization and change: An information-processing approach.* Hillsdale, NJ: Erlbaum.

Wyer, R. S. (1975). Functional measurement analysis of a subjective probability model of cognitive functioning. *Journal of Personality and Social Psychology, 31,* 94–100.

Wyer, R. S. (1976). An investigation of the relations among probability estimates. *Organizational Behavior and Human Performance, 15,* 1–18.

Wyer, R. S. (2003). *Social comprehension and judgment: The role of situation models, narratives and implicit theories.* Mahwah, NJ: Erlbaum.

Wyer, R. S., & Bodenhausen, G. V. (1985). Event memory: The effects of processing objectives and time delay on memory for action sequences. *Journal of Personality and Social Psychology, 49,* 304–316.

Wyer, R. S., Clore, G. L., & Isbell, L. M. (1999). Affect and information processing. In M. P. Zanna (Ed.), *Advances in experimental social psychology* (Vol. 31, pp. 1–77). San Diego, CA: Academic Press.

Wyer, R. S., & Goldberg, L. (1970). A probabilistic analysis of the relationships among beliefs and attitudes. *Psychological Review, 77,* 100–120.

Wyer, R. S., & Gruenfeld, D. H. (1995). Information processing in social contexts: Implications for social memory and judgment. In M. P. Zanna (Ed.), *Advances in experimental social psychology* (Vol. 27, pp. 49–91). San Diego, CA: Academic Press.

Wyer, R. S., & Hartwick, J. (1980). The role of information retrieval and conditional inference processes in belief formation and change. In L. Berkowitz (Ed.), *Advances in experimental social psychology* (Vol. 13, pp. 241–284). New York: Academic Press.

Wyer, R. S., & Hartwick, J. (1984). The recall and use of belief statements as bases for judgments: Some determinants and implications. *Journal of Experimental Social Psychology, 20,* 65–85.

Wyer, R. S., & Radvansky, G. A. (1999). The comprehension and validation of social information. *Psychological Review, 106,* 89–118.

Wyer, R. S., & Srull, T. K. (1989). *Memory and cognition in its social context.* Hillsdale, NJ: Erlbaum.

# 9

# The Cognitive Guidance of Behavior

*Shulamith Kreitler*

## Prologue

I assume no one starts out as a social psychologist. Anyway, I did not. I remember how surprised I was back in the mid-70s when I first met Bill McGuire at Yale and he treated me not only as a social psychologist, but as one engaged in innovative work. Little did I know at the time that cognitive orientation would turn into the big adventure of my love and life with my husband Hans. From my point of view, what Hans and I were trying to do then was solve the personally bothersome discrepancy between our personal conviction that values and opinions are important and research findings indicating that attitudes and behaviors were unrelated. Notably, the discrepancy did not consist in the classical contradiction between data and theory: The findings that cognitions were unrelated to behaviors were fully consistent with the dominant theories at the time—behaviorist theories no less than Freudian. Yet, from the outside view, Hans and I were doing several scientifically unconventional—at least at that time—things. For one, we started observing people engaged in behaviors rather than relying on self-reports of behaviors, because although self-reports are easier and publish better, they rarely match the actual behaviors. Furthermore, we considered the meaning people attributed to situations rather than assuming that their and our meanings were identical.

Looking back, I can discern several stages in doing social psychological research. In the first stage of working on cognitive orientation, we were concerned with whether it could be shown at all that cognitions are related to behaviors. It generated many findings demonstrating that using the right beliefs yielded good predictions of behavior and that changing beliefs resulted in changing behaviors.

In the second stage, we were concerned with devising a procedure for identifying the right kinds of beliefs guiding behavior. The solution came in the form of a method based on the meaning system that we had developed in another context. It demanded some scientific chutzpah to insist on the laborious task of preparing questionnaires for each type of behavior at a time when psychologists lauded brief all-purpose tools; nevertheless our questionnaires provided reliable predictions of varied behaviors and suggested guidelines for behavior change.

In the third phase, we were concerned with theory construction. The initial question about whether cognitions guide behavior metamorphosed into new questions: "What is the motivation for behavior? How is behavior stimulated and evoked?" This has led us not only to the field of motivation but also into other domains, such as psychopathology, cognition, and health psychology, when we applied cognitive orientation to emotions, cognition, mental health, and physical disorders. This apparent straying into other domains often led me to confront the issue of what it means to be a social psychologist and whether despite all these exciting wanderings I am still a social psychologist—as I was diagnosed by Bill so long ago.

However it may be, I have learned that research is an experience, an adventure, and fun. Personally, I am very grateful for having had the chance to have experienced it, done it, and through it, contributed to the store of human knowledge in my little personal present.

* * *

## What Is the Problem?

A major problem that has beset social psychology for decades concerns the attempt to unravel the relations between different kinds of cognitive contents and behavior. This issue, which came to be called "attitudes and behavior," has evoked an inordinately large amount of interest because of the special social and cultural stakes dependent on the results.

Belief in the importance of what people think, know, believe, and desire is common to all ideologies, religions, and sociopolitical systems. It plays a particularly salient role in the humanistic–liberal approach of Western culture and provides the ideological justification for the diffusion of information and education for values. The assumption underlying these approaches is that "attitudes" are related to behavior: What good are attitudes if they have nothing to do with behavior? Demonstrating that attitudes are related to behaviors also has implications for many fields in psychology, such as persuasion, behavior change (based on attitude change), education (for values), learning (of information), morality, and even personality (when opinions are considered as part of personality traits).

With this background, it becomes clear how shocking the results of experiments were that showed that attitudes were unrelated to behaviors. Not surprisingly, the attitudes involved in the best-known of those early studies had moral (see studies on honesty or deception, Corey, 1937) or social (see studies on racism, LaPiere, 1934) connotations.

The significance of the negative findings was enhanced by the theoretical biases rooted in the two major theoretical approaches that dominated the scene: the behaviorist approach on the one hand and the psychodynamic approach on the other hand, both of which relegated cognitive contents to a secondary status and denied their role in guiding behavior.

The negative results led many to seriously consider abandoning the attitude concept (e.g., Wicker, 1971) or playing down its behavioral connotations (McGuire, 1969).

## Attempts to Resolve the Attitude–Behavior Problem

Not surprisingly, the issue of attitudes and behavior could not be condemned to repression. From the early 1970s on, valiant attempts were made to overcome the disturbing inconsistency by searching for variables defining conditions under which attitudes could be shown to be related to behavior. Some of the suggestions were to reduce maximally the time interval between the assessment of attitudes and behaviors (Davidson & Jaccard, 1979) or to base attitudes on direct experience (Fazio & Zanna, 1978).

Studies of this kind focused on filling in the gap between attitudes and behavior with different additional variables. Although far from resolving the problem, they mitigated it to an extent that sufficed to prompt the next phase of dealing with the issue, which consisted in developing models of the cognitive guidance of behavior. The attempts were inspired by Lewin's (1951) and Tolman's (1932) theories that described organisms as moving *purposefully* in their life spaces in line with constructed *maps*. These theories already had two cognitive elements important for cognitive guidance of behavior: goals and representations of reality.

Moving on with the task of constructing theories of the cognitive guidance of behavior required first adjusting to the conception that cognition could play any role at all in regard to motivation. Up to the beginning of the 80s (Weiner, 1980), the scene of motivation was dominated by stimuli and drives. The separation of cognition and motivation was so complete that motivational concepts were rejected and were replaced by the "faulty computer" conception of information processing (Nisbett & Ross, 1980). Awareness of the motivational role of cognition was promoted, for example, by the distinction drawn between cognitive and motivational information processing (Kuhl, 1986) and by identifying conscious experience as basic for a theory of motivation (Weiner, 1980).

In addition, it was necessary to prepare the concepts that would serve as building blocks for cognitive theories of behavior. Advances along these lines were clarifying the motivational role of concepts, such as the self (Higgins, 1987), goals (Emmons, 1989), values (Feather, 1988), expectancy (Rotter, 1966), and representations of the environment such as causal schemata (Kelley, 1972), attributions (Weiner, 1980), or personal constructs (Kelly, 1955). Notably, the building blocks included the self, goals, values, and beliefs about reality.

The next phase consisted in model building. The earliest attempts were partial or context-bound models, such as the achievement motivation model (Atkinson & Feather, 1966), which emphasized expectancy and the value of success. Carver and Scheier (1990) added to these the concept of goals. A turn toward more comprehensive models was taken by Gollwitzer (1993), who described the process of action from the predecisional phase to the postactional phase. Similarly, the theory of reasoned action (Ajzen, 1985) is based on the assumption that behavior arises from a careful weighing of available information. The major tenet is that behavior intentions cause behaviors and are affected by attitudes, norms, and perceived control as well as by a host of additional personality and demographic variables.

Several prominent models of cognitive motivation were developed in health psychology. The best known is the health belief model (e.g., Becker,

1974), in which behavior is considered as the product of weighing of benefits and barriers. The major variables are perceived threat and efficacy of behavior, which are amended in each study by a host of demographic, situational, and personality variables added ad hoc. Similarly, the assumption in the subjective expected utility theory (e.g., Ronis, 1992) is that motivation for behavior is based on a calculation of probability estimates and severity judgments in regard to health outcomes, precautions, and current behaviors, as well as on perceived costs and barriers to action.

Cognitive therapies have also contributed to the acceptance of the motivational role of cognition. According to the relatively simple underlying motivational model, faulty behavior follows (or mirrors?) faulty beliefs (Beck, 1976) or inadequate resolution of personal problems (Mahoney's "personal scientist" paradigm, 1974). Hence, changing faulty beliefs such as "I should excel in everything" is expected to cure the disorder.

## General Critical Remarks in Regard to the Resolution Attempts

The brief description of major resolution attempts of the attitude–behavior problem shows that they are deficient in different respects. First, the assumption in most models is that individuals will take action when behavior leads to an outcome that is valued and when they expect that it can be attained. This value-expectancy assumption is based on the conception that human beings are reasonable animals whose decisions about what action to take are based on systematic processing and utilization of the information they have (Fishbein & Middlestadt, 1989, p. 95). They carefully weigh the expected benefits and costs of the behavior, considering fine differences in probabilities, and act only after the decision about the most reasonable alternative has been made. Yet the fact that humans could be reasonable and could utilize available information is not sufficient basis for assuming these elements to be the major characteristics of human motivation. A large body of research shows that people hardly behave according to the information they get about what is best for them (e.g., Stevens, Hatcher & Bruce, 1994).

Second, another assumption in most of the models is that behavior elicitation is caused by a person's deliberate decision. Again, the fact that we may be able to make decisions should not mislead us into assuming that all or most behaviors spring from decisions. Indeed, very few do, and these are often based on unreasonable considerations (Kahaneman, Slovic, & Tversky, 1982) and do not represent the best alternative in terms of costs and benefits (Baron, 1994). Third, an implicit assumption in many of the models is that cognitive motivation has to be conscious. Because most cognitive processes occur without consciousness, it is not justified to assume that precisely cognitive processes involved in motivation would be conscious. Moreover, this assumption introduces the expectation of volitional control over behavior, which has no empirical basis.

Fourth, most of the models do not deal with predicting or changing actual behavior. They replace behavior either with self-reports of behavior or with intentions for behavior, both of which were shown not to be identical with actual behavior (e.g., Heckhausen & Kuhl, 1985).

Fifth, most of the models are incomplete insofar as they often leave major links, such as how wishes get transformed into intentions or intentions into actions, unspecified. Furthermore, they leave broad margins for the addition of a host of other factors unrelated theoretically to the model, defining special conditions to account for success or failure of predictions or change of behavior. This produces the impression of apparent simplicity of the models, which is illusory because each application requires theoretical adjustments and changes.

However, the critical remarks should not blind us to the major advances that have taken place. The main ones are, first, that the motivational role of cognition has been accepted, and second, that major concepts mediating the impact of cognition on behavior have been elaborated. These constitute a healthy basis for the further development of a cognitively based theory of motivation.

## The Cognitive Orientation (CO) Theory: Major Assumptions

The CO is a model of behavior designed to provide an account of major processes intervening between input and output and to enable understanding, predicting, and changing behavior. It shares with the other cognitive models the basic assumption that cognitive contents, namely beliefs, meanings, or attitudes guide behavior but does not share with them the assumptions of rationality, realism, reasonableness, decision making, and voluntary control. Instead, it focuses on the major construct of meaning and shows how behavior proceeds from meanings and clustered orientative beliefs. The beliefs may orient toward rationality but also in other directions, and the outcome may seem rational or not regardless of the beliefs that oriented toward it. Furthermore, the theory focuses on actual, observable overt behaviors as distinct from intentions, self-reported behaviors, and commitments or decisions to act.

Meaning is a concept that plays a major role in the CO theory. It is defined as a pattern of cognitive contents (e.g., a color, an emotion) focused on some input (e.g., a stimulus, an object) that is expressed verbally or nonverbally and forms, together with the input or subject, a meaning unit, e.g., "The house—is gray" (Kreitler & Kreitler, 1990b). In a given context, meaning consists of a sequence of meaning units, each of which may be characterized in terms of the contents (e.g., causes, sensory qualities) assigned to the subject (e.g., an object) and relations between it and the subject (e.g., its directness, generality). Meaning includes the more interpersonal part as well as the more personal–subjective part and may vary in contents, structure, variety, and complexity. In fact, the various phases of progression from input stimulation to behavioral output consist of different kinds of elaboration of meanings.

Finally, another assumption of the CO theory is that any act in the human system is a function of a motivational disposition and the actual implementation of that disposition. The disposition provides the directionality, and it answers, as it were, the questions "what" or "where to," whereas the enactment is the operational manifestation of the directionality, and answers, as it were, the questions "how," "in which manner," or "with which means." The motivational disposition and operational implementation differ greatly in their constituents and dynamics. Cognition plays a different role in regard to each of them, whereby its contribution is more pronounced in the formation of the motivational disposition than in the actual enactment.

## The CO Theory: How Does It Function?
## Major Theoretical Stages

The CO theory was first formulated in the late1960s and underwent several extensions, the latest in regard to health phenomena (Kreitler & Kreitler, 1965, 1972, 1976, 1982, 1991a, 1991b). In the present context, only a brief description is provided.

The CO theory provides detailed descriptions of the processes intervening between input and output. These can be grouped into four stages, each characterized by metaphorical questions and answers. The *first stage* is initiated by an external or internal input and is focused on the question "What is it?" It consists in identifying the input in terms of a limited and primary "initial meaning" as one of the following: (a) a signal for a defensive, adaptive, or conditioned response, (b) a signal for molar action, (c) irrelevant in the present situation, or (d) new or especially significant and hence a signal for an orienting response.

The *second stage* is initiated by feedback indicating failure to cope with the situation by conditioned or unconditioned responses, by a meaning signaling the need for molar action, or by an input that has failed to be sufficiently identified despite the orienting response. It is focused on the question "What does it mean in general and what does it mean to or for me?" An enriched process of meaning generation sets in, based on extended elaboration of both interpersonally shared and personal kinds of meaning in terms of meaning units in the form of beliefs. By examining the extent to which the person's goals, norms, beliefs about self, and reality are involved, meaning generation eventually leads to a specification of whether action is required or not.

A positive answer initiates the *third stage,* which is focused on the question "What will I do?" The answer is sought by means of relevant beliefs of four types: (a) *beliefs about goals*, which express actions or states desired or undesired by the individual (e.g., "I want to be respected by others"); (b) *beliefs about rules and norms*, which express ethical, aesthetic, social, and other rules and standards (e.g., "One should be assertive"); (c) *beliefs about self*, which express information about oneself, such as one's habits, actions, or feelings (e.g., "I often get angry," "I was born in Israel"); and (d) *general beliefs*, which express information concerning others and the environment (e.g., "The world is a dangerous place"). Formally, the beliefs differ in the subject (in beliefs about self and goals the subject is the self; in general beliefs and norms it is nonself) and in the relation between subject and predicate (in beliefs about self and general beliefs it is factual; in norms it is the desirable and in goals the desired).

The cognitive elaborations in the third stage refer to beliefs that represent deep underlying meanings of the involved inputs rather than their obvious and explicit surface meanings. The meaning elaborations consist in matchings and interactions between beliefs ("belief clustering") based on clarifying the orientativeness of the beliefs (i.e., the extent to which they support the indicated course of action). If the majority of beliefs of a certain type support the action, then that belief type is considered positively oriented in regard to that action. Alternately, it may be negatively oriented or lack any orientativeness. If all four belief types support a certain action or at least three support it and the fourth is neutral, a cluster of beliefs is formed ("CO cluster") orienting toward a particular act. It generates a unified tendency orienting toward the performance of an action, which is called behavioral intent, and can be considered as a vector representing the motivational disposition toward a given behavior. When there are not enough beliefs in at least two belief types orienting toward the course of action, no CO cluster will form. Other possible results are the formation of two CO clusters that give rise to two behavioral intents ("intent conflict"), the retrieval of an almost complete CO cluster on the basis of past recurrences of similar situations, the formation of incomplete clusters because of a paucity of beliefs of a certain type, and the formation of an inoperable cluster caused by the inclusion of "as if" beliefs in one or more belief types that may orient toward daydreaming.

The *fourth stage* is initiated by the formation of the behavioral intent and is focused on the question "How will I do it?" The answer is in the form of a behavioral program, namely a hierarchically structured sequence of instructions governing the performance of the act, including both the more general strategy and the more specific tactics. Different programs are involved in executing an overt molar act, a cognitive act, an emotional response, a daydreamed act, conflict resolution, and so on. There are four basic kinds of programs: (a) innately determined programs (e.g., controlling reflexes), (b) programs determined both innately and through learning (e.g., controlling instincts and language behavior), (c) programs acquired through learning (e.g., controlling culturally shaped behaviors [e.g., running elections] or personal habits [e.g., forms of relaxing, arranging one's cupboards], and (d) programs constructed by the individual ad hoc in line with contextual requirements. Implementing a behavioral intent by a program requires selecting and retrieving a program and, often, adapting it to prevailing circumstances. A "program conflict" may occur between two equally adequate programs or between one that is about to be enacted and another still in operation.

## The Example of Dieting:

*Illustrating the Four Stages of the CO Theory*

Let us imagine a person who is on a diet spotting a piece of delicious pastry in a supermarket aisle. This is the input initiating the first stage of the CO theory. The input evokes the question "What is it?" Viewing the displayed object brings about meaning values, such as "sweet" and "soft," leading up to identification by means of the label "pastry." The primary identification indicates that the adequate response could not be made by means of a conditioned or unconditioned response but calls for molar action. The second stage is initiated by the question "What does it mean in general and for me?", which evokes a deeper process of meaning generation by means of beliefs such as "This is a delicious pastry," "It contains about 3000 calories," "I love these pastries," "I want to eat it," and "A person on a diet should not eat pastries." The evoked beliefs about goals, self, and norms show that the person is involved; hence, action is required. Accordingly, the third stage is initiated with the question "Which action?" The likely focal belief is "I want to eat the pastry." Deeper personal meanings of the action "eating the pastry" are evoked, for example, "acting with self-control," "viewing the world as a safe place," "accepting limitations," "self-destructiveness," "acting impulsively," and "succumbing to physical desires." Concerning each of these themes, four types of beliefs are evoked. Each belief either orients toward eating the pastry or not. The beliefs are organized in terms of the four types in line with their orientativeness. If there are enough beliefs (say, about half of those evoked in that belief type) orienting toward eating the pastry in at least three belief types, a CO cluster forms. In this case, there are a few beliefs in each belief type orienting toward eating the pastry but not enough to pass the threshold so that the belief type could be considered supporting the action of eating the pastry. Accordingly, no CO cluster forms and no behavioral intent can emerge. The process ends with no action. However, this valiant act may be stored in the person's memory if he or she has a CO cluster supporting memory for behaviors supporting one's decisions in general and dieting in particular (Kreitler & Chemerinski, 1988).

## The CO Theory: Predicting and Changing Human Behavior

A large body of research demonstrates the predictive power of the CO theory in a variety of domains, e.g., arriving on time, reactions to success and failure, curiosity, achievement, planning, assertiveness, conformity, cheating, overeating, anorexia, breastfeeding, cessation of smoking, self-disclosure, rigidity, defensive responses, undergoing tests for the early detection of breast cancer, sexual responses, compliance in diabetes patients, and so on. All studies refer to actual observed behaviors. The participants were adults, adolescents, children, mentally disabled individuals, schizophrenics, individuals with different physical disorders, and so on (Kreitler, Bachar, Canetti, Berry & Bonne, 2003; Kreitler, Chaitchik, Kreitler & Weissler, 1994; Kreitler & Chemerinski, 1988; Kreitler & Kreitler, 1976, 1982, 1988, 1990c, 1991a, 1993, 1994a, 1994b; Kreitler, Schwartz & Kreitler, 1987; Kreitler, Shahar, & Kreitler, 1976; Lobel, 1982; Nurymberg, Kreitler, & Weissler, 1996; Tipton & Riebsame, 1987; Westhoff & Halbach-Suarez, 1989).

All studies confirmed the hypothesis that behavior would occur if it was supported by at least three belief types and if a behavioral program was available. The success of the predictions is based on applying the special standardized procedure developed in the framework of the CO theory (Kreitler & Kreitler, 1982). The procedure consists in assessing the motivational disposition for the behavior (viz. behavioral intent) by means of a CO questionnaire and then examining the availability of a behavioral program for implementing the intent. A CO questionnaire assesses the degree to which the participant agrees with relevant beliefs orienting toward the behavior in question or rejects those that are not oriented toward it. The beliefs differ in content and form. With regard to content, they refer to themes that represent meanings underlying the behavior in question (called "themes"). In form, they refer to the four types of beliefs, namely beliefs about goals, beliefs about rules and standards (or norms), beliefs about self, and beliefs about others and reality (or general beliefs). The themes and belief types together define a prediction matrix, whereby the beliefs form the columns and the themes form the rows. Thus, a CO questionnaire mirrors the prediction matrix. It usually consists of four parts presented together in random order, each representing one of the four types of beliefs. Each part contains in random order beliefs referring to the different themes. The participant is requested to check on a four-point scale the degree to which each belief seems true (or correct).

The themes of the CO questionnaire are identified by means of a standard procedure applied to pretest participants that do or do not manifest the behavior in question. The procedure consists in interviewing the participants about the personal–subjective meanings of the key terms and then in turn sequentially (three times) about their responses. Repeating the questions about meanings leads to deeper meanings, out of which those that recur in at least 50% of the interviewees are selected for the final questionnaire. Examples of themes for arriving on time are respect for others and careful planning. It is important to emphasize that the beliefs in the questionnaire do not refer directly or indirectly by evoking associations to the behavior in question but only to the themes that represent the underlying meanings. Identifying the themes is followed by constructing a CO questionnaire that has to be examined for its psychometric properties, including reliability and validity, before it is ready for application.

It is evident that for every kind of behavior, it is necessary to construct a specific CO questionnaire. This represents the "bad news." The "good news" is that a single CO questionnaire predicts a broad range of relevant behaviors, for example, the CO questionnaire of curiosity yielded significant predictions of 14 different curiosity behaviors (Kreitler & Kreitler, 1994a). The availability of the behavioral program is established by means of questionnaires, observation, and information from others or role-playing.

Predicting behavior by means of the CO theory enabled mostly correct identification of 70%–90% of the participants manifesting the behavior of interest, 79% of 619 women who underwent mammography (Kreitler, Chaitchik et al., 1994), and 88% of those who persevered with dieting (Kreitler & Chemerinski, 1988).

The advantages of the prediction procedure generated by the CO theory are the following: (a) It has provided a great number of significant predictions of actual behaviors; (b) the predicted behaviors were of many different kinds and from different domains; (c) the participants whose behaviors were predicted were of different ages and intelligence levels, even cognitively challenged individuals; (d) applying the procedure does not require any special "mindset," preparation, intention, or even average intelligence on the part of the participants; (e) the procedure does not enable the participants to tailor their responses so that they would or would not correspond to their behaviors because it is impossible to unravel from the statements in the CO questionnaire the kind of behavior involved; (f) the procedure may be applied to any behavior, provided that it can be assessed; and (g) applying the prediction procedure is straightforward and does not require the involvement of additional criteria or constructs or assumptions or the creation of particular conditions with regard to any behavior.

The CO theory has also enabled successful modifications of behaviors such as rigidity, impulsivity, curiosity, and eating disorders (Bachar, Latzer, Kreitler & Berry, 1999; Kreitler & Kreitler, 1988; 1990a; 1994a; 1994b; Zakay, Bar-El & Kreitler, 1984). The essential components of the procedure consist in mobilizing sufficient support for the desired course of action by evoking in the participant beliefs orienting toward this course of action. The major conditions on which success of the intervention depends are that the evoked beliefs (a) refer to the themes (viz. underlying meanings of the action), (b) refer to all four types of beliefs (viz., goals, norms, self, and general), and (c) that they originated with the participant through a process of meaning generation. The procedure for intervention or changing behavior has been standardized and can be applied in individual or group sessions (Kreitler & Kreitler, 1990a). Again, there is no limitation on the types of behaviors or of participants to which it can be applied.

*A Note on the Attitude–Behavior Gap*

According to the CO theory, there is no gap between attitudes and behavior. When so-called attitudes are properly conceptualized and assessed, they are expected to correlate with the corresponding behaviors. In order to better understand the reasons for the frequent failures to demonstrate the correlation and to outline the relation between the CO theory and the attitude–behavior studies, a careful analysis of these studies was carried out (Kreitler & Kreitler, 1976, chapter 12). The analysis was guided by the assumption that attitudes correspond to statements reflecting beliefs in form and content. Analysis of 117 studies (the selection criteria were availability of full attitude scale, assessment of actual behavior) showed that the mean numbers of belief types in the scales of the studies showing positive ($N = 34$), mixed ($N = 15$), or negative ($N = 68$) attitude–behavior relations were 3.2, 2.3, and 1.4, respectively. Furthermore, the representation of the belief types was closer to equal in the positive relation studies than in the mixed and negative relations. The analyses showed that the chances for demonstrating a positive attitude–behavior relation increased when the attitude scale used had statements referring to three or four belief types and when the numbers of statements representing the belief types were similar. An analysis of 413 commonly used and psychometrically acceptable attitude scales showed that their statements included a mean of 2.1 belief types, mostly general beliefs and norms. Hence, the chances of demonstrating a relation with behavior when using one of the common scales was—and probably still is—slim. At best, the relation would be mixed.

## Future Directions

According to the CO theory, behavior is a function of a motivational disposition and a behavioral program. This also applies to the behavior of doing science. The progress in regard to the cognitive guidance of behavior that has been attained by the CO theory opens new vistas of potential development in this field that could lead to the shaping of a new comprehensive theory of human behavior. At this juncture, let me present at least in rough outline some of the directions to be taken by the CO theory specifically and the cognitive guidance of behavior at large.

There are three major foci of future development within the framework of the CO theory. The first concerns the extension and application of the CO theory in additional domains of psychological processes and actions. By this is meant not simply application in new domains of content, such as health behaviors, which fall within the range of the regular described CO model of behavior, but domains that require specific adjustments and extensions within the CO model. The physiological processes involved in physical disease and health constitute one domain within which progress has already been made. The resulting "CO model of physical wellness" applies the principles of the CO theory, specifically those concerning the cognitive guidance of behavior, to physical disorders, such as diabetes, asthma, ischemic heart disease, and cancer (Drechsler, Brunner, & Kreitler, 1987; Figer, Kreitler, Kreitler, & Inbar, 2002; Kreitler & Kreitler, 1991a, 1991b; Kreitler, Kreitler, & Carasso, 1987).

Other domains in which beginnings of theoretical extensions have been done are emotions (e.g., falling in love, being scared), cognitive behavior (e.g., problem solving; Kreitler & Kreitler, 1987a, 1987b; Kreitler & Nussbaum, 1998; Kreitler, Zigler, Kagan, Olson, & Weissler, 1995), social behavior, and psychopathological disorders (e.g., paranoid behavior, being depressive; Kreitler & Kreitler, 1997). An important domain that requires development concerns behaviors of groups, starting with dyads and moving up to small and bigger groups at least up to the level of organizations. The emerging image is of an encompassing CO theory that will provide the theoretical understructure for more specific models that will be developed for particular domains.

The second focus consists in defining the role of psychological constructs from other fields, mainly emotions and personality, within the context of the CO theory. Emotions may be already involved, at the level of meaning action for example, as a prominent element in the primary identification of the input and at the level of meaning generation as an important component of the personally relevant meanings and beliefs emerging at this stage. Furthermore, emotions may figure in the themes and beliefs that constitute the CO cluster. The role of personality tendencies and traits is probably even larger. Because personality traits were shown to correspond to particular preferred (or non-preferred) meaning assignment tendencies (Kreitler & Kreitler, 1990b), the impact of personality traits on meaning assignment at all stages is highly important. In addition, personality traits are bound with particular beliefs in diverse fields (e.g., beliefs about other people, about spending money, optimism, etc.) as well as with tendencies to assign greater or lesser weight to particular belief types (e.g., to goals or to reality or to norms) that may contribute to shaping the CO cluster, the conditions under which it will arise and the direction of the behavioral intent. Of no lesser importance are the personally shaped almost-complete CO clusters that are evoked by diverse inputs and need only to be adjusted to a particular situation before they give rise to the behavioral intent. Such clusters (e.g., in regard to achievement, social behavior) are person-specific and often figure as personality tendencies or properties. Finally, there are the personally shaped habits and behavior schemes that fulfill an important role as behavioral programs.

The third focus of future developments is the further elaboration of key terms in regard to the cognitive guidance of behavior. The elaboration includes a study of the development of the construct, its sources, its structure, and its motivational implications. A so-far unequalled paradigm has been provided by McGuire and McGuire's work on the self (McGuire & McGuire, 1988). Other major constructs that stand in need of similar elaborations include meaning, norms, goals, and reality. An evolutionary analysis is another major means of clarifying the deeper layers of the constructs making up the matrix of the cognitive guidance of behavior (Kreitler, 2001).

The major future directions that have been outlined are not necessarily bound to the CO theory. They may be embedded within the framework of another cognitive theory of motivation. We may not know which theory it will be, but we do know at present with fair certainty that there will be such a theory for the simple reason that we need it. Moreover, we know something about the characteristics of this theory. First, it will be or will eventually develop into a comprehensive theory of human behavior. The reason is that motivation is not simply one domain among many in psychology. Rather, it is intertwined within each of the other domains, fulfilling the major role of accounting for the "why," "where to," and "how" of behavior. Hence, the comprehensive theory of motivation stands a chance of becoming the general theoretical framework, which has been missing in psychology for many decades. Second, in this comprehensive theory of motivation, cognition will fill an important and basic role. The reason for this is that the evidence about the motivational contribution of cognition is ubiquitous and compelling and cannot be overlooked regardless of one's theoretical biases and leanings. Thus, the future points in the direction of a general theory of motivation within which cognition will play a highly important role. Yet the theory will be identified neither as a theory of motivation nor as cognitive but simply as *the* theory of human behavior.

# References

Ajzen, I. (1985). From intentions to action: A theory of planned behavior. In J. Kuhl & J. Beckman (Eds.), *Action control: From cognition to behavior* (pp. 11–40). Berlin: Springer-Verlag.

Atkinson, J. W., & Feather, N. T. (Eds.). (1966). *A theory of achievement motivation.* New York: Wiley.

Bachar, E., Latzer, Y., Kreitler, S., & Berry, E. M. (1999). Empirical comparison of two psychological therapies: Self psychology and cognitive orientation in treatment of anorexia and bulimia. *Journal of Psychotherapy Practice and Research, 8,* 115–128.

Baron, J. (1994). *Thinking and deciding* (2nd ed.). New York: Cambridge University Press.

Beck, A. T. (1976). *Cognitive therapy and the emotional disorders.* New York: International Universities Press.

Becker, M. H. (1974). The health belief model and personal health behavior. *Health Education Monographs, 2,* 324–508.

Carver, C. S., & Scheier, M. F. (1990). Principles of self-regulation: Action and emotion. In E. T. Higgins & R. M. Sorrentino (Eds.), *Handbook of motivation and cognition: Foundations of social behavior* (Vol. 2, pp. 3–52). New York: Guilford.

Corey, S. M. (1937). Professed attitudes and actual behavior. *Journal of Educational Psychology, 28,* 271–280.

Davidson, A. R., & Jaccard, J. (1979). Variables that moderate the attitude-behavior relation: Results of a longitudinal survey. *Journal of Abnormal and Social Behavior, 37,* 1364–1376.

Drechsler, I., Brunner, D., & Kreitler, S. (1987). Cognitive antecedents of coronary heart disease. *Social Science and Medicine, 24,* 581–588.

Emmons, R. A. (1989). The personal striving approach to personality. In L. A. Pervin (Ed.), *Goal concepts in personality and social psychology* (pp. 87–126). Hillsdale, NJ: Erlbaum.

Fazio, R. H., & Zanna, M. P. (1978). Attitudinal qualities relating to the strength of the attitude-behavior relationship. *Journal of Experimental Social Psychology, 14,* 398–408.

Feather, N. T. (1988). From values to actions: Recent applications of the expectancy-value model. *Australian Journal of Psychology, 40,* 105–124.

Figer, A., Kreitler, S., Kreitler, M. M., & Inbar, M. (2002). Personality dispositions of colon cancer patients. *Gastrointestinal Oncology, 4,* 81–92.

Fishbein, M., & Middlestadt, S. E. (1989). Using the theory of reasoned action as a framework for understanding and changing AIDS-related behaviors. In V. E. Mays, G. W. Albee, & S. F. Schneider (Eds.), *Primary prevention of AIDS: Psychological approaches* (pp. 93–110). Newbury Park, CA: Sage.

Gollwitzer, P. M. (1993). Goal achievement: The role of intentions. *European Review of Social Psychology, 4,* 142–185.

Heckhausen, H., & Kuhl, J. (1985). From wishes to action: The dead ends and short cuts on the long way to action. In M. Frese & J. Sabini (Eds.), *Goal-directed behavior: The concept of action in psychology* (pp. 134–159). Hillsdale, NJ: Erlbaum.

Higgins, E. T. (1987). Self-discrepancy: A theory relating self and affect. *Psychological Review, 94,* 319–340.

Kahaneman, D., Slovic, P. & Tversky, A. (Eds.). (1982). *Judgment under uncertainty: Heuristics and biases.* New York: Cambridge University Press.

Kelley, H. H. (1972). Attribution in social interaction. In E. E. Jones, D. E. Kanouse, H. H. Kelley, R. E. Nisbett, S. Valins, & B. Weiner (Eds.), *Attribution: Perceiving the causes of behavior.* Morristown, NJ: General Learning Press.

Kelly, G. A. (1955). *A theory of personality: The psychology of personal constructs.* New York: Norton.

Kreitler, S., Bachar, E., Canetti, L., Berry, E., & Bonne, O. (2003). The cognitive orientation theory of anorexia nervosa. *Journal of Clinical Psychology, 59,* 651–671.

Kreitler, S. (2001). An evolutionary perspective on cognitive orientation. *Evolution and Cognition, 7,* 81–97.

Kreitler, S., Chaitchik, S., Kreitler, H., & Weissler, K. (1994). Who will attend tests for the early detection of breast cancer? *Psychology and Health, 9,* 463–483.

Kreitler, S., & Chemerinski, A. (1988). The cognitive orientation of obesity. *International Journal of Obesity, 12,* 471–483.

Kreitler, H., & Kreitler, S. (1965). *Die Weltanschauliche Orientierung der Schizophrenen* [The cognitive orientation of schizophrenics]. Munich/Basel: Reinhardt.

Kreitler, H., & Kreitler, S. (1972). The model of cognitive orientation: Towards a theory of human behavior. *British Journal of Psychology, 63,* 9–30.

Kreitler, H., & Kreitler, S. (1976). *Cognitive orientation and behavior.* New York: Springer-Verlag.

Kreitler, H., & Kreitler, S. (1982). The theory of cognitive orientation: Widening the scope of behavior prediction. In B. A. Maher & W. A. Maher (Eds.), *Progress in experimental personality research* (Vol. 11, pp. 101–169). New York: Academic Press.

Kreitler, S., & Kreitler H. (1987a). The motivational and cognitive determinants of individual planning. *Genetic, Social, and General Psychology Monographs, 113,* 81–107.

Kreitler, S., & Kreitler, H. (1987b). Plans and planning: Their motivational and cognitive antecedents. In S. L. Friedman, E. K. Scholnick, & R. R. Cocking (Eds.), *Blueprints for thinking: The role of planning in cognitive development* (pp. 110–178). New York: Cambridge University Press.

Kreitler, S., & Kreitler, H. (1988). The cognitive approach to motivation in retarded individuals. In N. W. Bray (Ed.), *International Review of Research in Mental Retardation* (Vol. 15, pp. 81–123). San Diego, CA: Academic Press.

Kreitler, H., & Kreitler, S. (1990a). Cognitive primacy, cognitive behavior guidance and their implications for cognitive therapy. *Journal of Cognitive Psychotherapy, 4,* 155–173.

Kreitler, S., & Kreitler, H. (1990b). *The cognitive foundations of personality traits.* New York: Plenum.

Kreitler, S., & Kreitler, H. (1990c). The cognitive orientation determinants of sexual dysfunctions. *Annals of Sex Research, 3,* 75–104.

Kreitler, S., & Kreitler, H. (1991a). Cognitive orientation and physical disease or health. *European Journal of Personality, 5,* 109–129.

Kreitler, S., & Kreitler, H. (1991b). The psychological profile of the health-oriented individual. *European Journal of Personality, 5,* 35–60.

Kreitler, S., & Kreitler, H. (1993). The cognitive determinants of defense mechanisms. In U. Hentschel, G. Smith, W. Ehlers, & J. G. Draguns (Eds.), *The concept of defense mechanisms in contemporary psychology: Theoretical, research and clinical perspectives* (pp. 152–183). New York: Springer-Verlag.

Kreitler, S., & Kreitler, H. (1994a). Motivational and cognitive determinants of exploration. In H. Keller, K. Schneider, & B. Henderson (Eds), *Curiosity and exploration* (pp. 259–284). New York: Springer-Verlag.

Kreitler, S., & Kreitler, H. (1994b). Who will breastfeed? The cognitive motivation for breastfeeding. *International Journal of Prenatal and Perinatal Psychology and Medicine, 6,* 43–65.

Kreitler, S., & Kreitler, H. (1997). The paranoid person: Cognitive motivations and personality traits. *European Journal of Personality, 11,* 101–132.

Kreitler, S., Kreitler, H., & Carasso, R. (1987). Cognitive orientation as predictor of pain relief following acupuncture. *Pain, 28,* 323–341.

Kreitler, S., & Nussbaum, S. (1998). Cognitive orientation and interest: The motivational understructure for achievement in mathematics. In L. Hoffmann, A. Krapp, K. A. Renninger, & J. Baumert (Eds.), *Interest and learning* (pp. 377–386). Kiel, Germany: Institut fuer die Pedagogik der Naturwissenschaften an der Universitaet Kiel.

Kreitler, S., Schwartz, R., & Kreitler, H. (1987). The cognitive orientation of expressive communicability in schizophrenics and normals. *Journal of Communication Disorders, 20,* 73–91.

Kreitler, S., Shahar, A., & Kreitler, H. (1976). Cognitive orientation, type of smoker and behavior therapy of smoking. *British Journal of Medical Psychology, 49,* 167–175.

Kreitler, S., Zigler, E., Kagan, S., Olson, D., & Weissler, K. (1995). Cognitive and motivational determinants of academic achievements and behavior in third and fourth grade disadvantaged children. *British Journal of Educational Psychology, 65,* 297–316.

Kuhl, J. (1986). Motivation and information processing: A new look at decision making, dynamic change, and action control. In R. M. Sorrentino & E. T. Higgins (Eds.), *Handbook of motivation and cognition: Foundations of social behavior.* (Vol. 1, pp. 404–434). New York: Guilford.

LaPiere, R. (1934). Attitudes versus actions. *Social Forces, 13,* 230–237.

Lewin, K. (1951). *Field theory in social science.* New York: Harper.

Lobcl, T. (1982). The prediction of behavior from different types of beliefs. *Journal of Social Psychology, 118,* 213–233.

Mahoney, M. (1974). Cognition and behavior modification. Cambridge, MA: Ballinger.

McGuire, W. J. (1969). The nature of attitudes and attitude change. In G. Lindzey & E. Aronson (Eds.), *The handbook of social psychology* (2nd ed., Vol. 3, pp. 136–314). Reading, MA: Addison-Wesley.

McGuire, W. J., & McGuire, C. V. (1988). Content and processes in the experience of self. In L. Berkowitz (Ed.), *Advances in Experimental Social Psychology, 21,* 97–144.

Nisbett, R., & Ross, L. (1980). *Human inference: Strategies and shortcomings of social judgment.* Englewood Cliffs, NJ: Prentice-Hall.

Nurymberg, K., Kreitler, S., & Weissler, K. (1996). The cognitive orientation of compliance in short- and long-term type 2 diabetic patients. *Patient Education and Counseling, 29,* 25–39.

Ronis, D. L. (1992). Conditional health threats, health beliefs, decisions, and behaviors among adults. *Health Psychology, 11,* 127–134.

Rotter, J. (1966). Generalized expectancies for internal versus external control of reinforcement. *Psychological Monographs, 80* (1, Whole No. 609).

Stevens, V. M., Hatcher, J. W., & Bruce, B. K. (1994). How compliant is compliant? Evaluating adherence with breast self-examination positions. *Journal of Behavioral Medicine, 17,* 523–534.

Tipton, R. M., & Riebsame, W. E. (1987). Beliefs about smoking and health: Their measurement and relationship to smoking behavior. *Addictive Behaviors, 12,* 217–223.

Tolman, E. C. (1932). *Purposive behavior in animals and men.* New York: Appleton-Century.

Weiner, B. (1980). *Human motivation.* New York: Holt, Rinehart & Winston.

Westhoff, K., & Halbach-Suarez, C. (1989). Cognitive orientation and the prediction of decisions in a medical examination context. *European Journal of Personality, 3,* 31–71.

Wicker, A. W. (1971). An examination of the "other variables" explanation of attitude-behavior inconsistency. *Journal of Personality and Social Psychology, 19,* 18–30.

Zakay, D., Bar-El, Z., & Kreitler, S. (1984). Cognitive orientation and changing the impulsivity of children. *British Journal of Educational Psychology, 54,* 40–50.

# 10 ⸻⸻⸻⸻⸻⸻⸻⸻⸻⸻⸻⸻⸻

# The Opposite of a Great Truth Is Also True: Homage to Koan #7

*Mahzarin R. Banaji*

## Prologue

The *Handbook of Social Psychology*, the 1968 edition, was my portal from South India into the foreign land of experimental social psychology. I had purchased the five-volume set out of mild curiosity in the content but mainly because it seemed like a lot of book for the money (they were being offered at a dollar apiece). Until then, I had flip-flopped between an arcane psychophysics, which was the core of training in general psychology, and Marxian sociology, which exhilarated the soul but disappointed the mind. The 1968 *Handbook* filled the orienting role of teacher. From the writings of McGuire, Zajonc, Janis, and Abelson, I learned not as much about the content of social psychology (that was too much to grasp with no background) as I did about a particular way of thinking about the relationship between mind and society. The handbook told me that somewhere far from South India, a tribe existed for whom ordinary aspects of social behavior, how people thought and felt, seemed to be respectable topics of study and investigation in much the way that physical entities were in other sciences—through experimental analysis. This seemed so remarkable and so right that I had to do it myself, even if it meant leaving an intellectually rich environment to testify at the American embassy in New Delhi that I was not now, nor had ever been, a member of a communist party.

The issues raised in this paper emerged from the work of students past and present: Irene Blair, Nilanjana Dasgupta, Curtis Hardin, Jason Mitchell, and Brian Nosek, whose view of the power of the immediate situation and the context in which thoughts and feelings are elicited challenge theory about the nature of implicit social cognition, and William Cunningham, whose belief that attitude unification in personality is an equally important element produced new tests and interpretations. The research and writing were supported by grants from the National Science Foundation (SBR 9709924) and the National Institute of Mental Health (MH 57672), as well as by grants from Yale University and Harvard University. A rare instance of genuine oppositional thinking in my work is a collaboration with John Jost, in which he advanced the idea that the extreme strength of ingroup favoritism also suggests the presence of its opposite, outgroup favoritism. I am grateful to him for comments on this manuscript. I am also grateful to Brian Nosek and Shari Stout for comments on an earlier draft.

At Ohio State, I acquired tools from scientists who took their trade seriously and who had a point of view about everything. Here, in the company of remarkable graduate students and faculty, I learned how to decipher what I found to be exciting and challenging, to separate it from the rest, and to be able to articulate the difference. At Yale, where I took my first job, the environment was one of tolerance for all points of view (it was, after all, the place where it had been possible to join learning theory and psychoanalysis). Such tolerance, accompanied by a benign neglect of junior faculty, often regarded as an unpleasant aspect of life at Yale, turned into a much-needed freedom to select problems and methods without the burden of worrying about the fluctuating opinions of senior colleagues or about tenure. The learning in social (with McGuire, Abelson, and Salovey) and cognitive psychology (with Bob Crowder) that continued at Yale was juxtaposed with different ways of thinking on the part of colleagues in history and women's studies. It was in their joint company that the ideas about separate memory systems and of a social world marked by hierarchy and inequality suggested a melding. The idea was to assume a parallel between unconscious memory and unconscious attitudes and beliefs.

Doing it my way, as Bill McGuire would urge, has involved taking some risks—to continue to work with one's mentor was regarded as an act of suicide. If that were not enough, to regularly visit the women's studies program and even take on administrative duties there was considered a surefire way to turn oneself into cannon fodder in psychology. But learning to have a perspective and articulating it, being prepared to meld dramatically different viewpoints, and being slow to choose a problem to settle on were all possible because I had the privilege of being in great environments. Among the features of great environments such as Ohio State and Yale is that they provide the opportunity to develop one's preferences in the company of superb models, as well as the opportunity to learn to articulate those preferences to those who do not necessarily share them. Both environments did that for me, and in the discourse they facilitated, I was surely the beneficiary.

* * *

In 1973, William J. McGuire produced a gem. Entitled "The Yin and Yang of Progress in Social Psychology: Seven Koan," the paper was based on an address given at the Nineteenth Congress of the International Union of Scientific Psychology in Tokyo and written to stimulate hope in the face of growing pessimism about the state of social psychology and its future. The location of the meeting in the Far East perhaps suggested the use of a form that defied conventional notions of logic—the koan.[1] Using seven of them to

---

[1]Koan, derived from the Chinese *kung-an*, is defined as a public statement or proclamation. Koans are Zen challenges or riddles that defy conventional use of logic because they "cannot be grasped by a bifurcating intellect" (Kapleau, 1989). They are pithy sayings that contain

> patterns, like blueprints, for various inner exercises in attention, mental posture, and higher perception, summarized in extremely brief vignettes enabling the individual to hold entire universes of thought in mind all at once, without running through doctrinal discourses or disrupting ordinary consciousness of everyday affairs. (Cleary, 1994)
>
> To people who cherish the letter above the spirit, koans appear bewildering, for in their phrasing koans deliberately throw sand into the eyes of the intellect to force us to open our Mind's eye and see the world and everything in it undistorted by our concepts and judgments. (Kapleau, 1989)

speak of the creative early stages of research, of ways to find pattern in chaos, of observing people (not data), and of unexpected opportunities inherent in constraints, McGuire captured the possibilities that arise from permitting more than one way of thinking about all aspects of doing research. Some years later, in complex configuration, these ideas developed into his treatises on contextualism and perspectivism.

In the early 1980s, I was in graduate school at Ohio State when Bill McGuire gave a lecture on his work in progress on contextualism, a lecture that made my hair stand on end, so exciting were the ideas and so lyrical the delivery. McGuire, the senior Irish Catholic American, speaking a strangely familiar Eastern language of paradoxes, of 49 ways to generate hypotheses and turn them on their head, inspired this junior Zoroastrian Indian, whose colonial education had dulled all appreciation of the delicacy of oppositional thinking. We talked over Chinese food—that is to say, he talked and I attended to every word and nuance, because it was obvious to me that an encounter with a mind such as his was rare. Some years later, during my job interview at Yale, he recognized me with the greeting "You ate all the Kung-Pao chicken!" and gently prepared me for meetings with his colleagues through sketches of their personalities that were sufficiently accurate as to be unrepeatable. From that day on and for the past 16 years, Bill McGuire has been my outrageously brilliant colleague, silent and kind benefactor, and trusted confidante on the darkest of days. From "Yin and Yang," I select the seventh koan to pay homage.

## The Importance of Oppositional Thinking

McGuire captured the seventh and final koan in "Yin and Yang" not with the words of a Zen Buddhist but rather with those of a quantum physicist. From Niels Bohr, he drew the idea that "There are trivial truths and great truths. The opposite of a trivial truth is plainly false. The opposite of a great truth is also true" (McGuire, 1973). McGuire used Bohr's popular statement to acknowledge that the multiple paths he had suggested in "Yin and Yang" for recovery from malaise may themselves be internally contradictory. Over the next 15 years, his profound and practical guides to conducting research, captured by the term *perspectivism,* came to contain a complex set of guidelines about doing research (McGuire 1983, 1986, 1989). In brief, perspectivism is an approach to doing science, and it arrives, historically, as the newest in a line of major epistemological orientations. Dogmatism, rationalism, positivism, and logical empiricism each include assumptions about how one can know or understand, and the perspectivist approach poses a challenge to logical empiricism (exemplars being Carnap, Hempel, Feigl, and Popper), by advocating a system of greater flexibility that acknowledges the complexity of what is to be discovered and the reality of the practice of science.

Most centrally, perspectivism explicitly requires that any a priori hypothesis must be accounted for by multiple theories and that the scientist generate a contradictory and opposing hypothesis that should itself be derived from multiple theories. More radically, perspectivism assumes that because every proposition is generally wrong so also is its contradictory, and therefore every proposition is occasionally true, at least in certain contexts viewed from certain perspectives. . . . This postulate, that all knowledge formulations are true, is perspectivism's pons *asinorum*, its hardest-to-accept principle. Perspectivism maintains that the task of science, in its *a posteriori* as well as *a priori* aspects is not the dull and easy job of showing that a fixed hypothesis is right or wrong in a given context. Such a modest project is suggested by Popperian inversion of the null hypothesis and his inadequate understanding that the task of current science is to account for covariance rather than, as in antiquity, to establish category membership. Science has the more exciting task of discovering in what senses the hypothesis and its theoretical explanations are true and in what senses false. . . . Perspectivism assigns a higher purpose to the empirical confrontation, that it continue the discovery process, creating new knowledge by revealing, not whether one's fixed *a priori* hypothesis is correct or not, but what that hypothesis means, namely, the pattern of contexts (constituting interacting variables) in which it does and does not obtain, and the mix of reasons for which it obtains in any one context. (McGuire, 1999, p. 407)

## The Elusiveness of Oppositional Thinking: A Confession

Because I was raised on the ideas of contextualism and perspectivism, I have self-consciously relied on these principles in my teaching and, I had assumed, in the practice of my research as well. The myth that continues and needs to be rectified, I knew, is that there is a fixed a priori hypothesis and that experiments are conducted to reveal whether the hypothesis is supported or refuted. Yet, as the following two examples demonstrate, my thinking reveals a dissociation between endorsing the nuances of perspectivism and following its principles in the practice of daily research. My surprise at two unexpected results is evidence that I had fallen short of constructing the opposite of an expected pattern of results because of strong assumptions about the nature of implicit social cognition. Had I explicitly followed the perspectivist exercise, I would, more naturally, have predicted these outcomes as well. I undertake the self-imposed "outing" of this lapse publicly, while memory still serves. In each case, I was brought to see the fuller picture by the work of students past and present, and hence the moral of the story also includes a message about the benefit of paying attention to voices of dissent, especially from those who are intellectually closest and themselves deeply engaged in the work.[2]

## Association or Dissociation Between Explicit–Implicit Social Cognition?

When verbal behaviors of feeling and thinking do not map onto other behavioral indicators of the same feelings and thoughts, the following options immediately arise as explanations. First and not interesting, it is possible that one

---

[2]All students, not just fortunate ones, must feel safe and even elated when a result shows the opposite of what an advisor has predicted or is antagonistic to a theoretical position with which the laboratory is engaged. In order to do this, environments in which oppositional thinking is advocated and explicitly rewarded must be created by all advisors, not just excellent ones.

of the two measures does not represent a faithful rendition of the construct or that the two are mismatched in one of a variety of ways, such as their specificity. Alternatively, the lack of correspondence is expected a priori because the two measures are expected to tap theoretically distinct constructs. Each measure captures a particular state of affairs and each has, as William James said, its field of application and adaptation, but what it applies to or predicts is not the same. Here, the lack of correspondence between measures does not cause worry; rather the experimenter actually takes delight in specifying it a priori as a test of discriminant validity. This is how I approached the relationship between conscious and unconscious social cognition. I assumed that they were theoretically distinct constructs and so a lack of correspondence between them was expected, especially when considering certain attitude objects: (a) when the object naturally elicits strong social demand leading the explicit attitude to be in line with what one consciously aspires to feel or think and (b) when the attitude is not elaborated and the opportunities for linkages between conscious and unconscious feeling and thoughts are not present.

When the research using various implicit measures of social cognition began in my lab in the late 1980s (judgment tasks, priming, Implicit Association Test [IAT]), measures of explicit cognition were usually included and correlations between implicit and explicit measures were routinely assessed. Across dozens of studies using different attitude and belief objects, we discovered strong dissociations between conscious and unconscious attitudes and beliefs. For at least a large subset of attitude objects, neutral to positive attitudes toward socially disadvantaged outgroups were obtained using self-report measures of conscious attitude. An opposing and quite strong negative attitude was obtained on measures that bypassed conscious awareness or control. The same held for measures of beliefs or stereotypes of social groups.

In both cases of attitudes and stereotypes, when the group averages for conscious and unconscious measures were placed side-by-side using a common metric, wide divergences were observed, as was expected. In other words, the theoretical framework within which these data were analyzed supported such a disparity. Just as with other mental constructs, most obviously memory, it appeared that a useful distinction between conscious and unconscious components could be offered (see Banaji, 2001). Explicit attitudes presumably reflected feeling states on which the conscious mind could reflect and report, in a complex response to private and public standards of who one is, who one ought to be, or who one desires to be. These attitudes, I believed, would have their application in circumstances that appropriately elicited them. For example, there should be a high expectation that a relatively positive explicit attitude toward one political candidate over another ought to predict support for that candidate on other measures such as voting.

On the contrary, implicit attitudes presumably reflect feelings that may be equally influential but manage to escape the glare of the conscious eye. These feelings are relatively inaccessible to conscious thought, but their existence can nevertheless be tapped by means other than introspection and deliberate reflection. From their different evolution to their different modes of elicitation, implicit and explicit attitudes are not expected to fall in line with each other. Thus, implicit and explicit attitudes were not only expected to be unrelated, they were, under particular conditions, expected to be opposed to each other. Larry Jacoby, in an elegant series of experiments in the 1980s, showed just how much the conditions present at learning and testing led to stark dissociations in memory. If the meaning of a word is attended to, tasks that engage semantic meaning, such as generation tasks, rather than tasks that do not (e.g., a reading task), produce superior memory on conscious measures such as recognition but not on priming. On the other hand, tasks that create traces of the physical features of a word (such as reading but not generation) produce superior memory on measures such as priming but not on recognition (Jacoby, 1983). Just as memory may depend on the type of manipulation performed at the moment of engagement with the material (at encoding) and the type of measure used to draw out the material (at retrieval), so also it may be with attitudes. Depending on which aspect of the attitude is in question, the traces of past experience that are detected may vary, sometimes sharply enough to be evaluatively opposed. This is indeed one side of the truth about the relationship between implicit and explicit attitudes.

Other possibilities about the relationship between these two types of attitudes were simply not under consideration as perspectivist thinking would have advised. Instead, the assumption of attitudes as being fundamentally separate or divergent based on their status in consciousness came to be acceptable because it fit with an a priori hypothesis about their distinct nature, the different paths of their development, and the unique manner in which they were expressed or elicited. This explained why, when the mean valence of attitudes toward disadvantaged outgroups pointed in opposite directions (neutral or positive on explicit measures, negative on implicit measures), there was no rush to seek out conditions in which that would not be the case. This view was further strengthened by the use of low-powered, small $n$ designs. In part because small $n$ designs were sufficient to show differences between the two conditions of the implicit measure (faster pairings of Group A+good/Group B+bad than vice versa) and because the analogous computation on the explicit measure did not reveal the same effect, another measure of association, the *correlation* between the two, took second place. The data at the level of group means may show divergence, and yet there could easily be a relationship at the individual level—that is, an individual who scores relatively more negatively on the implicit measure may also score relatively more negatively on the explicit measure. Correlations were routinely conducted to test the association between the conscious and unconscious measure, and they were often small and insignificant or small and significant—nothing striking enough to change my mind about the dissociation or separateness of the two types of attitude being the only story.

Two pieces of evidence led me to a somewhat different place in understanding this relationship. First, data from a Web site had the advantage of large $n$s and standardized tasks. For each task, a simple explicit question was asked about the relative liking for two groups that could be correlated with the implicit measure. The analyses across tasks showed two clear findings: There was a good deal of variability in the correlation between explicit and implicit attitude across tasks, but there were sizable correlations between the two types of measures on a large subset of tasks (Nosek & Banaji, 2002). In fact, new analyses had produced a sizable enough increase in the already high explicit–implicit correlation for the Bush–Gore attitude to elevate it to almost .80. This discovery and others like it led to Brian Nosek's dissertation research in which he explored two factors that may affect the strength of implicit–explicit attitude correlations: the degree of social demand created by the nature of the attitude object (lower relationships for higher demand attitude objects) and the degree of elaboration (lower relationships for less well-elaborated attitudes). Thus, relations between implicit and explicit attitudes should be relatively low for racial attitudes (high demand) and for insect–flower (low elaboration) but higher for attitudes toward math or science (low demand, high elaboration) and political candidates (Bush–Gore; low demand, high elaboration preceding the election). A preliminary analysis gave support to the idea that both these factors may be operating.

First and foremost, relationships between implicit and explicit attitudes were expected to be about zero, and standard laboratory research with small $n$s had confirmed that result. The occasional large correlation could be written off as a Type I error. It was a series of Web-based data collections with large $n$s across many different tasks that gave the pattern credibility and demanded to be taken seriously—that is, to first accept that they were meaningful reflections of a positive relationship between implicit and explicit attitudes. In no case was the relationship negative or even zero: It was always positive, ranging from small to large.

Coming to the question with a different orientation, Wil Cunningham examined this issue as well (see Cunningham, Nezlek, & Banaji, 2003; Cunningham, Preacher, & Banaji, 2001). If social situations provoke similar experiences over time, individual differences in orientation toward social groups that are relatively stable modes of responding should develop. Cunningham favored a style of research that used (a) multiple measures of an attitude object, (b) multiple attitude objects to develop a strong measure of the underlying factor, (c) large $n$s, and (d) covariance structural modeling analysis as the statistical technique. The logic of Cunningham's experiments required that a single individual provide data on more than one occasion using more than one measure in each of the implicit and explicit categories and about multiple attitude objects.

Using a cluster of five social groups (American–foreign, Black–White, gay–straight, Jewish–Christian, rich–poor) Cunningham showed, as did the early researchers interested in prejudiced personality, that there is indeed an underlying latent factor of ethnocentrism when examining explicit attitudes toward multiple social groups. In other words, those whose attitudes are negative toward the outgroup (also more socially disadvantaged), also tend to have negative attitudes toward other such groups.

Two new findings emerged from Cunningham's work. First, an underlying latent factor, labeled "implicit ethnocentrism," in parallel, emerges. In other words, speed to respond to combined pairings of group+positive and group+negative shows a consistency in favoring all advantaged groups over relatively disadvantaged groups. For the issue under consideration, there is another, more important finding. The latent factor capturing explicit ethnocentrism is highly correlated (~ .45) with the latent factor that captures implicit ethnocentrism. This relationship is weak on examination of the single group correlations between implicit–explicit measures, but it is robust when measurement error is removed and the measure of association is computed on the latent factors of implicit and explicit ethnocentrism.

Remarkably, the factor structure is such that a single factor solution (one that assumes no uniqueness between implicit and explicit constructs) does not fit the data. A two-factor solution provides the best fit. In other words, implicit and explicit ethnocentrism are indeed unique constructs, but the opposite of this proposition is also true: They are also strongly related. In this case, it is not a matter of finding separate experimental conditions under which the two alternatives are each true. Rather, the same data set reveals, depending on the type of analysis, evidence for two seemingly contradictory findings that are not actually so.

From these data, no simplistic conclusion can be reached—that the two families of conscious and unconscious attitudes are fully independent or that they are identical constructs. Rather, these data are beginning to more faithfully reflect what may be the actual state of affairs regarding their relationship, at least as it pertains to analyses of the social groups under study. First, the two constructs of implicit and explicit attitude can be seen as unrelated (if the sharp divergence in the valence of the group means is the focus), and this most successfully tells the story of practiced feelings: that practiced values of egalitarianism, fairness in judging individuals and groups, lead to genuine shifts in explicit attitudes. Yet a learning system like that of humans also carries information about the world (accurate and inaccurate) that is acquired within a culture and mediated through personal experience. The end product of these processes need not be consistent, and, in fact, one measure of the evolution of a society may indeed be the degree of separation between conscious and unconscious attitudes—that is, the degree to which primitive implicit evaluations that disfavor certain social groups or outgroups are explicitly corrected at the conscious level at which control is possible.

The correlational data indicate that a given individual's standing on explicit attitude measures is always unrelated to that individual's standing on implicit attitude measures. Yes, there are the usual constraints of type of attitude object (elaborated, high in demand, etc.), but the fact is that a deep association between the two systems is possible (e.g, the .80 Bush–Gore IAT-explicit correlation). Both answers are true: There is a discrepancy between conscious and unconscious attitudes toward social groups (with the unconscious family of attitudes being more negative). There is wide agreement at the individual level such that there is positive covariation between implicit and explicit attitudes.

## Attitudes Are Not Things But Construals of the Moment

As early as the first explorations on this topic, my collaborators and I were nudged to think about the malleability of implicit attitudes. Jim Sherman and his colleagues first reported that an internal state produced changes in implicit attitude (Sherman, Presson, Chassin, Rose, & Koch, 2003). Heavy smokers showed negative associations to smoking, as did nonsmokers, but not when they had abstained from smoking. This early report led me to test myself by varying states of water deprivation—no liquid consumption for 24–36 hours. Aiden Gregg created the tests of evaluation for water versus food, and I showed, as the Sherman data indicated, greater implicit preference for water over food in this state of water deprivation. We were not able to replicate this finding with a larger group even though Gregg heroically tried various states of food and water deprivation and various locations such as gymnasiums in which the test was conducted (Gregg & Banaji, 1999).

Thus the view that implicit attitudes were not susceptible to intervention grew, and theory supported that view. Explicit attitudes are part of a system that is susceptible to conscious control and hence is capable of changing on demand. Implicit attitudes, in contrast, are disengaged from conscious thought and are unlikely to shift in response to the willful call for change. This assumption about the difference between the nature of the two constructs still holds, almost by definition, because tasks are constructed to vary in exactly this way. A related assumption that incorrectly led me to view implicit attitudes as invariant across social situations came to be associated with this belief. In particular, I was unprepared for data that showed that the influence that minor variations in social situations, such as the presence or absence of a person, can play in defining the attitude object itself—the different construals possible of seemingly the same attitude object. Prior to the studies I now describe, it would be accurate to say that I would not only have failed to predict their outcomes, I would have advised against putting in the effort to test such an effect. Fortunately, I was not consulted.

The most helpful presentation here may be to summarize the findings from three laboratories, which issued full reports in the November 2001 issue of the *Journal of Personality and Social Psychology*. Buju Dasgupta conducted studies in which participants performed a matching task of descriptions to pictures. The pictures and descriptions to be matched contained either admired Black individuals (Martin Luther King, Jr.) and unadmired White individuals (Timothy McVeigh) or vice versa. After completing one of these or a control task in the experimental conditions, participants were given a standard race IAT using faces of unknown individuals representing the two groups. The task has been widely used and is known to reliably and robustly produce positive evaluation of White Americans relative to Black Americans (see Nosek, Banaji, & Greenwald, 2002a). In the admired Black condition, subjects showed a significantly weaker race bias than in the control and opposite prime conditions (see Dasgupta & Greenwald, 2001).

Curtis Hardin and colleagues reached a similar conclusion by a more natural manipulation that varied the race of the experimenter. They showed that the mere presence of a Black experimenter reduced the automatic negative evaluation of that category (Lowery, Hardin, & Sinclair, 2001). Irene Blair (2002) used yet another manipulation, that of mental imagery, to show a similar effect on the gender–strength association. These studies showed, for the first time using the IAT as a dependent variable, that ordinary experiences such as the presence of a person or imagery could change implicit attitude and stereotypes that were not responsive to the dictates of a more effortful conscious desire to invoke change. This was intriguing because by their very nature, measures of implicit evaluation were expected to be tapping accumulated cognitions and therefore thought to be insensitive to trivial mental reorderings.

Knowledge of these findings long before they appeared in print did not persuade me but kept me sufficiently prepared to understand an outcome obtained in my own collaboration with Brian Nosek. For several years, we have conducted numerous studies of implicit academic orientations, in particular attitudes toward math and science as a function of implicit gender identity and gender stereotypes of a natural association between male (rather than female) with math and science. As we demonstrated, there is a strong gender difference in automatic attitudes toward math and science, with women showing more negative attitudes than men (Nosek, Banaji, & Greenwald, 2002b). This effect, obtained many times over, was not one that we were prepared to see disappear, but it did in a recent experiment, a finding that proved baffling. A finer-grained analysis of the data showed that the standard pattern of a gender difference was obtained but only when a male experimenter conducted the study. An opposite effect, with female participants showing positive implicit attitudes toward math, was obtained when a female experimenter performed the study. Since this serendipitous discovery, we have found that other laboratories predicted and detected similar effects on math attitudes and math performance. Blair (2002) provided a meta-analysis of 50 experiments that show evidence of such malleability.

Experiments such as these challenge the naïve view, one that I may have harbored, that measures of implicit social cognition would not be sensitive to such interventions. This view had a reasonable basis in the position that implicit social cognition reflects routinized expressions of a slow learning system, one whose function is to reflect the output of long-term experience. Given this assumption, it was expected that, putting aside uninteresting variations that reflect measurement error, measured implicit attitudes ought to be relatively impervious to situational demand. After all, these evaluations had developed over long periods of time and were resistant to simple attempts at faking (Kim & Greenwald, 1998). Why then should something as mundane as consideration of positive African American exemplars (and negative European American ones) produce weaker negative implicit attitudes toward African Americans as a group? Why should such a brief event lead to an automatic evaluation that is more positive than the typical one obtained in the control condition? The mistake may have been to assume that a representation that is not amenable to the dictates of conscious will is impervious to other inputs as well, and the implication of this may be more far-reaching than is possible to recognize at this time. The first error was to assume that more of our thoughts and feelings are within conscious control than may be the case. Having demonstrated the presence of automatic and unintended thought, however, we came to believe that if uncontrollable via conscious will, the attitude is also unlikely to be influenced through other, less willful efforts. Yet, as the work of Bargh and colleagues has demonstrated so significantly (see Bargh & Chartrand, 1999, for a review), influences that come from outside of oneself can produce direct effects on behavior. The surprising finding common to the studies discussed here is that mild intervention could influence a behavior that is itself assumed to be automatic: implicit preferences for or against a given social group.

When are such effects likely to occur? It seems worth suggesting that effects of malleability may vary as a function of the elasticity of the attitude object. A social group or a person (or any social object for that matter) has many facets, some of which are positive and others negative. It is the case that implicit attitudes toward African Americans compared with European Americans are more negative, but that is because the typical circumstance under which the attitude is elicited pulls for the default or habitual evaluation of the group. Social groups, however, do not have a single evaluation attached to them: Multiple features are available, and each of them has the potential to influence the momentary representation that is formed and that constitutes the basis of the automatic evaluation. To ask one's attitude toward Chinese Americans will produce quite differing outcomes depending on the task but also on the particular features that represent the group—names, faces, maps, personality traits, food, cultural practices. The experiments that I described in this section reveal that there is a plethora of ways to define a social group and that the mental shaping of the evaluative and stereotypical aspects of the group can shape the attitude that follows. To ask the "real attitude to please stand up" would be to assume that there is both a real attitude and that there is one attitude. Neither of these assumptions is supported by the current evidence, although that idea has intuitive appeal.

Because these are recent studies, they do not yet provide an interpretation of the nature of what they reveal. When an implicit attitude or stereotype appears to shift (e.g, a typically negative attitude toward Black Americans is reduced in negativity or a typically high association between gender and strength is attenuated), it intuitively feels as if the particular attitude has "changed." My assessment at this time is that there is no reason to assume that attitude "change" has occurred in the traditional sense. Rather it seems most parsimonious to conclude that the situations present in the experiments described in this chapter reveal the importance of situational construal of attitude. Mitchell, Nosek, and Banaji (2002) suggested that assuming a connectionist stance in thinking about mental representation can lead to a quite different manner of thinking about social cognition. Instead of thinking of an attitude as a thing that sits on a mental shelf, attitudes can be thought of as patterns of activation that reveal the presence of repeated learning and their reconstruction in a particular environment. If we psychologists can muster the imagination to think this way about attitudes, then such shifts need not suggest that "change" in the traditional sense has taken place. Rather—as Asch (1940) pointed out in his simple demonstrations of how we come to think positively or negatively of politicians (by construing of them in response to two different types of exemplars)—the very representation of an attitude is shaped by the features that exist in a given elicitation condition. The experiments by Blair, Dasgupta, Hardin, Nosek, and Mitchell indicate a renewed and even more rigorous emphasis on the acute properties of social situations. They also ought to suggest caution in succumbing to the intuitive appeal of "attitude change" in the sense in which we mean it colloquially, that is to say, when we refer to conscious attitude change which can be accompanied by the intuition of a change from time 1 to time 2.

Mitchell, Nosek, and Banaji (2002) showed that attitudes toward exactly the same exemplars can be dramatically different as a function of the frame for processing or as a function of the construal of the object. The previous studies have shown some change in valence, such as the lowering of the otherwise positive bias toward White Americans or the lowering of the otherwise stereo-typic association between male and strength. Mitchell, Nosek, and Banaji sought to create circumstances in which a more dramatic shift in automatic evaluation can be detected. They focus on retaining the same exemplars to denote race groups, but they shift the manner in which those exemplars are viewed. For example, Black and White males and females can be viewed either through the lens of race or gender. The particular lens that is used can produce noticeable shifts (i.e., from negative to positive) in the evaluation of the attitude object. When viewed through the race lens, Black females receive negative evaluation (as do Black males), but when viewed through the gender lens, Black females are viewed positively because females as a group are viewed more positively, especially by females.

In other words, given the many dimensions inherent in any attitude object, the particular one that is drawn out by the forces of situation or personality can determine the outcome. To speak of Black Americans as a group as eliciting a single attitude is not merely simplistic. It also leads to an incorrect assessment that such an attitude requires deep-rooted change. Getting away from the notion of change will get away from questions regarding how long the type of "change" seen in these studies will last. Instead, it will focus on a far more important consequence of this discovery: that even implicit attitudes can be sit-uationally created. The experiments reviewed indicate a different mode for non-dominant attitudes to be created: repeated, pervasive, and even minor interventions. The findings support those who have claimed that the shape and content of the immediate environment—the gender of the calculus teacher, the accent of the defense lawyer, the ethnicity of the janitor, the nationality of the scientist—matter. To extrapolate, what sits on our screensavers, the pictures that hang in our hallways, the advertisements that fill almost every social vacuum, and so on have the potential to influence not just our consciously framed ideas and feelings but perhaps especially our automatic and uninten-tional ones. When particular evaluations come to be repeatedly paired with an object in a given culture, they create the appearance that a single attitude exists—by being so easily and "naturally" evoked. The fact that the experiments described here demonstrate the potential for even mild interventions to produce shifts on measures of automatic attitudes suggests, optimistically, the potential to effect deviations from ingrained cultural learning of attitudes and stereo-types. To do that will require understanding that environments constantly signal who can be what, and it appears that our minds are surprisingly sensi-tive to detecting such information and yielding to it.

## Conclusion

This chapter is concerned with two discoveries that later revealed their oppo-sites as well. If implicit and explicit attitudes were disjointed, it seemed at first that they could not also be strongly associated. Likewise, if implicit attitudes were automatic and relatively uncontrollable, it seemed that environmental probes could not shape or shift them. It now appears, however, that each of these original discoveries and their opposites are true. Conscious and unconscious forms of evaluation are both independent and associated. Implicit attitudes may not bend to the instruction of conscious will, but they seem to be elastic in their response to even subtle suggestions in the environment. Theories of implicit social cognition must take these oppositional truths into account.

Oppositional thinking in science is not a dominant response. It is an acquired taste, and as such, it needs to be cultivated—attention from deliberative thought and repeated practice. Even in the well-intentioned, it can easily fall to the side as repeated tests of single hypotheses gain from their simplicity, ease, and please-all quality. Yet, as McGuire proposed 30 years ago, appreciating the virtues of paradoxical propositions, even fully contradictory ones, must become part of the daily activities of science (McGuire, 1973). The difficulty of practicing oppositional thinking in spite of consciously approving of its benefits, of reaching for the skill but never quite mastering it, is perhaps itself a process that fits into this evolving, never quite complete, view of doing science.

I have paid homage to the seventh koan but not to its author. To do so, I move a few thousand miles west to a different culture from which McGuire began the "Yin and Yang" paper in the Far East—the Indian epic of unparalleled length and complexity, the *Mahabharata,* which revolves around the battle of Kurukshetra, between the saintly Pandavas and their evil cousins, the Kauravas. In one scene, each side has sent its most prominent leader to their cousin Krishna, an avatar of god Vishnu, to persuade him to join their side in the war. Arjuna, the Pandava hero, is asked to choose first: The Pandavas can have Krishna's entire army "large and almost invincible" or Krishna himself who "shall wield no weapon and take no part in actual fighting" (Rajagopalachari, 1951). Without hesitation Arjuna picks the unarmed Krishna, leaving the evil Duryodhana happy at the prospect of gaining a full army. Those who know which side won also know a whole lot more: about Krishna and Arjuna's dialogues that address the primary duty of a human being, the distinction between self and group, questions of when war is moral, and the demands and limits of personal loyalty. If I had Arjuna's choice, I would without hesitation pick Bill bearing no weapons in favor of the most invincible army in psychology. Bill and his teachings—in "Yin and Yang," and also in other works addressing contextualism and perspectivism and his reviews of attitude theory and research, not to mention his contributions to understanding thought systems—give us the same gift as Krishna gave to Arjuna: words of a particular sort at moments of crisis, not answers but deeper questions, not instructions but revelations, not dismay but hope, not about his way to do it but about the discovery of yours.

# References

Asch, S. E. (1940). Studies in the principles of judgments and attitudes: II. Determination of judgments by group and by ego standards. *Journal of Social Psychology, 12,* 433–465.

Banaji, M. R. (2001). Implicit Attitudes Can Be Measured. In H. L. Roediger, I. N. Nairne, and A. M. Suprenant (Eds.), *The nature of remembering: Essays in honor of Robert G. Crowder* (pp. 117–149). Washington, DC: American Psychological Association.

Bargh, J. A., & Chartrand, T. L. (1999). The unbearable automaticity of being. *American Psychologist, 54,* 462–479.

Blair, I. V. (2002). The malleability of automatic stereotypes and prejudice. *Personality and Social Psychology Review, 6,* 242–261.

Cleary, T. (1994). *Instant Zen—Waking up in the present.* Berkeley, CA: North Atlantic Books.

Cunningham, W. A., Nezlek, J., & Banaji, M. R. (2002). *Conscious and unconscious ethnocentrism: Revising the ideologies of prejudice.* Unpublished manuscript, Yale University, New Haven, CT.

Cunningham, W. A., Preacher, K. J., & Banaji, M. R. (2001). Implicit attitude measures: Consistency, stability, and convergent validity. *Psychological Science, 12,* 163–170.

Dasgupta, N., & Greenwald, A. G. (2001). Exposure to admired group members reduces automatic intergroup bias. *Journal of Personality and Social Psychology, 81,* 800–814.

Gregg, A. & Banaji, M. R. (1999). Malleability of attitudes as a function of biological states. Unpublished data.

Jacoby, L. L. (1983). Remembering the data: Analyzing interactive processes in reading. *Journal of Verbal Learning and Verbal Behavior, 22,* 485–508.

Kapleau, R. P. (1989). *The three pillars of Zen.* New York: Doubleday.

Kim, D-Y., & Greenwald, A. G. (May, 1998). Voluntary controllability of implicit cognition: Can implicit attitudes be faked? Paper presented at meetings of the Midwestern Psychological Association, Chicago.

Lowery, B. S., Hardin, C., & Sinclair, S. (2001). Social influence effects on automatic racial prejudice. *Journal of Personality and Social Psychology, 81,* 842–855.

McGuire, W. J. (1973). The Yin and Yang of progress in social psychology: Seven koan. *Journal of Personality and Social Psychology, 26,* 446–456.

McGuire, W. J. (1983). A contextualist theory of knowledge: Its implications for innovation and reform in psychological research. In L. Berkowitz (Ed.), *Advances in experimental social psychology* (Vol. 16, pp. 1–47). New York: Academic Press.

McGuire, W. J. (1986). A perspectivist looks at contextualism and the future of behavioral science. In R. Rosnow and M. Georgoudi (Eds.), *Contextualism and understanding in behavioral science: Implications for research and theory* (pp. 271–301). New York: Praeger.

McGuire, W. J. (1989). A perspectivist approach to the strategic planning of programmatic scientific research. In B. Gholson, W. R. Shadish, Jr., R. A. Neimeyer, & A. C. Houts (Eds.), *The psychology of science: Contributions to metascience* (pp. 214–245). New York: Cambridge University Press.

McGuire, W. J. (1999). *Constructing social psychology.* New York: Cambridge University Press.

Mitchell, J. P., Nosek, B. A., & Banaji, M. R. (2002). Contextual variations in implicit evaluation. Unpublished manuscript, Harvard University, Cambridge, MA.

Nosek, B. A., & Banaji, M. R. (in press). (At least) two factors mediate the relationship between implicit and explicit attitudes. In R. K. Ohme & M. Jarymowicz (Eds.), *Natura automatyzmow.* Warszawa: WIP PAN & SWPS.

Nosek, B. A., Banaji, M. R., & Greenwald, A. G. (2002a). Harvesting implicit group attitudes and beliefs from a demonstration Web site. *Group Dynamics: Theory, Research, and Practice, 6,* 101–115.

Nosek, B. A., Banaji, M. R., & Greenwald, A. G. (2002b). Math = Male, Me = Female, therefore Math ≠ Me. *Journal of Personality and Social Psychology, 83,* 44–59.

Rajagopalachari, C. (1951). *Mahabharata.* Bombay, India: Bharatiya Vidya Bhavan.

Sherman, S. J., Presson, C. C., Chassin, L., Rose, J. S., & Koch, K. (2003). Implicit and explicit attitudes toward cigarette smoking: The effects of context and motivation. *Journal of Social and Clinical Psychology, 22,* 13–37.

# Part IV

## Language and the Self-Concept

# 11

# The Self-in-Talk: Toward an Analysis of Interpersonal Language and Its Use

*Gün R. Semin*

## Prologue

One could say that the task of social psychology is to uncover the sources that contribute to regularities in social behavior. For me, the fascination of social psychology has always been to understand the interplay between psychological and social sources that contribute to the regularities of social behavior. A particular methodological angle for the examination of such sources of regularity is to focus on socially created media such as language, by means of which we synchronize and coordinate our everyday social interactions. Language is the chief—albeit not only—medium by which the coordination and synchronization of social interaction is possible, providing an ideal platform for studying the interplay between the social and the psychological.

Much of my research has been dedicated to understanding the properties of language as a *tool,* which is a metaphor that has origins in diverse schools of thought. This was first and foremost a methodological commitment, although it may not appear to be so at first. My purpose was to get a quantifiable handle on the cognitive properties of language and to map the type of knowledge that interpersonal language (interpersonal verbs and adjectives) contains. The aspiration was also to go beyond charting lexical knowledge. In that sense, what emerged finally as the Linguistic Category Model was a model of the cognitive properties of language, a model that was aimed at capturing the generic features of a social source that contributes to regularities in social behavior.

The Linguistic Category Model (LCM) is in fact not a psychological model but a model of interpersonal language that has been developed to analyze communicative acts. One could therefore say that the LCM is a methodological device. The model is useful once it is put into use in a communication context that analytically distinguishes among speakers, messages, and receivers and between psychological processes of message production and reception (comprehension). Conceptualizing these processes in terms of interdependent communicative agents introduces analytic handles that can lead to innovative psychological theories that are socially informed. Exploring ways of getting a systematic handle on the media by which communication (coordina-tion and synchronization of social behavior) is achieved constitutes—in my view—a crucial step toward realizing this goal.

\* \* \*

Talk is the medium through which people enter the public arena. The partic-ular ways in which we address others are also the ways we dress ourselves as persons with distinctive identities. Our speech acts reveal deeds, beliefs, likes, and dislikes, as well as our areas of ignorance and competence. With these speech acts we give pledges, take vows of allegiance and eternal partnership, but we also commit the worst of crimes—in short, we lay our *selves* bare in talk: How we talk reveals our "selves." Yet revelation is not always what is written on the surface of what we say. We are also highly skilled in monitor-ing our verbal plumage because talk and its subtle uses are something that we have modulated and refined ever since our early childhood. Early on, we learn that saying some things makes us good boys or girls and that other forms simply do not come up to scratch. We know implicitly, or rather tacitly (Polanyi, 1967), that some forms of self-talk are more appropriate on some specific occasions or situations than on others. Nevertheless, I argue that although we are highly skilled in the art of public deception, we reveal more than we bargain for. This chapter is thus intended to examine features of self-in-talk that go beyond the surface of "monitored self-talk." This is possible, I believe, through examination of the linguistic tools that we use in self-talk, their "cognitive" properties in particular. Such a linguistic incision constitutes one set of means that allow us to uncover hidden agendas behind "motivated self-talk."

Self-in-talk and its analysis have diverse facets, some of which have a long history, mainly in a tradition that is often referred to as sociological social psy-chology (cf., Semin & Manstead, 1983, chap. 2, for a review of this work). There is another tradition that is firmly anchored in mainstream (or psycho-logical) social psychology. Broadly speaking, this tradition has a specific research agenda for the investigation of "self-talk." It is based on an analytic and procedural distinction between linguistic tools and their use (Semin, 1998). In this view, one treats linguistic devices much like tools (e.g., hammers and chisels) and examines their properties in the first instance. In a second step, one examines the types of tools people prefer to use over others in, for example, self-talk. The research program by McGuire and his colleagues on the self is—to my knowledge—the first example of such an approach. The question that guides this program has to do with the types of linguistic tools that are important in self-talk. The specific tools in this research program are nouns and verbs. The specific questions are: "What are the properties of these tools?" "How are they used 'strategically' in spontaneous self-descriptions?" and "What does this strategic use mean?"

I begin by providing a overview of this work and then proceed with recent developments in the social psychology of language that dovetail well with McGuire's seminal contributions, although to my knowledge this link has never been made explicitly. My primary focus in this section is an examination of the properties of interpersonal language. Next I draw out their implications for the analysis of self-in-talk, along with a few research examples. The analytic framework that drives the overall approach is what can be referred to as the "tool and tool use model" (TATUM; Semin, 1998). This simply consists of (a) treating language as a tool, (b) discovering the properties of these tools, and (c) examining how these tools are used spontaneously in experimentally controlled contexts. I should point out that I am interested in communicative acts (i.e., messages or narratives) and their properties, as well as the psychological processes involved in their production and reception (comprehension, behavioral consequences; e.g., Semin, 2000b). Nevertheless, the main part of this chapter is about message properties. Knowing precisely what message properties are is, in my view, critical for an informed examination of both message production and comprehension processes. I nevertheless venture a few remarks in closing on the relationship between the explicit and the implicit (or rather tacit) in social cognitive processes—a dominant theme in self-research since the discovery of the significance of implicit memory and its relevance for social cognition and by implication the self (e.g., Bosson, Swann, & Pennebaker, 2000; Greenwald & Banaji, 1995).

## Breaking in the Self in Self-Talk

One of the great advantages that an analysis of self-in-talk presents is the minimization of the reactive nature of dominant methodology in social psychology, which until recently relied predominantly on self-report measures. In contrast, self-narratives contain a wealth of information. This information can get lost when specific types of methodological considerations constrain data collection. Moreover, such constraints can also drive and narrow down the type and range of feasible conceptual frameworks about the self. As McGuire and McGuire (1988) noted:

> Psychological research often has a reverse-Midas touch in that it turns to dross such topics of golden promise as self, love, anxiety, etc., by cutting the topic to fit a Procrustean bed of conventional methods, even at the price of extirpating the bases of the topic's interest, so that it is dead on arrival at the laboratory. (p. 97)

In contrast, spontaneous speech or self-narratives dissolve the investigator-imposed response straitjacket. Such a permissive research strategy, which is driven by open-ended probes such as "Tell us about yourself" or "Tell us about your family or school," produces rich material.

Acknowledging the wealth of information in a permissive research strategy is one thing, but taming such wealth into theoretically informative, as well as empirically and objectively accessible, data is an entirely different thing. It calls for, among other things, a creative conceptual framework that drives and regulates an innovative methodical handle suitable for the analysis of self-narratives. What this comes down to is a theoretically informed analysis of language and its relevant properties first and then a theoretically driven approach to what the psychological significance of language use in such self-narratives means. This is precisely what William McGuire and his associates introduced with their contributions to this subject (e.g., McGuire & McGuire, 1986, 1988; McGuire, McGuire, & Cheever, 1986). One of the most innovative aspects of the research program is the methodological angle. Participants were asked to "describe themselves" spontaneously. Such a permissive method allows participants to use their own words and choose their own dimensions. As anyone who has used similar methods will know, this is also a very onerous path.

This path is not only onerous because of the transcribing and coding that it involves; it is also onerous because it requires the development of an informed analytic framework of what the linguistic tools in self-talk mean. Answers to "Tell us about yourself!" contain a wealth of narrative information about the self that needs to be "captured." To this end, McGuire's research program makes a distinction between *content* and *processes* of the phenomenal self. An examination of the *nouns* used in free descriptions provides insights into the *content*, such as the salience of different categories described above, and the use of *verbs* is regarded as reflecting *processes* of the phenomenal self. Process refers to the situated (or synchronic) manifestation of multiple self-concepts as a function of social contexts, such as school or home, as well as to diachronic analyses of the self-concept.

An early example of this can be found in the work on the distinctiveness of self-characteristics as a function of context. This research is driven by distinctiveness theory, which has broader applications than merely the domain of the self (cf. McGuire, 1999, p. 263) and is seen as exemplifying a more general process of cognitive economy that operates by focusing on the information-rich (i.e., distinctive) aspects of complex stimuli. Translated into the self-domain, this "strictly cognitive distinctiveness postulate yields predictions that people tend to perceive themselves (and other stimuli) in terms of their peculiarities" (p. 264). What would such a pattern of outcomes look like if one were merely asked to "describe yourself"? An analysis of noun use in the open-ended answers to this question reveals the following reliable finding. Peculiar self-characteristics that are salient to a person are a function of the distinctiveness of this characteristic in a *social context*. Basically, this research shows that the types of categories (e.g., those relating to gender, ethnicity) that people deploy in spontaneous self-descriptions depend on the degree to which it is peculiar in one's *situated* reference group. Thus, you are significantly more likely to mention your weight, birthplace, gender, or ethnic membership if you are heavier than the rest of your reference group, were born in an exotic town, or are in a minority in your reference group regarding gender or ethnicity (e.g., McGuire & McGuire, 1988).

The methodological handle for the examination of the *process* aspect of the self relied on a classification of verbs. An extensive dictionary of verbs based on this classification was then used to analyze subject–verb-complement thought segments in self-narratives. The fundamental distinction in this classification is based on a generally shared dichotomy (e.g., Abelson & Kanouse, 1966; Brown & Fish, 1983; Semin & Fiedler, 1988) regarding interpersonal verbs—namely between action and state verbs. McGuire (see McGuire & McGuire, 1988) then introduced additional subtle distinctions within these two categories with specific verb types that fall into each category. These classificatory divisions are unique to the McGuire system. Thus, for state verbs a distinction is made between "being states" and "becoming states." In the case of action verbs, a distinction between overt and covert actions is introduced. Overt actions are then split into "physically acting" versus "socially interacting" and covert actions are split into "cognitive" and "affective." This taxonomy served as a framework to establish a master dictionary that was then used to analyze thought segments in self-narratives. This dictionary was applied to examine (a) diachronic processes that reflect the increasing sophistication of self-conceptualizations, (b) processes that reflect the situated nature of self-conceptualizations as a function of social context, and (c) processes that are observed in comparisons of self with others.

By using the six verb categories and affirmations versus negations, McGuire and colleagues showed the following systematic and reliable findings. In the diachronic study (McGuire & McGuire, 1988), self-descriptions of children

> shifted from concrete verbs to becoming states, from superficial overt actions to sophisticated covert reactions, from simple physical actions to demanding social interactions, from primitive affective reactions to analytic cognitive reactions, and from simple affirmations of what one is to more complex negations that specify what one is not. (p. 140)

Another study (McGuire, McGuire, & Cheever, 1986) demonstrated the situated nature of self-conceptualizations, specifically that self-conceptualizations in a family context (regarded as nurturing and unchallenging) gave rise to a subdued or passive view of the self (as indicated by a higher ratio of state verbs relative to action verbs and a higher ratio of simple physical actions relative to those action verbs that are taken to be indicative of demanding social interactions). Opposite patterns were detected in a school context, which is regarded as more challenging, competitive, and achievement-oriented. An analysis of the six verb categories showed that the school context leads to narratives with a more dynamic and sophisticated sense of self.

Finally, a third verb study (McGuire & McGuire, 1986) focused on the examination of self–other comparisons and relied on the postulate that one has more differentiated knowledge about one's self. This study showed the expected differences in modes of thinking about self. For example, it was found that the more differentiated nature of the self-narratives is reflected in the higher ratio of concrete verbs of action relative to abstract state verbs. Similarly, the ratio of dynamic states of *becoming* relative to static states of *being* was higher inter alia.

## Taming the Beast: Coming to Terms
## With Interpersonal Language

The analysis of interpersonal language has undergone some developments since McGuire's pioneering research program. Nevertheless, the guiding assumptions of these developments overlap with those that have driven

McGuire's program. Briefly stated, the guiding assumption of the "tool and tool use model" is, "Understand the nature of the linguistic tools that people use and then examine how they use them and the systematic ways in which they select specific linguistic tools over others." In the next sections, I outline these developments first by focusing on *properties of the linguistic tools* that are used in talk about interpersonal events, and then I turn to how what we know about interpersonal language can be and has been applied to understand self-related processes and phenomena.

## Tools and Their Properties: Propositional and Structural Knowledge

Talking about any interpersonal event entails a linguistic representation that has two correlated properties (Semin, 2000a). These are the (a) *propositional* properties and (b) *structural* properties of a message. These correlated features are best illustrated by an example. Consider witnessing the following event: "John's fist travels with high speed in space, only to make violent contact with David's chin and thus knock him out flat." A large range of options is available to represent this event linguistically. Here are a few: "John punched David," "John hit David," "John hurt David," "John damaged David," "John dislikes David," "John hates David," "John is aggressive." All these sentences express a proposition that preserves a truth reference to the event that has taken place. No one who has witnessed the event would doubt the verity of these sentences. This captures the meaning of what is to be understood by propositional properties: They represent semantic information about events or persons. Moreover, the truth value or reference of such propositions can be checked. It is important to note that the propositional features of a message will vary as a function of the event to be represented. A different event, such as Jack assisting an older gentleman cross the street, will necessitate semantically different representations. Thus, propositional properties of messages vary as a function of the type of event that is represented in verbal utterances.

## The Linguistic Category Model

The example sentences in the previous section have a feature that is orthogonal to the specific propositional properties. Some of the sentences preserve perceptual features of the event (e.g., John *punched* David). Other sentences refer to the actual event but do not preserve its perceptual features (John *hit* David). Others are removed from the precise act (John *hates* David, John is *aggressive*). They are nevertheless valid representations of the event. An event can thus be represented with sentences that vary in their degree of abstraction. The *Linguistic Category Model* (LCM; Semin & Fiedler, 1988, 1991) captures this metasemantic or structural property of language. The LCM is designed to identify the general cognitive functions of various linguistic devices (predicates), namely interpersonal verbs and adjectives. It furnishes the *means* to investigate the properties of message structure and thereby the interface between psychological processes underlying message production, message structure, and message comprehension (Semin, 2000a, 2000b). This model makes a distinction among four different levels of abstraction. These categories are, respectively,

- *Descriptive action verbs*, which are the most concrete terms. These are used to convey a noninterpretive description of a single, observable event and to preserve perceptual features of the event (e.g., "A punches B").
- *Interpretive action verbs* also describe a specific event but are more abstract in that they refer to a general class of behaviors and do not preserve the perceptual features of an action (e.g., "A hurts B").
- *State verbs* constitute the next category in degree of abstraction and describe an emotional state and not a specific event (e.g., "A hates B").
- The most abstract predicates are *adjectives* (e.g., "A is aggressive"). Adjectives generalize across specific events and objects and describe only the subject. They show a low contextual dependence and a high conceptual interdependence in their use. In other words, the use of adjectives is governed by abstract, semantic relations rather than by the contingencies of contextual factors, with the opposite being true for action verbs (e.g., Semin & Fiedler, 1988).

The most concrete terms retain a reference to the contextual and situated features of an event. The dimension of abstractness–concreteness has been operationalized in terms of a number of different inferential features or properties. Some of these inferential properties are (a) the degree to which a dispositional (trait) inference can be made, (b) the ease and difficulty of confirming and disconfirming statements constructed with these predicates, (c) the temporal duration of an interpersonal event depicted by these terms, and (d) the likelihood of an event reoccurring at a future time (Maass, Salvi, Arcuri, & Semin, 1989; Semin & Fiedler, 1988).

These variables have been shown to form a concrete–abstract dimension on which the four categories of the LCM (Semin & Fiedler, 1988) are mapped systematically. Thus, one way of using language as a structuring resource is by resorting to how concretely or abstractly an event is represented in communication. For example, the same event can be described as somebody *hitting* a person or *aggressing* toward a person (actions), *hating* a person (state), or simply being *aggressive* (adjective). This way, it is possible to calibrate different inferences that people can make regarding a number of inferential properties, such as those listed above. When talking about social events, we rely on other critical features of persons and events without which it would be impossible to convey meaning. These features, time and space, are critical and are grammatically coded in interpersonal language. A number of studies (e.g., Semin & de Poot, 1997; Semin & Smith, 1999) have shown that the concreteness–abstraction dimension also represents these critical features. Thus, one can linguistically manipulate the spatial and temporal features of interpersonal events and relationships. Abstract event representations convey inferences that the event lasted longer than concrete event representations. Similarly, relative to concrete representations, abstract representations of interpersonal events and relationships convey the impression that the relationship is an enduring one or that the event is the result of an enduring relationship.

There is a substantial amount of research (for reviews see Semin, 1998; Semin & Fiedler, 1991) showing that interpersonal predicates also systematically mediate inferences about *agency, salience,* and *induced emotionality,* as well as *volition* and *responsibility.* These are also systematic inferences that are mediated by the different linguistic categories and constitute a second dimension (agency–volition dimension) that is orthogonal to the abstraction–concreteness one.

Abstraction–concreteness and agency–volition are not the only structural features of language. Language is not merely for representation, processing, and computation. As William James (1890) suggested, "Thinking is for doing," (p. 187) and one of the main tools for doing is language. One can therefore say that language *is essential(ly) for action:* It is a tool for doing. It is true that language is a tool to construct and represent meaning, but it is also true that language is a tool to transform reality by conveying meaning. All acts of communication entail a transformation of some reality. Generally, such transformation is achieved by resorting to the propositional properties of language. I might say things such as, "What time is it?" "Do you want to come to dinner tonight?" and "Please get me the application." Such *perlocutionary* acts (Austin, 1962) shape your behavior (verbal or otherwise) by the propositional properties of the statement alone. However, there are structural properties of —for example—interpersonal verbs that "tacitly" (Polanyi, 1967) contribute to the shape of a verbal response. When I ask "Why do you trust John?" I am actually asking to find out something about *John* and not about you. The verb in this question serves as a structuring device that directs the theme of the communicative exchange, and consequently the focus of the answer, primarily—though not exclusively—to John rather than to you. It would be a violation of diverse conversational maxims (Grice, 1975) should the answer be only about yourself. In contrast, take a comparable question in which the verb "trust" is replaced by "confide in": "Why did you *confide* in John?" In this case, I am really not interested in receiving information about John but rather about you. The choice of verb in such formulations functions as a structuring resource and directs the thematic focus of the conversation. Diverse research findings (see Semin, 2000a for a review) have suggested that sentences constructed with *verbs of action* (help, cheat, buy, sell, pay) direct the *thematic focus of a verbal exchange* to the sentence subject. In other words, the agent of the sentence with an action verb, and not the sentence object (the patient), becomes the thematic focus. In contrast, sentences with *verbs of state* (like, hate, abhor, respect, fear) direct the thematic focus of the verbal exchange to the sentence object (the stimulus role) and not the sentence subject (the experiencer role). The important point here is that these types of speech acts are not only about representing a proposition, posing a question, or structuring the linguistic representation of an event: They also issue tacit instructions about how somebody should structure a verbal response or direct attention to comprehend the sentence. These verbs have behavioral consequences and are resources for structuring verbal exchanges.

So far I have outlined the structural properties of linguistic devices in the interpersonal domain. It must be kept in mind that the properties of the linguistic devices are distinct from their affordances (Gibson, 1977), namely the variety of uses one can put them to. The number of properties of a linguistic device is limited, but the uses of that device are unlimited (Semin, 1998). This section of the chapter is intended to outline the *constraints* of interpersonal language by focusing on the properties of these linguistic tools. The next section is designed to sketch how these linguistic tools can be deployed in the service of presenting the self. Now I shall address creative production instead of constraints. The domain of the self constitutes one possibility of illustrating the range of creative production possibilities. There are others, such as how people use language strategically in the communication of stereotype-related information (see Maass, 1999). This research field shows how people make creative use of language in the production of messages by introducing subtle and systematic linguistic biases in order to transmit and maintain stereotypes. I very briefly refer to this literature as well.

## Resources to Structure Self-in-Talk

How can a person play with these linguistic devices to present himself or herself? The structural properties of interpersonal language provide a large range of possibilities. Knowing these properties provides psychological insights regarding hidden agendas that drive the choice of devices. Imagine a situation in which a secretary gives the wrong document to be signed by his boss. Noticing this mistake, the secretary returns with a corrected version to be signed again. He may say, "You signed the wrong document. Can you sign this one, please?" implying that the mistake was not his but his boss's. Alternatively, he could say, "I gave you the wrong document to sign. Can you sign this one, please?" implying that it was his mistake and responsibility. Imagine a vice squad officer interviewing a rape victim and inquiring about the events preceding the critical incident. The officer can ask a question such as "Did you two dance that evening?" The victim has a number of options, such as "Yes, I did dance with him," "Yes, he did dance with me," and "Yes, we danced that evening." The implications of these sentences are very different. The first implies the agency of the victim. The second implies the agency of the perpetrator. The third leaves the agency issue open (Semin, 2000a). These are just a few illustrations of the number of ways in which self and other presentations can be manipulated in talk and self-talk. There are four basic and one composite linguistic strategies that can be employed in self-talk. These linguistic strategies are

1. *The manipulation of agency and thematic focus.* This is achieved by verb choice such as in the examples provided previously (e.g., "Why do you trust John?" vs. "Why did you confide in John?"). Choice of verb type (action versus state) facilitates the manipulation of the agentic focus on an event (who initiated it). It also introduces what has been termed by some linguists "perspectivization" or "topicalization" on an event (e.g., Fillmore, 1971; Kay, 1996) or a device to introduce "thematic perspective" (e.g., Chafe, 1970; Comrie, 1989; Fillmore, 1971). The choice of action verbs in transitive sentences focuses the agentic theme on the sentence subject: The sentence subject is seen as

the instigator of the event. In contrast, the choice of state verbs in representing the same event focuses the agentic theme (the initiator of the event) on the sentence object.

2. *Subject–object position as a structuring device.* A simple way of modifying agentic focus for the same event is by changing the sentence subject and object references. Thus you use a verb from the same class (e.g., action) and insert different persons in the subject or object position, such as in the example regarding the document that was mistakenly signed or mistakenly given to be signed (i.e., "I signed it" versus "I gave it to you"). Another example is the one about the type of answers that a rape victim provides.

3. *Verbs within a verb class as a structuring device.* Another way of manipulating the communication of agentic focus is by using different verbs from a specific semantic domain. These verbs can all be of the same type—action verbs, for example—but choosing a specific verb rather than another from a particular propositional domain may mean privileging one agentic focus over another. Take, for example, the semantic domain of economic transaction verbs such as buy, sell, pay, give, take, and purchase. These verbs allow the perceiver to construct diverse linguistic representations of the same economic transaction. The choice of a specific action verb can lead to the purchaser being the agentic focus, as in "I bought an antique clock from the dealer." Another action verb, however, can mean that the salesperson becomes the agentic focus, as in "The dealer sold me the antique clock." The preferred formulation is likely to change if the clock turns out to be a cheap imitation or a unique piece.

4. *Adjectives as a structuring device.* For any event, it is possible to focus the agency by unambiguously suggesting the dispositionality of a person as the origin of the event. Thus, one can represent an event such as "A hit B," implying that A initiated the event (action verb). Alternatively, one can say "A hates B," implying that something about B initiated the event. The use of an adjective draws attention to only one person by means of using an enduring trait as the explanation for why the event came about ("A is aggressive" or "B is loathsome").

5. *Calibration in talk.* The examples provided in 1 to 4 are single sentence examples. Of course, when talking about the self or others, we use a number of sentences, each of which can be examined with respect to the type of device employed . Nevertheless, the way talk is stringed together is indicative of how the author is designing the calibration of the entire message. Thus, each piece of self-talk will employ a combination of these four devices. Each message composition will differentially imply agency, responsibility, volition, dispositionality, and the likelihood of the behavior being repeated, and will also give information about the regulation of social interaction by providing hints about the proper event duration and so on.

What I have argued so far should not lead to the erroneous conclusion that interpersonal predicates are responsible for driving cognitive inference processes, although a number of researchers have drawn this conclusion (e.g., Brown & Fish, 1983; Rudolph & Försterling, 1997). *Interpersonal predicates in their own right do not drive any cognitive processes at all.* Interpersonal predicates on their own or in the form of simple sentences do not convey any information. It is only in communicative contexts or settings with the addition of intended conversational goals that they acquire specific or contextualized meanings (e.g., Schwarz, 2000; Semin, 2000b). However, it is impossible to know the types of inferential uses to which interpersonal predicates can be put without first knowing their propositional and structural properties.

## Analyses of Self-in-Talk

One of the early applications of the LCM occurred in two studies examining the actor–observer discrepancy in experimentally induced narratives about the self and other (Semin & Fiedler, 1989). The analysis of the narratives shows that people use significantly more abstract predicates in describing and explaining important choices others make than in describing their own. Moreover, descriptions of self utilize interpersonal verbs that locate causes more frequently in sources outside the "self," whereas descriptions of a friend employ sentences with interpersonal verbs in which the friend is frequently in the agent rather than the patient position. Similar outcomes were observed in a second study (Semin & Fiedler, 1989) in which participants were given a number of retrieval cues and were asked to generate descriptions of events in which either they or some other person was the protagonist. The linguistic devices used in describing the self and other differed systematically, with more abstract terms used more frequently in the observer perspective than in the actor perspective. Moreover, the sentence constructions indicated differential agency patterns. The "other" was more often the initiator of the event than the "self." In another set of studies Fiedler, Semin, and Koppetsch (1991) examined the actor–observer discrepancy and the egocentric bias (e.g., Ross & Sicoly, 1979). Whereas the former has been concerned primarily with systematic differences in *dispositional* attribution, the latter has focused the respondent's attention implicitly, if not explicitly, to *activities or actions.* Fiedler et al. (1991) were able to show by means of linguistic analysis of free descriptions that narratives that involve one's own and one's partner's behaviors display both tendencies. The actor–observer discrepancy was reflected in a substantially greater number of adjectives (traits) ascribed to partners than to the self. Simultaneously, an egocentric bias shows up in an asymmetry at the more concrete and context-bound level of action verbs, whereby manifest actions are ascribed to the self rather than the partner. This type of differentiated linguistic analysis has the added advantage of elucidating "latent theoretical conflicts," such as those that could be seen between two independently developed attribution theories, by showing that both biases are present, albeit with predicates at different levels of abstraction (see also Fiedler, Semin, Finkenauer, & Berkel, 1995). Taris (1999) later examined how positive and negative behaviors are linguistically represented as a function of who the target in the narrative is (self vs. others) and whether the behavior is publicly verifiable or not. Positive behaviors of self and negative behaviors of others were linguistically represented more abstractly than the negative behaviors of self and the positive behaviors of others. This is precisely the pattern of outcomes observed in other domains, such as the transmission of stereotypes (cf. Maass, 1999). Taris' (1999) research on self and others' positive versus negative behavior reproduced the typical linguistic response pattern obtained in the linguistic intergroup bias area.

The linguistic intergroup bias, or LIB (Maass et al., 1989), refers to the finding that an ingroup member who engages in desirable behavior and an outgroup member who engages in undesirable behavior are described at a relatively high level of linguistic abstraction (e.g., "The ingroup member is polite" and "The outgroup member is hostile"). In contrast, the same undesirable behavior of an ingroup member and the same desirable behavior of an outgroup member are described at a relatively low level of linguistic abstraction (e.g., "The ingroup member pushes someone" and "The outgroup member opens the door for someone").

The linguistic representation of the same desirable or undesirable behaviors more concretely or abstractly conveys different implicit meanings, as mentioned previously. Relative to concrete descriptions, abstract descriptions lead to generalizations about the targets of such messages. Abstract representations are more informative about the properties of a person and less informative about a social context (Maass et al., 1989, Exp. 3; Semin & Fiedler, 1988). In contrast, concrete messages lead to a particularization of the event. Thus, the examples given previously imply that desirable behavior is typical for an ingroup member, whereas undesirable behavior is typical for an outgroup member. This research has shown the subtle but powerful way linguistic strategies by are used in the representation and transmission of stereotypes. I previously mentioned the significance of understanding the properties of interpersonal language and the structural properties of a message for both comprehension and production processes. Research (see Semin, 2000b) has shown that such variations in the abstraction level of a message lead to precisely the expected inferences in readers of such descriptions. These research examples show the importance of investigating subtle but systematic differences in the use of interpersonal language both in the way a message is structured and how a message is received and comprehended by listeners.

More important, the precise charting of the systematic differences in message composition permits researchers to have a more informed understanding of the processes that lead to message production. This is one of the issues that has been addressed in some detail in the LIB literature. Two distinctive models have been advanced to explain the production of the LIB pattern observed in messages. One relies on ingroup protective motives (Maass et al., 1995) and is derived from social identity theory (Tajfel & Turner, 1986). The argument suggests that when an ingroup is threatened, the LIB serves to maintain a positive ingroup image even in light of disconfirming evidence. This account has received support from intergroup settings in which the ingroup identity is severely threatened, such as the highly competitive context of the Palio races in Italy (Maass et al., 1989). The other model is a cognitive one. This argument is that expectancy-consistent behavior is generally described at a higher level of abstraction than is expectancy-inconsistent behavior. Indeed, research shows that this is true. Thus, both mechanisms appear to operate independently (see Maass, 1999, for an overview).

## The Tacit, the Implicit, and the Explicit

I have singled out two specific and related fields (self-talk and LIB) to illustrate the use of the LCM and how structural features of language identified by the LCM can be useful in the systematic investigation of not only the properties of messages (communicative act) but also of production and comprehension processes. Other research with these linguistic categories has indicated that the structural feature of language (e.g., abstractness–concreteness) can have fundamental, often unexpected effects on judgment and social memory (e.g., Semin & Smith, 1999). It is also known from previous research that producers of such messages are not aware of how they use the structural properties of a message. Research conducted within the context of the LIB has shown that although structural features of messages are related to implicit, unobtrusive measures of discrimination and stereotyping, they are not related to explicit measures (see Maass, 1999). The implication in this work is that propositional properties of a message can be kept in check deliberately, but structural properties of language elude such control. They are automatic (e.g., Bargh, 1994; Wegener & Bargh, 1998) and implicit, or rather they constitute "tacit knowledge" (Polanyi, 1967). Nevertheless, structural and propositional knowledge are not unrelated. One important point is that they constitute twin features of communicative acts. That is, structural and propositional features of a communicative act are modulated simultaneously when one is describing an interpersonal event for whatever purpose (e.g., the LIB). These twin features of a message are simply not independent. Yet the relationship between the two regarding their conscious accessibility is of considerable interest. The propositional properties of communicative acts are *domain specific,* as I mentioned previously. This aspect of language is always deliberately monitored. So, I may be speaking of an act of aggression committed by a friend or a foe. I cannot deny the act, but how I represent it in a message can be consciously controlled. In one case, I may not wish to offend. In another, I may wish to avoid being rebuked, and so on.

In contrast, structural features are *generic* (Semin, 2000b). They are recurrent features of language across all interpersonal domains. Thus, structural features of language (e.g., direction of thematic focus by type) are used across all types of event representations. By implication, structural features of interpersonal language must be less accessible because they are more frequently used and attract less—if any—conscious attention in comparison to propositional features of language, which are always event-specific and used deliberately.

If one particular quality of the proposed language analysis were to be highlighted, it would have to be the fact that structural and propositional features of language use are not independent and that both are *situated.* There is deliberate access and monitoring of one (propositional), but explicit access to the other (structural) is much less likely. However, both are modulated jointly—because structure and proposition are married to each other linguistically. You can divorce them analytically—as has been done here—but not in practice. Furthermore, diverse studies (e.g., Douglas & Sutton, 2003; Semin, de Montes, & Valencia, 2003) have shown that the structural features of messages are driven by the situated constraints that are operative. The cases of motivated self-talk and the LIB are good examples of this. The structural features of language are modulated as a function of the situation (e.g., whether a positive action is performed by an ingroup or an outgroup). Therefore, one can argue that the structural features of language use provide an interesting entry to situated implicit processes.

This analysis of structural features of language presents an interesting contrast with implicit measures of, for example, self-esteem or prejudice. The different implicit measures that have been developed to investigate self-esteem or prejudice (e.g., Bosson et al., 2000; Greenwald & Banaji, 1995) as such leave very little room—if any at all—for the operation and influence of situated constraints. The methods that are employed allow for maximum experimental control with substantially less room for contextual influences, unless these are experimentally induced. Therefore, one can argue that implicit indicators (e.g., prejudice or self-esteem) impose a heavy reliance on associative memory-based constraints when responding. In contrast, examination of the structural features of language in context allows for an optimally permissive research strategy—which is a methodological strategy that is very much in line with the type of recommendation McGuire would advance. Identifying tacit features of language use allows one to tap *situated or contextualized features* of, for example, self-expression in talk and to go beyond the surface of "monitored self-talk." It is thus possible to uncover hidden agendas behind "motivated self-talk" by attending to the manner in which structural features of self-presentation are disguised behind propositional features. Moreover, the issue of the interface between implicit measures and behavior becomes a nonissue simply because it is the situated behavior (verbal) that is examined in terms of its tacit (structural) properties that also provides an indication of the "hidden agenda" (i.e., prejudice, or self-enhancement).

This is very much in line with the research program initiated by McGuire, namely investigating variations in the representation of self as a function of different contexts. The main difference is in the type of analysis regarding language. It is possible to think of the propositional–structural distinction as potentially adding a link between the explicit and implicit whereby the recent reference to implicit derives from the implications of implicit memory for social cognition in general and for the self in particular. The assumption in the communication perspective advocated here is that the "tacit" is a situated and an integral part of ongoing speech acts. Having said that, one should not " . . . blur the distinction between the product and the process," as Broadbent (1973, p. 183) put it some time ago. The fact that self-talk can be analyzed this way "does not mean that the psychological processes which produce or understand them should be described in corresponding ways" (Broadbent, 1977, p. 187). I have therefore not only concentrated on the propositional and structural features of the product but have made some references to the psychological processes that drive the production and comprehension of such messages as well. This is obviously a broader subject that eludes detailed discussion here (Semin, 2000b).

## Conclusions

It is important to draw attention to the fact that the abstract–concrete dimension is a *tacit, structural* feature of interpersonal language (Semin, 2000a) and is independent of specific semantic domains or fields (e.g., economic exchange, prosocial behavior). This is one of the insights that emerge from a systematic examination of interpersonal language. The broader implications of such a linguistic analysis become apparent in the research applying the LCM in the self-talk domain but also in examinations of the LIB. In such applications of the LCM, it becomes necessary to include both the communication context and production and comprehension processes that come into play. The LCM is a methodological device for the analysis of communicative acts, but it forces one to think about social behavior in ways that make it possible to tame it methodologically and theoretically. The following points constitute an example of the steps that have been used to reach such domestication.

1.  Modeling the properties of interpersonal language (LCM) and examining the properties of messages permits an entry into quantitative investigations of communicative acts in the interpersonal domain.
2.  Knowledge of the structural properties of a message, along with the context in which it is produced (e.g., intergroup context), permits one to examine systematically how message properties are modulated (e.g., LIB).
3.  Knowledge of such variations furnishes the possibility of a systematic analysis of message impact, namely how it is comprehended and the linguistic factors that influence message comprehension.
4.  Knowledge of the systematic ways in which message structure is subtly shaped allows us to systematically investigate production processes (e.g., cognitive and motivational processes involved in message production).

These steps provide one avenue to systematically investigate the link among production processes that are responsible for a communicative act, the features of the communicative act itself (message structure), and how the message is received (comprehension processes). Thus, the current approach constitutes a move toward examining the cycle of social interaction by decomposing it down to specific constituent elements, analyzing these components, and reconstituting the link between the psychological and the social.

## References

Abelson, R. P., & Kanouse, D. E. (1966). Subjective acceptance of verbal generalizations. In S. Feldman (Ed.), *Cognitive consistency: motivational antecedents and behavioral consequences.* (pp. 171–197). New York: Academic Press.

Austin, J. L. (1962). *How to do things with words* (2nd ed.). Cambridge, MA: Harvard University Press.

Bargh, J. A. (1994). The four horsemen of automaticity: Awareness, intention, efficiency, and control in social cognition. In R. S. Wyer & T. K. Srull (Eds.*), Handbook of social cognition.* (2nd ed., Vol. 1, pp. 1–42). Hillsdale, NJ: Erlbaum.

Bosson, J. K., Swann, W. B., & Pennebaker, J. W. (2000). Stalking the perfect measure of implicit self-esteem: The blind men and the mice revisited. *Journal of Personality and Social Psychology, 79,* 631–643.

Broadbent, D. (1973). *In defense of empirical psychology.* London: Methuen.

Broadbent, D. (1977). Levels, hierarchies and the locus of control. *Quarterly Journal of Experimental Psychology, 29,* 181–201.

Brown, R., & Fish, D. (1983). The psychological causality implicit in language. *Cognition, 14,* 237–273.

Chafe, W. I. (1970). *Meaning and the structure of language.* Chicago, IL: The University of Chicago Press.

Comrie, B. (1989). *Language universals and linguistic typology.* Chicago, IL: The University of Chicago Press.

Douglas, K. M., & Sutton, R. M. (2003). Effects of communication goals and expectancies on language abstraction. *Journal of Personality and Social Psychology, 84,* 682–696.

Fiedler, K., Semin, G. R., & Koppetsch, C. (1991). Language use and attributional biases in close relationships. *Personality and Social Psychology Bulletin, 17,* 147–155.

Fiedler, K., Semin, G. R., Finkenauer, C., & Berkel (1995). Actor–observer bias in close relationships: The role of self-knowledge and self-related language. *Personality and Social Psychology Bulletin, 21,* 525–538.

Fillmore, C. J. (1971). Verbs of judging: An exercise in semantic description. In C. J. Fillmore & D. T. Langendoen (Eds.), *Studies in linguistic semantics* (pp. 273–296). New York: Holt, Rinehart & Winston.

Gibson, J. J. (1977). The theory of affordances. In R. Shaw & J. Bransford (Eds.), *Perceiving, acting and knowing: Toward an ecological psychology* (pp. 67–82). Hillsdale, NJ: Erlbaum.

Grice, H. P. (1975). Logic and conversation. In P. Cole & J. L. Morgan (Eds.), *Syntax and semantics* (Vol. 3, pp. 44–58). New York: Academic Press.

Greenwald, A. G., & Banaji, M. R. (1995). Implicit social cognition. Attitudes, self esteem, and stereotypes. *Psychological Review, 102,* 4–27.

James, W. (1890). *Psychology.* New York: Holt.

Kay, P. (1996). Inter-speaker relativity. In J. J. Gumpertz & S. C. Levinson (Eds.), *Rethinking linguistic relativity* (pp. 97–114). New York : Cambridge University Press.

Maass, A. (1999). Linguistic intergroup bias: stereotype perpetuation through language. In M. P. Zanna (Ed.), *Advances in Experimental Social Psychology* (Vol. 31, pp. 79–122). NewYork: Academic Press.

Maass, A., Salvi, D., Arcuri, L., & Semin, G. R. (1989). Language use in intergroup contexts: The linguistic intergroup bias. *Journal of Personality and Social Psychology, 57,* 981–993.

Maass, A., Milesi, A., Zabbini, S., & Stahlberg, D. (1995). The linguistic intergroup bias: Differential expectancies or ingroup protection? *Journal of Personality and Social Psychology, 68,* 116–126.

McGuire, W. J. (1999). *Constructing social psychology.* New York: Cambridge University Press.

McGuire, W. J., & McGuire, C. V. (1986). Differences in conceptualizing self versus conceptualizing other people as manifested in contrasting verb types in natural speech. *Journal of Personality and Social Psychology, 51,* 1135–1143.

McGuire, W. J., & McGuire, C. V. (1988). Content and process in the experience of self. In L. Berkowitz (Ed.), *Advances in experimental social psychology* (Vol. 21, pp. 97–144). New York: Academic Press.

McGuire, W. J., McGuire, C. V., & Cheever, J. (1986). The self in society: Effects of social contexts on the sense of self. *British Journal of Social Psychology, 25,* 259–270.

Polanyi, M. (1967). *The tacit dimension.* London: Routledge.

Ross, M., & Sicoly, F. (1979). Egocentric biases in availability and attribution. *Journal of Personality and Social Psychology, 37,* 322–336.

Rudolph, U., & Försterling, F. (1997). The psychological causality implicit in verbs: A review. *Psychological Bulletin, 121,* 192–218.

Schwarz, N. (2000). Social judgment and attitudes: Warmer, more social, and less conscious. *European Journal of Social Psychology, 30,* 149–176.

Semin, G. R. (1998). Cognition, language, and communication. In S. R. Fussell & R. J. Kreuz (Eds.), *Social and cognitive psychological approaches to interpersonal communication* (pp. 229–257). Hillsdale, NJ: Erlbaum.

Semin, G. R. (2000a). Language as a cognitive and behavioral structuring resource: Question-answer exchanges. In W. Stroebe & M. Hewstone (Eds.), *European Review of Social Psychology,* (pp. 75–104). Chichester, England: Wiley.

Semin, G. R. (2000b). Agenda 2000: Communication: Language as an implementational device for cognition. *European Journal of Social Psychology, 30,* 595–612.

Semin, G. R., & de Poot, C. J. (1997). The question-answer paradigm: You might regret not noticing how a question is worded. *Journal of Personality and Social Psychology, 73,* 472–480.

Semin, G. R., & Fiedler, K. (1988). The cognitive functions of linguistic categories in describing persons: Social cognition and language. *Journal of Personality and Social Psychology, 54,* 558–568.

Semin, G. R., & Fiedler, K. (1989). Relocating attributional phenomena within the language-cognition interface: The case of actor-observer perspectives. *European Journal of Social Psychology, 19,* 491–508.

Semin, G. R., & Fiedler, K. (1991). The linguistic category model, its bases, applications and range. In W. Stroebe & M. Hewstone (Eds.), *European Review of Social Psychology,* (Vol. 2, pp.1–30) Chichester, England: Wiley.

Semin, G. R., & Manstead, A. S. R. (1983). *The accountability of conduct.* London: Academic Press.

Semin, G. R., de Montes, G. L., & Valencia, J. F. (2003). Communication constraints on the Linguistic Intergroup Bias, *Journal of Experimental Social Psychology, 39,* 142–148.

Semin, G. R., & Smith E. R. (1999). Revisiting the past and back to the future: Memory systems and the linguistic representation of social events. *Journal of Personality and Social Psychology, 76,* 877–892.

Tajfel, H., & Turner, J. C. (1986). The social identity theory of intergroup behaviour. In S. Worchel & W. G. Austin (Eds.), *Psychology of intergroup relations* (pp. 7–24). Chicago: Nelson-Hall.

Taris, T. W. (1999). Describing behaviors of self and others: Self-enhancing beliefs and language abstraction level. *European Journal of Social Psychology, 29,* 391–396.

Wegner, D. M., & Bargh, J. A. (1998). Control and automaticity in social life. In D. T. Gilbert, S. T. Fiske, & G. Lindzey (Eds.), *The handbook of social psychology.* (Vol. 1, pp. 446–496). Boston, MA: McGraw-Hill.

# 12

# (Self-)Conceptions as Social Actions

*Curtis D. Hardin*

## Prologue

My life as a student of social psychology evolved from my identification with a series of mentors who think for a living, including Bill and Claire McGuire, who adopted me as one of a more or less motley group of devotees during my graduate study at Yale from 1988 to 1993. Unlike that of my precocious comrades—especially Irene Blair, John Jost, and Alex Rothman—my appreciation of McGuire's approach came slowly. I fought it and thought I had rejected it as incompatible with science, even as Bill mentored me, with what must have been divine patience, all the way through the completion of my dissertation (under the supervision of Mahzarin Banaji, a miraculously patient and wise mentor in her own right). Indeed, I do not believe I recognized the degree to which I had internalized and accepted tenets of perspectivism until my own students began complaining about the arguments in which they repeatedly found themselves. Doesn't everybody know that theories are inherently incomplete, that experimental effects are inherently conditional, that phenomena are multiply determined and have multiple consequences, that for every empirical yin there is a yang, and that conditional truths are nevertheless meaningfully true? Sometimes it is your offspring who reveal most clearly your debt to your parents. Thank you Stacey Sinclair, Leah Spalding, Terri Conley, Christine Reyna, Lien Pham, John Hetts, Dan Ortiz, Karen Cheng, and Brian Lowery. Thank you, Bill, and thank you, Mahzarin.

The effects of my identification with Bill on my approach to social psychology are especially pronounced, I think, because the Yale school of social psychology at the time was a veritable culture of perspectivism, living and breathing in the work of my fellow graduate students as well as in the approaches of my other teachers. One of Bill McGuire's greatest influences on the program has been his model of methodological, theoretical, and topical eclecticism. There, I learned that one of the glories of social psychology is the view from its perch at the nexus of so many elements of the human condition. (In my

This chapter was prepared with the support of a UCLA Academic Senate Grant. The best parts of my scholarly work reflect a deep indebtedness to my teacher, Bill McGuire. I would like also to acknowledge my debt to another mentor, the late William Kessen, who taught me to seek connections among ideas, and to Mahzarin R. Banaji, who taught me how to capture connections among ideas in the scientific experiment. For useful comments on a draft of this chapter, I thank Karen Cheng, John Jost, Ludwin Molina, M. Park, Lien Pham, and Stacey Sinclair.

research, I have focused most on the interpersonal foundations of cognition, with a particular focus on communication and language in the dynamics of attitudes and memory as expressed in social judgment and self-understanding.)

Another glory of social psychology is that it affords the study of the human condition within the language of science, which, among the great human religions, may be the one most consistently devoted to creating the conditions of common experience. The scientific experiment, for example, imposes a particular kind of systematic interaction with the world that can be shared. Indeed, the ultimate scientific criterion is that one's experiment is reproducible by others to identical effect. Hence, the benefits of the scientific experiment flow not so much from control over reality as from the creation of a more or less definable circumstance, which, because it is definable, can be reproduced by anyone. The well-articulated experiment is an experience that many people—with their varieties of history, experience, biases, and so on—may share. In short, the experiment is a method for creating that most elusive yet necessary human experience: intersubjectivity, which is sometimes misleadingly called "objectivity." This perspective suggests to me that although as scientists, we may be relatively ecumenical about interpretations or implications of a given experiment (e.g., as it relates to theory or hypothesized generalizability), we might benefit from being somewhat more dogmatic about the integrity of descriptions of our experiments, whose replicability makes them brute facts of a type. Indeed, my guess is that the embarrassing problem of the difficulty of replicating some social psychological experiments, which is usually attributed to the instability of the phenomenon in question, is perhaps more often caused by incomplete understanding of the effective conditions defined by the experiment. Perhaps this supposition reflects the most important thing I've learned from Bill: that the vicissitudes of research results are to be embraced as moments of potential discovery rather than as ephemeral errors of inconvenience.

* * *

What is the sense of one mind thinking?

The Zen koan poses a peculiar kind of question—one that invites exploration yet defies resolution. As such, William James McGuire teaches, the koan is an apt metaphor for another peculiar kind of question—the scientific hypothesis, which is never forever confirmed or disconfirmed but rewards the wise with reiterative riches (e.g., McGuire, 1983, 1997, 1999). From this perspective, the hypothesis is a proposition awaiting the kind of theoretical and empirical exploration that will reveal its conditional truths as well as its conditional falsehoods. Even cursory use of McGuire's perspectivist method—such as turning a hypothesis on its head, manipulating its expression, or exploring potential mediating and moderating conditions—proves that each hypothesis is provisional and self-subverting, situated in an ever-evolving web of related ideas. As a graduate student, I initially misapprehended perspectivism as a clever variation of nihilism. I was wrong. Perspectivism may be the most scientifically useful expression of epistemological pragmatism to date (Dewey, 1922/1976–1983; James, 1907/1956; Mead, 1936; Peirce, 1903). Perspectivism facilitates scientific progress by providing tools that help connect one's mind to the minds of others, as well as by freeing the scientific theory from the anchor of metaphysical absolutism to find its most practical applications. To make the case, I first situate perspectivism in its pragmatic roots and conclude with a demonstration of the capacity of the perspectivist method to yield a novel hypothesis in one of the most studied topics of psychology.

## Conceptions as Social Actions

The term "pragmatism" was coined by William James (1898)—as a tribute to his friend, Charles Peirce (Menand, 2001)—to describe theories of knowledge that postulate that ideas are not metaphysical constants awaiting discovery but socially created tools people use to cope with a dynamic world. From this perspective, the value of an idea is not the degree to which it accurately represents objective reality but rather the degree to which it enables groups of people to understand and navigate their circumstance—that is, the degree to which the idea enables people to productively solve the problems to which it is applied. A hammer is useful for pounding a rusty nail into a board but not as useful for sawing a board in half. Although it makes little sense to ask how "true" a tool a hammer is, it does make sense to ask the degree to which it is useful for the task at hand. Likewise, the idea that the self is an evaluative attitude has proved useful in studying people's responses to failure and success, among other things, but not as useful for understanding the extent and nuance of self-related phenomenology—where the net of free description has captured more than the ball-peen hammer of self-evaluation (McGuire & McGuire, 1988).

To suggest that perspectivism is an expression of pragmatism is not to suggest that McGuire's approach is identical to the classical expressions of pragmatism. At minimum, perspectivism is a concrete implementation of what are largely philosophical abstractions in the writings of James, Peirce, and Mead. However, it is more than a practical implementation of pragmatic philosophy. The smug comfort that one's hypothesis is a provisional tool may make little difference in practice if it remains a mere metaphysical assumption. Positivists, too, assume that the hypothesis is provisional, albeit in the pursuit of some objective "Truth" (e.g., Popper, 1945).[1] Although it is accepted in perspectivism that an idea is a tool, proponents of this theory are encouraged to break out the whole toolbox. Why be content to pound pins into planks with a hammer when one can also pry them out? Why settle for the assumption that one's hypothesis is like a hammer—and then proceed as a positivist—when one's research can benefit from the simultaneous use of multiple

---

[1] Perhaps this explains in part why many scientists believe that they are positivists when their practice is so easily described in pragmatic terms (e.g., Kuhn, 1962/1970). Important however, is that from the pragmatic perspective, scientific positivism is not problematic because it is wrong; it is problematic only to the degree that it inhibits productive scientific work. Perspectivism is perhaps the most powerful demonstration to date of the practical limits of the positivist paradigm, in a tradition begun by Dewey's (1896/1967–1972) reconstruction of the "reflex arc."

hypotheses, like so many pliers, planes, saws, and squares? Perspectivism enhances the utility of the pragmatic assumption by facilitating the scientist's capacity to multiply the number of conceptual tools applied to a given problem, thereby providing a recipe for scholarship in its fullest sense.

There is another sense in which the perspectivist method is pragmatic in character: the way that it liberates the hypothesis or theory from the stultifying burden of being right about life, the universe, and everything—or else doomed to the footnotes of failure in dusty textbooks. Embracing the notion that the scientific idea, like any other idea, is a tool whose utility is determined by the degree to which it enables one to productively address issues of interest, liberates one to make use of many theories (including old theories), as well as to discover and create scientific uses for one's favorite theories—secure in the knowledge that one theory cannot, and hence need not, be useful for every problem. Identifying the conditions in which a theory fails need not be cause for worry—or, worse, for overly defensive attempts to salvage it—but rather cause for celebration. Knowing the limits of a theory's applicability is practical knowledge. Knowing exactly where the theories of others are required to complement one's own theory is practical knowledge. Systematic exploration of the conditions in which a theory succeeds in relation to the conditions in which it fails is a sure route to the identification of new syntheses of scientific understanding.

In sum, perspectivism not only shares the pragmatic assumption that scientific conceptions are social actions—whose values are defined by their practical social (scientific) uses—but also provides a system of exploration that efficiently enables one to benefit from the social nature of scientific practice. Implementing the tools of perspectivism inevitably connects one to the ideas of others in dynamic new combinations, making the method a practical advance over the method of the solitary tiller who plods along one row at a time, for the sense that one mind can make is as elusive as the sound of one hand clapping.

## Self-Conceptions as Social Actions

Just as perspectivism embraces the conditional nature of knowledge at the level of epistemology, one may apply the perspectivist method to find ways in which kinds of knowledge more typically studied by psychologists also operate in the social web. Hence, in the spirit of constructive contradiction, I now outline a specific application of perspectivism to one of McGuire's favorite topics: the self. If ever there were a topic in danger of being fully tapped, it would have to be the self (for reviews see Banaji & Prentice, 1994; Baumeister, 1998). For example, Ashmore and Jussim (1997) identified 31,550 abstracts on the self from 1974 to 1993 alone. Banaji and Prentice (1994) identified more than 5000 articles published from 1987 to 1994 alone. Despite the large number of publications on the self, the application of just a few simple perspectivist heuristics elicits a novel hypothesis yet to be directly tested, though interesting enough to warrant additional empirical exploration. Just as scientific theories represent social contracts, so too may self-conceptions.

## Deriving a Novel Hypothesis From a Truism

McGuire (1961) demonstrated that many seemingly deep-rooted values, including cultural truisms, can crumble to pieces with even a cursory challenge because people have rarely had occasion to establish foundations of the values' existence. However, the same is unlikely to be said of one of social psychology's favorite truisms—i.e., that self-conceptions are a function of social recognition, feedback, and interaction—because the literature is replete with demonstrations that the self is a dynamic social construction (inter alia Andersen & Glassman, 1996; Aron, Aron, Tudor, & Nelson, 1991; Baldwin, Carrell, & Lopez, 1990; Baumeister, 1998; Cooley, 1902; Hardin & Higgins, 1996; Leary, Tambor, Terdal, & Downs, 1995; Markus & Kitayama, 1991; Mead, 1934; Morse & Gergen, 1970; Ross, Amabile, & Steinmetz, 1977; Sullivan, 1953; Tice, 1992). Although the hypothesis that the self is a social creation is demonstrably true in many ways, the perspectivist approach revels in contradiction and delights in the empirical sparks that fly when even well-founded dogma is turned on its head in a process that inevitably reveals the connections of one's new hypotheses to the ideas of others.

Hence, McGuire and McGuire's (1988) wry observation that the self is everyone's favorite topic may reflect less about rampant narcissism than about its opposite: the universal human need to establish and maintain interpersonal relationships. Although theorists in both West and East have long contraposed egoistic and social motivations (Allport, 1955; Doi, 1971; Freud, 1933; James, 1890/1955; Markus & Kitayama, 1991; Plato, 360 B.C.E./2003), applying the perspectivist method to the notion that to be true to the self and to society are mutually exclusive indicates that individual expression and interpersonal obligation may not be opposites so much as two sides of the same coin. Not only is self-knowledge a product of social interaction, but the opposite may also be true: To know the self is to affirm some particular interpersonal relationship or set of relationships. The hypothesis is hereby hardly proved but rather derived and briefly considered.

According to McGuire (see Appendix), hypothesis exploration is facilitated by first putting it into a form that is easily manipulated and transformed. Hence, the truism that the self is a social creation may be represented by a simple declarative proposition in which "society" is the independent variable (IV) and "self" is the dependent variable (DV). Here, I employ a verbal proposition to represent the social psychological truism that the self is created by society, although one benefits further by exploring other representational modalities such as graphs, tables, and mathematical formulae, as well as example caricatures and prototypes (heuristic 21[2]).

Society (IV) creates the self (DV).        (P1)

One useful way to explore and refine one's hypothesis is to explore its linguistic representation through strategic searches for concepts related to each element of the proposition (heuristic 15). "Society" is related to many other

---

[2]Heuristics are identified by their location in Table 1 of McGuire (1997), which is reprinted in part in chapter 12 of McGuire (1999).

terms, including *people, (in)significant others, friends, enemies, culture, interpersonal relationships, impersonal relationships,* and so on. "Self" is related to many other terms, including *phenomenology, social identity, ego, superego, id, self-awareness, self-esteem, self-understanding, self-conceptions, self-knowledge, self-deception, self-affirmation, self-hate,* and so on. "Creates" is related to other terms, including *causes, structures, affirms, constrains, destroys, enables,* and so on. Generating lists of synonyms, antonyms, and closely related terms—especially boundary terms—often yields modified propositions truer to one's interest while also indicating parts of the conceptual landscape in which the focal proposition may live. Hence, there are many ways to clarify this proposition. Here's mine:

> Interpersonal relationships (IV) affirm self-conceptions (DV).     (P2)

The senses in which P2 is demonstrably true include research suggesting that (a) self-esteem is a function of the approval of others (e.g., Leary et al., 1995), (b) cognitive representations of the self overlap with representations of significant others (e.g., Aron et al., 1991), (c) self-concepts are actively protected to the degree that they are perceived to be validated by significant others (e.g., Hardin & Higgins, 1996), and (d) self-evaluation is made more negative by thoughts of disapproving significant others (e.g., Baldwin et al., 1990).

To those uninitiated to the perspectivist approach, merely fathoming the possibility that the opposite of one's cherished hypothesis might also be true may seem difficult, at least at first. Yet one of McGuire's most useful analytical tropes is to embrace contradiction by exploring inversions of the relation and reversing the implied causal direction of the relation (heuristic 11). Here the IV and DV replace each other to form a new proposition with reversed causality:

> Self-conceptions (IV) affirm interpersonal relationships (DV).     (P3)

Another useful way to turn a hypothesis on its head is to invert the IV–DV relationship. For example, interpersonal relationships may disaffirm or subvert self-conceptions as well as affirm them, and self-conceptions may disaffirm or subvert interpersonal relationships as well as affirm them. P3 is therefore just one deserving possibility. Notably, iterating and reiterating the hypothesis-contextualizing process in its entirety adds considerable texture to the theoretical and empirical landscape and may yield a modification of one's initial hypothesis, or inspire new direction entirely.

## Quixotic Defense of an Unlikely Hypothesis (Heuristic 32)

A common response to a novel hypothesis is a failure to engage it seriously—often by rejecting it as out-of-hand on self-evidentiary grounds. This may be especially true when the new hypothesis is a product of the kind of bald derivation prescribed by perspectivism. Yet much is gained by scrutinizing novel hypotheses related to one's focal interest, particularly with attention to possible conditions that might cause the novel hypothesis to obtain. This attitude is represented by McGuire's (1999) axiom that "every hypothesis is occasionally true, at least in certain contexts viewed from certain perspectives."

In what sense, therefore, might the proposition that self-conceptions affirm interpersonal relationships possibly be true? The idea suggested here is that the act of endorsing a particular characteristic as true of the self may have the consequence of affirming some particular interpersonal relationship or set of relationships. For example, one conception I have of myself is that I am a cook. The way that social psychologists currently understand such self-descriptions is primarily in representational terms, which may vary in objective truth value but nevertheless are essentially the province of one's cognitive structure as a function of one's social context (e.g., Baumeister, 1998; Greenwald & Pratkanis, 1984; Higgins & Bargh, 1987; Markus & Wurf, 1987; Turner & Oakes, 1986). Why do I say I am a cook? According to contemporary theory, and broadly congruent with P2, it is because I have been given opportunities to cook, have been rewarded for cooking, or have been required to cook as part of my cultural or interpersonal roles. I say I am a cook because "cook" is linked to my cognitive representation of myself, which may be more or less accessible depending on how often I cook or how relevant cooking is to the situation in which I describe myself as cook. However, as derived from this application of the perspectivist method, another function of describing myself as a cook may be to affirm my social connection with somebody else—to affirm my allegiance to, identification with, or liking or love for someone.

It turns out that, for me, conceiving of myself as a cook is relatively new and primarily associated with my role as a father. My young son Simon thinks I am a cook. When he was a year and a half old, he would say things such as, "Daddy cook! Simon cook too! Pour it! Stir it! Round and round and round! Simon see Daddy cook! Simon help Daddy cook!" Clearly, part of the reason I describe myself as a cook is because at least one person in my life identifies me as a cook, congruent with my emerging duties as a father as well as with the proposition that interpersonal relationships affirm self-conceptions (P2). However, this may also illustrate the proposition in which causality flows in the opposite direction, i.e., that to describe myself as a cook affirms my relationship with Simon (P3). For example, for me to deny that I am a cook is to deny what my son thinks about me, thereby betraying my relationship with him by implying that *I think* he is mistaken, deluded, or naïve. Moreover, to deny that I am a cook would be to forsake a trait my son apparently admires in me. Not cooking is to fail to live up to a standard my son has set for me. Hence, despite the fact that I am unlikely to ever run a four-star kitchen, I *am* a cook. I must be a cook to identify with my son and to affirm or respect my relationship with him.

Direct tests of the hypothesis that self-conceptions affirm interpersonal relationships would include experiments that manipulate the self-concept and assess consequences on relevant relationships. For example, if I were experimentally induced to describe myself as a cook, my relationship with my son might loom large on any number of interesting assessments—such as judgments of closeness to Simon, response latencies to perceive his little face, persistence on tasks framed to benefit him, and so on. Alternatively, if I were induced to describe myself as a social psychologist, relationships with my mentors, students, and academic colleagues might loom large. This hypothesis might be explored further by testing potential mechanisms of the phenomenon as well as its conditionality. Are the associations among self-conceptions and interpersonal relationships symmetrical? Is a given association strengthened or weakened if self-conceptions are relevant to multiple relationships? Can self-descriptions be functionally abstracted away from the relationships in which they were originally founded? If so, is there a way to characterize which ones are and which ones are not? What happens under conditions in which one self-conception is associated with one relationship but an opposite self-conception is associated with a different relationship? Might commitment to one relationship be strengthened if associated self-conceptions are validated (or subverted) by others? Of course, these are just a few of the possible ways in which the hypothesis could be empirically and theoretically explored.

Affirming the inherently social nature of the perspectivist method, most of the possibilities would engage extant theory and research on the self, social interaction, and cognitive representation. Yet, to my knowledge, there has been no experimental test of the hypothesis that self-conceptions affirm interpersonal relationships Hence, a simple, McGuirean twist on a social psychological construct studied tens of thousands of times yields a novel hypothesis rich enough to inspire many plausible basic demonstrations, as well as innumerable elaborations should the phenomenon be captured. This fact in itself demonstrates the utility of the perspectivist method.

The hypothesis resonates in a broader way with the pragmatic character of McGuire's inspiration. It suggests that having self-conceptions is functional, that self-conceptions exist in a dynamic process of living in the web of others' influence, and that self-conceptions facilitate understanding and navigation of the world by connecting us with others (cf. Swann, 1990). This perspective also implies that self-conceptions will be endorsed and acted upon to the extent that they work—i.e., by productively regulating interpersonal relationships: I *must* care for my son. That care may require regular validation that I acknowledge and reciprocate his experience of me and the world we inhabit together (e.g., Hardin & Conley, 2001; Hardin & Higgins, 1996). I care for my son in part by acknowledging that I am a cook. By the same token, because social regulation is not a one-way street, self-conceptions may be cherished for their relation to enemies as well as loved ones. I may identify myself as a cook in part because my enemy believes that culinary artistry is an effete affectation. Also, even though being a cook may be part of the behavioral circuit of loving my son (or hating my enemy) now, it need not be for perpetuity. Circumstances may arise in the future that make my culinary aspirations irrelevant to my relationships—e.g., that make it an ineffective way to act on my relationship with my son. When that time comes, I will be something else to him and for him. Hence, in a sense analogous to James' (1907/1956) definition of "truth," self-conceptions may be as true as they demonstrate themselves to be—for the purposes of acting on the requirements of one's dynamic social environment.

## Circumstantial Evidence of Self-Conceptions as Relationship Affirmations

Although no experimental tests of the hypothesis that self-conceptions are interpersonal affirmations exist, there is indirect theoretical and empirical evidence bearing on its promise. The study of human development reveals that the self-concept is at root bound up with social regulation. Most agree that the self-concept is predicated on social interaction (e.g., Ainsworth, 1964; Bowlby, 1969; Freud, 1933; Mead, 1934; Sullivan, 1953). For example, development of the capacity for self-awareness and the capacity for perspective taking co-occur; this is consistent with the notion that an act of self-awareness may be predicated on perspective taking (e.g., Mead, 1934). It is only upon the acquisition of self-awareness at this age that the child is capable of experiencing expressly social emotions such as embarrassment, envy, empathy, pride, guilt, and shame (e.g., Lewis, Alessandri, & Sullivan, 1992). This is the age at which the "language explosion" occurs (e.g., Golinkoff, Hirsh-Pasek, & Hollich, 1999), in which the child graduates from apishly learned, associative labeling to astronomical rates of lexical and grammatical language acquisition associated with the rudimentary use of communicative pragmatics, on which the cooperative, meaning-making linguistic activity of adults is known to be predicated (e.g., Clark, 1998; Krauss & Fussell, 1996; Sperber & Wilson, 1986). By the end of the second year, social standards are known and the anxiety associated with failure first appears (Kagan, 1984; Sullivan, 1953). Psychodynamic theorists have taken similar findings from case studies as evidence that the self-system emerges as an adaptive outcome of the need to manage the anxiety associated with social disapproval (Bettelheim, 1987; Bowlby, 1969; Freud, 1933; Sullivan, 1953). Moreover, as individuals become strongly identified with others, they tend to emulate the others' thoughts, feelings, and behaviors in an apparent attempt to maintain the social connection, as well as to gain the others' love and acceptance (e.g., Freud, 1933; Kelman, 1961). Hence, although much of this research is consistent with the social psychological truism that the self-concept is a product of social relationships, it is also consistent with the hypothesis that self-concepts may function as affirmations of social relationships.

Like the developmental research linking the self-concept to the social approval of significant others, research on adults is broadly consistent with the possibility that self-conceptions function as social affirmations. For example, at a fundamental level, the hypothesis that self-conceptions are social affirmations would appear to be predicated on the assumption that self-conceptions and interpersonal relationships are represented with some minimal level of modularity. Hence, if the hypothesis were true, one might also expect the reverse association to hold, i.e., that different relationships should elicit different self-conceptions. Several findings corroborate this hypothesis. For example, Baldwin and Holmes (1987) demonstrated that people's responses to failure or to reading a sexually permissive piece of fiction were qualitatively different depending on the cognitive salience of parents versus friends. In subsequent experiments, Baldwin and colleagues found that self-evaluation varied as a function of the cognitive salience of significant others (Baldwin et al., 1990).

More telling evidence in support of the proposition that self-conceptions are social affirmations comes from research demonstrating that effects of interpersonal relationships on self-understanding are enhanced to the degree to which one is required to establish or maintain the relationship. For example, Tice (1992) found that participants internalized their own behavior (either emotional expressiveness or emotional stability) as more true of themselves when it was expressed to a peer than when it was expressed anonymously. In a second experiment, participants who behaved in an introverted or extraverted manner publicly internalized the behavior more than participants who performed the identical behavior privately. Baldwin et al. (1990) found that negative self-evaluations as a function of subliminal exposure to the Pope's frowning face obtained for Catholics but not for non-Catholics.

My colleagues and I have found evidence for the proposition that self-concepts are linked to particular social relationships, in particular to the degree that they are high in relationship motivation (Hardin & Conley, 2001). For example, we found that self-evaluations of academic ability are related to the degree to which one's ethnic versus gender identity is salient—along ingroup stereotype-consistent lines—and also that this relationship is mediated by the degree to which one thinks one's significant others believe the ethnic and gender stereotypes are applicable to the self (Sinclair, Hardin, & Lowery, 2002). We also found evidence that self-judgment assimilates to the perceived views of interpersonal acquaintances or imagined others to the degree that one is motivated to get along with the other (Sinclair, Huntsinger, Skorinko, & Hardin, 2003). Finally, we found evidence that motivation to excel in school is enhanced to the degree that one takes the perspective of one's parents as opposed to the perspective of a lazy peer (Pham & Hardin, 2003). In short, although the hypothesis that self-conceptions function as interpersonal relationship affirmations has received no direct experimental test to date, circumstantial evidence indicates that empirical exploration is warranted.

## Conclusion

One can readily discern the pragmatic principles in the empirical work of the classical pragmatists (e.g., Dewey, 1922/1976–1983; James, 1890/1955; Mead, 1934). To do so, however, is an exercise in philosophy. One contribution of McGuire's perspectivism is the formalization of a systematic approach to any empirical problem, thereby transforming philosophy of science into generative scientific practice. For example, even in rudimentary form, it was used to derive the novel hypothesis that self is everyone's favorite topic because it connects one with others. Yet the most persuasive arguments in favor of perspectivism are found in McGuire's empirical explorations of attitudes, language, and the self (collected in McGuire, 1999). Aside from descriptions of now canonical social psychological phenomena, one finds in them that McGuire's method is characterized by a proclivity for paradox and revelation in contradiction, perhaps not seen in science since Marx. Indeed, a famous Marxian aphorism may be adapted to capture McGuirean praxis: "The hypothesis is dead. Long live the hypothesis!" Embracing the provisional character of the hypothesis liberates it, allowing the scientist to find its most useful and inspiring place, as well as to exploit its potential to elicit genuine novelty. Yet the creativity perspectivism inspires is not empty sophistry; it is the most practical of pragmatisms. This is its signature contribution, for in perspectivism, McGuire offers more than just another philosophy of truth without a capital T. He demystifies scientific genius—his method is a metatheory for the scientific masses.

# References

Ainsworth, M. D. S. (1964). Patterns of attachment behavior shown by the infant in interaction with his mother. *Merrill-Palmer Quarterly, 10*, 51–58.

Allport, G. W. (1955). *Becoming: Basic considerations for a psychology of personality*. New Haven: Yale University Press.

Andersen, S. M., & Glassman, N. (1996). Responding to significant others when they are not there: Effects on interpersonal inference, motivation, and affect. In R. M. Sorrentino & E. T. Higgins (Eds.), *Handbook of motivation and cognition* (Vol. 3, pp. 272–331). New York: Guilford Press.

Aron, A., Aron, E. N., Tudor, M., & Nelson, G. (1991). Close relationships as including other in the self. *Journal of Personality and Social Psychology, 60*, 241–253.

Ashmore, R. D., & Jussim, L. (1997). Toward a second century of the scientific analysis of self and identity: Introduction. In R. D. Ashmore & L. Jussim (Eds.), *Self and identity: Fundamental issues* (pp. 3–19). New York: Oxford University Press.

Baldwin, M. W., Carrell, S. E., & Lopez, D. F. (1990). Priming relationship schemas: My advisor and the Pope are watching me from the back of my mind. *Journal of Experimental Social Psychology, 26*, 435–454.

Baldwin, M. W., & Holmes, J. G. (1987). Salient private audiences and awareness of the self. *Journal of Personality and Social Psychology, 52*, 1087–1098.

Banaji, M. R., & Prentice, D. A. (1994). The self in social contexts. *Annual Review of Psychology, 45*, 297–332.

Baumeister, R. F. (1998). The self. In D. T. Gilbert, S. T. Fiske, & G. Lindzey (Eds.), *The handbook of social psychology* (4th ed., Vol. 1, pp. 680–740). New York: Oxford University Press.

Bettelheim, B. (1987). *A good enough parent*. New York: Vintage.

Bowlby, J. (1969). *Attachment and loss*. New York: Basic Books.

Clark, H. H. (1998). Communal lexicons. In K. Malmkjaer and J. Williams (Eds.), *Context in language learning and language understanding* (pp. 63–87). New York: Cambridge University Press.

Cooley, C. H. (1902). *Human nature and the social order*. New York: Scribner's.

Dewey, J. (1967–1972). The reflex arc concept in psychology. In Jo Ann Boydston (Ed.), *The early works, 1882–1898*. Carbondale: Southern Illinois University Press. (Original work published 1896)

Dewey, J. (1976–1983). Experience and nature. In Jo Ann Boydston (Ed.), *The middle works, 1899–1924*. Carbondale: Southern Illinois University Press. (Original work published 1922)

Doi, T. (1971). *The anatomy of dependence*. Tokyo: Kodansha International.

Freud, S. (1933). New introductory lectures on psycho-analysis (W. J. H. Sprott, Trans.). London: Hogarth Press.

Golinkoff, R. M., Hirsh-Pasek, K., & Hollich, G. (1999). Emergent cues for early word learning. In B. MacWhinney (Ed.), *The emergence of language*. Mahwah, NJ: Erlbaum.

Greenwald, A. G., & Pratkanis, A. R. (1984). The self. In R. S. Wyer, Jr., & T. K. Srull (Eds.), *Handbook of social cognition* (Vol. 3, pp. 3–26). Hillsdale, NJ: Erlbaum.

Hardin, C. D., & Conley, T. D. (2001). A relational approach to cognition: Shared experience and relationship affirmation in social cognition. In G. B. Moskowitz (Ed.), *Cognitive social psychology: The Princeton symposium on the legacy and future of social cognition* (pp. 3–21). Mahwah, NJ: Erlbaum.

Hardin, C. D., & Higgins, E. T. (1996). Shared reality: How social verification makes the subjective objective. In R. M. Sorrentino & E. T. Higgins (Eds.), *Handbook of motivation and cognition* (Vol. 3, pp. 28–84). New York: Guilford Press.

Higgins, E. T., & Bargh, J. A. (1987). Social perception and social cognition. *Annual Review of Psychology, 38*, 369–425.

James, W. (1955). *Principles of psychology* (Vols. 1 & 2). New York: Dover Publications. (Original work published 1890)

James, W. (1956). *The will to believe and other essays in popular philosophy*. New York: Dover Publications. (Original work published 1907)

James, W. (1975–1988). Philosophical conceptions and practical results. In F. H. Burkhardt (Ed.), *Pragmatism: The works of William James*. Cambridge, MA: Harvard University Press. (Original work published 1898)

Kagan, J. (1984). *The nature of the child*. New York: Basic Books.

Kelman, H. C. (1961). Processes of opinion change. *Public Opinion Quarterly, 25,* 57–78.

Krauss, R. M., & Fussell, S. R. (1996). Social psychological approaches to the study of communication. In E. T. Higgins & A. W. Kruglanski (Eds.), *Social psychology: Handbook of basic principles.* New York: Guilford Press.

Kuhn, T. (1970). *The structure of scientific revolutions.* Chicago: University of Chicago Press. (Original work published 1962)

Leary, M. R., Tambor, E. S., Terdal, S. K., & Downs, D. L. (1995). Self-esteem as an interpersonal monitor: The sociometer hypothesis. *Journal of Personality and Social Psychology, 68,* 518–530.

Lewis, M., Alessandri, S., & Sullivan, M. (1992). Differences in shame and pride as a function of children's gender and task difficulty. *Child Development, 63,* 630–638.

Markus, H. R., & Kitayama, S. (1991). Culture and the self: Implications for cognition, emotion, and motivation. *Psychological Review, 98,* 224–253.

Markus, H., & Wurf, E. (1987). The dynamic self-concept. *Annual Review of Psychology, 38,* 299–337.

McGuire, W. J. (1961). The effectiveness of supportive and refutational defenses in immunizing and restoring beliefs against persuasion. *Sociometry, 24,* 184–197.

McGuire, W. J. (1983). A contextualist theory of knowledge: Its implications for innovation and reform in psychological research. In L. Berkowitz (Ed.), *Advances in experimental social psychology* (Vol. 16, pp. 1–47). New York: Academic Press.

McGuire, W. J. (1997). Creative hypothesis generating in psychology: Some useful heuristics. *Annual Review of Psychology, 48,* 1–30.

McGuire, W. J. (1999). *Constructing social psychology: Creative and critical processes.* New York: Cambridge University Press.

McGuire, W. J., & McGuire, C. V. (1988). Content and process in the experience of self. In L. Berkowitz, (Ed.), *Advances in experimental social psychology* (Vol. 21, pp. 97–144). New York: Academic Press.

Mead, G. H. (1934). *Mind, self, and society: From the standpoint of a social behaviorist* (C. W. Morris, Ed.). Chicago, IL: University of Chicago Press.

Mead, G. H. (1936). *Philosophy of the act* (C. W. Morris, Ed.). Chicago, IL: University of Chicago Press.

Menand, L. (2001). *The metaphysical club.* New York: Farrar, Straus & Giroux.

Morse, S., & Gergen, K. J. (1970). Social comparison, self-consistency and the concept of the self. *Journal of Personality and Social Psychology, 16,* 148–156.

Peirce, C. S. (1903). What pragmatism is. *Monist, 15,* 161–181.

Pham, L., & Hardin, C. D. (2003). *The role of social (dis)identification in self-regulation.* Unpublished manuscript, University of California, Los Angeles.

Plato. (2003) *The republic.* (D. Lee, Trans.). New York: Penguin. (Original work published ca. 360 B.C.E.)

Popper, K. R. (1945). *The open society and its enemies.* London: Routledge.

Ross, L. D., Amabile, T. M., & Steinmetz, J. L. (1977). Social roles, social control, and biases in social-perception processes. *Journal of Personality and Social Psychology, 35,* 485–494.

Sinclair, S., Hardin, C. D., & Lowery, B. (2002). *Implicit self-stereotyping in the context of multiple social identities.* Unpublished manuscript, University of Virginia, Charlottesville.

Sinclair, S., Huntsinger, J., Skorinko, J., & Hardin, C. D. (2003). *Social tuning of the self: Consequences for the self-evaluations of stereotype targets.* Unpublished manuscript, University of Virginia, Charlottesville.

Sperber, D., & Wilson, D. (1986). *Relevance: Communication and cognition.* Oxford: Blackwell.

Sullivan, H. S. (1953). *The interpersonal theory of psychiatry.* New York: Norton.

Swann, W. B., Jr. (1990). To be adored or to be known? The interplay of self-enhancement and self-verification. In R. M. Sorrentino & E. T. Higgins (Eds.), *Handbook of motivation and cognition: Foundations of social behavior* (Vol. 2, pp. 408–441). New York: Guilford Press.

Tice, D. M. (1992). Self-concept change and self-presentation: The looking glass self is also a magnifying glass. *Journal of Personality and Social Psychology, 63,* 435–451.

Turner, J. C., & Oakes, P. J. (1986). The significance of the social identity concept for social psychology with reference to individualism, interactionism, and social influence. *British Journal of Social Psychology, 25,* 237–252.

# Stereotyping, Prejudice, and Intergroup Relations in Society

# 13

# Vicissitudes of Societal Psychology

## *Willem Doise*

> It may be best if each of us, with glances at paths made by travelers who
> have gone before, makes his or her own way (McGuire, 1999, p. 432).

## Prologue

Some years ago, I had occasion to study a set of published and unpublished
reports on empirical studies of social representations. In these studies, several
authors who defined social representations as shared meaning systems used,
without any justification, factor analytic methods to assess their content.
Methods used for studying the organization of interindividual differences were
used rather bluntly to describe more or less consensual beliefs or opinions.
From this evolved the project conceived by Alain Clémence, Fabio Lorenzi-
Cioldi, and myself to make an extensive survey of different data-analytic techniques used in research on social representations.

The study resulted in a book (Doise, Clémence, & Lorenzi-Cioldi, 1993).
The primary aim of our joint endeavor was to evaluate the general principles
of various quantitative data-analytic techniques in terms of their usefulness
for studying essential characteristics of these representations. Studying social
representations always implies the description of shared meaning systems,
the analysis of differences of individual positioning in relation to this system,
and the explanation of these differences.

Not every study on social representations combines the three kinds of
analyses. In some studies, data-analytic techniques reveal the aspect of
common knowledge. Social representations are viewed as mental maps that
are endowed with a quasi-material existence and are peculiar to a given population. Data-analytic methods serve primarily to draw these common maps
out from individual responses in which they do not appear as distinctly. In our
view, descriptions of these objectified representations are major contributions
of statistical analyses as long as researchers remain aware that social representations are not confined to such objectifications, which usually do not take
into account variability that may characterize them.

This is exactly where the paradox lies: Techniques used to obtain common
representations are actually based on a study of material that is characterized
by varying degrees of interindividual variations. The sole aim of social representation research is not to show how scattered and varied fragments of
opinions can be integrated into a coherent whole. Systematic sources of varia-

tions among individuals must be studied on their own with appropriate research methods whose very use obliges researchers to revert to the problem of interindividual differences. Showing that social representations involve organizing principles of differences in individual positioning is an important contribution of the appropriate use of factor analysis.

Differences in positioning remain to be explained. Various methods are explicitly designed for detecting preferential links between individual response modalities and other characteristics of respondents, such as their general beliefs or value choices, their views on other aspects of society, and their group memberships. In this sense, anchoring processes at work in social representations are in evidence.

To conclude, shared meaning systems, organizing principles, and anchoring are the key concepts of the three-phase model that was elaborated on the basis of a study of the existing literature in the realm of social representations. Furthermore, since completion of this study, the three-phase model has oriented several research programs, such as the one studying human rights as social representations (Doise, 2002).

* * *

Let me tentatively define societal psychology as the analysis of individual psychological functioning within the framework of social relationships that are organized around important issues at stake in a society. More specifically, I am interested in the analysis of individual *cognitive* functioning in the framework of *symbolic* social relationships that are organized around important issues, such as power or status relationships between groups, the sexual division of labor, and national or ethnic group memberships.

The need for societal psychology was commonly acknowledged at the beginning of the 20th century. Suffice it here to refer to authors such as Cattaneo (1864), Orano (1902), and Baldwin (1913). The societal perspective reemerged on several occasions in psychology, including in publications of the early 1930s by Piaget (1932), Mead (1934), Vygotsky (1962), and, more recently, Himmelweit and Gaskell (1990), who devoted an edited volume to the issue.

Let me try to avoid a misunderstanding from the beginning. In pleading for a more societal social psychology, I do not want to convey the opinion that such would be the authentic social psychology to the exclusion of all other manifestations of this discipline. On the contrary, I have described and practiced different levels of analysis in social psychology, and there are many ways of articulating these levels (Doise, 1986a). Hence, I remain convinced that social psychology is intrinsically pluralistic.

The theoretical foundations of this pluralism are nowhere outlined in a more direct and convincing way than in McGuire's (1983) chapter on "A contextualist theory of knowledge." I was very impressed by this chapter and have taken the opportunity (Doise, 1986a) to quote it because the ideas in this text supported me in the conviction that every explanatory model in social psychology is always insufficient on its own and needs the intervention of other explanations to account more fully for the conditions that are necessary for the dynamics described by the model to function. I remain convinced that "empirical confrontation is a discovery process to make clear the meaning of the hypothesis, disclosing its hidden assumptions and thus clarifying circumstances under which the hypothesis is true and those under which it is false" (McGuire, 1983, p. 7).

The whole idea of articulating levels of analysis is based on the assumption

> that an adequate understanding of either a phenomenon or a theory requires that it be investigated through a program of research planned to reveal the wide range of circumstances that affect the phenomenon and the rich set of implicit assumptions that limit the theory, thus making explicit the contexts in which one or another relationship obtains. (McGuire, 1983, p. 22)

Implicit assumptions of researchers become hypotheses or theoretical conjectures when they are explicitly invoked to explain modifications of psychological processes or when they are used to describe more exhaustively the manifold conditions under which processes under investigation will hold. One of my "guiding idea theories" (to use McGuire's terminology) is that such implicit assumptions often bear on societal dynamics and involve ideas on symbolic relationships between social actors and groups. They may activate conceptions about social justice, individual responsibility, cultural differences, value priorities, and beliefs about the nature of social conflict.

When analyzing "Social Institutions as Attitude Determinants," McGuire had the following to say:

> Institutions may affect attitudes, not only by their explicit persuasive communications, but also by their structures' determining the stimulus situations to which the person is exposed, the response options made available, the level and type of motivation aroused, and the schedules of reinforcements administered. (1999, p. 103)

He illustrated such effects as they are produced in a half-dozen varied types of institutions: family, peer groups, ideological schooling, legislation, mass media, art and rituals, and total institutions.

One could consider, as the French sociologist Bourdieu (1979) does, that all these institutions are very powerful and efficient in shaping individual dispositions or "habitus." Societal positioning, the specific insertion of an individual in social and symbolic relationships characteristic of a society, also has influence, often mediated by the institutions analyzed by McGuire. Important objects of study for societal psychologists should be the degrees of congruence and antagonism between the influences of these different institutions in the realm of societal issues.

In order to become more specific and before returning to other aspects of McGuire's writings, I first illustrate how societal approaches have been developed in social representation theory and in social identity theory. Whereas the first example shows the historical continuity of a societal approach, the second teaches us how such an approach is sometimes difficult to sustain. Thereafter, I briefly present some other examples of the relevance of societal analyses for a better understanding of social psychological processes.

## Social Representation Theory

I will not develop here various aspects of social representation theory as I have already done on too many occasions. On this occasion, I choose to stress one challenge that must be met in order to fulfill the conditions for a further development of the theory: the challenge of disciplinary pluralism or, to use Moscovici's words, of

> creating a science capable of linking and stitching together its components hitherto scattered among social sciences. I have in mind the psychology of economics, the psychology of politics, mass psychology, ethnomethodology, as well as interactionist symbolism. . . . Not to be omitted are certain aspects of the psychology of language . . . and child psychology, both of which are closely related to social psychology. (Moscovici, 1989, p. 409)

Are not many of these different areas thoroughly explored by McGuire? In this aspect as well, he is outstanding, as he often explores fields of study associated with other disciplines.

In my view, social psychology is not to be considered just a branch of psychology, and here I quote Moscovici (1989, p. 409) again, who noted that the first to have defined its objectives were sociologists such as Durkheim, Simmel, and Tönnies, and, perhaps even more important, ". . . the psychologists who were its founders—take Wundt, Tarde, Freud, McDougall, Baldwin, Mead, Lewin—thought of it as a means of establishing continuity with the other sciences, notably anthropology."

Social psychology, when becoming a subsidiary branch of psychology, moves away from social analyses. Therefore, social psychology is no longer thought of as a "bridge toward other branches of knowledge" (Moscovici, 1989, p. 409), and hence the necessity of reinventing links with other social sciences. Social psychology, using its own methods, should evolve into an anthropology of modern culture and society. In other words, it should become once again a societal psychology.

This has important methodological consequences for practitioners of societal psychology. According to issues under study, they should borrow cognition harvested by colleagues from sociology, political science, history, anthropology, economics, and eventually still other disciplines. Such a condition is necessary for building bridges with other disciplines and for producing knowledge of more general relevance: "Extrapolation is justified as long as exchanges are maintained with other disciplines which raise the same questions, provide a set of data and give some theoretical guidelines" (Moscovici, 1989, p. 411). I want to emphasize this quotation from the initiator of social representation theory. It is a strong claim in favor of interdisciplinary collaboration, to be practiced by social psychologists interested in constructing societal psychology generally and social representation theory more specifically.

## Social Identity Theory

What an exciting story indeed is the one of social identity theory. It originated in a "Gestaltist" conception of a theory on accentuation of contrasts in perception, leading Tajfel (1959) to reorganize a whole set of research on quantitative judgments and to formulate a model on the effects of categorization in perception (Tajfel & Wilkes, 1963) and in intergroup stereotypes (Tajfel, Sheikh, & Gardner, 1964).

Thereafter, a study by Tajfel and colleagues on the minimal conditions for producing intergroup discrimination (Tajfel, Billig, Bundy & Flament, 1971) became an important landmark in intergroup relations research. I would not feel it necessary to add some new paragraphs to the abundant literature on social identity in intergroup relations were it not for the fact that in most of these writings, an important aspect of Tajfel's theorizing has been neglected: the societal analysis.

In a first presentation of the results of the now famous Klee/Kandinsky experiment, the societal explanation can be considered minimalist.

> It will be clear that we interpret our results in terms of a "generic" norm which guided the Ss' choices. This was so because they classified the social situation in which they found themselves as one to which this norm was pertinent, in which categorization *ought* to lead to discriminatory intergroup behaviour rather than to behaviour in terms of alternatives that were offered to them. (Tajfel et al., 1971, p. 174)

However, Tajfel (1972) soon developed a theory on the search for positive social identity in intergroup comparison settings. In more theoretical articles (Tajfel, 1974, 1975), he established a link between these social identity processes and the ideology of social change adopted by groups that could not improve their fate without recourse to collective action to change established relationships between groups. He distinguished between a condition of intergroup relations in which there is the possibility of individual social mobility and intergroup relations in which such mobility is not possible and only collective change can improve the fate of group members:

> One of the important determinants of an individual's choice to act in terms of self rather than in terms of his group is what we shall refer to in this discussion as "social mobility" as contrasted with "social change." The former refers to situations in which it is relatively easy to move individually from one social group to another; so that if a group does not contribute adequately to an individual's social identity, one of the more obvious solutions for him is to move, or attempt to move, to another group. In the latter class are those situations in which, for whatever reasons, passing from one group to another is very difficult or impossible. It may be expected that, in these situations, there will be many occasions (and constraints) leading an individual to act as a member of his group, or at least in the knowledge that he is categorized as such. Social change (as distinct from social mobility) refers therefore in this discussion to changes in the relationships between the groups as a whole, to expectations, fears or desires of such changes, to actions aiming at inducing or preventing them, or to intentions and plans to engage in these actions (Tajfel, 1974, p. 78).

Of even greater importance for a putative societal psychology is the fact that this distinction is explicitly associated with different ideological systems as described by the economist Hirschman (see Tajfel, 1975, p.107).

Such analyses clearly are societal, and the paradox is that they are invoked to explain the behavior of pupils in a comprehensive school in the Bristol area who filled in strange matrices in a rather bizarre setting. Tajfel's explanation, however, is relevant if one considers with him that these pupils participated in a situation in which access to a positive social identity was only possible by changing the relative status of their temporary membership group.

I am sure that a systematic study of the social identity literature would show that conjectures in terms of social change and individual mobility have almost completely disappeared from the social identity literature. One could ask why this is the case and if there is not a kind of fatality inherent in the experimental method, which tends to eliminate from the researchers' analyses all that is not directly produced and controlled in the experimental setting. If researchers are to practice societal psychology, explanatory theories must take into account variables that exist prior to the experimental situation, such as power relations, relative dominance of social categories, and ideological preconceptions. Experimental social psychologists often are not interested in analyzing the societal dynamics in which their paradigms are embedded.

Nevertheless, I should mention a minority of authors on intergroup relations who have referred to these societal ideas of Tajfel. These ideas were, for instance, further elaborated by Ellemers (1993), Guimond and Tougas (1994), Jost, Burgess, and Mosso (2001), and Taylor and Moghaddam (1987). However, such exceptions do not prevent social identity theory from being now often assimilated to Turner's (1987) self-categorization theory, which no longer makes reference to societal hypotheses.

In a review of studies on the intertwining of regional, national, and European identities using self-categorization theory (Doise & Devos, 1999), I showed that this theory is incapable of explaining the observed patterns of identification without referring to the general ideas held by respondents concerning relationships among regional, national, and European entities supposed to foster or impede realization of important economic and political goals. In other words, in order to investigate social identity hypotheses in this setting, one should also elaborate hypotheses in relation to the views individuals have developed on the intra- and intersociety relationships in which they are involved. Simply put, one should introduce societal perspectives in the explanation of identification processes.

## Other Examples

Popular wisdom is, of course, correct in stating that the proof of the pudding is in the eating but not in overeating. To not overfeed you, I will present in a much shorter way more examples of societal analyses practiced by social psychologists. What they have in common is that I was able to directly observe their coming into being.

In the fall of 1967, I had the chance to observe in life an instance of creative perspectivism before the term was christened by McGuire. I was working on a bibliography of social influence studies and shared with other junior researchers the space of a painter's atelier transformed into an office next door to Moscovici's office. Moscovici suddenly entered the room with a question: "Are the experiments by Asch really to be considered experiments on majority influence?" Of course, he had his own answer that he wanted to test:

> They are not experiments on majority influence, because what Asch considers to be a majority of three stooges giving a wrong answer unanimously compared to the "naive" subject is in fact a minority compared to the immense majority of people who would give the same answer as the subject.

Indeed, if one looks at the Asch situation of pressure to conformity outside its societal context, one could suppose that his experiments deal with majority pressure, but the responses of the numerical majority in the experiment are very strongly those of a deviant minority, when looked at in a broader context. Thereafter, Moscovici (1976) studied in a series of experiments the specific effects of influence attempts that ran counter to the dominant norms in a given society. Mugny (1981) looked more specifically at the influence exercised by a minority when faced with "populations" that subscribed to themes characteristic of the dominant ideology.

A more recent conundrum in social psychology pertains to recurrent failures in confirming the hypothesis that people ascribe more homogeneity to outgroups than to ingroups. According to Lorenzi-Cioldi (1998), a systematic trend of ascribing more heterogeneity to high-status groups than to low-status groups can account for many of these exceptions to the general trend, hence his general assumption that

> a group's social status accounts for the tendencies of the group members to perceive themselves, and to be perceived by outgroup members, as interchangeable exemplars of the group or as persons endowed with unique attributes. High-status or dominant groups tend to promote the heterogeneity of their members. . . . Conversely, low-status or subordinate groups tend to conceal interpersonal variation and promote the group members' depersonalization and interchangeability (pp. 32–33)

He reported several experiments demonstrating that membership in high-status versus low-status groups moderates perceptions of ingroup homogeneity in the predicted sense. Of special interest is his historical study (Lorenzi-Cioldi, 1996) on the evolution of paradigms used by psychologists to analyze sex-typed attributes and their ascription across the borders of gender groups. Clearly, societal changes have accompanied and even oriented the evolution of scientific approaches. At one time, the display (by the same person) of both sex-typed attributes was considered a symptom of psychological maladjustment, but in contemporary society, an individual manifesting attributes characteristic of both genders is often considered psychologically better adapted than a typical feminine or masculine person.

Important societal issues revolve around gender relations. In contemporary Western societies, equality has become a societal norm supposed to regulate these relationships inside as well as outside the family. However, gender inequality and status differences subsist even among partners in a family. Even when they are employed full-time out of the home, relatively more women than men have to assume a larger share of domestic chores. Women readily acknowledge and even denounce this inequality at a general level: They admit that women are often discriminated against at home as well as in professional settings. When asked about their individual fate, however, they do not feel personally discriminated against. Roux (1999) reported evidence concerning these differences, and her interpretation is this: While well aware of the general societal norm of equality, women still feel that they are more responsible for maintaining good relationships, especially at home. This awareness leads them to underestimate the gender discrimination they experience in personal settings, because it would not be acceptable to try to maintain good relationships with a partner who is discriminating against them forcefully. Evaluations of personal relationships are to be studied in the frame of normative conflict at the societal level.

Jean-Léon Beauvois (1994), in his treatise on "Liberal serfdom," and Nicole Dubois (1994), in her studies on internality, reinterpret in a societal framework the internality norm analyzed by different authors in the wake of Rotter's (1966) famous studies on internalism and externalism. Modern society rests on the idea of free and autonomous persons, and the experiments by Beauvois and Dubois, two colleagues, are based on the assumption that important institutions continuously reaffirm the internality norm in evaluating individuals. Evaluations of these kinds extend across societal borders, because they underlie discriminatory judgments of third world and nondemocratic countries (Staerklé, Clémence, & Doise, 1998). Symbolic relations in which individual judgments are embedded span the world; however, they are easily inflected by ethnocentric uses of normalized societal concepts such as democracy or human rights (see Moghaddam & Vuksanovic, 1990).

Nevertheless, the vision of human rights as such is a powerful social reality. Accordingly, human rights were studied as normative social representations by myself and a group of colleagues (see Doise, 2001). Our general assumption was that human rights representations were generated historically in specific settings of relationships of interdependence that interlink human beings all over the world.

More specifically, three hypotheses were investigated. The first hypothesis concerned the existence of a common meaning system about human rights that is shared to some extent by respondents of different national and cultural origins. A second hypothesis dealt with individual positioning. The existence of a common frame of reference does not imply consensual attitudes, and therefore systematic variations of individual positioning should be analyzed. Organizing principles of these variations in positioning are related, first to the relative importance attributed to individual rights versus social, economic, and political rights, and second to the beliefs in the efficacy of individuals and institutions to have these rights respected. A third hypothesis concerned the anchoring of individual differences in value choices and in experiences of social injustice and intergroup conflicts. An overall view of results confirming these hypotheses has been presented (Doise, 1998, 2002).

## A Decisive Contribution by William McGuire

Bill McGuire was one of the few American social psychologists with whom I had the opportunity to develop a working relationship. It was during a joint teaching experience at a Summer School run by the EAESP in Bologna, Italy, from August 17 to September 6, 1986. As stated in the prologue, I was at that time already interested in his contextualist and perspectivist approach, and for this reason, I asked the Committee of the European Association, chaired during this period by Geoffrey Stephenson, to invite McGuire as a member of the staff. McGuire and I were together in charge of organizing a series of seminars in common.

While I was reading his book *Constructing Social Psychology*, his remarks (1999, p. 335) on the so-called European social psychology revived in my memory an event that occurred during one of our joint seminars. To get to the significance of this episode, let me first remind you that in the pages of this book, originally published in the *European Journal of Social Psychology*, he basically described the "cause" of European social psychology as a cultural reaction to, if not a cultural revolution against, American colleagues who promoted social psychology in Europe:

> Predictably, by the late 1960s the most favored European social psychologists who had at first welcomed the missionaries (or at least the gifts they bore) became embarrassed by their acceptance of this cultural colonization and disenchanted with the obsolescent models that had been foisted upon them. A number of European social psychologists of that generation endeavored in the 1965 to 1985 period to promote a more distinctively European social psychology, forged out of everything from a Marxist–Leninist historical materialism to a Durkheimian collective representational idealism (Israel & Tajfel, 1972). This nationalistic reaction is understandable. . . . (McGuire, 1999, p. 331)

Of course, I feel myself concerned, having been a member of the executive committee of the European Association from 1975 to 1981, the period during which, according to Bill, the nationalistic reaction was still raging. I come now with some feeling of embarrassment to the event revived in my memory. It had to do with social representation theory and with World War II.

During our joint seminars, I was assigned to present social representation theory, which I introduced as a "typical European theory." Bill was not at all happy with this expression and told me something like, "Scientific theories are universal and not national, and for defending this universalistic idea I drove a tank from Sicily to Germany at the end of World War II." I quote from memory, as I did not write this down nor tape it at the time. Let me say, first of all, that since that day I have never used the term "European theory" again, although I still may use the expression "theory of European origin," just to be, if I may say so, contextualist in presenting the theory. Basically, I remain convinced, as I already was before (see Doise, 1986a) that it is not a heuristically useful idea to oppose European and American social psychology.

Extolling such an antagonism could well lead to the deadlocks that McGuire described in the same paper in rather vivid terms. Personally, I tried to follow the recommendation he addressed to his European colleagues: "Rather than jousting against abandoned windmills they might better devote their talents to the third, structuralist, attitudinal flourishing in the 1980s and 1990s as it struggles to describe knowledge constructions of experienced life" (Doise, 1986a, p. 332).

I doubt that Bill considers, as I do, social representation theory as belonging to this third generation of attitudes theory. However, I agree with his idea that scholars whose main interest is choosing antagonists in order to construct their own identity can easily become trapped in sterile fights. On the other hand, systematically complying with dominant trends may lead to the same dead end. Within that framework, Bill's lessons on creativity and perspectivism and, more generally, the whole of his intellectual endeavors are invaluable, because they endow us with practical devices for avoiding overcompliance as well as overantagonism in our thinking.

## Conclusion

Let me quote Bill once more:

> There is a witticism that psychologists have made two great discoveries, that all people are basically the same and that everyone is fundamentally different. It was exhibited in these early years by the simultaneous popularity of the Wundtian *Völkerpsychologie* and Durkheimian *représentations collectives* notions on the Continent, while the Spearman, Bogardus, and Thurstone individual-differences scaling work flourished in the Anglo-American offshore provinces. The two efforts are supplementary in that collective representations focus on within-group homogeneity and among-group contrasts, whereas individual-difference attitudinalists focus on variability both within and among groups. (McGuire, 1999, pp. 326–327)

Some social psychologists have paid a high price for not seriously considering the articulation of the two approaches, for not integrating analyses of individual variation and collective homogeneity. One social psychologist who made this error is Paolo Orano. On the continent, if not in the world, he was probably the first to have published a book, *Psicologia Sociale*, with the sole name of our discipline as the title (Orano, 1902). For him, society was clearly more important than the individual. He became cofounder, with Mussolini, of the Italian Fascist Party, and he inspired Mussolini's politics in relation to the church, education, and the Jews (see Doise, 1986b).

History has shown that Orano's ideas were at the root of the ideological themes that were going to dominate Italian political life for many years. For better or for worse, the lesson to draw is that a collectivistic and nationalistic conception of mankind, described by Orano as a sociopsychological conception, can successfully orient politics for many years. Unfortunately, this type of large-scale field experiment has been repeated only too often at prohibitively high costs. As a researcher, I doubt that the general ideas developed in Orano's social psychology will be very useful in solving the problem of how to construct a societal psychology that satisfactorily integrates a social and an individual approach. These general ideas drew attention to one part of the explanandum but offered no detailed analysis of how individual psychology both produces and is produced by collective dynamics.

When Bill McGuire started his first journey through Europe, Paolo Orano was probably still alive. He had been promoted as Rector of the University of

Perugia, and at the end of World War II, he died in an American prisoner-of-war camp. It was a regime based on ideas of this Italian scholar that the American soldier named William J. McGuire had to fight.

Years later, McGuire's studies on the history of attitude research convinced me that it is always necessary in studying social representations to introduce a phase of analyzing differences in individual positioning, as well as their anchoring in relevant views on social and societal reality. As is probably understood by now, there are important reasons of a societal psychological nature that led me to organize this chapter in honor of Bill McGuire around the idea of societal psychology.

# References

Baldwin, J. M. (1913). *History of psychology. From John Locke to the present time* (Vol. 2). London: Watts.

Beauvois, J.-L. (1994). *Traité de la servitude libérale* [A treaty of liberal serfdom]. Paris: Dunod.

Bourdieu, P. (1979). *La distinction* [The distinction]. Paris: Minuit.

Cattaneo, C. (1864). Dell'antitesi come metodo di psicologia sociale [On antithesis as a method in social psychology]. *Il Politecnico, 20,* 262–270.

Doise, W. (1986a). *Levels of explanation in social psychology.* Cambridge: Cambridge University Press.

Doise, W. (1986b). Mass psychology, social psychology and the politics of Mussolini. In C. F. Graumann & S. Moscovici (Eds.), *Changing conceptions of crowd mind and behaviour* (pp. 69–82). New York: Springer-Verlag.

Doise, W. (1998). Social psychology and human rights. *European Review, 6,* 341–347.

Doise, W. (2001). Human rights studied as normative social representations. In K. Deaux & G. Philogene (Eds.), *Social representations: Introductions and explorations* (pp. 96–112). Oxford: Blackwell.

Doise, W. (2002). *Human rights as social representations.* London: Routledge.

Doise, W., Clémence, A., & Lorenzi-Cioldi, F. (1993). *The quantitative analysis of social representations.* London: Harvester Wheatsheaf.

Doise, W., & Devos, T. (1999). Identité et interdépendance: Pour une psychologie sociale de l'Union Européenne [Identity and interdependence: Toward a social psychology of the European Union]. *Psychologie et Société, 1,* 11–27.

Dubois, N. (1994). *La norme d'internalité et le libéralisme* [The norm of internalism and liberalism]. Grenoble: Presses Universitaires de Grenoble.

Ellemers, N. (1993). The influence of socio-structural variables on identity management strategies. In W. Stroebe & M. Hewstone (Eds.), *European Review of Social Psychology* (Vol. 4, pp. 27–57). Chichester: Wiley & Sons.

Guimond, S., & Tougas, F. (1994). Sentiments d'injustice et actions collectives: La privation relative [Feelings of injustice and collective action: On relative deprivation]. In R. Y. Bourhis & J. P. Leyens (Eds.), *Stéréotypes, discrimination et relations intergroupes.* [Stereotypes, discrimination, and intergroup relations]. Liège, France: Mardaga.

Himmelweit, H., & Gaskell, G. (1990). *Societal psychology.* London: Sage.

Israel, J., & Tajfel, H. (1972). *The context of social psychology: A critical assessment.* London: Academic Press.

Jost, J. T., Burgess, D., & Mosso, C. (2001). Conflicts of legitimation among self, group, and system: The integrative potential of system justification theory. In J. T. Jost & B. Major (Eds.), *The psychology of legitimacy: Emerging perspectives on ideology, justice, and intergroup relations* (pp. 363–388). New York: Cambridge University Press.

Lorenzi-Cioldi, F. (1996). Psychological androgyny: A concept in search of lesser substance. Towards the understanding of the transformation of a social representation. *Journal for the Theory of Social Behaviour, 26,* 1–19.

Lorenzi-Cioldi, F. (1998). Group status and perceptions of homogeneity. In W. Stroebe & M. Hewstone (Eds.), *European Review of Social Psychology* (Vol. 9, pp. 31–75). Chichester: Wiley & Sons.

McGuire, W. J. (1983). A contextualist theory of knowledge: Its implications for innovation and reform in psychological research. *Advances in Experimental Social Psychology, 16,* 1–47.

McGuire, W. J. (1999). *Constructing social psychology. Creative and critical processes.* Cambridge: Cambridge University Press.

Mead, G. H. (1934). *Mind, self and society.* Chicago: University of Chicago Press.

Moghaddam, F., & Vuksanovic, V. (1990). Attitudes and behavior towards human rights across different contexts: The role of right-wing authoritarianism, political ideology and religiosity. *International Journal of Psychology, 25,* 455–474.

Moscovici, S. (1976). *Social influence and social change.* London: Academic Press.

Moscovici, S. (1989). Preconditions for explanations in social psychology. *European Journal of Social Psychology, 19,* 407–430.

Mugny, G. (1981). *El poder de la minorias* [The power of minorities]. Barcelona: Rol.

Orano, P. (1902). *Psicologia sociale* [Social psychology]. Bari, Italy: Gius. Laterza & Figli.

Piaget, J. (1932). *The moral judgment of the child.* New York: The Free Press.

Rotter, J. B. (1966). Generalized expectancies for internal versus external control of reinforcement. *Psychological Monographs: General and Applied,* No 80. Washington DC: American Psychological Association.

Roux, P. (1999). *Couple et égalité: Un ménage impossible* [Couples and equality: Impossible marriages]. Lausanne, Switzerland: Réalités Sociales.

Staerklé, C., Clémence, A., & Doise, W. (1998). Representation of human rights across different national contexts: The role of democratic and non-democratic populations and governments. *European Journal of Social Psychology, 28,* 207–226.

Tajfel, H. (1959). Quantitative judgement in social perception. *British Journal of Psychology, 50,* 16–29.

Tajfel, H. (1972). La catégorisation sociale [Social categorization]. In S. Moscovici (Ed.), *Introduction à la psychologie sociale* [Introduction to social psychology; pp. 272–302]. Paris: Larousse.

Tajfel, H. (1974). Social identity and intergroup behaviour. *Social Science Information, 13,* 65–93.

Tajfel, H. (1975). The exit of social mobility and the voice of social change. *Social Science Information, 14,* 101–118.

Tajfel, H., Billig, M., Bundy, R. P., & Flament, C. (1971). Social categorisation and intergroup behaviour. *European Journal of Social Psychology, 1,* 149–178.

Tajfel, H., Sheikh, A. A., & Gardner, R. C. (1964). Content of stereotypes and the inference of similarity between members of stereotyped groups. *Acta Psychologica, 22,* 191–201.

Tajfel, H., & Wilkes, A. L. (1963). Classification and quantitative judgment. *British Journal of Psychology, 54,* 101–114.

Taylor, D. M., & Moghaddam, F. M. (1987). *Theories of intergroup relations: International social psychological perspectives.* New York: Praeger.

Turner, J. C. (1987). *Rediscovering the social group: A self-categorization theory.* Oxford: Basil Blackwell.

Vygotsky, L. S. (1962). *Thought and language.* Cambridge, MA: MIT Press.

# 14

# Social Stereotypes and "Implicit Social Theory"

## György Hunyady

### Prologue

It is a naked fact that the Hungarian world of science did not play a pioneering role in the development and formation of social psychology, but in the prehistory of social psychology, ideas of nation characterology did appear in Hungary as well. After World War II, the lucid-minded and effective writer Ferenc Mérei transmitted the intellectual stimuli of Lewin and Moreno to us, but only to the extent that his political exclusion and imprisonment allowed it. Hungarian psychology was paralyzed in the aftermath of the war, and almost two decades passed before new signs of life began to appear and grow in the borderland of psychology and sociology. It is relevant to the nation's bitter history, however, that beginning in the late 1960s, the science policy of the state party supported—with its limited and restrictive methods—social psychological research and application. In this period of recovery, William McGuire was a key figure in this field of science, as anybody familiar with the authoritative American social psychology could see. His undertaking and message provided the first definitive impression—or imprinting, as we say in the specific language of psychology—for many of us.

I visited Bill McGuire at Yale University as the first station of my first visit to the United States—as part of an exchange program between the Hungarian Academy of Sciences and the National Academy of Science—in 1981. I was led by intellectual eagerness, and, as a representative of rising Eastern European societies, I felt entitled to take up his time. Since that time, I have been able to follow and get to know his work more thoroughly. I was conducting research in the area of the organization and change of stereotypes, which was neither very distant from his field nor identical with it. There was no important theoretical starting point or successful methodological solution in which I did not feel that he had been there before me. This includes the systematic organization of beliefs and the functional explanation of cognitive stability and change, as well as the peculiar role of negation in judgment and evaluation, the advantages of noninvasive research methods, and the recognized importance of grasping non-linear relationships among measured variables. The list of examples could continue. Nothing characterizes our intellectual relationship better than an anecdotal event: When historical changes took place in Hungary and the multiparty system was initiated, it seemed justified for me to move from the more theoretical questions of social psychology to the recently unfolding applied field of political psychology. My report to Bill was soon followed by his letter: He found this change in the direction of my interest to be a good idea, and at the same time he was sending me a book on this topic that he and Shanto Iyengar had edited that had just been published and that included his excellent historical summary of the field of political psychology.

One of the most recent self-avowals made by Professor McGuire, "Doing Psychology My Way," was published in a volume edited by R. J. Sternberg in 2002. Here he reported that it is worth breaking with research styles, topics, and the one-sidedness of methodological fashions, and he encouraged us to do so. In this way, he also demonstrated that he is not the kind of master who seeks and educates followers; rather he wishes to tune us to originality through the example of originality. I myself, however, have not been able to set out on a course in social psychology and its adjoining territories that he had not already hunted down with considerable success. Thus, it is not easy to take his appealing advice and to chart an original course in cognitive social psychology that differs from his, for he is a living, active, and impressive classic in the field.

In the spirit of this idea and in order to make it more pronounced, his summary work was published in Hungary in the series "Classics in Social Psychology" under my editorship. This edition is based on the summary volume that he himself compiled and that was published by Cambridge University Press. This is the most authentic source, because Bill McGuire does not let contemporary admirers and the succeeding generations freely ravage the interpretation of his works but does this himself for them with light courtesy. The Hungarian title of the book, *The Unyielding Beliefs and the Dynamics of Persuasion,* is an attempt to give an idea of the novelty that the author has brought to the eternal social psychological topic of attitude: the study of the resistance of beliefs on one hand and the subtle analysis of attitude-forming persuasion on the other. However, the reader can learn much more than that from such an exceptional mentality and a fertile style of research.

\* \* \*

Implicit social theory is not a customary concept. An Eastern European social psychologist is not a customary figure. The joint appearance of the two may become—in accordance with David Hamilton's illusory correlation paradigm that is so well known and thoroughly studied in stereotype research—the accidental starting point of stereotype formation about the tendency of Eastern European scientists to generate unclear concepts. To prevent this unfounded overgeneralization, I'd like to win Walter Lippmann over to my side right from the introduction of the concept. He is to be thanked for the elaborated concept of stereotype, and he himself can be considered as the prototypical exemplar of the autonomous American thinker. In his classic work, he gave the following example about the stereotypical thinking of Clemenceau, the great French statesman who dictated peace after World War I:

> He saw the (German) type, and among the reports that came to him from Germany, he took to heart those reports, and, it seems, those only, which fitted the type that was in his mind. If a junker blustered, that was an

authentic German, if a labor leader confessed the guilt of the empire, he was not an authentic German. (Lippmann, 1922, p. 55)

Lippmann illustrated the working and genesis of national stereotypes with examples of momentous consequences in world history. Thus, two social types are concealed in the background. It is the perceived system of relationships of national and social categories that are expressed in national characterization—and it is this system of the relationships I called "implicit social theory" in the title.

In this summary of related ideas, I present three basic assumptions, three selected research topics, and three concluding remarks.

## 1. Assumption: Stereotypes May Have More Than One Useful Function

Stereotype research has been a triumphant field of social psychology since the early 1980s: Radical changes have taken place, new paradigms have gained ground, and new conceptual constructions have been created (Hunyady, Hamilton, & Nguyen Luu, 1999). One of the main outcomes of research is the convincing evidence that *stereotypes* linked to social categories have a *function* in *person perception* (Fiske & Pavelchak, 1986; Brewer, 1988). These stereotypes include general assumptions, knowledge, and expectations we apply to a person identified as a member of a category. This is done when we have insufficient motivation to build an individualized image of the person or if we do have the motivation but lack sufficient intellectual capacity to do so. This practical function of stereotypes explains and justifies their existence and also takes the edge off the pejorative connotation of the expression—and we have not even mentioned the standpoint of the self-categorization theory (Oakes, Haslam, & Turner, 1994; Turner, 1987), according to which knowledge that is fixed in stereotypes definitely provides some information in addition to that momentarily available in the process of person perception. Some people can see that stereotypes do have a function as a part of self-image, and many believe that the maintenance of stereotypes stems from their normative role in intergroup relationships.

Nevertheless, the functional approach of stereotypes that exists at this point does not take into account the fact that the categories of persons and the related *stereotypes do not stand on their own* but rather are components of some kind of a system. To put it more metaphorically, stereotypes are the mosaic pieces of a picture formed of the whole society. One not only gets to know his individual companions or groups of his companions but also *tries to get a comprehensive view of the entire human world and of society*, in which he and his fellows have a place and a more or less stable environment. In his classic work in which he introduced the concept of stereotype, Lippmann (1922) implied the importance of developing expectations associated with familiarity and intimacy. Stereotypes create the basis of orienting oneself in society, in space and time filled by society and endowed with meaning, and thus they decrease the feeling of loss arising from unpredictability and contribute to self-awareness rooted in certainty.

## 2. Assumption: Stereotypes Hide Category Comparisons

Categories are meaningful not in themselves but only relative to each other. Let us take the cases of the most simple, basic, and inherently dichotomous categorizations. If we as social perceivers want to formulate or indicate on a scale what characterizes women, we will—implicitly or explicitly—contrast them with men. We *do not simply* draw an inference on the basis of the *common features found* in females *but rather we identify and sharpen* those *variances* that distinguish them from men in general.

Standard social psychological literature deals with the interdependence and comparative and relative nature of categories and stereotypes almost exclusively within the context of the distinction between *ingroup* and *outgroup*. In this respect, the literature contains important conclusions regarding both the evaluative charge of perception and the variability of perception of groups. However, the fact that outgroups do not merge into each other at all but show a differentiated image (Hagendoorn, 1995) is rarely considered. No matter what the source is, we see differences among groups that are alien to us; these differences can be bad, good, or even exemplary by the standards of the ingroup.

## 3. Assumption: There Is a Categorization of Categories Hidden in the System of Stereotypes

If we accept as a starting point that there are comparisons hidden behind the stereotyped characterization of categories, the next question is which category should be compared with which. It should not be overlooked that groups of categories such as gender, age, occupation, and nationality are evidently differentiated. It can be assumed that relevant comparisons across categories are made mostly within fields. Intuitively, in this way we can reach the hypothesis about implicit and explicit categorization of categories. For example, the concept of nation covers a multitude of groups. It is used by people and with competence. When asked to define it, even less-educated people can name state-forming ethnic groups they consider a typical nation. For a long time, the prototype of *nation* used to be the French, but later, among European intellectuals, people were inclined to differentiate and consider the so-called cultural nation—taking the Germans as a model—in addition to the so-called political nation.

Although social psychology so far has not dealt directly and specifically with the categorization of categories, it gets very close to this when the concept of cognitive domain is introduced and applied. The concept of cognitive domain is linked to the research on cognitive complexity. William Scott and colleagues (1979) played an important role in this when they extended the description and measurement of cognitive structures to national categories in addition to person perception.

Distinguishing the cognitive domains makes it meaningful to ask what the relationship is among various domains. Naturally, the expression "interrelationship of domains" could mean a lot of things. To mention two extremes, on one hand, it could mean a preference announced as the profession of a world-view ("The national belonging of myself and others is more important to me than the social status of myself and others"); on the other hand, it could also mean the relative role of the categories that represent the different domains in the actual process of cognition and judgment formation. The series of studies by Eagly and colleagues (Eagly & Kite, 1987; Eagly & Steffen, 1984; Eagly & Wood, 1982) presented a rare and valuable example of this; they devoted their study to gender categorization so as to find its basis and derive its consequences in other cognitive areas. Focusing on the perceived characteristics of women, they traced them back to household occupational categories. They used the method of cross categorization, which—by its provocative nature—offers a particularly good opportunity to study these complex questions. The most striking results of this method were achieved when the categories of gender and nation were combined and it could be demonstrated that the category of gender left its mark on the characterization of women and the category of national group left its mark on the characterization of men. Eagly and colleagues thus revealed a segment of implicit social theory.

Having given these assumptions, let me turn to my own research (Hunyady 1998a, 1998b). My research conducted in the past three decades lies somewhere between Scott's and Eagly's approaches, that is, between the conceptual frame of the cognitive domain and the analysis of between-category content relations trying to bridge the gap between them.

I feel uneasy to admit in the Festschrift for Bill McGuire that I have conducted a large number of studies in which the respondents had to judge persons and categories on closed scales in prestructured trait dimensions. Without doubt, this belongs to a dark period in my past (even if I attempted to compensate by using noninvasive methods later). Picking an MDS map from 1991 (see Figure 14.1), I would only like to give a visual impression that the categories representing various cognitive domains differ strikingly from one another and from the characterization of concrete persons. This is true even if negative evaluation detaches the objects of criticism from their circles and mixes them up. Behind this, one can find well-documented differences among cognitive domains: (a) The level and polarization of evaluation are distinct, (b) the role and relationships of trait judgments are different, and (c) the cognitive complexity of the individual characterizations of the whole domain is varied. The studied cognitive domains that are present in the thinking of individuals, groups, and the public represent *distinct units* with their own aspects.

I omit everything else and mention only three research topics relevant to the *interrelations* of the different category domains.

## 1. Research Topic: The Mental World Map of Continents

When asked to indicate European countries, the majority of Hungarian respondents marked Germany (75%) and France (60%), half indicated Hungary as a typical European country, and only then came Great Britain,

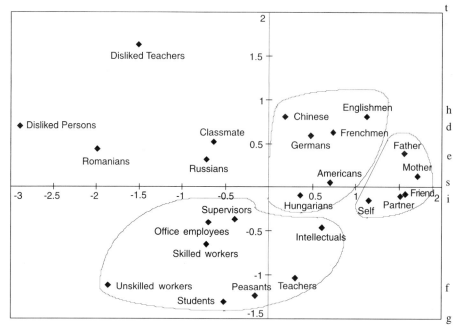

**Figure 14.1.** MDS map of all characterized objects, 1991. Key: d = diligent, e = educated, f = friendly, g = good humored, h = honest, i = intelligent, s = self-assertive, t = patriotic.

with nearly 50%. The evaluation and ranking of countries and nations do not always match each other in every respect, but in the evaluation of being European, they do.

So, what are "Europeans" like—as the mental anchor of these comparisons? I found that regardless of the method of characterization used—fixed or free—a typical trait profile emerges (see Figure 14.2). In 1991 and 2000, students and a sample of respondents representing the adult population of Hungary described Europeans very similarly: Intellectual values, erudition, feeling of self-worth, and the ambitious safeguarding of one's interests are the strong positive sides of the characterization, and moral values and emotional and social openness are relatively less prominent. Thus there exists a European stereotype, just as there are stereotyped characterizations of other continental and subcontinental (e.g., the Balkan) categories. It is understandable why the continental categories fit well into the value hierarchy of national categories or into the MDS map reflecting the relationships of nation characterizations (see Figure 14.3). The figure, based on the data received in 1994, shows that on one hand, the "Balkan people," the "Asians," and the "Europeans" are systematically differentiated in the multidimensional characterizations, and on the other hand, the descriptions of the continental categories are usually relatively close to the characterization of the national groups that live there. I received additional support for the fact that people see an overlap between geographical categorization and national characterization; these results seem interesting and need further interpretation.

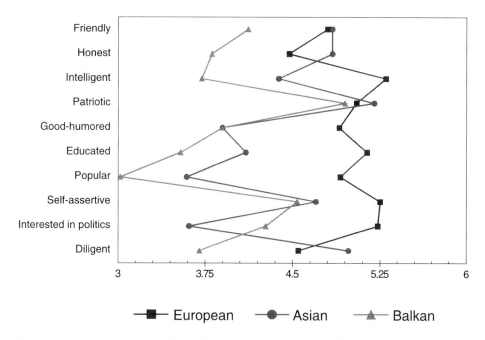

**Figure 14.2.**   Characterization of the continental types, 1991.

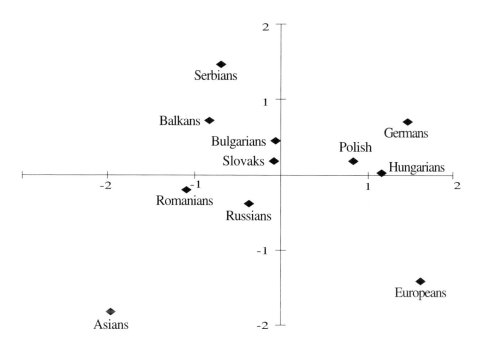

**Figure 14.3.**   Common MDS map of the nations of the region and continental types, 1994.

## 2. Research Topic: The Human and Social Meaning of the Points of the Compass

International literature on stereotypes has already dealt with the psychological significance of the points of compass, but no attention has been given to a different dimension, in the literal sense, from what we found to be relevant in Hungary. The North–South divide has a rich and systematic documentation (Pennebaker, Rimé, & Blakenship, 1996). Even within larger countries, people in the North are seen as being more reserved and self-controlled than the more passionate and unrestrained Southerners are (Peabody, 1985). The interpretation of this finding can be traced back to Montesquieu's notion of the relationship between climate and temperament.

Samples of people from the Hungarian population, however, perceived greater and more distinct differences between East and West than between North and South. The difference is not manifested in the judgments regarding temperament but in contrasting Eastern sociability, sense of community, and work ethic with Western erudition, intellect, and self-assertiveness. The duality of Asia and Europe seems to come from Hungary's past and from the geopolitical position of the country in the Carpathian basin. A relevant social controversy is a part of the Hungarian heritage: The progressive upper classes all took their ideals from the developed West (France, Great Britain, Germany), and the dissatisfied opponents of the direct Austro–German influence and sometimes compulsory social-economic changes attempted to counterbalance them by emphasizing the Eastern origin and community.

This view of the world belongs to the national and social identity of the Hungarians; it is from here that they look at the developments of the world. The intellectual, economic, and social center of the world keeps shifting: It used to be the Mediterranean region, then it became the two shores of the Atlantic Ocean, and it may yet be the Pacific region. The latter possibility is barely present in the Hungarian perspective; in this respect, Earth is not spherical in Hungarians' mental geometry, but is situated between an Eastern and a Western end.

The content of the stereotypes related to the social categories may offer a key to the explanation of the perceived differences. To summarize these investigations, it can be said that our respondents saw essentially similar differences between (economically successful) intellectuals and (unqualified) workers as between Western and Eastern nations. The question arises whether this is a simple parallel or whether the social–occupational model is really inherent in the conception of the national categories or if it might even mediate between national categories and trait characteristics.

In 1991, I asked respondents to associate occupations to names of continents and nations. Conversely, in 2000 I asked members of a national representative sample what nations and ethnic groups they thought of when various occupations were named. The results of the two investigations were similar in that there were *systematic and subtle connections* between the categories belonging to these different cognitive areas, between nations and occupations.

In almost 50% of the associations given by the respondents, "Asians" had an agricultural occupation. The significantly less-often mentioned workers represented the two extremes of manufacture and modern electronics. In the occupational structure of "Romanians" and "Russians," the proportions of peasants and animal breeders were still rather large (38% and 29%, respectively). Regarding the "Russians," workers and miners appeared equally often, and soldiers, policemen, and secret agents, with 17%, seemed to be specific to that nation. The picture was completely different for "Europeans": One-third of their occupations were intellectual professions, and another third was related to business. It is noteworthy that "Hungarians"—the name of the ingroup—was the only nation in which intellectual occupations predominate, with teachers, physicians, engineers, scientists, and inventors figuring at the top. This was followed by business life, mainly entrepreneurial. Workers came before the agricultural sphere. The unemployed were mentioned here alone and in association with the Romanians.

In contrast, in the Western part of Europe, in the case of "the English," the emphasis shifted from intellectual occupations to business activities, which made up 37%. Politicians and diplomats occurred frequently, and aristocrats were also mentioned. The United States is even more to the west than Western Europe; in this relation, half of the typical occupations were related to business life, the economy, and trading. It is an interesting and subtle difference in this respect that the Englishmen were more often bankers and bank clerks, and Americans were businessmen, managers, industrialists, and even brokers. Farmers and cowboys represented agricultural life, and intellectual life was represented by actors. This is the only place in which athletes and criminals are mentioned.

## 3. Research Topic: Social Models in the Images of Nations

The frequency of associations in the mass of respondents is only one index among many possible ones. Other procedures were also applied to study this question. For example, a different approach was employed in 1991. With the use of cross categorization, we asked for characterizations of national types, occupational types, and the combination of the two (see Figure 14.4). As the telling MDS figure shows, the national categories of "Romanians" and "Russians" are definitely closer to the "Romanian workers" and "Russian workers" than to the subtype of intellectuals, and not only the "English" but "English workers" and not only "Germans" but "German workers" tend to carry the characteristics of the intellectual occupations.

Otherwise, I can demonstrate that there is a clear logic in the organization based on similarity of the entire field of characterizations made up of 17 objects by 10 traits. The judgments of national and occupational cross categories are influenced by both the occupational and the national components. The relationship between pure occupational categories and their national subcategories deserves special attention. It is striking that the subcategories belonging to the respondents' own national group are the most similar to—or even identical with—the pure, abstract, general occupational categories. This has two far-reaching consequences. On one hand, it can be hypothesized that the occupational subcategories of other nations and the model of their society are probably constructed on the basis of impressions formed of the occupational

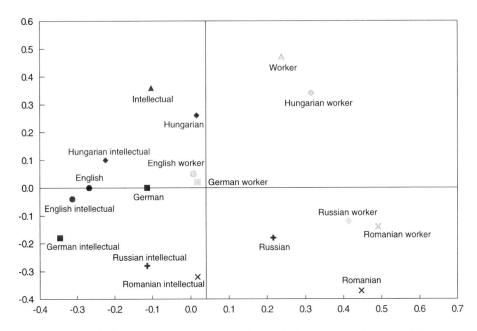

**Figure 14.4.**  MDS map of complex categories and the characterization of the components, 1991.

groups of our own nation, which is then *projected* onto the other nation. On the other hand, it can be proven that the stereotyped characterization of the subcategories of one's own national group and that of other nations are organized according to different principles.

The appropriate method for the study of a network of the trait judgments was finally found in the so-called canonical factor analysis (see Table 14.1). It is remarkable that in the case of outgroups, the national component is a strong—actually the stronger—determinant of the characteristics of the combined categories. In the case of the ingroup, however, the occupational component becomes almost totally dominant; this is what marks the whole of the combined subcategory. If a "worker" is Hungarian, national specification will not add anything new to the meaning of the occupational category, but if a "worker" is "German," it will essentially influence the overall image of the combined category. This asymmetry is in accordance with the experimental results of the perceived variability of the ingroup, and it also casts light on the filtered perceptual effects of national identity: The integrative force of the national autostereotype is relatively small.

## 1. Concluding Remark: The Two Implicit Theories Are Interlaced

When introducing the concept of "implicit social theory," I am not only playfully referring back to the term "implicit personality theory," already estab-

**Table 14.1.**   Canonical Analysis of "German Skilled Workers" and "Hungarian Skilled Workers"

| Factor structure (value: over .50) | | | | | | | | | | | | |
|---|---|---|---|---|---|---|---|---|---|---|---|---|
| 1. factor<br>.26 – v.e. – .20 | | | | | 2. factor<br>.18 – v.e. – .10 | | | | | 3. factor<br>.10 – v.e. – .05 | | |
| GS | fri | .768 | .717 | fri G | GS | pat | -.639 -.600 | pat G | GS | dil | -.926 -.646 | dil G |
| GS | hum | .701 | .691 | hum G | GS | pro | -.560 -.592 | pro G | | | | |
| GS | int | .621 | .606 | int G | | | | | | | | |
| GS | hon | .510 | .592 | pro G | | | | | | | | |
| | | | .551 | pop G | | | | | | | | |
| 1. factor<br>.40 – v.e. – .27 | | | | | 2. factor<br>.11 – v.e. – .06 | | | | | 3. factor<br>.11 – v.e. – .06 | | |
| HS | int | .752 | .746 | int S | HS | pro | -.563 | | HS | hum | -.611 -.600 | hum S |
| HS | hon | .738 | .717 | hon S | | | | | | | | |
| HS | pat | .725 | .678 | pat S | | | | | | | | |
| HS | edu | .648 | .677 | edu S | | | | | | | | |
| HS | pro | .624 | .612 | fri S | | | | | | | | |
| HS | hum | .603 | .602 | dil S | | | | | | | | |
| HS | fri | .553 | .586 | hum S | | | | | | | | |
| HS | pol | .508 | .573 | pol S | | | | | | | | |
| | | | .558 | pro S | | | | | | | | |
| | | | .503 | pat H | | | | | | | | |

*Note:* v.e. = variance extracted, G = German, GS = German skilled worker, H = Hungarian, HI = Hungarian intellectual, HS = Hungarian skilled worker, S = skilled worker, dil = diligent, edu = educated, fri = friendly, hon = honest, hum = good humoured, int = intelligent, pat = patriotic, pol = interested in politics, pop = popular, pro = proud

lished in the literature. I return to the model that was created and used by Bill McGuire (1989) to grasp the basic structure of the more or less complex attitude/thought systems. The basic elements are dimensions for the location of the subjects and the subjects to be judged on the dimensions. In the case of stereotypes, the dimensions are bipolar trait constructs for the anthropomorphic characterization of the subjects, and the subjects are categories referring to social groups to be characterized. The implicit personality theory notion means that the judgments on bipolar trait dimensions are not independent of each other. There are ordered relationships among them: maybe inclusive categorization and supplementary functions, perceived causal determination, and evaluative coherence.

This implicit social theory notion means only that the categories are not independent from each other, and once again, there are ordered relationships among them, such as inclusive categorization and supplementary functions, perceived historical–causal determination, and evaluative coherence. These systems are studied as more or less conscious structures, and, apparently, they work together in information processing in an interacting way.

It was Ashmore (1981) who raised the idea that the network of relationships perceived among traits also contains categories and that dichotomous categories such as gender can occupy some kind of position in the system of relationships of traits. Ashmore came to this idea by applying the method of multidimensional scaling, and his conclusion was that stereotyping (as a system of relationships among categories and traits) is itself an implicit personality theory, or a part of it. I think the problem is a little more complicated, taking into consideration the multicategory cognitive domains as well.

On one hand, we have some evidence that there are no universal relationships among the traits. More than a single implicit personality theory exists: There are as many (and as many kinds) of them as there are cognitive domains (where the relationship of dimensions is studied). The role and network of traits depend on whether persons, nations, or social–occupational categories are characterized. On the other hand, extending Ashmore's train of thought, we can accept that there is a tendency even in social categorization toward dimensional arrangements (see the East–West divide as an example). At the same time, the cognitive literature related to the representation of traits reveals them to be categories that comprise a set of individual features. In this way, the researchers of the field also conceive of a network of social categories and psychological categories.

## 2. Concluding Remark: The Change of Stereotypes Depends on the Effects of Implicit Social Theory

I stated that stereotypes are parts of a social image. If this is true, then the internal consistency of social conception will *maintain* stereotypes as long as the world—reflected in the overall image—does not change dramatically according to individual experience and public thinking formed in communication. As long as that social constellation remains intact, in which stereotypes fit and work effectively, no radical changes in the content of those stereotypes will be generally expected.

According to evidence in the literature, the effect of personal contact experience and intergroup communication—despite expectations based on the inductive approach to stereotype formation—is rather poor and deficient. Several profound changes appear, however, after changes in the social constellation—as forecast by the previously outlined deductive approach to stereotype formation—even without coming across the representatives of the given categories. This was exemplified by the historical social transformation we could call—to paraphrase Spranger's book title—the decline of the East. As a single example taken at random: Between 1981 and 1991, the personal contact between the student respondents and the skilled laborers did not change; it did not become more or less frequent or more or less pleasant. Nevertheless, the stereotyped image of skilled workers was modified, its level of evaluation decreased, and the profile of characterization became more marked (see Figure 14.5).

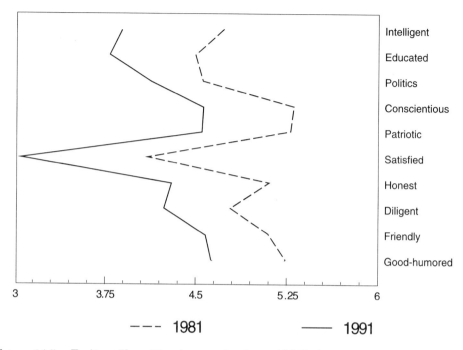

Intelligent

Educated

Politics

Conscientious

Patriotic

Satisfied

Honest

Diligent

Friendly

Good-humored

3        3.75        4.5        5.25        6

--- 1981            —— 1991

**Figure 14.5.**   Trait profiles of the characterizations of "skilled workers," 1981 and 1991.

## 3. Concluding Remark: Explicit Ideology Can Penetrate Implicit Social Theory and Vice Versa

By way of introduction, I tried to deny that there is a distinctive feature of the infrequent category of Eastern European social psychologists. What I cannot deny, however, is that Eastern European social scientists have a distinctive common experience, namely a unifying ideological pressure. For decades, Eastern European societies were ruled by coercive power, which prescribed how social relationships must be conceived and what one had to think about them. Explicit ideology is more elaborated, more conscious, and more abstract than implicit social theory: It is an open question as to how deeply explicit ideology can penetrate implicit social theory in public thinking. In this historical context, Bill McGuire's warning, which—based on American research— expressed doubts about the social–political awareness of common people, was probably less valid. Here, perhaps the other extreme may become a threat: that we belittle the ideological sensitivity and reactivity of common people. Perhaps we could avoid both extremes and discover public thinking that was formed behind and also partly influenced by ideology and that developed somewhat spontaneously.

Finally, we may turn our attention to a classical topic of social psychology that has been studied from several aspects already: the description of comprehensive social systems of beliefs. Naturally, this can take place in many ways. The general trend of the endeavor, however, perhaps stands the test of time and in fact, may even be timely. If I am correct, it fits the prediction formulated by Bill McGuire (1993, pp. 34–35) in his fundamental chapter on the past and future of the poly-psy affair: At the turn of the millennium, the time has come to study the cognitive systems that play a role in the evaluation and formation of intergroup relationships. Whom should we believe if not him?

# References

Ashmore, R. D. (1981). Sex stereotypes and implicit personality theory. In D. L. Hamilton (Ed.), *Cognitive processes in stereotyping and intergroup behavior* (pp. 37–82). Hillsdale, NJ: Erlbaum.

Brewer, M. B. (1988). A dual process model of impression formation. In T. K. Srull & R. S. Wyer (Eds.), *Advances in social cognition* (Vol. 1, pp. 1–36). Hillsdale, NJ: Erlbaum.

Eagly, A. H., & Kite, M. E. (1987). Are stereotypes of nationalities applied to both women and men? *Journal of Personality and Social Psychology, 53,* 451–462.

Eagly, A. H., & Steffen, V. J. (1984). Gender stereotypes stem from the distribution of women and men into social roles. *Journal of Personality and Social Psychology, 46,* 735–754.

Eagly, A. H., & Wood, W. (1982). Inferred sex differences in status as a determinant of gender stereotypes about social influence. *Journal of Personality and Social Psychology, 43,* 915–928.

Fiske, S. T., & Pavelchak, M. A. (1986). Category-based versus piecemeal-based affective responses: Developments in schema-triggered affect. In R. M. Sorrentino & E. T. Higgins (Eds.), *The handbook of motivation and cognition: Foundation of social behavior* (pp.167–203). New York: Guilford Press.

Hagendoorn, L. (1995). Intergroup biases in multiple group systems: The perception of ethnic hierarchies. *European Review of Social Psychology, 6,* 199–228.

Hunyady, Gy. (1998a). *Stereotypes during the decline and fall of communism.* (International Series of Experimental Social Psychology). London and New York: Routledge.

Hunyady, Gy. (1998b). *Characterization of social categories in psychological and societal context.* Budapest: Eötvös University Press.

Hunyady, Gy., Hamilton D. L., & Nguyen Luu, L. A. (1999). *Csoportok percepciója* [Perception of groups]: *Vol. XVII. Pszichológiai tanulmányok* [Studies in psychology]. Budapest: Akadémiai Kiadó.

Lippmann, W. (1922). *Public opinion.* New York: Harcourt, Brace, Jovanovich.

McGuire, W. J. (1989). The structure of individual attitudes and attitude systems. In A. R. Pratkanis, S. J. Breckler, & A. G. Greenwald (Eds.), *Attitude structure and function* (pp. 37–69). Hillsdale, NJ: Erlbaum.

McGuire, W. J. (1993). The poly-psy relationship: Three phases of a long affair. In S. Iyengar & W. J. McGuire (Eds.), *Explorations in political psychology.* (pp. 9–35) Durham, NC: Duke University Press.

McGuire, W. J. (2002). Doing psychology my way. In R. J. Sternberg (Ed.), *Psychologists defying the crowd: Stories of those who battled the establishment and won.* Washington, DC: APA Books.

Oakes, P. J., Haslam, S. A., & Turner, J. C. (1994). *Stereotyping and social reality.* Oxford: Blackwell.

Peabody, D. (1985). *National characteristics.* Cambridge: Cambridge University Press.

Pennebaker, J. W., Rimé, B., & Blakenship, V. E. (1996). Stereotypes of emotional expressiveness of northerners and southerners: A cross-cultural test of Montesquieu's hypothesis. *Journal of Personality and Social Psychology, 70,* 372–380.

Scott, W. A., Osgood, D. W., & Peterson, C. (1979). *Cognitive structure theory and measurement of individual differences.* New York: Wiley.

Turner, J. C. (1987). Rediscovering the social group. In J. C. Turner, M. A. Hogg, P. J. Oakes, S. D. Reicher, & M. S. Wetherell (Eds.), *Rediscovering the social group: A self-categorization theory.* Oxford: Blackwell.

# 15

# The Commonsense Psychology of Changing Social Groups

## Alice H. Eagly and Amanda B. Diekman

### Prologue[1]

In Bill McGuire's perspectivist theory of knowledge, science is depicted as inevitably flawed, producing representations that are hazy, fuzzy, and incomplete. McGuire encourages scientists to exploit this ambiguity by exploring the array of contexts in which hypotheses and their opposites are often both true. I suggest that perspectivism is best realized by regarding science not as an individual process that is fueled by a single scientist's skill and imagination but as a deeply collective process whereby many scientists working semi-independently produce varied tests of related hypotheses. The most challenging part of science is exploiting this collective process by fitting studies together into larger patterns to produce a generalizable set of answers to a question. Within the matrix of answers yielded by many research programs, it can often be seen that both a hypothesis and its opposite have produced confirmations but in different contexts.

To illustrate the collective nature of psychological science, consider the issue of whether attitudes influence memory for attitude-relevant information, a question that has intrigued researchers since the beginning of work in social psychology. It seemed to early researchers that attitudes surely would affect memory in the form of the *congeniality hypothesis,* whereby people remember information better to the extent that it is congenial with their attitudes. This hypothesis was not consistently confirmed, and researchers left a trail of diverse findings in the wake of their attempts to understand the relation between attitudes and memory. This morass of findings provided an opportunity to recover the contribution of this blighted research area with the aid of meta-analytic methods. Telling this story required new theoretical insights as well as methodological expertise. With my collaborators Shelly Chaiken, Serena Chen, and Kelly Shaw, I spent countless hours contemplating the studies in this research literature as we sought to understand the contexts in which memory favored congeniality or its opposite. Eventually we published an article that displayed the strengths and weaknesses of this research literature and illuminated its findings (Eagly, Chen, Chaiken, & Shaw-Barnes,

---

[1]The prologue to this chapter was written by Alice H. Eagly.

1999). Like most research integrations, ours told an unfinished story, because this meta-analysis is only a way station along the route to achieving an understanding of the many ways in which attitudes can influence memory.

Meta-analysis allows researchers to realize McGuire's perspectivist vision far more thoroughly than they could within their own research programs. The integrators of research are forced to contemplate the hypothesis confirmations and disconfirmations that emerged along with many methods for testing hypotheses. In contrast, when a single investigator conducts a series of studies, it is impossible to know whether the results are generalizable or whether the particular context of the studies created fairly unique conditions that were critical to obtaining these results. The knowledge produced is no doubt partial and flawed, but the sense in which that is so is initially hidden. After other researchers produce more studies, the larger sets of findings can address issues of generalizability and context. With skill and luck, those reviewers who seek larger patterns in the findings will discover them and generate the broader theory that makes sense of the whole. Overcoming McGuire's perspectivist dilemma at least to some extent, the theory produced on top of contextually varying findings is a far more complete theory.

Since the early 1980s, I have divided my life as a researcher between meta-analytic projects that integrate research and primary research projects that produce new findings. In primary research, I have few methodological preconceptions except for a belief that, in an ideal world of unlimited resources, researchers would use multiple methods that converge on a question from differing directions. Although I have favored experimental methods in my primary research because of my training and disciplinary positioning in a psychology department, I believe that these methods represent only one of many useful approaches to research. As Bill McGuire has so wisely stated, all methods produce incomplete insights. Psychologists therefore have much to gain not only from using diverse methods but also from reaching out to allied disciplines to grasp their contribution to understanding human behavior.

* * *

A psychology of how people understand the future is one of the products of Bill and Claire McGuire's research on thought systems (McGuire, 1990; McGuire & McGuire, 1991). In their project, they showed that people have coherent thoughts about future personal and societal events. In this chapter, we feature research that also examined construals of the future (Diekman & Eagly, 2000). However, rather than inducing people to think about their personal futures or the future of social problems as did the McGuires, we asked them to think about the future of social groups and also about groups' pasts. In planning the research, we assumed that people have considerable awareness of groups' trajectories in time. Just as people think about their own past and future, they also think about the past and future of social groups.

Our research has shown that when people think about the future of groups, they think like sociologists, not like psychologists, because they shift to a societal level of analysis and manifest what Hunyady (chapter 14 of this volume) terms an *implicit social theory*. At this societal level, social perceivers do not contemplate the antecedents and consequences of groups in the manner that McGuire and McGuire (1991) showed that perceivers contemplate the antecedents and consequences of events. Because groups are the entities of the social world in the sense that rocks, trees, and the sky are entities of the physical world, groups are merely present in the environment, and people reflect on their attributes. Perceivers' inferences about group members' attributes—that is, their stereotypes—follow from their commonsense understanding of how groups fit into their society.

The word *stereotype* derives from the term applied to the metal plates or forms once used in printing. It is in this spirit that in traditional theorizing in psychology (e.g., Allport, 1954), stereotypic beliefs were assumed to rigidly fix the attributes of members of social groups in perceivers' minds. However, in this chapter we argue that, in contrast to this traditional treatment of stereotypes, beliefs that members of a group have certain characteristics do not imply belief in the immutability of these characteristics. Stereotypes are social facts, contrary to Lippmann's (1922) idea that they are like *biological facts*. Because the social world changes, people have a fluid conception of some social groups as changing entities that can manifest different characteristics in the past and future than in the present. Before explaining how social perceivers project groups through time, we discuss the more basic issue of how people ascribe characteristics to social groups—in other words, the matter of stereotype content.

## What Accounts for the Content of Stereotypic Beliefs?

Psychology textbooks typically describe stereotypes not only as rigid but also as misguided, perhaps reflecting a *kernel of truth* but driven by prejudices and biases. Although stereotypes can exaggerate reality, it is productive for theorists to think about them in a less judgmental framework by regarding social perceivers as observers of the behavior of people whom they have categorized into social groups. Everyday thinking about social groups reflects the correspondent inference principle that is basic to reasoning about the meaning of observed behavior. Social perceivers thus assume correspondence between the types of behaviors that members of groups typically engage in and their inner dispositions (see Eagly, Wood, & Diekman, 2000; Gilbert, 1998). Because most behaviors are enacted in the context of social roles, stereotype content reflects the most typical roles held by members of social groups—that is, the roles that they occupy more often than members of other social groups do. Because stereotypes are correspondent inferences from representative role behavior, they mirror the qualities that group members commonly enact in these roles. Stereotypes are thus emergents from observed role behavior even though people's observations of some groups are mainly indirect, communicated by the media and cultural traditions more generally.

Supporting the principle of correspondent inference from role behavior, research has demonstrated social perceivers' failure to give much weight to the constraints of social roles in inferring role players' dispositions (e.g., L. Ross, Amabile, & Steinmetz, 1977) or to situational constraints in inferring group members' traits (e.g., Schaller & O'Brien, 1992). In a similar vein, Hoffman and Hurst (1990) argued that stereotypes function as rationalizations for existing role distributions, as did Jost and Banaji (1994) in their analysis of stereotypes as providing *system justification*. These analyses agree that to understand stereotypes, social scientists must understand how groups are positioned in society.

Our research on stereotypes about men and women has followed this logic in indicating that gender stereotypes stem from the distribution of the sexes into social roles (Diekman & Eagly, 2000). Several distributional features stand out: (a) the male–female division of labor between domestic work and wage labor, (b) the relative sex segregation of paid occupations, and (c) the gender hierarchy by which roles yielding high levels of power and status are male-dominated. Because the roles performed more by one sex than by the other have somewhat different requirements and demands, perceivers ascribe different characteristics to the sexes.

Social perceivers assume that women and men accommodate to their family and employment roles by acquiring role-related skills and traits, such as women learning domestic skills and nurturance and men learning skills that are useful in paid occupations, particularly in male-dominated occupations. Research on gender stereotypes has thus shown that the characteristics thought to typify homemakers are ascribed to women in general and that the characteristics thought to typify providers are ascribed to men in general (Eagly & Steffen, 1984). Women's association with the domestic role and female-dominated occupations thus lends the female role a pattern of interpersonally facilitative behaviors that can be termed communal. In particular, the assignment of the majority of child rearing to women leads people to expect women to have communal tendencies, including nurturance that facilitates care for children. The importance of close relationships to women's nurturing role favors inferences that women possess superior interpersonal skills and the ability to communicate nonverbally. In contrast, men's association with the employment role, especially in male-dominated occupations, produces expectations of more assertive and independent behaviors that can be termed agentic.

The distribution of men and women in roles obviously requires a more complex description than a division between domestic and wage labor. In the United States and many other nations, the majority of women are employed outside of the home, and paid occupations show wide variation in the kinds of activities that they require. Therefore, if people's observations of role behavior account for the content of gender stereotypes, something of a match should exist between gender stereotypes and the types of activities associated with the typical paid occupations of men and women. Indeed, to the extent that occupations are male-dominated, success in them is perceived to require agentic personal qualities, whereas to the extent that occupations are female-dominated, success in them is perceived to require communal personal qualities (Cejka & Eagly, 1999). The physical qualities ascribed to men and women, such as greater size and physical strength to men and beauty and sensuality to women, are also reflected in the perceived demands of sex-segregated occupational roles.

Differences in the power and status of the typical roles of men and women also are reflected in gender stereotypes. Especially related to status and power are perceivers' divergent expectations for dominant and submissive behavior (Eagly & Wood, 1982). Because people in more powerful roles are expected to behave in a more dominant style, gender stereotypes include this belief as well. Men are expected to be more controlling, assertive, and relatively directive and autocratic, and women to be more compliant to social influence, less overtly aggressive, and more cooperative and conciliatory. Reflecting the societal tendency for women to have less power and status than men, gender stereotypes encompass beliefs about these dominant and subordinate aspects of behavior (Conway, Pizzamiglio, & Mount, 1996).

The theory that stereotype content reflects correspondent inferences from role behavior provides a general theory of the content of stereotypes of social groups. Therefore, it is not surprising that similar principles have been invoked by researchers investigating stereotypes based on ethnicity, race, nationality, age, and income (see Johannesen-Schmidt & Eagly, 2002).

## How Do Perceivers Think About Groups Over Time?

Sometimes the social roles of groups change over time. For example, immigrant groups often initially take jobs involving menial and low-status wage labor but typically rise in the social structure by becoming better-represented in higher-status roles. The attributes of members of such groups seem to change because their stereotypes are emergents from perceivers' observations of them in their typical roles. These dynamic aspects of stereotypes thus follow from perceived change in the placement of groups in the social structure. Perceivers function as implicit role theorists by noting change in role distributions and inferring corresponding change in stereotypic characteristics.

Attention to beliefs about change is sparse in the psychological literature, yet in addition to McGuire and McGuire's (1991) research on perceptions of future events, M. Ross (1989; M. Ross & Newby-Clark, 1998) has examined people's perceptions of their own personal histories. This research suggested that people first evaluate their present tendencies and then gauge their past by invoking an implicit theory of stability or change depending on the available cues. Entrance into roles cues theories of personal change because of the expectation that a new role evokes new behaviors. Similar processes occur at the group level: When a substantial number of group members enter new roles, the stereotype for that group changes because social perceivers understand that new roles evoke new behaviors. The relatively rapid shift of women into paid employment in the second half of the 20th century should thus cue an implicit theory of change; perceivers should view women as different in the past than in the present. In contrast, the relative lack of change in men's roles should cue an implicit theory of stability; perceivers should view men as similar in the past and in the present. Whether people would project these trends into the future was more in question in our research project.

In a research program addressing the construal of groups over time, we examined the beliefs that social perceivers have about the characteristics of women and men of the past, the present, and the future (Diekman & Eagly, 2000). To the extent that women or men or, for that matter, members of any social group are perceived to change their characteristics over time, they should acquire a cultural representation that incorporates this change. They would be regarded as a group on the move or, in our terminology, they would have a *dynamic stereotype*.

We hypothesized that, because of the increasing similarity of the lives of women and men, perceivers would discern convergence in their characteristics. However, this increased role similarity is primarily a product of women's increased wage labor, which has occurred without a commensurate change in men's domestic labor, and of women's entry into male-dominated occupations, which has occurred without a similar shift of men into female-dominated occupations. Although sex differences should be perceived as eroding, the one-sided direction of this social change implies that the stereotype of women is more dynamic than that of men.

In our experiments, we examined beliefs about the attributes of women and men projected 50 years into the past and 50 years into the future. Research participants living at the turn of the 21st century thus reflected on the characteristics of men and women in 1950, 1975, the present, 2025, and 2050. The data were as expected: Women have a dynamic stereotype; our participants regarded them as fluidly changing over time. In contrast, men have a static stereotype; our participants regarded them as staying basically the same over a century of time.

The particulars of these dynamically rendered women were clear when projected onto three dimensions of gender stereotyping: personality characteristics, cognitive abilities, and physical attributes. Women were perceived as progressively taking on the personality, cognitive, and physical characteristics that are more typical of men. Women and men were thus perceived to converge strongly in their masculine personality characteristics (e.g., competitive, dominant) and masculine cognitive characteristics (e.g., analytical, good with numbers) and moderately in their masculine physical characteristics (e.g., rugged, muscular). As we had hypothesized, this convergence in masculine characteristics reflected perceived change mainly in women. Although there was no convergence in feminine cognitive characteristics (e.g., imaginative, intuitive) or physical characteristics (e.g., cute, petite), there was modest convergence in feminine personality characteristics (e.g., gentle, kind) that was predominantly a product of women's perceived loss of these characteristics.

The commonsense psychology of gender thus features belief in considerable malleability over a 100-year time span, with the trends that people project over time primarily reflecting the belief that women's attributes are changing. People believe that women of the present are more masculine than women of the past and that women of the future will be more masculine than women of the present. This perceived shift in women's attributes even encompassed masculine personality characteristics that are unfavorably evaluated. Women were thus described as becoming more egotistical and arrogant as well as more assertive and independent. Belief in complementary change by which men increase their feminine tendencies appeared to be weak, as was belief in change by which women decrease their feminine tendencies. We predicted these results because the increasing similarity in the roles of women and men is primarily a product of change in women's roles. Because the modal situation for women now incorporates paid employment along with domestic responsibilities, perceivers should believe that women's masculine attributes have shifted to incorporate the personal characteristics identified with men and employees but that their feminine attributes have remained relatively constant.

Various features of our findings support our reasoning that people reason as implicit social theorists. In particular, it is unlikely that a simpler process took place whereby asking participants about a past or future year suggested that they should respond in terms of changed characteristics. If this demand were inherent in our questioning, participants should have responded in terms of changed characteristics for both sexes instead of predominantly for women. Another concern is that responding to the stereotype measure in terms of changed characteristics might have suggested corresponding shifts in roles, producing an artifactual association between stereotypes and roles. Contrary to this reasoning, even those participants who rated men, whom they perceived as changing rather little, also indicated that role distributions were different in the past and will be different in the future. Thus, our participants were competent intuitive sociologists who recognized that one-directional change in roles implies that women's but not men's personal characteristics would change.

Functioning as implicit role theorists, people apparently believe that personal characteristics adapt to social structure. Path analyses were consistent with the assumption that perceptions of role distributions mediated the impact of the context year on beliefs about the characteristics of women and men. When social change takes the form of a substantial proportion of a social group changing its roles, people observe these changes and believe that the characteristics of these group members also change to meet the requirements of the new roles.

Because projections that actual, observed change will continue in the future are of course not derived from observations of future events, it is especially revealing of people's implicit theories that they predict additional change in the future. In our research, perceptions of changes in future characteristics were mediated by beliefs that social roles will continue to change in the next 50 years at about the same rate that they changed in the past 50 years. Perceivers' theories thus project role change into the future, allowing them to infer corresponding future changes in women's personal attributes.

## Are Dynamic and Static Stereotypes Accurate?

The research on stereotype content that we have described raises the issue of stereotype accuracy. This question deserves more sensitive exploration than it has ordinarily received. Stereotypes can obviously produce erroneous judgments of individuals because within-group variability in most characteristics is quite large. The more difficult issue is whether stereotypes accurately reflect average group differences in characteristics. Although the case for inaccuracy in the perception of group differences has been made in laboratory experiments (e.g., Hoffman & Hurst, 1990), in natural settings people are socialized for their futures as adult occupants of the roles that are typical of their group. For example, in virtually all societies, the socialization of girls is arranged to give them practice in childcare and nurturing to ensure their accommodation to mothering as an adult role (Wood & Eagly, 2002). Moreover, engaging in behavior that meets the requirements of adult roles affects personal dispositions through processes such as expectancy confirmation and self-regulation by means of internalized role requirements.

In general, groups that are positioned differently in the social structure acquire different characteristics, reflecting their typical roles. For example, girls become more nurturant than boys, as assessed by personality tests (see Feingold, 1994), even if they were not intrinsically more nurturant. This reasoning about the power of social roles is consistent with Gilbert's (1998) argument that effects that appear as inferential errors in social psychology experiments do not necessarily have counterparts in natural settings. The erroneous inferences that participants in laboratory experiments make about the group members' typical or average attributes when they reason from their role performances thus may diminish substantially in natural settings because of the power of prolonged occupancy of social roles to mold inner dispositions. Research has thus shown that people are often at least moderately accurate in perceiving group members' characteristics at the level of a group average (e.g., Hall & Carter, 1999).

Whether perceivers have an accurate theory of change in group members' attributes from the past to the present is an especially demanding question. Has research on personality, social behavior, and cognitive abilities produced evidence of actual change over time in the personal attributes of women? Such evidence is difficult to produce because it requires the collection of data over long time periods, as well as adjustments of findings for changes in research methods. Despite these challenges, in research literatures in which studies extend over several decades, the hypothesis that sex differences are decreasing in size is amenable to testing by relating the year that the data were collected to studies' outcomes.

From the perspective of the commonsense psychology of sex differences, convergent male and female secular trends should be observed most clearly in behaviors that reflect masculine—but not feminine—personality, cognitive, and physical dispositions, and this convergence should be accounted for mainly by change in women. A considerable number of findings support these predictions. For example, the career plans of male and female university students showed a marked convergence from 1966 to 1996 that is accounted for mainly by changes in women's career aspirations (Astin, Parrott, Korn, & Sax, 1997). Also, a meta-analysis showed that job attributes such as freedom, challenge, leadership, prestige, and power became relatively more important to women, in comparison with men, from the 1970s to the 1980s and 1990s (Konrad, Ritchie, Lieb, & Corrigall, 2000). As the gender barriers to opportunity declined during this period, women's aspirations to obtain jobs with these attributes rose. Also, a meta-analysis of self-report measures of masculine and feminine personality traits showed that women's masculinity increased linearly with the studies' year of publication (Twenge, 1997). Men's masculinity showed a weaker increase with year, and their femininity increased slightly as well.

Some meta-analyses of sex differences in specific domains of stereotypically masculine behavior also showed a decrease in the magnitude of these differences. For example, a meta-analysis of sex differences in risk-taking behavior observed a decrease over time in the tendency of men to engage in riskier behavior than women (Byrnes, Miller, & Schafer, 1999). A meta-analysis of leader emergence in small groups reported a decrease over time in the tendency for men to emerge more than women (Eagly & Karau, 1991). Twenge (2001) found that women increased in self-reported dominance and assertiveness from 1931 to 1945, decreased from 1946 to 1967, and increased from 1968 to 1993, whereas men's self-reports were relatively invariant across these time periods. Studies of performance on tests of cognitive abilities demonstrated some declines in the size of sex differences favoring males on tests of mathematics and science but no decline in the size of differences favoring females on tests of reading and writing (e.g., Campbell, Hombo, & Mazzeo, 2000; Hedges & Nowell, 1995; Hyde, Fennema, & Lamon, 1990). Also, the marked increase in women's athletic participation (National Collegiate Athletic Association, 2001) indicates that women may even be physically stronger than in the past. Finally, aggregate statistics reveal women's increasing representation in violent crime (U.S. Department of Justice, 2000). On balance, in view of evidence of actual convergence in masculine personal characteristics and behaviors, perceivers may be reasonably accurate not only about the current attributes of the sexes but also about changes in these attributes.

Even though people believe that women are changing, stereotypes are not perfectly matched to the external reality of the present. This possibility would be consistent with the limited shifts in gender stereotypes revealed by comparing data sets from different years (e.g., Lueptow, Garovich-Szabo, & Lueptow, 2001; Spence & Buckner, 2000). Although *bookkeeping* models of stereotype change that presume constant updating of stereotypes indicate that stereotypes change at the same pace as external realities, other models suggest mechanisms for maintaining stereotypes, such as the formation of subtypes to encompass deviating cases (see Hilton & von Hippel, 1996). Moreover, because concepts of male and female are conveyed by many cultural forms that change slowly (e.g., literature, ritual, religion), the drag of culture causes stereotypes to lag somewhat behind the realities of social roles (Brinkman & Brinkman, 1997; Ogburn, 1922/1964).

## Conclusion

Thoughtful observers of social life would not be at all surprised to find that change in men and women over time appears to be asymmetrical, with women adopting masculine characteristics without much reciprocal change whereby men adopt feminine characteristics. Men's characteristics will not actually change or be perceived to change until they change their social roles by accepting substantially more domestic responsibility, entering female-dominated occupations, and ceasing to dominate high-power roles. Any changes in this direction have been small; therefore, there is little basis for predicting that men have adopted or will adopt more feminine characteristics. Groups alter their actual characteristics as they prepare for and occupy roles that have new demands:

Women but not men have undergone such transitions on a major scale in recent decades in the United States and many other industrialized nations.

Benjamin DeMott (2000), an attentive social critic, has published a book about this one-sided gender shift, titled *Killer Woman Blues*. DeMott complained about women adopting male culture with its toughness and aggressiveness—taking on what he terms the *kick-butt* culture. DeMott shares a theory of change with everyday perceivers but added his politically conservative censure of these changes without much understanding of the broader socioeconomic changes that are responsible for greater change in women's than men's roles. Moreover, whether everyday perceivers would join DeMott in disapproval of women's masculine shift is an issue that we have also investigated (Diekman & Goodfriend, 2002). Helpful in making predictions about this issue is McGuire and McGuire's (1991) treatment of the intertwining of evaluation and likelihood. Their *rationalization postulate* suggests that likely events become good, and their *wishful-thinking postulate* suggests that good events become likely. Thus, by rationalization, those who, like most of our participants, regard changes in gender relations as quite likely may come to approve of the shift. Consistent with this postulate, our research participants attached predominantly favorable evaluation to the increase that they perceived in women's masculine personality and cognitive attributes over the 1950 to 2050 time period. Also, by wishful thinking, those who approve of the ongoing changes toward nontraditional gender relations should come to regard as very likely both future change toward gender equality and the associated masculine shift in women's attributes.

Another possible direction of social change is that roles change to accommodate new role occupants. For example, in relation to the managerial roles that women have entered in large numbers, rather than women conforming to the typical behaviors of male managers, the managerial role might change by encompassing the more relational qualities of women (see Eagly & Karau, 2002). Although many social roles are flexible enough to accommodate a range of behavioral styles, the accommodation of newcomers to the requirements of roles may override roles' accommodation to the characteristics of newcomers, if only because the newcomers are at least initially only a small minority. However, if the proportion of new occupants of a social role increases very substantially, so that the role becomes dominated by the new group, the role may change greatly in its requirements, wage structure, and cultural representation (e.g., Preston, 1995).

The construals of the future revealed by our research are important because people's ideas about the future influence their behavior in the present. The commonsense belief that women will continue to change may foster continued upward change in the status of women. Despite some resistance to the shifts in women's roles, especially among more politically conservative social groups, the shared belief that women will augment their masculine personality, cognitive, and physical characteristics in the future should expand women's access to male-dominated roles and to the socialization experiences and training opportunities that will allow them to assume these roles. Similarly, to the extent that other societal groups, especially immigrant groups, have dynamic stereotypes, this perceived dynamism should expand their opportunities. It is thus likely that stereotypes' representation of change in group members' characteristics functions in the service of social change despite the potential for stereotypes' representation of group members' present characteristics to justify the status quo.

Finally, our research, in relating stereotypes to social structure in order to understand their content, reflects a societal theme in social psychology that has been more popular among European than American social psychologists in recent years (e.g., Himmelweit & Gaskell, 1990; Torregrosa, in press). Doise (chapter 13 of this volume) provides an eloquent statement of how and why social psychology would be enriched by the inclusion of societal relationships in its theories along with individual psychological factors. Explaining the content of stereotypes surely requires a societal social psychology, as illustrated by the work that we present in this chapter as well as by the research of Hunyady (chapter 14 of this volume, 1998a, 1998b) and other psychologists (e.g., Fiske, Xu, Cuddy, & Glick, 1999; Jost & Banaji, 1994). This attention to explaining stereotype content by understanding groups' positioning in the social structure may signal the dawning of a new era in which societal and individual themes become intertwined in social psychology.

# References

Allport, G. W. (1954). *The nature of prejudice*. Reading, MA: Addison-Wesley.

Astin, A. W., Parrott, S. A., Korn, W. S., & Sax, L. J. (1997). *The American freshman: Thirty year trends*. Los Angeles: Higher Education Research Institute, University of California, Los Angeles.

Brinkman, R. L., & Brinkman, J. E. (1997). Cultural lag: Conception and theory. *International Journal of Social Economics, 24,* 609–631.

Byrnes, J. P., Miller, D. C., & Schafer, W. D. (1999). Gender differences in risk taking: A meta-analysis. *Psychological Bulletin, 125,* 367–383.

Campbell, J. R., Hombo, C. M., & Mazzeo, J. (2000). *NAEP trends in academic progress: Three decades of student performance* (U.S. Department of Education, Office of Educational Research and Improvement, National Center for Educational Statistics, NCES 2000-469). Washington, DC: U.S. Department of Education. Retrieved May 15, 2001, from http://nces.ed.gov/ NAEP/site/home.asp.

Cejka, M. A., & Eagly, A. H. (1999). Gender-stereotypic images of occupations correspond to the sex segregation of employment. *Personality and Social Psychology Bulletin, 25,* 413–423.

Conway, M., Pizzamiglio, M. T., & Mount, L. (1996). Status, communality, and agency: Implications for stereotypes of gender and other groups. *Journal of Personality and Social Psychology, 71,* 25–38.

DeMott, B. (2000). *Killer woman blues: Why Americans can't think straight about gender and power*. Boston: Houghton Mifflin.

Diekman, A. B., & Eagly, A. H. (2000). Stereotypes as dynamic constructs: Women and men of the past, present, and future. *Personality and Social Psychology Bulletin, 26,* 1171–1188.

Diekman, A. B., & Goodfriend, W. (2002). *Attitudes toward social groups in motion: The evaluative content of dynamic and static gender stereotypes*. Manuscript submitted for publication.

Doise, W. (2004). Vicissitudes of societal psychology. In J. Jost, M. Banaji, & D. Prentice (Eds.), *Perspectivism in social psychology: The ying and yang of scientific progress*. Washington, DC: American Psychological Association.

Eagly, A. H., Chen, S., Chaiken, S., & Shaw-Barnes, K. (1999). The impact of attitudes on memory: An affair to remember. *Psychological Bulletin, 125,* 64–89.

Eagly, A. H., & Karau, S. J. (1991). Gender and the emergence of leaders: A meta-analysis. *Journal of Personality and Social Psychology, 60,* 685–710.

Eagly, A. H., & Karau, S. J. (2002). Role congruity theory of prejudice toward female leaders. *Psychological Review, 109,* 573–598.

Eagly, A. H., & Steffen, V. J. (1984). Gender stereotypes stem from the distribution of women and men into social roles. *Journal of Personality and Social Psychology, 46,* 735–754.

Eagly, A. H., & Wood, W. (1982). Inferred sex differences in status as a determinant of gender stereotypes about social influence. *Journal of Personality and Social Psychology, 43,* 915–928.

Eagly, A. H., Wood, W., & Diekman, A. (2000). Social role theory of sex differences and similarities: A current appraisal. In T. Eckes & H. M. Trautner (Eds.), *The developmental social psychology of gender* (pp. 123–174). Mahwah, NJ: Erlbaum.

Feingold, A. (1994). Gender differences in personality: A meta-analysis. *Psychological Bulletin, 116,* 429–456.

Fiske, S. T., Xu, J., Cuddy, A. C., & Glick, P. (1999). (Dis)respecting versus (dis)liking: Status and interdependence predict ambivalent stereotypes of competence and warmth. *Journal of Social Issues, 55,* 473–489.

Gilbert, D. T. (1998). Ordinary personology. In D. T. Gilbert, S. T. Fiske, & G. Lindzey (Eds.), *The handbook of social psychology* (4th ed., Vol. 2, pp. 89–150). Boston: McGraw-Hill.

Hall, J. A., & Carter, J. D. (1999). Gender-stereotype accuracy as an individual difference. *Journal of Personality and Social Psychology, 77,* 350–359.

Hedges, L. V., & Nowell, A. (1995). Sex differences in mental test scores, variability, and numbers of high-scoring individuals. *Science, 269,* 41–45.

Hilton, J. L., & von Hippel, W. (1996). Stereotypes. *Annual Review of Psychology, 47,* 237–271.

Himmelweit, H. T., & Gaskell, G. (Eds.). (1990). *Societal psychology.* London: Sage.

Hoffman, C., & Hurst, N. (1990). Gender stereotypes: Perception or rationalization? *Journal of Personality and Social Psychology, 58,* 197–208.

Hunyady, Gy. (1998a). *Characterization of social categories in psychological and societal context.* Budapest, Hungary: Eötvös University Press.

Hunyady, Gy. (1998b). *Stereotypes during the decline and fall of Communism.* London: Oxford University Press.

Hunyady, Gy. (2004). Social stereotypes and "implicit social theory." In J. Jost, M. Banaji, & D. Prentice (Eds.), *Perspectivism in social psychology: The ying and yang of scientific progress.* Washington, DC: American Psychological Association.

Hyde, J. S., Fennema, E., & Lamon, S. J. (1990). Gender differences in mathematics performance: A meta-analysis. *Psychological Bulletin, 107,* 139–155.

Johannesen-Schmidt, M. C., & Eagly, A. H. (2002). Diminishing returns: The effects of income on the content of stereotypes of wage earners. *Personality and Social Psychology Bulletin, 28,* 1538–1545.

Jost, J. T., & Banaji, M. R. (1994). The role of stereotyping in system-justification and the production of false consciousness. *British Journal of Social Psychology, 33,* 1–27.

Konrad, A. M., Ritchie, J. E., Jr., Lieb, P., & Corrigall, E. (2000). Sex differences and similarities in job attribute preferences: A meta-analysis. *Psychological Bulletin, 126,* 593–641.

Lippman, W. (1922). *Public opinion.* New York: Harcourt, Brace.

Lueptow, L. B., Garovich-Szabo, L., & Lueptow, M. B. (2001). Social change and the persistence of sex typing: 1974–1997. *Social Forces, 80,* 1–36.

McGuire, W. J. (1990). Dynamic operations of thought systems. *American Psychologist, 45,* 504–512.

McGuire, W. J., & McGuire, C. V. (1991). The content, structure, and operation of thought systems. In R. S. Wyer, Jr. & T. K. Srull (Eds.), *Advances in social cognition* (Vol. 4, pp. 1–78). Hillsdale, NJ: Erlbaum.

National Collegiate Athletic Association. (2001). *1982–2000 participation statistics report.* Indianapolis, IN: Author.

Ogburn, W. F. (1922/1964). Social change with respect to culture and original nature. Gloucester, MA: Peter Smith.

Preston, J. A. (1995). Gender and the formation of a women's profession: The case of public school teaching. In J. A. Jacobs (Ed.), *Gender inequality at work* (pp. 379–407). Thousand Oaks, CA: Sage.

Ross, L., Amabile, T. M., & Steinmetz, J. L. (1977). Social roles, social control, and biases in social-perception processes. *Journal of Personality and Social Psychology, 35,* 485–494.

Ross, M. (1989). Relation of implicit theories to the construction of personal histories. *Psychological Review, 96,* 341–357.

Ross, M., & Newby-Clark, I. R. (1998). Construing the past and the future. *Social Cognition, 16,* 133–150.

Schaller, M., & O'Brien, M. (1992). "Intuitive analysis of covariance" and group stereotype formation. *Personality and Social Psychology Bulletin, 18,* 776–785.

Spence, J. T., & Buckner, C. E. (2000). Instrumental and expressive traits, trait stereotypes, and sexist attitudes. *Psychology of Women Quarterly, 24,* 44–62.

Torregrosa, J. (in press). Social psychology: Social or sociological? In A. H. Eagly, R. M. Baron, & V. L. Hamilton (Eds.), *The social psychology of group identity and social conflict: Theory, applications, and practice.* Washington, DC: American Psychological Association.

Twenge, J. M. (1997). Changes in masculine and feminine traits over time: A meta-analysis. *Sex Roles, 36,* 305–325.

Twenge, J. M. (2001). Changes in women's assertiveness in response to status and roles: A cross-temporal meta-analysis, 1931–1993. *Journal of Personality and Social Psychology, 81,* 133–145.

U.S. Department of Justice, Federal Bureau of Investigation (2000). *Crime in the United States, 1999.* Washington, DC: Author. Retrieved May 15, 2001, from http://www.fbi.gov/ucr/Cius_99/99crime/

Wood, W., & Eagly, A. H. (2002). A cross-cultural analysis of the social roles of women and men: Implications for the origins of sex differences. *Psychological Bulletin, 128,* 699–727.

# 16

## A Perspectivist Looks at the Past, Present, and (Perhaps) the Future of Intergroup Relations: A Quixotic Defense of System Justification Theory

### John T. Jost

### Prologue

My first encounter with the discipline of social psychology was on foreign soil as an exchange student in London in the summer of 1987. The idea of creating a microcosm of society in the controlled circumstances of a laboratory seized me, and I have sought to pursue this image in my own work. Beginning with my dissertation research under the supervision of Bill McGuire, I developed an experimental paradigm to manipulate perceived socioeconomic status differences between groups in order to investigate their effects on the contents of social stereotypes (e.g., Jost, 2001; Jost & Burgess, 2000).

I deferred my admission to the PhD program at Yale University, with Bill's blessing, to do graduate work in analytic philosophy for one year, much as he had done almost 40 years before. When I finally arrived at Yale in 1990, it was by sheer luck that I happened into an environment that was almost perfectly conducive to my nascent interests in social and political psychology. My hopes for an intellectually stimulating graduate school experience were realized not only in lectures, seminars, colloquia, and interdisciplinary research teams, but also in darkened, wood-paneled bars, pizza places, and cafés, where a small group of students savored the writings of Marx, Mead, Dewey, Simmel, Vygotsky, Wundt, James, Köhler, Wittgenstein, Mannheim, Lewin, Allport, Hovland, Asch, Festinger, Milgram, and many others.

My preoccupations with ideology, justice, and intergroup relations did not obviously fit with those of Bill McGuire, but I finally convinced him, after weeks of persuasive attempts, to become my advisor. He read and commented tirelessly on every draft of every manuscript I wrote, and for that I can only offer my undying gratitude and sincere apologies (to him and the world of social psychology) for his lost time. I learned the perspectivist method for building theory and planning research from its creator, repeating again and again the worksheets contained in the appendix of this volume until I (almost) got them right. In this chapter, I illustrate the ways in which Bill's teachings and writings have influenced and inspired some of my own quixotic, theory-driven work on stereotyping, intergroup relations, and system justification.

The first statement of system justification theory was coauthored with my other Yale mentor, Mahzarin Banaji, and was published in 1994 in the *British Journal of Social Psychology*, a fitting outlet given that my social psychological odyssey began in Britain. Through Bill and Mahzarin, I acquired an abiding respect for the (short) scientific history and innovative methods of social cognition. Although I have always been more enamored of the intricacies of collective social processes than of individual mental processes per se, my research proclivities generally favor experimental machinations over public opinion surveys. Thus, as an experimental social psychologist, I aim to isolate and trap evidence of justification, rationalization, and other psychological defense mechanisms exercised on behalf of the social system. In the perspectivist tradition, I am a social constructionist who believes in using empirical methods to investigate, among other things, the processes by which reality is socially constructed (see Jost & Kruglanski, 2002). I see my work as descended from "old school" social cognition, in which society and the mental lives of individuals are inextricably linked. I also keep the faith, as did the original Yale attitude change researchers, that social psychology, if conducted rigorously and critically, may help to diagnose and, ultimately, even solve problems of society.

\* \* \*

## Introduction

> He was but seven-and-twenty, an age at which many men are not quite common—at which they are hopeful of achievement, resolute in avoidance. . . . But, one vacation, a wet day sent him to the small home library to hunt once more for a book which might have some freshness for him: in vain! unless, indeed, he took down a dusty row of volumes with grey-paper backs and dingy labels. . . . They were on the highest shelf, and he stood on a chair to get them down . . . the moment of vocation had come, and before he got down from his chair, the world was made new to him by a presentiment of endless processes filling the vast spaces planked out of his sight by that wordy ignorance which he had supposed to be knowledge. (Eliot, 1872/2000, pp. 134–136)

I once asked Bill McGuire, as dutiful graduate students of seven-and-twenty occasionally do, if I should read anything in advance of our next research meeting. "Yes," he replied with a mischievous smile, "*Middlemarch* by George Eliot." Like Kurt Lewin, Bill believed that reading academic psychology generally served to limit the imaginations of psychology students and that focusing too narrowly on the published scientific literature would lead one almost inevitably to the fate of conducting studies about studies rather than studies about people and the "endless processes filling the vast spaces" within them and between them. Serious measures of vigilance are continually needed to force one's mind to be open and creative in pursuit of human understanding, and that is why McGuire (1997) lists no fewer than 49 heuristics for "jolting one's conceptualizing out of its usual ruts" and other methods for provoking new insights and drawing innovative hypotheses. "The goal," he told me, "is to find out what it is that *YOU* think." My moment of vocation had begun.

Bill McGuire is probably the greatest list maker that psychology has ever seen, and his (1997) list of creative heuristics represents the culmination of a quarter-century of formal and informal teaching and writing on his perspectivist philosophy of science (1973, 1983, 1986, 1989, 1997). Although my years as his graduate student make it possible for me to recite better than the rosary most if not all of the 49 heuristics, in this chapter I will focus on just 7 of them. Specifically, I will address the benefits of following these McGuirean principles: (a) accounting for deviations from the general trend, (b) accounting for the contrary of a banal hypothesis, (c) conjecturing interaction variables that qualify a relation, (d) quixotically defending a theory, (e) multiplying insights by conceptual division of independent and dependent variables, (f) reconciling conflicting outcomes, and (g) considering nonmonotonic relations as a function of separate monotonic relations. Each of these research strategies, I suggest, either has contributed or will contribute significantly to the past, present, and future of intergroup relations.

Next to list making and poetry reading (especially Blake, Yeats, Wordsworth, and Hopkins), Bill's third favorite pedagogic activity is describing and delineating "eras" of research, including some eras of social and political psychology that have yet to take place (e.g., McGuire, 1985, 1993, 1999). In 1993, for example, after successive waves of intrapersonal research in political personality (1940s–1950s), political attitudes and voting behavior (1960s–1970s), and political ideology (1980s–1990s), he predicted that "macroresearch is likely to grow relative to microresearch due to growing interest in intergroup issues" (McGuire, 1999, p. 365). I do not know whether the era of intergroup relations has begun yet, but I have certainly tried my best to hasten its arrival (e.g., Jost, 2001; Jost & Banaji, 1994; Jost & Burgess, 2000). If the era of intergroup relations ever does regain its Lewinian splendor, we perspectivists should be ready to learn from the past in order to make the most of present opportunities and guarantee creative directions for the future. Adopting each of these different time perspectives in turn, I consider the past, present, and future of intergroup relations.

## The Past: The Yin and Yang of Intergroup Relations

> Perhaps that was a more cheerful time for observers and theorisers than the present; we are apt to think it the finest era of the world when America was beginning to be discovered, when a bold sailor, even if he were wrecked, might alight on new kingdom. . . . (Eliot, 1872/2000, p. 139)

Observers of scientific trends typically reach the same conclusion that observers of other kinds of social trends usually reach, which is that tastes and interests swing back and forth between one set of concerns and assumptions and their opposite. This is the "pendulum" argument famously advanced by McGuire (1973) in his celebrated article on "The Yin and Yang of Progress in Social Psychology." A prime example of the waxing and waning of research interests, which often follow broader societal patterns (see also McGuire, 1999), pertains to the study of intergroup relations. Although Kuhn (1962) saw different scientific paradigms as largely incommensurable with one another and paradigm shifts as brought on by nonrational, social forces, a case can be made that scientific *progress* has taken place in intergroup relations because of perspectivist practices: New theories build on the insights of earlier theories by incorporating old variables and past hypotheses and reconciling them with new and opposing variables, hypotheses, and relations. That is, societal trends may drive changes in interests, but perspectivist methodology allows for our knowledge to be cumulative.

## The Era of Group Self-Hatred

From 1935 to 1965, it was a virtually indisputable assumption of the emerging field of intergroup relations that members of disadvantaged groups could not help but internalize society's biases against them and adopt preferences for other, more advantaged groups (e.g., Allport, 1954/1958; Lewin, 1941/1948). The hypothesized result was an "inferiority complex" at the group level. This discovery represented an attempt to "account for deviations from the general trend" (McGuire, 1997); the "general trend," as psychologists then and now would agree, is to defend the ego against threat and adversity (Allport, 1954; Greenwald, 1980; Steele, 1988). Even Jean-Paul Sartre (1948/1976) got in on the act, joining social psychologists such as Kurt Lewin and Gordon Allport in diagnosing the syndrome of Jewish Anti-Semitism. Psychoanalytic work on "identification with the aggressor" indicated that among victims of injustice and deprivation there was, as McGuire (1985) put it, an implicit "resentment against one's own kind, who are, however unintentionally, the reasons for one's suffering" (p. 265).

This was also the famous conclusion reached by Clark and Clark (1947), whose research on African American children's preferences for White dolls is among the most influential social psychological work in history from the standpoint of social policy (e.g., Allport, 1954/1958). For more than three decades, social scientists documented the extent to which "self-hatred," as it was originally called, encumbered minority groups low in social status. Researchers did not blame members of oppressed groups for "hating" themselves and their peers. Rather, it was seen as a natural "expression of the situation in which the individual finds himsef" (Lewin, 1941/1948, p. 197), so that "some degree of in-group hate seems almost inevitable" (Allport, 1954/1958, p. 152).

## The Era of Strategic Identity-Enhancement

From approximately 1965 to 1990, these pessimistic conclusions yielded to the notion that members of disadvantaged groups strive (often successfully) to compete with members of advantaged groups for symbolic and material resources (e.g., Campbell, 1965; Sherif, 1966; Tajfel & Turner, 1979). The most influential theories of this period stressed motives for positive group distinctiveness and favorable social identification, which led members of low status groups to generally reject unfavorable stereotypes of their group in order to enhance their own individual and collective self-esteem (e.g., Brewer, 1979; Hogg & Abrams, 1988; Tajfel & Turner, 1979). Buoyed no doubt by the significant advances in terms of power and identity made by disadvantaged minority groups during the civil rights era, social identity theory documented the ways in which people rebound creatively and resiliently from the consequences of belonging to stigmatized groups (e.g., Tajfel & Turner, 1979).

Taking a page out of the perspectivist playbook, researchers turned received wisdom on its head, asking not about the ways in which deprived minorities suffered in terms of self-esteem but rather how and why members of disadvantaged groups acquired *elevated* levels of self-esteem (e.g., Crocker & Major, 1989; Porter & Washington, 1979). Not only did researchers of this middle era manage to account for the contrary of what had become a relatively banal hypothesis (that disadvantaged group members internalize a sense of inferiority), they proposed interaction variables to qualify the relation between stigma and self-esteem. Specifically, social identity theorists found that members of disadvantaged groups accept their inferiority on status-relevant but not status-irrelevant attributes (van Knippenberg, 1978) and when perceived legitimacy and system stability are high but not when they are low (e.g., Turner & Brown, 1978). Crocker and Major (1989) made good use of the concept of attributional ambiguity to handle "conflicting outcomes" (McGuire, 1997), such as the initially surprising evidence that African Americans possessed higher self-esteem than did European Americans (Porter & Washington, 1979). A series of ingenious experiments summarized by Crocker and Major (1989) revealed that members of disadvantaged groups show enhanced self-esteem when circumstances make it possible to attribute negative social feedback to prejudice and discrimination but not when circumstances prevent self-protective attributions from being made (e.g., when procedures are "colorblind").

## The Era of (Implicit) Outgroup Favoritism

By 1990 the pendulum had begun to swing back, as liberal social scientists concluded that the revolution was over and that the good guys had either lost or been bought off with stock options. Sexism, racism, and classism, one was obliged to finally admit, are enduring and even collaborative institutions. Not long after Mansbridge (1986) and others asked why we lost the Equal Rights Amendment and found that women were as responsible as men, social psychologists renewed attention to phenomena such as the "depressed entitlement effect" among women (Blanton, George, & Crocker, 2001; Jost, 1997; Major, 1994; Pelham & Hetts, 2001), the existence of consensual status hierarchies (Jackman, 1994; Jost & Banaji, 1994; Sidanius, Levin, & Pratto, 1996), and the persistence of outgroup favoritism among members of low status groups (Hinkle & Brown, 1990; Jost, 2001). Thus, after a flourishing of research on the strategies with which people successfully resist the social order—psychologically if not in every way—pessimism (or perhaps realism) returned to the study of intergroup relations. Inequality *is* internalized, at least to some degree, and members of disadvantaged groups are indeed affected by their subjugation (e.g., Glick & Fiske, 2001; Jost & Burgess, 2000;

Major, 1994; Sidanius, 1993). If the recent flurry of publications on implicit, nonconscious forms of outgroup favoritism (e.g., Jost, Pelham, & Carvallo, 2002; Nosek, Banaji, & Greenwald, 2002; Rudman, Feinberg, & Fairchild, 2002; Uhlmann, Dasgupta, Elgueta, Greenwald, & Swanson, 2002) is any indication, the future of research on intergroup relations is even more likely to return to its earlier appreciation of the internalization of inequality.

An astute perspectivist might have seen it coming: millennial researchers seeking to overturn what had become a relatively banal hypothesis (the ubiquity of ingroup favoritism) during the era dominated by social identity theory. System justification theory addresses "classic" phenomena such as group self-hatred by integrating previous findings and incorporating new scientific methods, including implicit, unobtrusive measures. What results is a more nuanced theoretical account that views people as striving (consciously and nonconsciously) to cope with and reconcile a set of potentially conflicting needs and motives, including the motive to rationalize the status quo. As perspectivists with an avid respect for historical lessons, we hope not merely to repeat prior "delusional systems," as McGuire (1973) would say, but rather to advance our own delusional systems to explore and justify, building on earlier insights and theories in seeking to reconcile seemingly contradictory outcomes and findings.

## Present Opportunities: A Quixotic Defense of System Justification Theory

> For in the multitude of middle-aged men who go about their vocations in a daily course determined for them much in the same way as the tie of their cravats, there is always a good number who once meant to shape their own deeds and alter the world a little. The story of their coming to be shapen after the average and fit to be packed by the gross, is hardly ever told even in their consciousness. . . . Nothing in the world is more subtle than the process of their gradual change! In the beginning they inhaled it unknowingly: you and I may have sent some of our breath towards infecting them, when we uttered our conforming falsities or drew our silly conclusions. . . .
> (Eliot, 1872/2000 pp. 136–137)

Emboldened by Bill McGuire's advice to find out what it is that *I* think and to explore the meaning of my own insights, I set out to develop a new theory of intergroup relations and political psychology (Jost, 1995; Jost & Banaji, 1994). My colleagues and I formulated system justification theory in order to integrate and expand on cognitive dissonance theory, justice research, social identity theory, and Marxist–feminist theories of ideology. In so doing, we drew very heavily on McGuire's (1983, 1989, 1997) perspectivism, in which researchers are implored to combine and integrate opposing hypotheses and alternative theories and "to interpret and integrate the empirical relationships that have been turned up by the recent deluge of studies, rather than simply adding new, undigested relationships to the existing pile" (McGuire, 1973, p. 455). Thus, the origins of system justification theory are integrative and pluralistic, perhaps even promiscuous, in their approach to theorizing about social and political behavior.

We proposed system justification theory mainly to account for the consensuality of stereotypes across group boundaries and the phenomenon of outgroup favoritism on the part of low status group members (Jost & Banaji, 1994). The guiding assumption of our theory was that people engage in a rationalization of the status quo (see Kay, Jimenez, & Jost, 2002). We were objecting to the one-sidedness (and, indeed, the banality) of the message that people universally favor members of their own group and discriminate against outsiders, even under "minimal" conditions involving laboratory groups with no history of interaction (e.g., Brewer, 1979; Tajfel & Turner, 1979). The hypothesis of ingroup favoritism, in any case, was a good one for a perspectivist to turn on its head, and so we, like a few other commentators (e.g., Hinkle & Brown, 1990; Sidanius, 1993), focused on the phenomenon of *out*group favoritism (Jost & Banaji, 1994). We argued that outgroup favoritism was one means by which members of disadvantaged groups accepted and even perpetuated the legitimacy of the existing system of hierarchy. For us, it was one piece of evidence that, to their own detriment, people could be "shapen after the average and fit to be packed by the gross," as George Eliot observed.

In a related line of research, my colleagues and I have sought to account for the contrary of the relatively banal hypothesis that people's social and political attitudes generally follow patterns of self-interest. Without rejecting the truthfulness or the utility of the self-interest assumption, we perspectivists set out to identify contexts in which people would hold attitudes that were opposite from what would be expected on the basis of objective self-interest. Specifically, we incorporated the logic of dissonance theory to predict that when the salience of personal and collective interests and esteem was low, members of disadvantaged groups would engage in system justification to an even greater degree than would members of advantaged groups, insofar as the latter group would have a greater need to justify their own suffering under the status quo. Support for this hypothesis came from five survey studies reported by Jost, Pelham, Sheldon, and Sullivan (2003).

## The Categorical Trap

By employing theoretical categories like outgroup favoritism and false consciousness (Eliot's "conforming falsities"), we often left ourselves open to an objection Bill raised in the margins of my manuscripts. The objection was that we were in danger of *reifying* an extremely subtle, complex, and dynamic social *process* whereby people are pulled by a great many factors in opposite directions both toward and away from the overarching social system. In raising this problem, Bill alluded to a classic article by Lewin (1931/1935) and accused me of being an "Aristotelian" rather than a "Galilean." Having been raised by a father who teaches ancient Greek philosophy, I did not immediately recognize this as criticism. Nevertheless, Bill was right that our conceptualization was too "categorical" and that one symptom of the problem was that we were often treating a continuous dependent variable (the difference between ingroup and outgroup evaluations) as a dichotomous one (either ingroup favoritism or outgroup favoritism). Lewin, who has probably been a greater influence on

Bill's perspectivist philosophy of science (e.g., McGuire, 1973, 1986, 1989, 1997, 1999) than has been recognized, wrote, somewhat hopefully, that

> the grouping of events and objects into paired opposites and similar logical dichotomies is being replaced by groupings with the aid of serial concepts which permit of continuous variation, partly owing simply to wider experience and the recognition that transition stages are always present. (p. 22)

I learned from Bill that the perspectivist should regard his or her task as detecting patterns of covariation in reality and that one needs a "pretzel-shaped theory for a pretzel-shaped universe" (see McGuire, 1968a, p. 178).

Rather than abandoning system justification theory in the face of skeptical challenges, I have sought to defend it quixotically. McGuire (1997) advocates "embracing and sticking with a theory, continuing to derive testable implications from it despite its superficial implausibility, its obvious oversimplification, or its poor empirical track record" (p. 21). In attempting to compensate for some of the shortcomings associated with the theory's Aristotelian origins, we found our way out of the "categorical trap" by adopting explicitly perspectivist strategies: conjecturing situational and dispositional moderating and interacting variables, reconciling conflicting outcomes and complementary theories, and multiplying insights by conceptual division of independent and dependent variables.

## Conjecturing Interaction Variables

After the first phase of research on system justification theory, in which we sought to demonstrate and theorize about the occurrence of outgroup favoritism, depressed entitlement, and false consciousness (e.g., Jost, 1995, 1997; Jost & Banaji, 1994), in the second phase we sought to identify variables that would moderate the expression of ingroup and outgroup favoritism among members of groups that differ in social status (see also Jost, Burgess, & Mosso, 2001). Following perspectivist prescriptions, we focused on both situational variables, such as perceived legitimacy, presence versus absence of explanation, and system threat (Haines & Jost, 2000; Jost, 2001; Jost et al., 2001), and on dispositional variables, such as the belief in a just world, political orientation, and social dominance orientation (Jost & Burgess, 2000; Jost et al., 2001; Jost & Thompson, 2000). Specifically, we found that the degree of (system justifying) outgroup favoritism among members of low status or powerless groups is increased when (a) explanations (or pseudoexplanations) are provided, (b) an ideological threat is directed at the system, or (c) perceived legitimacy is increased, and when people are high in (d) the belief in a just world, (e) social dominance orientation, or (f) political conservatism.

## Reconciling Conflicting Outcomes and Complementary Theories

From the beginning, proponents of system justification theory have sought not to deny but to embrace and incorporate ethnocentric motives to favor the ingroup, such as those documented by social identity theorists (Tajfel & Turner, 1979). Thus, my colleagues and I acknowledge that people are indeed motivated to maintain or enhance individual self-esteem (ego justification) and to maintain or enhance ingroup status and esteem (group justification), as previous theorists have argued (e.g., Brewer, 1979; Cialdini et al., 1976; Greenwald, 1980; Steele, 1988; Tajfel & Turner, 1979). Our contribution has been to suggest that there is also a motive to maintain or enhance the legitimacy and stability of the status quo (see also Lerner & Miller, 1978) and that this (system justification) motive may work in conjunction with or contradiction to ego justification and group justification motives. In general, system justification theory indicates that for members of high status groups, motives for ego justification, group justification, and system justification are consistent and complementary, whereas for members of low status groups, these motives are often in conflict with one another.

Jost and Burgess (2000) found that members of low status groups exhibited greater attitudinal ambivalence (or psychological conflict) directed at their own group than did members of high status groups. Here, the perspectivist sees an internal reconciliation (in the form of ambivalence) of conflicting or opposite motives (McGuire, 1989). Furthermore, we found that increased levels of system justification are associated with increased levels of ambivalence among members of low status groups (as the conflict is made worse) but with *decreased* ambivalence among members of high status groups, for whom group and system justification needs are consistent and reinforcing. By distinguishing clearly among motives of ego justification, group justification, and system justification (Jost & Banaji, 1994), our theory helps in understanding and integrating the complementary insights offered by other theorists and researchers of intergroup relations.

## Multiplying Insights by Conceptual Division

Always a fan of conceptual analysis, McGuire (1997) has advised researchers to partition independent and dependent variables into more specific submeanings in order to fully explore the richness of our theories. This is the strategy that Jost and Thompson (2000) took in dividing Pratto, Sidanius, Stallworth, and Malle's (1994) conceptualization and measurement of "social dominance orientation" into two variables or subscales: "group-based dominance" and "opposition to equality." The first of these, we argued, is a rough approximation of what Jost and Banaji (1994) referred to as group justification, whereas the second captures a specific form of system justification. By applying the above analysis concerning expected relations among ego, group, and system justification, we were able to generate new hypotheses concerning social dominance orientation.

Specifically, in four studies, Jost and Thompson (2000) found that a correlated, two-factor solution of the social dominance orientation scale provided a better fit for the data than did a one-factor solution. More significant, perhaps, we found that the two factors predicted different social and psychological outcomes for European Americans and African Americans. Consistent with Jost and Banaji's (1994) formulation, "opposition to equality" was related positively to self-esteem and ingroup favoritism for European Americans, but it was related *negatively* to self-esteem and ingroup favoritism for

African Americans. In contrast, "group-based dominance" was positively related to ingroup favoritism for both groups, as system justification theory would predict. By partitioning the variable of social dominance orientation into distinct subvariables, Jost and Thompson (2000) were able to learn something more about empirical relations involving structural inequality, political ideology, and personal and group attitudes.

Although we sought to use the system justification perspective constructively (as well as quixotically) as a way of forcing new insight into old problems (see also Kay et al., 2002), I fear that we have not yet done justice to the subtlety and complexity of dynamics that involve individual and collective tendencies toward rationalization and reactions to structural inequality. As George Eliot observed, "Nothing in the world is more subtle" than the "gradual change" whereby people go from wanting to "alter the world a little" to conforming like neckties to the mundane folds that society demands. Admittedly, system justification theorists are far from having captured this process of change in a fully satisfactory way or of demonstrating how people "send their breath" toward "infecting others" with ideology. A partial answer may be that we need to analyze open-ended, nonreactive, qualitative sources of data, as recommended by McGuire (1999).

In addition, researchers should explore ever more complex relations involving multiple variables and complex causality (McGuire, 1973). McGuire's (1968b, 1985) feats of list making remind us that any given behavioral outcome could be the product of 37 forces (or causal variables) pushing in one or more directions and 21 forces (or causal variables) pulling in other directions. For better or for worse, the professional journal publication system was not made for such complex uncertainty. Editors and reviewers typically require authors to demonstrate that effects are attributable to a single cause and to "rule out" all other possible influences, regardless of whether theory competition is intended or even possible (see Greenwald, chapter 20 of this volume).

Perspectivism helps manage the complexity, leading researchers to specify both monotonic and nonmonotonic relations among variables in isolation and in combination. Although perspectivism poses special theoretical and methodological challenges to understand and decompose nonmonotonic effects into separate monotonic relations (e.g., McGuire, 1997), the rewards in terms of understanding and prediction are great indeed (e.g., see Brewer, 1991; McGuire, 1968b). In the future, we would do well to reconcile different theoretical frameworks (e.g., social identification, social dominance, and system justification) and opposing findings (such as ingroup favoritism and outgroup favoritism) by appreciating the distinctive roles of separate motives and tendencies in determining human behavior and empirically observed relations among variables.

## Future Challenges: Exploring Nonmonotonic Relations Among Variables

News is often dispersed as thoughtlessly and effectively as that pollen which the bees carry off (having no idea how powdery they are) when they are buzzing in search of their particular nectar. (Eliot,1872/2000, p. 570)

In applying McGuire's (1973, 1986, 1999) dialectical methods to the domain of intergroup relations, I have already mentioned several of his favorite vehicles for reconciling conflicting hypotheses, theories, and outcomes. One that is powerful and underutilized has to do with accounting for nonmonotonic relations by decomposing a U-shaped or inverted U-shaped pattern into separate and opposite monotonic trends or processes (see McGuire, 1997). This technique has been used to great effect by McGuire (1968b) and Brewer (1991), but if the future is as curvaceous as it looks from here, more theory-driven researchers should ride the roller coaster.

In what is probably still the most famous example in social psychology (see Eagly & Chaiken, 1993), McGuire (1968b) sought to integrate conflicting findings pertaining to self-esteem and attitude change. Whereas Janis (1954) obtained a negative relation between receiver self-esteem and influenceability, McGuire and Ryan (see McGuire, 1999, p. 89) found the opposite. Complicating matters further were extant reports of both U-shaped and inverted U-shaped relations between influenceability and actual attitude change. McGuire (1968b) reasoned that self-esteem should be related positively to one mediator of attitude change, namely argument comprehension, but that it should be related negatively to another mediator, namely *yielding* in response to the argument. Multiplying these compensatory effects, one sees that the optimal level of persuasiveness exists at moderate levels of self-esteem (and intelligence, education, age, anxiety, and so on; see also McGuire, 1997, 1999). "Out of this nettle, confusion," McGuire (1999, p. 89) wrote, "our theory plucks the flower, truth."

Brewer (1991) sought to reconcile the eminently reasonable theoretical assumption that people are motivated to affiliate with others (e.g., Cialdini et al., 1976) with the equally plausible assumption that people are motivated to define themselves as unique and distinctive individuals (e.g., McGuire, 1999; Zimbardo, 1969). Brewer graphed each of these opposite, monotonic trends and reasoned that the optimal level of distinctiveness for meeting contradictory identity needs must lie in the middle, so that belonging to very small or very large groups will not be as satisfying as belonging to groups that are intermediate in size and therefore strike the best balance between contradictory needs for affiliation and uniqueness. This account was supported in several experimental studies (e.g., Brewer, Manzi, & Shaw, 1992), and the implications should continue to influence social identity theory for years to come.

To return to my "own particular nectar," which may or may not be "news" to others buzzing in the conceptual space of intergroup relations, what are the nonmonotonic opportunities awaiting the student of system justification? It seems to me that the effect of social status (e.g., socioeconomic status [SES], income, class, education) on political ideology—which has been the subject of theory and research for several decades (Adorno, Frenkel-Brunswik, Levinson, & Sanford, 1950; Centers, 1949)—is a perfect candidate for McGuirean treatment. Consistent with theories of self-interest and "class consciousness," some researchers have observed positive relations between SES and political conservatism (e.g., Centers, 1949; Sidanius, Ekehammar, & Lukowsky, 1983). Other studies have yielded no discernible effects of SES on conservatism (e.g., Sidanius & Ekehammar, 1979), and still others have turned up signs of *increased* levels of conservatism among those who are lower in social and economic status (e.g., Ray, 1990; Stacey & Green, 1971).

Providing still more evidence that we do indeed live in a "pretzel-shaped universe," data collected by Sulloway (personal correspondence, May 2, 2001) adhere to a U-shaped pattern of relations between social status and conservatism. In an archival study of 1408 participants in 28 scientific revolutions who lived between 1543 and 1967 (see Sulloway, 1996), Sulloway plotted the scientists' SES levels against a composite measure of conservatism with respect to religious and political attitudes. The results indicated that conservatism is highest when socioeconomic status is either very high or very low. Pushing further, Sulloway and I have discovered relatively general support for the quadratic hypothesis that conservatism increases at extreme levels of SES in either direction.

The integrative capacities of even the most earnest perspectivist are tested by four seemingly contradictory patterns: (a) a positive, monotonic relation between status and conservatism (e.g., Centers, 1949; Sidanius et al., 1983), (b) a negative, monotonic relation between status and conservatism (e.g., Ray, 1990; Stacey & Green, 1971), (c) no effect of status on conservatism (Sidanius & Ekehammar, 1979), and (d) a U-shaped pattern (Sulloway, personal correspondence, May 2, 2001). Without oversimplifying the case too dramatically, system justification theory may offer some assistance.

To the extent that political conservatism may be considered to be a kind of system-justifying variable (see Jost, Glaser, Kruglanski, & Sulloway, 2003), there are sound theoretical reasons for predicting opposite monotonic relations between social status and conservatism and, therefore, for reconciling them nonmonotonically. Jost et al. (2001) argued that self-interest motivation should lead members of high status groups to exhibit stronger levels of system justification than would members of low status groups. However, for very different reasons, having to do with dissonance reduction, one might suppose that members of disadvantaged groups would be *more* likely to support the existing social system, at least under some circumstances (Jost et al., 2003; Lane, 1959). Putting these opposing insights together in the manner of McGuire (1968b) and Brewer (1991), future-oriented system justification theorists would be well-poised to understand nonmonotonic relations such as the one observed by Sulloway.

Much of the mystery remains, however, for future researchers to explore. It is not yet clear from the analysis above when to expect that monotonic relations will hold and when nonmonotonic, U-shaped patterns will emerge. Presumably, additional mediators and moderators could be identified that would introduce further multiplicative effects (see McGuire, 1968b), perhaps even flip-flopping the pattern from one condition to the next. To incorporate historical and cultural variables, for example, Converse (1958) observed that social class affected voting behavior much more in 1945 than it did in 1956, and Robinson and Bell (1978) noted that social class had larger effects on political attitudes in Great Britain (where organized labor parties figure more prominently in local and national politics) than in the United States. Even more generally, it is reasonable to suppose that dissonance-related mechanisms would play a larger role in democratic societies (see Lane, 1959), in which political decisions are made under conditions of choice (or at least the illusion of choice), compared to societies in which authorities and systems are seen as imposed rather than chosen (see also Jost et al., 2003).

It may also be advisable to partition dependent variables such as conservatism (or system justification) into subvariables (see McGuire, 1997) to see whether different patterns emerge for stereotypes, beliefs about meritocracy, and support for the government. For example, Sidanius et al. (1983) reported a positive, monotonic relation between social status and political–economic conservatism, but they also found evidence of a nonmonotonic, U-shaped relation between social status and racism, thereby supporting Lipset's (1960/1981) hypothesis of "working class racism." The complexity of these considerations should make it clear that much of interest remains to be done in intergroup relations and neighboring territories and that McGuire's corpus of work shows us just how vast the spaces are and how to make the journey.

# References

Adorno, T. W., Frenkel-Brunswik, E., Levinson, D. J., & Sanford, R. N. (1950). *The authoritarian personality.* New York: Harper.

Allport, G. W. (1958). *The nature of prejudice.* Cambridge, MA: Addison Wesley. (Original work published 1954)

Blanton, H., George, G., & Crocker, J. (2001). Contexts of system justification and system evaluation: Exploring the social comparison strategies of the (not yet) contented female worker. *Group Processes and Intergroup Relations, 4,* 126–137.

Brewer, M. B. (1979). Ingroup bias in the minimal intergroup situation: A cognitive-motivational analysis. *Psychological Bulletin, 86,* 307–324.

Brewer, M. B. (1991). The social self: On being the same and different at the same time. *Personality and Social Psychology Bulletin, 17,* 475–482.

Brewer, M. B., Manzi, J. M., & Shaw, J. S. (1992). In-group identification as a function of depersonalization, distinctiveness, and status. *Psychological Science, 4,* 88–92.

Campbell, D. T. (1965). Ethnocentric and other altruistic motives. In D. Levine (Ed.), *Nebraska Symposium on Motivation* (Vol. 13, pp. 283–311). Lincoln: University of Nebraska Press.

Centers, R. (1949). *The psychology of social classes.* Princeton, NJ: Princeton University Press.

Cialdini, R. B., Borden, R. J., Thorne, A., Walker, M. R., Freeman, S., & Sloan, L. R. (1976). Basking in reflected glory: Three (football) field studies. *Journal of Personality and Social Psychology, 39,* 406–415.

Clark, K. B., & Clark, M. P. (1947). Racial identification and preference in Negro children. In E. E. Maccoby, T. M. Newcomb, & E. L. Hartley (Eds.), *Readings in social psychology* (pp. 602–611). New York: Holt, Rinehart, and Winston.

Converse, P. E. (1958). The shifting role of class in political attitudes and behavior. In E. E. Maccoby, T. M. Newcomb, & E. L. Hartley (Eds.), *Readings in social psychology* (3rd ed., pp. 388–399). New York: Holt, Rinehart and Winston, Inc.

Crocker, J., & Major, B. (1989). Social stigma and self-esteem: The self-protective properties of stigma. *Psychological Review, 96,* 608–630.

Eagly, A. H., & Chaiken, S. (1993). *The psychology of attitude change.* San Diego, CA: Harcourt Brace Jovanovich.

Eliot, G. (2000). *Middlemarch.* New York: Modern Library. (Original work published 1872)

Glick, P., & Fiske, S. T. (2001). An ambivalent alliance: Hostile and benevolent sexism as complementary justifications for gender inequality. *American Psychologist, 56,* 109–118.

Greenwald, A. G. (1980). The totalitarian ego: Fabrication and revision of personal history. *American Psychologist, 35,* 603–618.

Greenwald, A. G. (2004). The resting parrot, the dessert stomach, and other perfectly defensible theories. In J. Jost, M. Banaji, & D. Prentice (Eds.), *Perspectivism in social psychology: The ying and yang of scientific progress.* Washington, DC: American Psychological Association.

Haines, E. L., & Jost, J. T. (2000). Placating the powerless: Effects of legitimate and illegitimate explanation on affect, memory, and stereotyping. *Social Justice Research, 13,* 219–236.

Hinkle, S., & Brown, R. (1990). Intergroup comparisons and social identity: Some links and lacunae. In D. Abrams & M. A. Hogg (Eds.), *Social identity theory: Constructive and critical advances* (pp. 48–70). New York: Springer-Verlag.

Hogg, M. A., & Abrams, D. (1988). *Social identifications: A social psychology of intergroup relations and group processes.* London: Routledge.

Jackman, Mary R. (1994). *The velvet glove: Paternalism and conflict in gender, class, and race relations.* Berkeley: University of California Press.

Janis, I. (1954). Personality correlates of susceptibility to persuasion. *Journal of Personality, 22,* 204–218.

Jost, J. T. (1995). Negative illusions: Conceptual clarification and psychological evidence concerning false consciousness. *Political Psychology, 16,* 397–424.

Jost, J. T. (1997). An experimental replication of the depressed entitlement effect among women. *Psychology of Women Quarterly, 21,* 387–393.

Jost, J. T. (2001). Outgroup favoritism and the theory of system justification: An experimental paradigm for investigating the effects of socio-economic success on stereotype content. In G. Moskowitz (Ed.), *Cognitive social psychology: The Princeton symposium on the legacy and future of social cognition* (pp. 89–102). Mahwah, NJ: Erlbaum.

Jost, J. T., & Banaji, M. R. (1994). The role of stereotyping in system-justification and the production of false consciousness. *British Journal of Social Psychology, 33,* 1–27.

Jost, J. T., & Burgess, D. (2000). Attitudinal ambivalence and the conflict between group and system justification motives in low status groups. *Personality and Social Psychology Bulletin, 26,* 293–305.

Jost, J. T., Burgess, D., & Mosso, C. (2001). Conflicts of legitimation among self, group, and system: The integrative potential of system justification theory. In J. T. Jost & B. Major (Eds.), *The psychology of legitimacy: Emerging perspectives on ideology, justice, and intergroup relations* (pp. 363–388). New York: Cambridge University Press.

Jost, J. T., Glaser, J., Kruglanski, A. W., & Sulloway, F. (2003). Political conservatism as motivated social cognition. *Psychological Bulletin, 129,* 339–375.

Jost, J. T., & Kruglanski, A. W. (2002). The estrangement of social constructionism and experimental social psychology: History of the rift and prospects for reconciliation. *Personality and Social Psychology Review, 6,* 168–187.

Jost, J. T., Pelham, B. W., & Carvallo, M. (2002). Non-conscious forms of system justification: Cognitive, affective, and behavioral preferences for higher status groups. *Journal of Experimental Social Psychology, 38,* 586–602.

Jost, J. T., Pelham, B. W., Sheldon, O., & Sullivan, B. N. (2003). Social inequality and the reduction of ideological dissonance on behalf of the system: Evidence of enhanced system justification among the disadvantaged. *European Journal of Social Psychology, 33,* 13–36.

Jost, J. T., & Thompson, E. P. (2000). Group-based dominance and opposition to equality as independent predictors of self-esteem, ethnocentrism, and social policy attitudes among African Americans and European Americans. *Journal of Experimental Social Psychology, 36,* 209–232.

Kay, A., Jimenez, M. C., & Jost, J. T. (2002). Sour grapes, sweet lemons, and the anticipatory rationalization of the status quo. *Personality and Social Psychology Bulletin, 28,* 1300–1312.

Kuhn, T. S. (1962). *The structure of scientific revolutions.* Chicago: University of Chicago Press.

Lane, R. E. (1959). The fear of equality. *American Political Science Review, 53,* 35–51.

Lerner, M. J., & Miller, D. T. (1978). Just world research and the attribution process: Looking back and ahead. *Psychological Bulletin, 85,* 1030–1051.

Lewin, K. (1935). The conflict between Aristotelian and Galilean modes of thought in contemporary psychology. In K. Lewin (Ed.), *A dynamic theory of personality* (D. K. Adams & K. Zener, Trans.; pp. 1–42). New York: McGraw-Hill. (Original work published in 1931)

Lewin, K. (1948). Self-hatred among Jews. In K. Lewin (Ed.), *Resolving social conflicts: Selected papers on group dynamics* (pp. 186–200). New York: Harper & Brothers. (Original work published in 1941)

Lipset, S. M. (1981). Working-class authoritarianism. In S. M. Lipset (Ed.), *Political man: The social bases of politics* (pp. 87–126). Baltimore: Johns Hopkins University Press. (Original work published in 1960)

Major, B. (1994). From social inequality to personal entitlement: The role of social comparisons, legitimacy appraisals, and group memberships. *Advances in Experimental Social Psychology, 26*, 293–355.

Mansbridge, J. (1986). *Why we lost the ERA.* Chicago: University of Chicago Press.

McGuire, W. J. (1968a). Personality and attitude change: An information processing theory. In A. G. Greenwald, T. C. Brock, & T. M. Ostrom (Eds.), *Psychological foundations of attitudes.* New York: Academic Press.

McGuire, W. J. (1968b). Personality and susceptibility to social influence. In E. F. Borgatta & W. W. Lambert (Eds.), *Handbook of personality theory and research* (pp. 1130–1187). Chicago: Rand McNally.

McGuire, W. J. (1973). The yin and yang of progress in social psychology. *Journal of Personality and Social Psychology, 26*, 446–456.

McGuire, W. J. (1983). A contextualist theory of knowledge: Its implications for innovation and reform in psychological research. *Advances in Experimental Social Psychology, 16*, 1–47.

McGuire, W. J. (1985). Attitudes and attitude change. In G. Lindzey & E. Aronson (Eds.), *Handbook of social psychology* (pp. 233–346). New York: Random House.

McGuire, W. J. (1986). A perspectivist looks at contextualism and the future of behavioral science. In R. L. Rosnow & M. Georgoudi (Eds.), *Contextualism and understanding in behavioral science: Implications for research and theory* (pp. 271–301). New York: Praeger.

McGuire, W. J. (1989). A perspectivist approach to the strategic planning of programmatic scientific research. In B. Gholson, W. R. Shadish, Jr., R. A. Niemeyer, & A. C. Houts (Eds.), *The psychology of science: Contributions to metascience* (pp. 214–245). New York: Cambridge University Press.

McGuire, W. J. (1993). The poly-psy relationship: Three phases of a long affair. In S. Iyengar & W. J. McGuire (Eds.), *Explorations in political psychology* (pp. 9–35). Durham, NC: Duke University Press.

McGuire, W. J. (1997). Creative hypothesis generating in psychology: Some useful heuristics. *Annual Review of Psychology, 48*, 1–30.

McGuire, W. J. (1999). *Constructing social psychology: Creative and critical processes.* Cambridge, UK: Cambridge University Press.

Nosek, B. A., Banaji, M. R., & Greenwald, A. G. (2002). Harvesting implicit group attitudes and beliefs from a demonstration website. *Group Dynamics, 6*, 101–115.

Pelham, B. W., & Hetts, J. J. (2001). Underworked and overpaid: Elevated entitlement in men's self-pay. *Journal of Experimental Social Psychology, 37*, 93–103.

Porter, J. R., & Washington, R. E. (1979). Black identity and self-esteem: A review of studies of black self-concept, 1968–1978. *Annual Review of Sociology, 5*, 53–74.

Pratto, F., Sidanius, J., Stallworth, L. M., & Malle, B. F. (1994). Social dominance orientation: A personality variable predicting social and political attitudes. *Journal of Personality and Social Psychology, 67*, 741–763.

Ray, J. J. (1990). Racism, conservatism and social class in Australia with German, Californian and South African comparisons. *Personality and Individual Differences, 11*, 187–189.

Robinson, R. V., & Bell, W. (1978). Equality, success, and social justice in England and the United States. *American Sociological Review, 43*, 125–143.

Rudman, L. A., Feinberg, J., & Fairchild, K. (2002). Minority members' implicit attitudes: Automatic ingroup bias as a function of group status. *Social Cognition, 20*, 294–320.

Sartre, J. P. (1976). *Anti-semite and Jew.* New York: Schocken Books. (Original work published in 1948)

Sherif, M. (1966). *Group conflict and cooperation.* London: Routledge and Kegan Paul.

Sidanius, J. (1993). The psychology of group conflict and the dynamics of oppression: A social dominance perspective. In S. Iyengar & W. J. McGuire (Eds.), *Explorations in political psychology* (pp. 183–219). Durham, NC: Duke University Press.

Sidanius, J., & Ekehammar, B. (1979). Political socialization: A multivariate analysis of Swedish political attitude and preference data. *European Journal of Social Psychology, 9*, 265–279.

Sidanius, J., Ekehammar, B., & Lukowsky, J. (1983). Social status and sociopolitical ideology among Swedish youth. *Youth & Society, 14*, 395–415.

Sidanius, J., Levin, S., & Pratto, F. (1996). Consensual social dominance orientation and its correlates within the hierarchical structure of American society. *International Journal of Intercultural Relations, 20,* 385–408.

Stacey, B. G., & Green, R. T. (1971). Working-class conservatism: A review and an empirical study. *British Journal of Social and Clinical Psychology, 10,* 10–26.

Steele, C. M. (1988). The psychology of self-affirmation: Sustaining the integrity of the self. *Advances in Experimental Social Psychology, 21,* 261–302.

Sulloway, F. J. (1996). *Born to rebel: Birth order, family dynamics, and creative lives.* New York: Pantheon.

Tajfel, H., & Turner, J. C. (1979). An integrative theory of intergroup conflict. In W. G. Austin & S. Worchel (Eds.), *The social psychology of intergroup relations* (pp. 33–48). Monterey, CA: Brooks-Cole.

Turner, J. C., & Brown, R. (1978). Social status, cognitive alternatives, and intergroup relations. In H. Tajfel (Ed.), *Differentiation between social groups* (pp. 201–234). London: Academic Press.

Uhlmann, E., Dasgupta, N., Elgueta, A., Greenwald, A. G., & Swanson, J. (2002). Subgroup prejudice based on skin color among Hispanics in the United States and Latin America. *Social Cognition, 20,* 198–225.

van Knippenberg, A. (1978). Status differences, comparative relevance and intergroup differentiation. In H. Tajfel (Ed.), *Differentiation between social groups* (pp. 171–199). London: Academic Press.

Zimbardo, P. G. (1969). The human choice: Individuation, reason and order versus deindividuation, impulse, and chaos. In W. J. Arnold & D. Levine (Eds.), *Nebraska Symposium on Motivation* (Vol. 17). Lincoln: University of Nebraska Press.

# Part VI

# Political Communication and Mass Media

# 17

## Continuities and Contrasts in American Racial Politics

*David O. Sears*

### Prologue

The study of intergroup relations has a long history in social psychology. My approach has had three particular features. First, I use the case of relations between American racial and ethnic groups as a prism for understanding the problem of intergroup relations more generally. Second, I have focused on the political realm, because the political system has been the main lever of power in most efforts to improve intergroup relations, and efforts to provide a more egalitarian society more generally. Third, I have tried to assess continuity and change in those politics in response to two major, partially exogenous, societal events. One is the broad set of changes in relations between blacks and whites often associated with the so-called "civil rights era." The other is the sharp change in both the amount and source of immigration to the United States that began at about the same time. In this chapter, I briefly review the general theses I have worked with, the evidence (much of it recent) on the debates about them, and the main open questions.

\* \* \*

### The Black–White Model of Racial Conflict

The subordination of blacks[1] to whites dates virtually to the earliest years of European settlement in North America. Even at the dawn of the 18th century, blacks constituted a very large minority group, almost all in slavery. For the past two centuries, they have been the largest minority group in America, though now the several distinct groups of Hispanic Americans rival them in size when aggregated. It is not surprising, then, that the pattern of black–white relations has long been the dominant model for thinking about intergroup relations in the United States, both in the general public and among social scientists.

That black–white model goes like this. Africans were captured and imported involuntarily to America. Then they were forcibly held in a lower caste role, first in the institution of chattel slavery and later in the various institutions of the Jim Crow system and its Northern parallels that ensured

---

[1]In this chapter, the terms black and white have been lowercased to honor the author's preference.

physical segregation of the races and formal discrimination in favor of whites. These institutions were supported by widespread racial prejudice among whites. Blacks were formally freed from this lower caste role during the civil rights era, although there is dispute about the extent to which white racism has truly been eliminated.

Social scientific research has arrived at four important findings relevant to this black–white model. First the "color line" has long been the dominating fact of relations between blacks and whites and is a line that historically has been dangerous for blacks to cross. It was embodied in law and almost all public and private institutions for many years. Today, the continuing resonance of the color line can be seen in the remarkably high level of residential segregation of blacks and whites and low level of intermarriage between them. No human institution is perfect, of course, not even the color line, and for a variety of reasons, our country contains many people of mixed race but long-standing American ancestry. Nevertheless, the absolutistic nature of the color line is illustrated by the quirk that those of mixed ancestry, if any (black) African ancestry is known, are customarily described as "black."

Second, for nearly a century, social scientists have used William Graham Sumner's (1906) language that distinguishes "ingroups" and "outgroups" in analyzing intergroup relations. Much research has tested for the influence of whites' animosity toward blacks, as their primary racial outgroup, on whites' political attitudes. Numerous surveys have shown that individual differences in racial prejudice have been correlated with political attitudes unfavorable to blacks on issues ranging from privatizing Southern public schools in the 1950s to affirmative action in the 1990s. The magnitude of those correlations is a matter of debate, however, as is their robustness with other variables controlled.

A third finding is the especially high level of group consciousness among blacks, as manifested in strong senses of group identity and common fate. Blacks' attitudes toward racial issues also generally display less variance and weaker associations with other demographic characteristics than is the case for whites, as if being black tends to trump social class, educational level, age, gender, and so on.

As a consequence of this white outgroup animosity and black ingroup solidarity, the races are highly polarized politically. Blacks have been the most solidary of all Democrats, giving more than 90% of their votes to Democratic presidential candidates since the mid-1960s, and Democratic presidential candidates have not attracted a majority of the white vote since 1964. The races are also highly polarized on manifestly racial issues, such as affirmative action. A surprising number of issues without manifest racial content have become racialized as well, among them attitudes toward the police, welfare, and even elements of "the American Dream."

Finally, to foreshadow some comments in following sections, race tends to have relatively direct effects on whites' political attitudes. Linear, main effect models do better than curvilinear or interactive models. Nor do such effects involve much that is paradoxical, mysterious, or subtle, aside from, in the post-civil-rights era, whites' increasing efforts to avoid expressing racial animosity directly.

Since World War II, important changes in American racial politics have been stimulated most dramatically by the civil rights movement of the 1960s and the subsequent surge in immigration from Asia and Latin America. Yet there is also much continuity in racial politics, at both the aggregate and individual levels. In this chapter, I first review recent evidence on a "black–white model" of intergroup relations, with a focus on debates surrounding the theory of symbolic racism. Then the extension of the black–white model to the case of the new immigrants, as developed by social structural theories, is counterposed to a "black exceptionalism" perspective that owes its lineage to symbolic politics theory. McGuire's "Seven Koan" is then reexamined in the light of this research.

## Continuity and Change in American Racism

The research on American racism conducted by my collaborators and myself has proceeded from the assumption that basic racial prejudices are among the most powerful and enduring products of preadult political socialization. Most of the evidence for this assumption is somewhat indirect. It includes demonstrations that basic racial prejudices are acquired in early childhood, as well as evidence of high levels of continuity over time in adult whites' racial attitudes (Sears, 1983; Sears & Levy, 2003).

We argue that although race has always been a major source of political tension in the United States, the two major political parties have been strongly polarized on racial issues only in three relatively brief historical periods: around the time of the Civil War, during the civil rights era, and in the contemporary period. That suggests the hypothesis that attitudes toward racial issues should have been important bases for whites' partisan choices in those three periods and not in other periods. Our quasi-experimental test of that hypothesis found high levels of continuity in presidential voting across those three periods but little continuity between those periods and any periods in between (Sears & Valentino, 2001).

That continuity mainly reflects heavy Southern voting for racially conservative candidates in all three racialized periods. The states that were most pro-slavery in the key antebellum election of 1856, the first one involving the Republican party and the last before the election of Abraham Lincoln, are the same as those voting most strongly for George W. Bush in 2000: Texas, Mississippi, Alabama, and Georgia. Continuity held for the North as well. Those states most strongly Republican in 1856 and most opposed to the extension of slavery were Al Gore's strongest supporters in 2000: Massachusetts, Rhode Island, New York, Vermont, and Maine. The border states, Missouri, Delaware, and Tennessee (Maryland and Kentucky are something of an exception), tend to fall in the middle. The Pearson $r$ for the correlation between the state-by-state votes in 1856 and 2000 was $-.68$.

More generally, the Bush–Gore results correlate most strongly with those in the two eras in which the parties were most polarized over racial issues: the antebellum period (the average correlation with the 1848 to 1860 elections was $r = -59$) and the civil rights era (the average correlation with the 1964 to 1972 elections was $r = .65$). Other results show that the election of 2000 is no exception: the 1984, 1988, and 1996 elections all fell out along this ancient American cleavage. However, the correlations with the year 2000 of the election outcomes for the years between the Civil War and the civil rights era are much lower, exceeding .30 only once and averaging (regardless of sign) $r = .12$.

Subsequent analyses have used public opinion data to make the case that whites' racial attitudes are at work in generating (or regenerating) this cleavage. In contemporary society, whites in the Deep South continue to be more prejudiced than whites in other regions, net of other variables (Valentino & Sears, 2000).

Despite such evidence of long-term continuity in the political power of race, especially in the South, we argue that the form and content of racial prejudice has changed. "Old-fashioned racism," so common before World War II and with its emphasis on stereotypes of blacks' biological inferiority and support for racial segregation and formal discrimination, has largely been replaced by a new "symbolic racism" involving four specific content components: a denial of continuing racial discrimination and beliefs that blacks show insufficient work ethic, make unfair demands for special treatment, and too often are given undue special attention (Henry & Sears, 2002). It presumably has been shown to have origins in a blend of racial prejudice with traditional and conservative non-racial values (Sears & Henry, 2003).

Symbolic racism has been shown to have potent influence over attitudes toward racially targeted policies such as busing or affirmative action, toward black political candidates and white candidates who "play the race card," and even toward welfare and tax and spending cuts in general (e.g., Kinder & Sanders, 1996; Sears, van Laar, Carrillo, & Kosterman, 1997). Consistent with the theory about its origins, symbolic racism is greatest among those exposed to both the long tradition of racial animus in the South and conservative religious values: Southern white evangelical Protestants, reared within Southern white culture and adhering to a religious tradition that is strikingly conservative (Sears & Valentino, 2001). Symbolic racism contributes to Republican Party identification considerably more strongly in the South than in the North, especially among Southern white Evangelicals, by far the most numerically dominant component of the Southern electorate.

This theory of symbolic racism has been challenged by critics who are, for the most part, more sympathetic toward racial conservatives than toward racial liberalism. Most of those critiques have been speculative rather than based on new and disconfirming empirical evidence. We have conducted much empirical research in recent years to check the validity of these critiques. The results have led us to conclude that the theory of symbolic racism is in fact on fairly solid ground, although some of the most important evidence has not yet reached print (for a review, see Sears, Henry, & Tarman, 2003). Here I will summarize that research. It centers on five general implications of the theory.

The first implication is that symbolic racism is now distinctively different from old-fashioned racism, is much more common, and holds far more influence over whites' political attitudes. The critics speculate, in contrast, that symbolic racism, as conceptualized and as usually measured, is not really new at all (Sniderman & Tetlock, 1986). However, we argue that it is quite different in content, sharing none of the elements of old-fashioned racism except the negative stereotype about blacks' work ethic. Empirically, the two prove to be statistically independent: Symbolic racism is far more common, and it is far more powerful politically (Sears & Henry, 2002; Sears et al., 1997; Tarman & Sears, 2003).

The second implication is that symbolic racism is a distinctive and coherent belief system independent of (though somewhat correlated with) the other usual suspects, that is, other values and attitudes relevant to racial politics, such as conservative ideology, old-fashioned racism, or inegalitarian or individualistic values. This has been challenged in two ways: first with the idea that a separate construct is not necessary because symbolic racism simply reflects these other well-known attitudes and second that symbolic racism is not internally a psychologically, conceptually, or operationally coherent construct (Sniderman & Tetlock, 1986). Our research has shown, on the contrary, that when factor analyzed with these other attitudes, all four components of the manifest content of symbolic racism load together on a separate, unique factor, whereas each of those usual suspects loads only on its own individual factor. Moreover, the symbolic racism belief system, considered by itself, forms a coherent single factor, though with two highly (negatively) correlated variants that distinguish individual from structural attributions for black disadvantage (Tarman & Sears, 2003).

A third implication is drawn from a broader symbolic politics theory (Sears, 1993). If attitude objects such as racial policies and black political candidates have highly salient racial features, they should all tend to evoke racial predispositions. Symbolic racism should therefore prove to be a strong and relatively uniform predictor of opposition to a wide variety of racial policies. The critics, however, argue that whites no longer respond to all racial policies with a knee-jerk racial prejudice but rather evaluate each on its own merits. As a result, conservatives' opposition to racially targeted policies should often stem more from their being bad policies than from their stimulation of racial animosity. The evidence does not favor that view; rather, symbolic racism has strikingly uniform effects across the variety of race-targeted policies (Sears et al., 1997). The critics go on to speculate that any such uniform effects arise either because preferences about such racial policies as affirmative action have been incorporated into measures of symbolic racism by definition or because symbolic racism is measured with items similar in content to those of the dependent variables it is intended to predict (Sniderman, Crosby, & Howell, 2000; Sniderman & Tetlock, 1986). The critics' views on the first point are outdated (though quite common), because such items have not been used in measures of symbolic racism since the early 1980s. On the second point, purging any such items from measures of symbolic racism proves consistently not to reduce the strength of its effects (Sears et al., 1997; Tarman & Sears, 2003). Whatever the differences among racial policies, they all seem to attract racial animosity in about the same measure.

A fourth implication is that the effects of symbolic racism on racial policy preferences also dominate those of more benign, race-neutral conservative values, though not necessarily to their exclusion. The critics believe that opposition to racial policies is centrally motivated by opposition to big government and therefore by conservative ideology, whereas those effects of symbolic racism result from its being a confounded mixture of prejudice and ideology (Sniderman & Tetlock, 1986). On the contrary, the evidence is that conservative ideology has little effect on such preferences with symbolic racism controlled, whereas controls on ideology diminish the effects of symbolic racism very little. Indeed, symbolic racism continues to explain a hefty amount of the variance in racial policies when entered in stagewise regression equations after all the other usual suspects have been considered (Sears et al., 1997).

A fifth implication is that the origins of symbolic racism lie in early-socialized attitudes, reflected in adulthood as a blend of racial animosity with individualistic values. The critics argue that symbolic racism has not been shown to originate in either racial animus or individualism, that the notion of a blend is unclear and unproven, and that in the end it is not clear what the origins of symbolic racism are (Sniderman et al., 2000; Sniderman & Tetlock, 1986). It is true that the correlations of symbolic racism with more traditional measures of racial prejudice, such as dislike of blacks or negative stereotypes, though significant, are not of overwhelming magnitude (e.g., Sears et al., 1997). Symbolic racism explains black-targeted policy preferences considerably better than it does preferences about nonracial policies or those targeted for other ethnic groups, indicating that it has a strong racial component elicited most strongly by specifically racial attitude objects (Kinder & Sanders, 1996; Sears, Citrin, Cheleden, & van Laar, 1999). More recently we have found evidence that blending racial affect and individualistic values in perceptions that blacks violate such values explains symbolic racism better than does treating them separately (Sears & Henry, 2003).

Although this research has resolved some important issues that had been raised about the theory of symbolic racism, it still leaves some open questions. Four of them seem to me most important. The assertion that conservatives' opposition to racially targeted policies stems from the nature of those policies and not from racial animosity poses one problem. Clearly, racial animus has an important role, because symbolic racism has strikingly uniform effects across the full variety of race-targeted policies. That does not explain differences in aggregate white support across diverse racial policies. Global item-wording variations do produce differences in the level of white support (Sniderman et al., 2000). The descriptions of various policies must therefore contain features other than racial symbolism that make them more or less attractive. No research so far has been successful in isolating the attitudes or values that would explain *why* those other features stimulate differences in aggregate support. One proposed reason does prove to be largely irrelevant: Whites' opposition to affirmative action cannot stem in very large measure from a genuine commitment to a color-blind society, because opposition to affirmative action is consistently associated with *in*egalitarian, not egalitarian, values (Sears, Henry, & Kosterman, 2000; Sidanius, Singh, Hetts, & Federico, 2000).

A second question concerns the possible underestimation of the contribution of racism to opposition to racial policies. As indicated, symbolic racism continues to have strong effects even when entered as a final stage in stage-wise regression equations after the other ostensibly race-neutral "usual suspects" have been considered. The problem is that the purportedly race-neutral factors, such as ideological conservatism, may themselves have become infected with racial prejudice, so such findings may actually underestimate the effects of racism. It is not clear how to answer this question with cross-sectional survey data.

The origins of symbolic racism pose the third open question. We do find evidence of a role for black individualism, blending antiblack affect with perceived violations of individualistic values (Sears & Henry, 2003)—but is individualism the only ostensibly nonracial traditional conservative value that symbolic racism draws on, or even the most important? What about traditional morality and various religious values? Racism permeated American society for more than 350 years and probably has wormed its way into the warp and woof of many of the ways we think about society. Black individualism probably does not exhaust that penetration. As mentioned previously, Valentino and Sears are beginning to find it linked closely to conservative religious beliefs in the South.

Finally, another approach to the origins of symbolic racism is to trace its course through the individual's life history. Longitudinal studies show that symbolic racism is highly stable through the adult years (Kinder & Sanders, 1996), but little else is known about its history. Perhaps, as originally hypothesized, early-socialized prejudices and values provide some fertile ground when the child is later exposed to beliefs about the broader society, such as those contained in the symbolic racism belief system. The standard adult cross-sectional survey represents a flimsy basis for reconstructing that life history.

## "Peoples of Color" and Black Exceptionalism

Since the 1960s, high rates of immigration have greatly expanded cultural diversity in the United States, especially of "peoples of color," such as Latinos and Asians. This raises questions about the future politics of cultural diversity, as well as presenting an opportunity to test more fundamental theories of intergroup relations.

The black–white model has been usefully extended to the case of this more diverse society by several social–structural theories, especially realistic group conflict theory, sense of group position theory, and social dominance theory (e.g., Bobo & Johnson, 2001; Sidanius et al., 2000). Although these theories have differences, they share four key assumptions. One is that the large census categories (whites, Asian Americans, Latinos, and African Americans) are also subjectively meaningful groups that most Americans use to carve up a diverse society, from the standpoints of ingroup and outgroup members alike. Running through those categories is an expanded color line, with whites on one side and the three peoples of color on the other. A consensual racial hierarchy or racial order exists, with whites of European ancestry at the top as the historically dominant group, followed by the other three subordinate groups ordered according to socioeconomic standing and social status. Finally, they generally assume that the groups exist in a competitive relationship with one another.

In our research on cultural diversity, we have found some evidence that accords with this general view of a competitive American racial hierarchy, arraying, in order, whites, Asians, Latinos, and blacks, each displaying ingroup favoritism in various ways (Citrin & Sears, 2003; Sears, 1994; Sears, Citrin, Cheleden, & van Laar, 1999). In the civil disorder in Los Angeles in 1992, almost all those arrested were members of the most subordinate groups, either blacks or Latinos, and their targets were mainly members of superordinate groups: the predominantly white police force and Asian merchants. Most blacks and Latinos sympathetically saw the disorder as a protest, whereas most Asians and whites thought it was caused by a criminal element. Other survey data showed that perceived discrimination against one's own group is highest among blacks, then Latinos, then Asians, and least among whites. Finally, these four large ethnic groups differ in the expected ways about policies relevant to their differing interests. The largely immigrant groups, Latinos and Asians, are the most supportive of liberal immigration and language policies. Blacks are the most supportive of affirmative action for blacks, and Latinos are the most supportive of affirmative action for Latinos. Whites as a group are the most opposed to all of these pro-minority redistributive policies.

As plausible as those theoretical ideas are, however, and as supportive as these findings are, I offer an alternative theoretical perspective that would send us in a somewhat different direction. Symbolic politics theory (Sears, 1993) focuses on the individuals' attitudinal environments in early life as determinants of their political socialization and, ultimately, of their adult political attitudes. That leads us to look more at different groups' histories than at their current structural relations. The shift of focus is easily applied in the black–white model. The history of the relationship between blacks and whites is unparalleled in the United States. No other minority group was enslaved so thoroughly or consigned to an explicitly lower caste role for so long. The history of the white population is very different, originating in the voluntary immigration over many years, mainly of Europeans, and then gradual assimilation into the cultural mainstream. Of course, those European immigrants were often initially subjected to segregation and discrimination, to which they often responded with ethnic solidarity and coalition building. Over most of the past century, they have shown reduced intraethnic political solidarity and increased assimilation to a broader white category. For example, the descendants of the "black" Irish immigrants of the mid-19th century are today considered whites without a second thought, quite a contrast from a century and a half ago.

Those using social–structural theories, when applying the black–white model to the new immigrant groups, seem to liken them to African Americans as fellow peoples of color, not to those now "white" European immigrants. Our (Sears, Citrin, et al., 1999) black exceptionalism perspective, in contrast, suggests separating two distinct phenomena. The largely involuntary immigrants from Africa and their descendants have been for most of their history forcibly relegated to lower caste status. Today's African Americans are almost all descended from that long history. On the other hand, most recent voluntary immigrants from Asia and Latin America entered communities with only relatively small numbers of descendants of earlier waves of immigration. These latter, of course, were frequently mistreated in ways analogous to (if not, on average, as extreme as) the mistreatment of blacks. The largest numbers of today's Asian American and Hispanic families, however, are recent immigrants. In this sense, their political future may be more analogous to the European immigrants' than to African Americans'. Let me review some of our research on this point.

First, today's new immigrant groups are indeed heavily composed of new immigrants, not descendants of the badly treated Chinese, Japanese, and Mexican workers of a century ago. More than half of the Asians and Latinos in Los Angeles in the 1990 census were foreign-born. If immigrating aliens are to find their place in a consensual American racial hierarchy, it should take some time to accomplish. Merely being a newly arrived Korean with few English language skills might not convey an understanding of that distinctive ethnic place automatically. So, do these new immigrants' ethnic identities become more important and more reflective of their place in the racial hierarchy the longer the immigrants are in the United States? Or does their distinctive ethnic identity in fact gradually diminish with time, like that of the earlier European immigrants? Some of our research on ethnic identity used a six-wave panel survey of most of the incoming UCLA freshman class of 1996 (Sears et al., 2003). The class was a richly diverse ethnic mixture: 36% Asian, 32% white, 19% Latino, and 6% black. Like their adult counterparts, the Asian and Latino students were predominantly of quite recent immigrant origin; half of the Asian students were themselves immigrants, and most of the Latino students were first or second generation, with no American-born ancestors. We have three findings consistent with the black exceptionalism view of Asians and Latinos.

Their spontaneous political identity did reflect those recent immigrant origins more than it reflected their position in an American ethnic hierarchy. Before the students actually enrolled, identity was assessed by asking, "What racial/ethnic group do you most closely identify with?" Of the Asian American students, almost two-thirds referred to their national origins, and only 12% used one of the politically constructed labels for their American ethnic group (Asian American or Pacific Islander). More than half of the Latinos referred to their national origin (almost all Mexican). That is, their ethnic identity was still tied to their national origin rather than to a place in the American racial hierarchy, unlike white and black students, who almost unanimously used the standard American ethnic labels (white, black, or African American), consistent with the black–white model.

Second, the Asians and Latinos with the strongest ethnic identity were themselves the most recent immigrants, with parents and grandparents most likely to have been born in another country, and were the most likely not to speak English at home. Those with families longer in the United States, who had learned the ropes and the frustrations of the American racial hierarchy, had weaker senses of ethnic identity. Third, Asian and Latino students' ethnic identities actually became somewhat weaker through the college years rather than strengthening as the students became more familiar with the American racial hierarchy (Sears, Fu, Henry, & Bui, 2003).

What about the adult new immigrant groups? As indicated previously, blacks remain politically quite distinctive almost four centuries since their importation to America began. The new immigrant groups in the aggregate show some of this same political distinctiveness, seemingly supporting their own group interests. Do the adult Asians and Latinos maintain or increase this distinctiveness with time over the years since immigration? Here our research is based on sample surveys of adults, in some cases of the nation as a whole, and in other cases of Los Angeles County (Citrin & Sears, 2004; Sears, Citrin, et al., 1999).

The short answer is that unlike blacks, Latinos and Asians show signs of increasing political acculturation over time in the United States in three ways. When asked, "On social or political issues, do you think of yourself as just an American or as a member of an ethnic or racial or nationality group?" about three-fourths of the Latinos and Asians responded, "just an American." Moreover, the most recent immigrants, not those with long experience with the American racial order, are the most likely to choose a more ethnic identity. That is, longer experience in the United States leads to stronger national identity and less ethnicized identity. A similar acculturation effect holds with the group-targeted policies discussed previously. The strongest supporters of the seemingly group-interested immigration and language policies are the recent immigrants, not those with years or generations of frustration with an ethnocentric American society.

In other words, the new immigrant groups are just that: Their sense of distinctive ethnicity is tied to their recent immigration rather than to their place in the American racial hierarchy, and it tends to wane with more exposure to American society. As with the European immigrant families of a century ago, lengthier experience in the United States results in less distinctively ethnicity-based political preferences, in contrast to the continuing race-based political stance of a black population with long tenure. The theoretical model is an imperfect fit, then. The obstacles to acculturation are fewer for the new immigrant groups because the color line is weaker and more permeable. Latinos and Asians may be more like newer versions of Italians and Jews than like slightly less stigmatized versions of African Americans.

## Ingroup Favoritism and Outgroup Antagonism

Another set of conflicts between these theories concerns ingroup favoritism and outgroup antagonism. In symbolic politics theory, both are contingent on socialization experiences specific to the historical context in question. In social–structural theories, both tend to be viewed as inherent products of the structure of intergroup relations. Three points follow.

Anti-black prejudices have historically been particularly strong in the United States, and, I believe, remain strong, though largely in changed form. A distinctive sense of white identity has perhaps not been very strong, however, outside of areas in which African Americans have been exceptionally numerous, such as the Black Belt in the South or concentrated black ghettos in large cities. That sense of white identity (or self-categorization as a white person) tends to have only weak effects on racial policy preferences (Sears & Jessor, 1996). Also, social–structural theories and social identity theory predict ingroup favoritism in group stereotypes. Empirically, that proves not to hold very reliably; rather there is quite a bit of consensus across groups in the stereotypes that rightfully apply to each, as the historical–contingency symbolic politics theory would suggest (Bobo & Johnson, 2001; Sears, Citrin, et al., 1999).

Social–structural theories usually assert that white opposition to racial equality is driven by a desire to maintain the existing racial hierarchy and its structural inequalities. This implies that a number of perceptions, such as recognition of that racial hierarchy, perceptions of whites' own privilege and of threats posed by subordinate groups, perceived common fate with other whites, and a desire to protect whites' privileged positions, should be both reasonably common and significant influences on racial policy preferences. Unfortunately, such perceptions rarely have been measured in the research done in this area. When measured, they often do not yield great support for these hypotheses. The perceptions that whites' gains would benefit oneself or that blacks' gains would hurt oneself seem not to be very common among whites, and they do not contribute to negative outgroup stereotypes or influence racial policy preferences. The exception is that whites do often perceive the gains of blacks as a group to have systematic negative effects on the well-being of whites as a group, and such perceptions generally are significantly associated with opposition to race-targeted policies (Bobo & Johnson, 2001; Kinder & Sanders, 1996; Sears & Jessor, 1996). That finding by itself, however, is not theoretically decisive, because it is consistent with either the social–structural account or with the continuing role of symbolic group prejudices.

Finally, the social–structural theories treat beliefs such as those involved in symbolic racism as mere myths that help legitimate the American racial hierarchy. The language of such theories implies that the cognitions just cited about a racial hierarchy should motivate acceptance of legitimating myths like symbolic racism or that complex cognitive processes would probably not be very common among preadults, where we would look for the historical roots of symbolic racism. To test between these views will require going beyond cross-sectional surveys of adults.

## The Seven Koan

Bill McGuire was my first mentor in graduate school in 1957. He later passed on some prematurely graybeard pieces of wisdom about the "yin and yang of progress in social psychology," in terms of "seven koan" (McGuire, 1973). It might be useful to assess how well his advice coincided with the directions this research area has taken.

Koan 1: Emphasize hypothesis development using (inter alia) case studies and analogies. This research has used the cases of American race relations and current immigration to the United States to illuminate theories of intergroup relations more generally. Perhaps my research has become so immersed in the history of the American case that it will never come out again, but then I was a history major as an undergraduate and old habits die hard or maybe never die at all.

Koan 2: Linear models have outlived their usefulness. The work described in this chapter has principally used linear models. I was taught a more complex approach at Yale by McGuire, Anderson, Hovland, Cohen, and others, but in this case, the evidence in front of me usually does not require it. This research has obtained mostly main effects; though interactions have often been tested for, they have rarely panned out. Perhaps that is because of the overwhelming power of race as a stimulus in the American political environment.

Koan 3: Observe people, not data. This literature is primarily based on surveys of ordinary people, using questions that have been drawn from the ambient language of day-to-day politics. It is intended to represent how ordinary people think in ordinary daily life. It is not raw human experience but perhaps more like it than is research using more artificial laboratory situations.

Koan 4: To see the future in the present, see the present in the past. The symbolic politics theory is, if nothing else, a paean to the past—both the historical past and the personal past—and how difficult it is for us to free ourselves from the inertial pull of past experience. The roots of today's racial politics still lie, I believe, in fateful legal and institutional decisions made 3 centuries ago. I am struck by the political continuity of even the Bush–Gore outcome with, of all things, the antebellum period. That one of the early decisive differences between Bush and Gore concerned the visibility of the Confederate battle flag in South Carolina is simply the kind of vivid example that our dry and statistical theories often lack. Time series data, whether from surveys or voting records, are essential for this kind of endeavor and are vastly more available and easier to access and analyze than they were in 1973.

Koan 5: New statistics for correlational research. Multiple regression models were becoming popular in 1973 and are critical for the multiply determined phenomena involved in this research. LISREL and other structural equation models were in their infancy then and are very useful for testing multistep models. I am skeptical that they will help much to pinpoint causal order in cross-sectional correlational data. Still, we have come a long way, baby.

Koan 6: The virtue of poverty. The data I rely on could not be gathered without extensive financial support. Fortunately, this has been recognized by the National Science Foundation and other institutions, including my own university. These data represent public goods, archived for all academic users—but they are expensive.

Koan 7: The opposite of a great truth is also true. I believe Bill McGuire had early religious and philosophical training in paradox and mystery that I missed out on. Even if I had been exposed to it, I probably wouldn't have enjoyed it as much as he does. I enjoy rooting for my own baseball team and political party, and underdog social groups, and see little that is magical or entertaining in their opponents' successes. Linearity again. I leave it to others to judge whether it comes from me or from the phenomena I study.

Overall, Bill's "Seven Koan," even if not a perfect fit in every case, seem to me remarkably prescient and appropriate for this research area, one I, almost 30 years later, feel sure he was not thinking of. Pretty impressive!

# References

Bobo, L., & Johnson, D. (2001). Racial attitudes in a prismatic metropolis: Mapping identity, stereotypes, competition, and views on affirmative action. In L. Bobo, M. L. Oliver, J. H.

Johnson, Jr., & A. Valenzuela, Jr. (Eds.), *Prismatic metropolis: Inequality in Los Angeles* (pp. 81–163). New York: Russell Sage Foundation.

Citrin, J., & Sears, D. O. (2004). *The politics of multiculturalism*. New York: Cambridge University Press.

Henry, P. J., & Sears, D. O. (2002). The symbolic racism 2000 scale. *Political Psychology, 23,* 253–283.

Kinder, D. R., & Sanders, L. M. (1996). *Divided by color: Racial politics and democratic ideals.* Chicago, IL: University of Chicago Press.

McGuire, W. J. (1973). The yin and yang of progress in social psychology: Seven koan. *Journal of Personality and Social Psychology, 26,* 446–456.

Sears, D. O. (1983). The persistence of early political predispositions: The roles of attitude object and life stage. In L. Wheeler & P. Shaver (Eds.), *Review of Personality and Social Psychology* (Vol. 4, pp. 79–116). Beverly Hills: Sage.

Sears, D. O. (1993). Symbolic politics: A socio-psychological theory. In S. Iyengar & W. J. McGuire (Eds.), *Explorations in political psychology* (pp. 113–149). Durham, NC: Duke University Press.

Sears, D. O. (1994). Urban rioting in Los Angeles: A comparison of 1965 with 1992. In M. Baldassare (Ed.), *The Los Angeles Riots: Lessons for the Urban Future* (pp. 237–254). Boulder, CO: Westview Press.

Sears, D. O., Citrin, J., Cheleden, S. V., & Van Laar, C. (1999). Cultural diversity and multicultural politics: Is ethnic balkanization psychologically inevitable? In D. Prentice & D. Miller (Eds.), *Cultural divides: The social psychology of cultural contact* (pp. 35–79). New York: Russell Sage Foundation.

Sears, D. O., & Henry, P. J. (2003). The origins of symbolic racism. *Journal of Personality and Social Psychology, 85,* 259–275.

Sears, D. O., & Henry, P. J. (2000, July). *Symbolic racism after thirty years: A current appraisal.* Paper presented at the 23rd annual meeting of the International Society of Political Psychology, Seattle, WA.

Sears, D. O., Fu, M.-Y., Henry, P. J., & Bui, K. (in press). The origins and persistence of ethnic identity among the "new immigrant" groups. *Social Psychology Quarterly.*

Sears, D. O., & Jessor, T. (1996). Whites' racial policy attitudes: The role of white racism. *Social Science Quarterly, 77,* 751–759.

Sears, D. O., & Levy, S. (2003). Childhood and adult political development. In D. O. Sears, L. Huddy, & R. Jervis (Eds.), *Handbook of political psychology* (pp. 60–109). New York: Oxford University Press.

Sears, D. O., & Valentino, N. (2001, September). *Race, religion, and sectional conflict in contemporary partisanship.* Paper presented at the annual meeting of the American Political Science Association, San Francisco.

Sears, D. O., Valentino, N. A., & Cheleden, S. V. (1999, September). *Long-term continuities in the politics of race.* Prepared for presentation at the annual meeting of the American Political Science Association, Atlanta, GA.

Sears, D. O., van Laar, C., Carrillo, M., & Kosterman, R. (1997). Is it really racism? The origins of white Americans' opposition to race-targeted policies. *Public Opinion Quarterly, 61,* 16–53.

Sidanius, J., Singh, P., Hetts, J. J., & Federico, C. (2000). It's not affirmative action, it's the blacks: The continuing relevance of race in American politics. In D. O. Sears, J. Sidanius, & L. Bobo (Eds.), *Racialized politics: The debate about racism in America* (pp. 191–235). Chicago, IL: University of Chicago Press.

Sniderman, P. M., Crosby, G. C., & Howell, W. G. (2000). The politics of race. In D. O. Sears, J. Sidanius, & L. Bobo (Eds.), *Racialized politics: The debate about racism in America.* Chicago, IL: University of Chicago Press.

Sniderman, P. M., & Tetlock, P. E. (1986). Symbolic racism: Problems of motive attribution in political debate. *Journal of Social Issues, 42,* 129–150.

Sumner, W. G. (1906). *Folkways: A study of the sociolological importance of usages, manners, customs, mores, and morals.* Boston: Ginn & Co.

Tarman, C., & Sears, D. O. (in press). The conceptualization and measurement of symbolic racism. *Journal of Politics.*

Valentino, N. A., & Sears, D. O. (2000, April). *Race, sectional conflict, and partisan realignment in the contemporary era.* Paper presented at the annual meeting of the Midwest Political Science Association, Chicago, IL.

# 18

# Engineering Consent: The Renaissance of Mass Communications Research in Politics

*Shanto Iyengar*

## Prologue

Since coming in contact with Bill McGuire, I have addressed in my work the role of the mass media (broadly speaking) in politics. In my "pre-McGuire" days, I was a practicing survey researcher who studied the political attitudes of Indian high school students. Bill's seminar on attitude change, which I sat in on as a postdoctoral fellow in 1980, convinced me of the importance of applying experimental methods to the study of political communication.

In the years since, my work has come to rely on experiments to capture ordinary citizens' encounters with the news media. As a practicing political scientist, however, I found that my professional survival necessitated a different form of experimentation, one that featured "real" stimulus materials, unobtrusive procedures and settings, and quasi-representative samples (e.g., a cross section of potential voters who watch political advertisements embedded in a television news program during a political campaign).

Over the years, I have used this approach to study the effects of exposure to national network news, local television news, political advertising (both broadcast and direct mail), and, most recently, "online" campaigns. Of course, the fact that these field experiments have gained legitimacy in a nonexperimental discipline is a testament to the viability of the recently emerged field of political psychology. As I point out in this chapter, Bill's work has contributed profoundly, in both theoretical and methodological terms, to the intellectual maturation of the field of political psychology.

\* \* \*

I began writing this chapter in the immediate aftermath of the 2000 presidential election. The election itself was without parallel in living memory, and the spectacle that followed, namely the regular appearance of the candidates and their spokespersons on network television to cast their individual "spin" on breaking events, was utterly predictable. The need to play to the public even spread to the U.S. Supreme Court. The day after the decision in *Bush v. Gore*, Justice Clarence Thomas, in the course of a televised appearance with high school students, claimed that partisanship was irrelevant to the Court's modus operandi.

As Election 2000 well illustrates, there have been fundamental changes in the American political process over the past 50 years. "Media politics" is now central, and the importance of political institutions traditionally entrusted with organizing and aggregating public preferences (political parties and interest groups) has correspondingly declined. Today, the use—even manipulation—of the mass media to promote political objectives is not only standard practice but in fact is essential to survival.

Given the new regime, the study of mass communications has become central to the study of politics. Because Bill McGuire is the foremost theoretician in the field of persuasion, his works are required reading for professors and politicos alike. My aim in this chapter is to provide an overview of the evolution of media politics, to identify the areas in which scholars have uncovered evidence of the effects of political communication while showing how Bill's insights have provided the necessary impetus and guideposts for the development of this work.

## The Rise of Media Politics

Placed in historical context, the current state of American politics represents a continuation of the third great age of persuasion (McGuire, 1979). The defining macro characteristic of this era has been the gradual atrophy of political institutions designed to organize political preferences and the replacement of those institutions by the mass media (Polsby, 1980, 1983). Old-fashioned forms of governing, which emphasized the formation of coalitions and bargaining between rival partisans, have been replaced by efforts to cultivate the appearance of effective and responsive leadership—through rhetorical posturing, credit claiming, and avoidance of blame (Kernell, 1993). The new "engineers of consent" are not party or interest-group leaders but the legion of pundits and spokespersons who make daily rounds on television news programs and the editorial pages of our newspapers.

The acceleration of "going public" can also be traced to the gradual encroachment of election campaigns on the policy process. Campaign techniques such as television advertising are now used long after Election Day. For example, the "Harry and Louise" ad campaign mounted by the health insurance industry proved instrumental in swaying moderate Democrats and Republicans in Congress against the Clinton health reform package. Following suit, the pharmaceutical industry launched a massive ad campaign in opposition to congressional attempts to extend prescription drug benefits to Medicare recipients. Elected officials and interest groups have accumulated considerable expertise in the use of public relations techniques while attempting to win elections, and it is only to be expected that they seek to capitalize on this expertise when formulating and debating legislation.

In the final analysis, media advocacy has thoroughly penetrated all governmental arenas, including the traditionally invisible judicial process, because it works. The nation's collective political consciousness is grounded in the content and form of news programming. For all but a tiny number of Americans, the news media represent the sole point of contact with the world of public affairs. Events and stories that fail journalistic tests of "newsworthiness" are, as is the proverbial tree falling in the forest, nonexistent.

Over the years, depending on technological and market-based factors, different news outlets have assumed the "spotlight" function of the media. Broadcast journalism dominated by network programming began to supplant the print media in the 1940s; more recently, the preeminent position of network newscasts has been challenged by the proliferation of cable channels, the expansion of local news programming, and, of course, the advent of online news outlets. Changes in the prominence of particular sources, not surprisingly, have resulted in changes in the nature of the news itself (Schudson, 1995). The substitution of television news for newspapers not only speeded up delivery time but also affected the content of news; more active or visual issues, such as crime and terrorism, became especially newsworthy. Moreover, as the number of media channels increased, so did competition for audiences. Increasingly, the need to entice and captivate audiences has taken precedence over the old-fashioned norm of journalism that informs (Kalb, 1998).

These dramatic changes in the shape of the industry and the product notwithstanding, it is taken as axiomatic that those in a position to shape the content and imagery of news improve their standing in the court of public opinion, and, in doing so, gain the upper hand in Washington, Hartford, Sacramento, or other policy arenas. Evidence supporting this axiom is described in the next section.

## Effects of News on the Mass Public

Early research on political communication seemed to indicate that mass communications had only "minimal consequences" on voting and public opinion (Klapper, 1960). The failure to detect traces of media influence stemmed from both conceptual and methodological limitations (for a recent inventory, see Iyengar & Simon, 2000). Initial research focused exclusively on persuasion effects and treated media messages as necessary and sufficient conditions. In addition to missing the key interdependencies among message, source, and receiver factors, researchers also ignored a variety of other highly relevant effects, including changes in the size and composition of the electorate, the transmission of information, and the setting of campaign agendas. Moreover, even if one were to accept persuasion as the benchmark for campaign effects, identifiable traces of persuasion were bound to be minimal because most campaigns feature offsetting messages, thus limiting observable effects to cases in which one candidate has a significant resource or skills advantage. This condition occurs rarely, if at all, in presidential campaigns, the races most often studied.

Methodological preferences also contributed to findings of minimal effects. Political communication researchers have been (and still are) limited by their dependence on survey methods. Like all scientific techniques, survey methods have weaknesses, of which the logic of treating respondents' self-reported exposure to campaign communication as a reliable surrogate for actual exposure is particularly dubious. People have notoriously weak memories for past events, especially when the "event" in question concerns an encounter with a particular political campaign (e.g., see Bradburn et al., 1987; Pierce & Lovrich, 1982), and the resulting measurement error in self-reports necessarily attenuates estimates of the effects of political campaigns (see Bartels, 1993, 1997). Also adding disarray to the literature, self-reported exposure to campaign messages is often motivated by political attitudes, including candidate preference. Those who choose to tune in to the campaign differ systematically (in ways that matter to their vote choice) from those who do not (for evidence, see Ansolabehere, Iyengar, & Simon, 1999). Unfortunately, most survey-based analyses fail to disentangle the reciprocal effects of self-reported exposure to the campaign and partisan attitudes or behaviors, thus undermining affirmative claims about the effects of campaigns.

As the subfield of political communication has matured, these limitations have been overcome, and over the past 50 years, there has been sufficient accumulation of evidence to warrant significant rethinking—if not wholesale abandonment—of the limited effects view. McGuire's own skepticism over the scope of mass media influence (McGuire, 1986) notwithstanding, his research has been central to this evolution.

At the very least, researchers can attest to two classes of media effects on public opinion. The first, offered by McGuire as a "salvaging" hypothesis in his dialectic account of the search for media influence (McGuire, 1986), may be termed *agenda control* or media-induced changes in the public's political priorities. The second class of effects is a direct extension of the classic McGuire studies on attitude change and corresponds to direct political persuasion.

## Agenda Control

Political scientists agree that ordinary citizens prefer to keep the world of public affairs at arm's length. As casual observers of the political scene, most Americans selectively attend to a few issues that appear important at the moment. Of course, apparent importance is very much a matter of what editors and journalists choose to cover or ignore. Thus, the prominence of issues in the news media is the major determinant of the public's perception of issue importance (see, for example, Dearing & Rogers, 1996; McCombs & Shaw, 1972). Because government officials (most notably the president) are the principal sources of news, they are in an especially advantageous position to simultaneously influence the media and public agendas (Behr & Iyengar, 1985).

Experimental studies (Iyengar & Kinder, 1987) provided the most unequivocal evidence on media agenda setting. These studies revealed that the insertion of only a modest degree of news coverage into network newscasts is sufficient to induce substantial shifts in viewers' beliefs about the importance of issues. In one experiment, for example, viewers were shown a series of newscasts containing three, six, or no stories dealing with U.S. dependence on foreign sources of energy. When exposed to no news coverage on this subject, 24% of the participants cited energy as among the three most important problems facing the country. When participants watched three stories on energy issues, *50%* of them regarded energy as an important problem. Finally, when the "dose" was increased to six stories, energy was cited as an important national problem by 65% of the viewers (Iyengar & Kinder, 1987, chap. 3).

Agenda-setting researchers have also identified several antecedent factors that condition the media's ability to shape the public's priorities. These include the personal relevance of the issue, the political involvement of the audience, and the prominence of coverage. In general, the more remote an issue or event is from direct personal experience, the weaker the agenda setting effect of news coverage (Erbring, Goldenberg & Miller, 1980). Thus, people who are personally affected by issues in the news are particularly likely to have their agendas set by the media. After being exposed to news reports detailing the financial difficulties confronting the social security fund, elderly viewers of network newscasts were found to be much more likely than younger viewers to nominate social security as one of the most important problems facing the country (Iyengar & Kinder, 1987).

Finally, the manner in which a news story is presented significantly affects that story's impact on the public agenda. Stories with greater prominence—front-page news, newspaper stories accompanied by photographs, or lead stories in television newscasts—tend to be particularly influential (Behr & Iyengar, 1985; Dearing & Rogers, 1996).

Agenda setting has important attitudinal consequences. The issues deemed significant by the electorate become the principal yardsticks for evaluating candidates and governmental institutions. This "priming" phenomenon (weighting issues in accordance with their perceived salience) has been documented in a series of experimental and nonexperimental studies (for reviews of priming research, see Krosnick & Kinder, 1990; Miller & Krosnick, 2000). For example, the news media's sudden preoccupation with the Iranian hostage issue in the closing days of the 1980 presidential campaign caused voters to think about the candidates' ability to control terrorism when choosing between Carter and Reagan (Iyengar & Kinder, 1987). Given his record in office, this logic proved disadvantageous to President Carter.

Because the average voter is known to employ only a few considerations, candidates are motivated to introduce and pursue issues on which they enjoy a comparative advantage. The candidate closer to the median voter on an issue such as tax reform would want to address that topic in preference to discussing issues on which he or she might be some distance away. Accordingly, a great deal of campaign rhetoric and strategy is designed to capitalize on this "disequilibrium of tastes" (Iyengar, 1993; Johnston, Blais, Brady, & Crete, 1992; Riker, 1980).

In sum, people pay attention to the world of public affairs through the media. Issues and events in the news are judged to be important and treated as relevant considerations for evaluating the caliber of public officials.

## Political Persuasion

Message learning theorists, including McGuire, analyzed persuasion from the perspective of "who says what to whom"; the major determinants of attitude change were source, message, and audience characteristics (McGuire, 1999, chap. 3). The immediate impact of this work on political science was less than dramatic because the pioneers in the empirical study of political campaigns were oriented more toward sociological than toward psychological explanations of political attitudes. As a result, survey and experimental research on attitudes were curiously compartmentalized and, for the most part, this pattern continued until quite recently.

Intellectual shifts in the social sciences, most notably an increasing openness to interdisciplinary synthesis, created opportunities for researchers working at the intersection of psychology, mass communication, and political science (this process is traced in McGuire's account of the development of the subfield of political psychology; McGuire, 1993). A growing number of researchers began to examine public opinion from more explicitly psychological perspectives. This line of research applied the "who says what to whom" logic of message learning theory to the study of political campaigns. As described in the next section, the evidence indicates that the effects of media messages (the "what" element) by themselves are insufficient; rather, persuasion requires a set of joint contingencies among message, receiver, and source factors.

## Receiver–Message Contingencies

In his classic paper on campaign effects, Converse (1962) demonstrated that both the most and the least attentive strata of the electorate were least affected by exposure to the presidential campaign. The former group encountered a host of campaign messages but rejected most of them (high exposure–low acceptance). The latter group, although predisposed to accept messages, was unlikely to receive them (high acceptance–low exposure). In short, moderately informed or aware citizens showed signs of greater instability over the course of the campaign than did either of the extremes.

Converse's discovery in the electoral arena of McGuire's "golden mean" maxim indicated that the susceptibility of particular receivers to persuasion is conditioned by their political awareness, the volume or intensity of particular messages, and the degree to which acceptance requires small or large shifts from the status quo (Zaller, 1992). When messages are less audible and convey unfamiliar points of view, for example, exposure dominates acceptance as a predictor of persuasion, and because awareness is positively related to exposure, the awareness–attitude relationship will be monotonic. Similarly, when message content is relatively congruent with the receiver's existing views (e.g., a liberal message and liberal audience), greater awareness will correlate with greater attitude change. When message content and existing views are incongruent (e.g., a liberal message directed at conservative receivers), however, greater awareness will correlate with less attitude change because more-aware receivers recognize the message as discrepant and discount it.

These message–receiver interactions become even more elaborate when both one- and two-sided flows of information are considered. In the case of consensual or one-sided news, more-aware receivers are more likely to conform to the "mainstream" perspective. However, when the news reflects "official" and "opposition" views, the public's attitudes are determined by the interaction of political awareness and partisan values. During the early years of the

Vietnam War, for example, news coverage was generally slanted in a hawkish direction. As a result, support for the war grew among less-aware liberals but declined among more-aware liberals. The former were able to receive the "loud" prowar message, but the latter were sufficiently attentive to receive the less-audible countervailing message. As news coverage became more antiwar, the same interaction occurred among conservatives; the less-aware shifted in the dovish direction, and the more-aware remained prowar (see Zaller, 1992).

## Source-Related Contingencies

While accepting the premise that the persuasive effects of political messages are conditioned by specific properties of receivers, some scholars have uncovered a different family of interactions, this time involving message and source factors. Their argument is that persuasion effects are conditioned by the degree of fit between the content of the message and the audience's evaluations of the source of the message. In the context of American political campaigns, the two major sources of news are the candidates of the Democratic and Republican Parties. It is well-established that most Americans have a sense of partisan identity. Acquired during early childhood, this psychological anchor is known to withstand the vicissitudes of events and the passage of time (Jennings & Niemi, 1981; Niemi & Jennings, 1991).

The relevance of voters' partisanship extends well beyond the mere fact that Democrats will be more responsive to the Democratic candidate and vice versa. Not only do most voters acquire a partisan identity, they also acquire beliefs about the groups served by the political parties and, by inference, about the issues or problems on which the parties will deliver (Petrocik, 1996). For example, the public generally considers Democrats more able than Republicans to deal with the problem of unemployment. Conversely, Republicans are seen as the party more likely to cut taxes. These stereotypes about the differential policy responsiveness of the parties influence campaign strategy. Campaigns that take advantage of (or resonate with) voters' expectations are considered more likely to be effective; a Democrat should be better off using appeals that emphasize his or her intent to strengthen job training programs, and a Republican should promote his or her support for lower taxes.

This "issue ownership" hypothesis has been tested experimentally through examination of differences in the persuasiveness of Democratic and Republican campaign advertisements concerning specific policy issues. In one set of experimental studies, the identical advertisement was attributed to either the Democratic or the Republican candidate running for U.S. Senate in California. Exposure to the unemployment ad elicited greater gains for the Democratic candidate, with the opposite pattern holding for crime (Ansolabehere & Iyengar, 1995). In a related study, voters rated campaign ads aired by candidates Dole and Clinton during the 1996 presidential campaign. Republicans were more likely to rate Dole's ads as informative (and less likely to rate them as misleading) when the ads addressed "Republican" issues. Conversely, Democrats were more impressed by Clinton's ads dealing with "Democratic" issues (Iyengar & Valentino, 2000). Thus, policy reputations are tantamount to assessments of source credibility.

The logic of differential credibility extends easily to attributes of the candidates other than their party affiliation. Gender is an especially visible attribute, and popular culture provides several cues about the traits of males and females, cues that are amply reinforced by the media's depiction of women candidates (Kahn, 1994). Given the availability of gender stereotypes, it might be anticipated that issues would have differential effects across male and female candidates. In fact, the evidence reveals that "masculine" issues, such as defense or crime, are especially persuasive as campaign material for male candidates, whereas preschool funding and other matters of educational policy work well for female candidates (Ansolabehere & Iyengar, 1995; Kahn & Gordon, 1997).

In short, campaign messages are not encountered in a vacuum and must blend in with voters' partisan motives and attitudes. Persuasion effects are thus inherently interactive—either involving interactions between the content or source of campaign messages on the one hand and voters' political predispositions on the other or involving higher-order interactions that also capture individual differences in exposure to campaign messages.

The evidence described previously indicates that the payoffs from media management are nontrivial. Either by directing the spotlight at particular issues or by providing more favorable exposure for a particular candidacy or point of view, media presentations affect public opinion.

## Conclusion

In the current regime, American politics is almost exclusively a mediated experience. The role of the citizen has evolved from occasional foot soldier and activist to spectator. Those who seek public office invest heavily in efforts to shape news coverage of their candidacy. The returns from this investment provide them with leverage over public opinion: By setting the public agenda or by projecting a general impression of competent leadership, elected leaders stay one step ahead of their would-be opponents.

Scholars are only just beginning to consider the broader implications of the new media-based regime. An obvious possibility is that elected leaders and the policies they pursue are more responsive to public opinion. On those issues for which clear majorities exist—as in the case of "law and order"—candidates must rapidly converge on the dominant position if they are to remain popular. Thus criminal justice policy, at both the federal and state level and no matter which political party is in the majority, has changed in the direction of greater punitiveness. The same pattern applies to civil rights legislation: The mass public and policy makers have both retreated from affirmative action.

Although media politics may have heightened the congruence between public policy and public opinion, the causal mechanisms and appropriate normative implications are far from clear (Page & Shapiro, 1992; Shapiro & Jacobs, 2000). The fact that large majorities of the public favor harsh treatment of violent criminals may reflect their response to one-sided news messages and the frequent use of crime as a campaign issue rather than any well-considered judgment over the pros and cons of punishment versus rehabilitation as potential remedies. Voters may follow rather than guide their elected leaders.

The potential for opinion leadership is especially significant because the views and pronouncements of political elites are rarely challenged in the mainstream media. The old-fashioned notion of watchdog or adversarial journalism that uses the press as a restraining force no longer applies. Instead, political elites enjoy a significant edge in their efforts to shape the news. Official sources provide the great majority of news reports even in the most prestigious of daily newspapers, such as the *New York Times* and *Washington Post* (Sigal, 1973). Nonofficial sources tend to be ignored, even in cases in which they may be especially knowledgeable (Bennett, 2000). Whereas the new class of elected leaders enjoys a surplus of communications resources (in the form of both staff and money), the degree of professionalism and substantive expertise among reporters has diminished. For a variety of reasons, including the rise of new and less rigorous forms of journalism and the explosion in online news sources, as well as the competitive requirements imposed by the marketplace, the contemporary news media is generally less able to actively resist official sources. Thus, a new form of "deferential" reporting has replaced the traditional ideal of independent journalists with the ability to challenge official sources (Bennett, 2000; Dorman & Farhang, 1987).

In short, the increased correspondence between the views of policy makers and ordinary citizens may reflect not a rejuvenation of direct democracy and electoral accountability but rather the increased control over media messages enjoyed by political elites. Today, the boundaries between news and political marketing are not at all clear.

Although the normative implications of media politics are debatable, the revisions to the minimalist view of media management are not. A major stimulus to this progression has been the increasing volume of traffic among political science, psychology, and allied disciplines. In this ongoing process of interdisciplinary exchange, Bill McGuire, in his incarnation as a communication theorist, has served as a beacon for the current generation of researchers in political communication.

# References

Ansolabehere, S. D., & Iyengar, S. (1995). *Going negative: How attack ads shrink and polarize the electorate*. New York: Free Press.

Ansolabehere, S. D., Iyengar, S., & Simon, A. F. (1999). Replicating experiments using aggregate and survey data: The case of negative advertising and turnout. *American Political Science Review, 93,* 901–910.

Bartels, L. M. (1993). Messages received: The political impact of media exposure. *American Political Science Review, 87,* 267–285.

Bartels, L. M. (1997). *Three virtues of panel data for the analysis of campaign effects*. Unpublished manuscript, Princeton University, Princeton, NJ.

Behr, R. L., & Iyengar, S. (1985). Television news, real-world cues, and changes in the public agenda. *Public Opinion Quarterly, 49,* 38–57.

Bennett, W. L. (2000). *News: The politics of illusion*. New York: Longmans.

Bradburn, N., Rips, L. J., & Shevell, S. K. (1987), Answering questions: The impact of memory and interference on surveys. *Science, 236,* 157–161.

Converse, P. E. (1962). Information flow and the stability of partisan attitudes. *Public Opinion Quarterly, 26,* 578–599.

Dearing, J. W., & Rogers, E. M. (1996). *Agenda-setting.* Thousand Oaks, CA: Sage.

Dorman, W. A., & Farhang, M. (1987). *The U.S. press and Iran: Foreign policy and the journalism of deference.* Los Angeles: University of California Press.

Erbring, L., Goldenberg, E. N., & Miller, A. H. (1980). Front-page news and real-world cues: A new look at agenda-setting by the media. *American Journal of Political Science, 24,* 16–49.

Iyengar, S. (1993). Agenda-setting and beyond. In W. H. Riker (Ed.), *Agenda formation* (pp. 211–230). Ann Arbor: University of Michigan Press.

Iyengar, S., & Kinder, D. R. (1987). *News that matters: Television and American opinion.* Chicago, IL: University of Chicago Press.

Iyengar, S., & Simon, A. F. (2000). New perspectives and evidence on political communication and campaign effects. *Annual Review of Psychology, 51,* 149–170.

Iyengar, S., & Valentino, N. A. (2000). Who says what? Source credibility as a mediator of campaign advertising. In A. Lupia, M. D. McCubbins, & S. L. Popkin (Eds.), *Elements of reason: Cognition, choice and the bounds of rationality* (pp. 108–129). New York: Cambridge University Press.

Jennings, M. K., & Niemi, R. G. (1981). *Generations and politics: A panel study of young adults and their parents.* Princeton, NJ: Princeton University Press.

Johnston, R., Blais, A., Brady, H. E., & Crete, J. (1992). *Letting the people decide: Dynamics of a Canadian election.* Stanford, CA: Stanford University Press.

Kahn, K. F. (1994). Does gender make a difference? An experimental examination of sex stereotypes and press patterns in statewide campaigns. *American Journal of Political Science, 38,* 162–195.

Kahn, K. F., & Gordon, A. (1997). How women campaign for the U.S. Senate. In P. Norris (Ed.), *Women, media and politics* (pp. 59–76). New York: Oxford University Press.

Kalb, M. (1998). The rise of the new news. (Discussion Paper D-34). Cambridge, MA: Joan Shorenstein Center, Harvard University.

Kernell, S. (1993). *Going public: New strategies of presidential leadership.* Washington DC: Congressional Quarterly Press.

Klapper, J. T. (1960). *The effects of mass communications.* New York: Free Press.

Krosnick, J. A., & Kinder, D. R. (1990). Altering the foundations of support for the president through priming. *American Political Science Review, 84,* 497–512.

McCombs, M. C., & Shaw, D. L. (1972). The agenda-setting function of mass media. *Public Opinion Quarterly, 36,* 176–187.

McGuire, W. J. (1979, September). Toward social psychology's second century. Paper presented at the 87th annual meeting of the American Psychological Association, New York, New York.

McGuire, W. J. (1986). The myth of massive media impact: savagings and salvagings. In G. Comstock (Ed.), *Public communication and behavior* (pp. 175–259). New York: Academic Press.

McGuire, W. J. (1993). The poly-psy relationship: Three phases of a long affair. In S. Iyengar & W. J. McGuire (Eds.), *Explorations in political psychology* (pp. 9–35). Durham, NC: Duke University Press.

McGuire, W. J. (1999). *Constructing social psychology: Creative and critical processes.* New York: Cambridge University Press.

Miller, J. M., & Krosnick, J. A. (2000). News media impact on the ingredients of presidential evaluations: Politically knowledgeable citizens are guided by a trusted source. *American Journal of Political Science, 44,* 295–309.

Niemi, R. G., & Jennings, M. K. (1991). Issues and inheritance in the study of party identification. *American Journal of Political Science, 35,* 970–988.

Page, B. & Shapiro, R. Y. (1992). *The rational public: Fifty years of trends in Americans' policy preferences.* Chicago, IL: University of Chicago Press.

Petrocik, J. R. (1996). Issue ownership in presidential elections, with a 1980 case study. *American Journal of Political Science, 40,* 825–850.

Pierce, J. C., & Lovrich, N. P. (1982). Survey measurement of political participation: Selective effects of recall in petition signing. *Social Science Quarterly, 63,* 164–171.

Polsby, N. W. (1980). The news media as an alternative to party in the presidential selection process. In R. A. Goldwin (Ed.), *Political parties in the eighties* (pp. 50–66). Washington, DC: American Enterprise Institute.

Polsby, N. W. (1983). *Consequences of party reform.* New York: Oxford University Press.

Riker, W. H. (1980). Implications from the disequilibrium of majority rule for the study of institutions. *American Political Science Review, 74,* 432–446.

Rivers, D., & Rose, N. L. (1985). Passing the president's program: Public opinion and presidential
influence in Congress. *American Journal of Political Science, 29,* 183–196.

Schudson, M. (1995). *The power of news.* Cambridge, MA: Harvard University Press.

Shapiro, R. Y., & Jacobs, L. R. (2000). Who leads and who follows? U.S. presidents, public opinion,
and foreign policy. In B. L. Nacos, R. Y. Shapiro, & P. Isernia (Eds.), *Decisionmaking in a
glass house: Mass media, public opinion, and American and European foreign policy in the
21st century* (pp. 223–246). New York: Rowman and Littlefield.

Sigal, L. V. (1973). *Reporters and officials: The organization of news reporting.* Lexington, MA:
D. C. Heath.

Zaller, J. R. (1992). *The nature and origins of mass opinion.* New York: Cambridge University Press.

# Part VII

# Theory and Metatheory in Social Psychological Science

# 19

# Clapping With Both Hands: Numbers, People, and Simultaneous Hypotheses

*Phoebe C. Ellsworth*

## Prologue

I am afraid that I have not lived up to Bill's recommendation that "one's way should be taken deliberately and egosyntonically" (McGuire, 1999, p. 432); I'm not even sure I know what "egosyntonically" means. I feel that I've been extraordinarily lucky to have been surrounded by interesting questions all my life, more than I could possibly address, enough to last forever. Bill was one of the people, along with Bob Zajonc and Bob Krauss, who demonstrated to me that a person could study a wide variety of topics and still have a rewarding career, and that realization was a source of joy and liberation for me. If I was feeling frustrated or unimaginative in my research on emotions, I could do a law and psychology study, doing interesting and useful work on a second topic while in the background my mind refreshed itself on the first. Sometimes I chose questions because of pure curiosity, sometimes because I wanted to change society—or at least bear witness to its shortcomings—sometimes because the question matched the interests of a particularly promising student. Usually I chose questions that were not "in the mainstream" because I figured that plenty of other smart people were already addressing those questions. Bill argued that there is a congestion of researchers around a few topics, while much of the rest of the universe of interesting questions is sparsely populated. I was happy to work in those wildernesses, where the questions were still new and territorial disputes over tiny theoretical points had not yet developed.

But sometimes I think that my "inner self" is a methodologist. I get as much joy out of figuring out how to answer a question as I do from answering it. When I was an undergraduate, various people told me that I had a talent for experimental design and procedure: I was devastated. I was an artist, damn it, and I wanted people to tell me I had a talent for fiction writing or painting, or even acting. I resisted the suggestion that my special gift was so small and dull. Eventually, I had to admit that my advisors had a point. When I read a study I would think, "No, no, no! That's not the best way to answer that question! A better way to do it would be to. . . ." I worried about plausible rival hypotheses and missing controls, and I worried about what the subjects were actually thinking and feeling when they were being studied. I came to recognize that a good social psychologist needs a whole range of skills from cold logic to sympathetic human understanding, needs them every time she plans a study. I realized that usually you have to sneak up on a hard problem through intelligent compromise and triangulation. If there is an alternative explanation for the results of your first study (and there usually is), you change your method and eliminate it in the next. It has all the excitement of hunting or competing except that you don't have to kill anything or beat anybody. Campbell and Stanley's (1966) little book taught me the beauty of the logic of experimental design, and, equally important, the beauty of finding the best possible combination of compromises when nature or ethics made the perfect design impossible. Elliot Aronson and others taught me the beauty of creating a situation that captured both the essence of the question and the full attention of the people being studied.

The recognition that good social psychological research requires every kind of skill suddenly made it seem like a worthy and inexhaustibly interesting enterprise, not just some sort of intellectual second best, and sometimes when I would read an experiment (and, I'll add immodestly, sometimes when I thought of one myself), I'd think, "Yes, yes, yes! That's so smart, that's so right, that's so beautiful!" And my pleasure was not just the pleasure of science, but of art.

* * *

Throughout his career, William J. McGuire has been a tireless advocate for the creative, generative, exploratory side of research, urging us to move away from the congested gridlock of popular topics into the uncharted wilderness (McGuire, 1999) and to care more about discovery than proof (McGuire, 1997). In McGuire's famous "Yin and Yang" article (McGuire, 1973), the very first of the seven koan tells us that we ought to focus more on generating hypotheses and less on testing them. He argues that

> at least 90% of the time in our current courses on methodology is devoted to ways of testing hypotheses and . . . little time is spent on the prior and more important process of how one creates these hypotheses in the first place. (McGuire, 1973, p. 450)

A long time has passed since Bill first suggested that we as methodologists should balance our preoccupation with hypothesis testing by devoting more attention to hypothesis generation and so achieve a more symmetrical yin and yang. Have we heeded his message? What do our writings and teachings about research methods look like today? In this chapter, I argue that we have done well by Bill's recommendations to add diversity and complexity to our methods but not so well on the "prior and more important" stages of thinking about ideas and human beings, or of entertaining multiple simultaneous hypotheses.

To begin with, we have failed to rise to the challenge of the first koan, failed rather spectacularly. If anything, we have moved in the opposite direction. Hypothesis generation may now be given a day at the beginning or a day at the end of a methods course, often with one of McGuire's pieces assigned, but it is certainly not an integral part of the course: It is one of those tacked-on topics like ethics. Instead of moving forward to consider the beginning stages of the research process, when the researchers are still trying to figure what exactly the question is and how to turn it into an empirical study, our attention is more and more exclusively focused on the final stages: measurement and data analysis.

In 2000, social psychology's first handbook of research methods was produced (Reis & Judd, 2000). It is 558 pages long and contains 19 chapters. Four of these are devoted to research design; eight to research procedures, of which six are concerned almost entirely with different types of measures; and seven to various techniques for data analysis. There are no index entries for "hypothesis generation," "ideas," or "questions" (although there are 27 for "questionnaire design") and only five for "theorizing."

This imbalance is probably disappointing to Bill, but not surprising. He recognized that people avoid teaching about the birth of hypotheses because they fear that "so complex a creative process . . . is something that cannot be taught" (1973, pp. 450–451). What worries me is that the imbalance in our attention to the earlier and the later stages of the research process seems to be becoming even more lopsided. Getting an idea is the very first stage, and we have never given much consideration to that mysterious process. But more and more we are neglecting the *other* early stages of research: the translation of our abstract question into a coherent set of procedures that makes sense to the subjects and holds their attention, the development of nonreactive treatments and measures that subjects care about and that mean what we want them to mean, and the exciting, frustrating trial-and-error iterations of pilot testing, when we finally get a feel for our research problem and for what works and what doesn't in transforming an idea into a concrete set of events that matter to people. Technicalities of measurement and data analysis, less messy and more quantifiable, are taking up more and more space in our courses and textbooks at the expense of some of the skills that made social psychologists famous (and interesting), most notably the recreation of significant social phenomena in a simplified but psychologically meaningful form.

I do not mean to single out the new *Handbook* for criticism. Its emphases and its oversights are not idiosyncratic but reflect the current emphases and oversights of the field as a whole. On the Society for Personality and Social Psychology listserv, for example, almost all of the methodological questions people ask are requests for off-the-shelf measures: Does anyone have a measure of mistrust of female executives, or attitudes toward mixed-race people, or chocolate addiction, or empathy for pets, or any of dozens of other traits and attitudes? Rarely do the requesters describe their study or ask about the context in which the original measure was used. The idea that a measure is interpreted in a context, and that the same instrument may make sense in one context but not in another, seems to be all but forgotten, despite excellent work by Schwarz and his colleagues (cf. Schwarz, Groves, & Schuman, 1998) showing that even responses to apparently straightforward measures like questions on a survey are affected by the context.

## The Three Koan on Complexity and Variety

Not all of the koan have fared as poorly as the first. In the second, fourth, and fifth koan, Bill urged us to add diversity to our methods and complexity to our theories and analyses, to decrease our reliance on the laboratory experiment, and to look to more complicated sources of data and analytical techniques. Laboratory experiments greatly restrict the number of independent variables we can examine simultaneously and encourage a focus on simple, unidirectional causal relationships. In any case, any field that relies on a single method is likely to be either impoverished (most notably by failing to address the many interesting questions that don't fit the method) or distorted (most notably by Procrustean efforts to fit inappropriate questions to a 2 x 2 design). And here I think that social psychology has begun to rise to Bill's challenge.

Since 1973, many social psychologists have ventured out of the laboratory, and others have brought new techniques into it, techniques capable of capturing some of the complexity that Bill advocated. In part, the proliferation of methods reflects a proliferation of the topics that interest social psychologists. As evolutionary theory, the role of culture, intimate relationships, and intergroup relations have attracted theoretical interest, the limitations of the laboratory experiment as the favored method have become apparent. The fields of health psychology (Salovey, Rothman, & Rodin, 1998) and psychology and law (Ellsworth & Mauro, 1998) have also expanded enormously since 1973, moving researchers from the laboratory to the hospital and the courtroom and diversifying our subject population.

Of course, social psychologists have not given up laboratory experimentation, nor should they. As long-standing advocates of the use of multiple methods to achieve convergent validity (Campbell & Fiske, 1959; Webb, Campbell, Schwartz, & Sechrest, 1966), we seek supplements, not substitutes, for our traditional methods. Nisbett and Cohen's (1996) work on the culture of honor in the North and the South is an excellent example of the creative combination of the traditional laboratory experiment with archival surveys and other nontraditional methods. The laboratory experiment allows us to unconfound variables that are commonly confounded, to present people with dilemmas that are theoretically important but rarely occur in the real world, to examine the responses of people from different cultural backgrounds to the same situation, and to add process measures, such as physiological measures, that are not available in most natural settings.

Not all of our methodological advances require messy real-world data. We have also developed methods for studying the details of complex processes without leaving the psychology department. Computer simulations can provide highly specific sequential accounts of both individual and group processes (Hastie & Stasser, 2000), and we have made substantial progress in differentiating the influence of the specific individuals who make up a group from emergent group-level properties (Kashy & Kenny, 2000). Psychophysiological measures are more numerous and more precise than they were in 1973, and some social psychologists have even begun to venture into the world of the brain—as complex a system as any we are likely to encounter.

These methodological innovations reflect an increasing desire to examine psychological processes directly rather than inferring them, and, in keeping with Koan 2, social psychologists have begun to develop more complex, non-linear theories "that involve parallel processing, nets of causally interrelated factors, feedback loops, bi-directional causation, etc." (McGuire, 1973, p. 452). In the field of emotion, for example, unidimensional theories were common in the 1950s (Lindsley, 1951), and in the 1960s, Schachter and Singer (1962) proposed a model that involved two variables—physiological arousal and cognition. Social psychologists now include several specific varieties of "cognition," as well as bodily responses, expressive behaviors, subjective feelings, and action tendencies, and envision emotions as unfolding over time, with each element capable of influencing the others in a recursive series of parallel processes (Ellsworth & Scherer, 2003). Complex models have replaced simpler ones in many areas of social psychology: attitudes, stereotyping, group behavior, aggression, and love.

This new theoretical complexity could not have been achieved, and certainly could not have moved beyond the realm of empty speculation, without the astonishing advances in our data analysis capabilities since the early 1970s. The most obvious one, now so taken for granted that its importance in shaping our theories as well as our analyses is almost forgotten, is the computer. We are not more complex thinkers than the social psychologists of past generations; we just have better tools. Some of us can remember doing 2 × 2 analyses of variance or simple linear regressions by hand. We had memorized the sums of squares up to 25 and we rarely calculated farther than one number to the right of the decimal point. A three-way mixed model analysis of variance on a single dependent variable could take all night. So of course our designs were simple. Now we can do a month's work of analyses in a minute, and the technology has made feasible a wealth of new data analytic techniques—factor analysis, multidimensional scaling, path analysis, covariance structure modeling, hierarchical linear modeling, and meta-analysis, for example—that have in turn made a wealth of new research questions tractable.

Koan 4 is more specific, recommending the creation and use of longitudinal data archives. Here, too, technological advances have made a tremendous difference, this time in the form of the Internet. Census data, public opinion survey data, and data on crime, disease, and a host of other specialized topics are readily available. Beginning in the 1990s, Samuel Gross and I carried out several analyses of trends and correlates of Americans' attitudes toward capital punishment (Ellsworth & Gross, 1994; Gross, 1998; Gross & Ellsworth, 2003). All of the national polls that have asked about death penalty attitudes are available (e.g., from the Roper Center for Public Opinion Research at the University of Connecticut) and can easily be correlated across time with data on demographic variables, other attitudes, views about the most serious problems facing the country, personal experience as a crime victim, or any of dozens of other variables a researcher might find interesting. With only a little extra effort, correlations with other national trends, such as the homicide rate (FBI Uniform Crime Reports), can be examined. For my first article on public opinion on the death penalty, published in 1974 (Vidmar & Ellsworth, 1974), it took many months to find the surveys that had been done, and there were some that we missed. In the recent studies, the basic data collection took only a few hours, and whenever we got a new idea we could log on and check it out, refining our questions as we went along. Archival data are still underused, but they have great potential.

We are doing well on the three koan related to complexity and variety: We are regularly using (a) a more diverse set of data sources and (b) a greater variety of far more sophisticated methods of data analysis to (c) study new domains and relationships among a larger number of variables. And, in a backhanded way, these developments have implications for the first koan. Although our courses and our textbooks devote no more attention to the creative generation of hypotheses than they ever did, new methods and new domains imply new hypotheses.

## Missing Persons: Koan 3

"Nevertheless: Oh, nevertheless:" (Agee & Evans, 1939). Something is drifting away, becoming indistinct and shadowy. Our absorption with analytic advances has to some extent distracted us from ideas, but because the techniques suggest new hypotheses, there is still hope for Koan 1. But it has also distracted us from human beings, and I am deeply concerned about Koan 3: "Observe. But observe people not data" (McGuire, 1973, p. 452). In 1973, in tones of eloquent frustration, Bill described the problem exactly:

> We have plunged through reality, like Alice through the mirror, into a never-never land in which we contemplate not life, but data. All too often the scientific psychologist is observing not mind or behavior but summed data and computer printout. (1973, p. 453)

The situation has not gotten any better since 1973; in fact, I think it has gotten worse. Textbooks and chapters on methods devote more and more attention to the data we analyze and less and less to the people we supposedly want to understand. We used to worry more about what was going on in the minds of our subjects, recognizing that they were reacting emotionally and intellectually to the events that happened to them in our laboratories, to the questions on our questionnaires, to the researcher's appearance and demeanor. Subjects may or may not become engaged in their experience, they may or may not try to figure out what the researcher is looking for, and they usually care about the impression they are making on us. Discussions of interview methods used to devote considerable attention to strategies for establishing rapport, to the delicate psychological task of creating a situation in which people would be motivated to give honest answers (Cannell & Kahn, 1968). Discussions of laboratory experiments were concerned with creating an involving situation in which the events made sense and would be interpreted in the same way by all or most people (Aronson & Carlsmith, 1968; Carlsmith, Aronson, & Ellsworth, 1976).

Even the methodological artifacts we worried about—demand characteristics, evaluation apprehension, experimenter bias—were human artifacts. We feared that our subjects' reactions to our treatments or measures or to the whole situation might be more complex and multidimensional than the reactions contemplated by our hypotheses. Subjects were seen as interested human beings, alert to subtle cues and consciously or unconsciously adjusting their responses to those cues. Discussion of these human artifacts has dwindled in recent methodological writings, replaced by ever-more sophisticated discussions of statistical artifacts. We have a hypothesis about the meaning of our study, and we unthinkingly assume that subjects will respond according to that hypothesis. We pay little attention to the possibility that subjects will either interpret the independent or dependent variables differently from what we had in mind or will analyze our intentions and adjust their behavior accordingly. We have come to treat our subjects as mindless units, passing through our procedures on a conveyor belt.

We don't really talk to our subjects any more: We don't try to find out what they think; we barely notice them. Traditionally, the best time to learn about what our research subjects are thinking was during pilot testing. During pilot testing, the researcher can find out how people interpret the procedures—the stated purpose of the research, the treatments, the questions on the questionnaire, the instructions, the relation between one part of the study and another. The researcher can look at separate pieces of the procedure in isolation, measuring immediate psychological responses before they are muddied by later events or by the subject's own responses to them: "So what did you think about the people in the story you just read?" "Which questions did you think were hardest to answer?" "What stood out to you most about this study/questionnaire/person?" "What do you think we were getting at in this study?" Of course, not all of what the pilot subjects tell us can be taken at face value: If people had such great insight into their own behavior, simple interviews would be all we needed for psychological research (Freedman, 1969; Nisbett & Wilson, 1977); however, a good deal of what they say is useful, forcing us to rethink our definitions, manipulations, procedures, and measures. In a study of the effects of emotions on performance, I once had the great idea of using typing as the behavioral measure, because all mistakes could be entered into the computer as they happened and we could skip the whole tedious task of coding. However, pilot testing made it abundantly clear that nobody cared about being a good or bad typist, so the subjects didn't experience any emotions at all, except maybe boredom.

Nowadays, when I tell students that I want to watch a couple of pilot subjects, many of them go all shifty-eyed. It is clear to me that some of them hadn't even thought of running pilot subjects, that the whole idea is unfamiliar to them. When I serve on dissertation committees, I am often surprised to find that the experiment got null results because the mood manipulation failed or because there were ceiling effects on the crucial measure. Pilot testing is designed to identify problems like these so that they can be fixed before the real research is conducted.

The other opportunity to talk to subjects is at the end of the experimental session, during debriefing. This is not as useful as talking to them during pilot testing, because it only allows us to discover our mistakes when it is too late, but it can be very helpful in making sense of results that don't fit our predictions or in identifying deviant subjects. Debriefing at my university has more or less degenerated into passing out a printed description of the study. When students come to me bearing a printout and ask whether it's legitimate to throw out a couple of outliers, I ask, "Did you notice anything weird about those subjects? What did they say?" On these occasions, the look I get says, "What do you think I am, a mind reader?" and it is clear that they know nothing at all about the person except what is on the printout.

This is a lost opportunity. Talking to our subjects can help us to learn from anomalies and paradoxes, as Bill recommended. If some subjects respond to our treatments very differently from the others, it is a clue that there may be an important moderator variable lurking out there. In contemporary psychology, when theoretically plausible items fail to correlate with the main thrust of our measure, nowadays we tend to just dump them without asking why in order to achieve a high alpha for the overall measure—but important psychological questions might be illuminated by these "bad items," and talking to the subjects about their answers could be helpful.

It is difficult to say why we have become so much less likely to think of our subjects as real human beings or to talk to them before and after the study. Part of the story may be academia's increasing emphasis on quantity over quality and the bureaucratic emphasis on standardization over imagination unwittingly created by Human Subjects Review Boards. Researchers feel pressured to publish many articles and to include many studies in each article. The time spent on pilot testing, on designing a really elegant and meaningful study, could be used to run one or two clones of the original study, which could be reported as "Study 2" and "Study 3," and the temptation to do so is hard to resist. Competition for lab space and subjects is heightened when multiple studies are required for publication, and we are reluctant to waste a subject hour gaining insight when we could be producing data. There is no need to talk to the subjects after the study; because the Human Subjects Review Board requires us to submit standardized, written descriptions of our debriefing materials, we might as well just hand copies of these to the subjects as they leave the room. During the 10 minutes we save by not talking to the subjects, we might even have time to administer another measure. McGuire has argued that the "preliminary thrashing around" (1999, p. 410) of pilot testing provides much richer and more interesting information than generating "one little study after another" (1973, p. 455), and perhaps the field should reward detailed reports of careful pilot work more highly than a series of uninteresting follow-up studies.

It has become politically correct to call the people we study "participants" rather than "subjects." I have not done so here because I don't think the new term represents genuine respect but is simply window dressing. In fact, we are treating them more as objects than as participants or even subjects. We don't think about their subjectivity. In some of our sister disciplines, most notably sociology, the all-consuming attention to quantitative analysis led to a rebellion on the part of those who wanted to capture the nuanced complexity of the thoughts and feelings of real human beings and finally to an acrimonious rift between the quantitative mainstream and the qualitative resistance movement, closing off communication and deeply wounding the field as a whole. Social psychology has so far avoided this bitter divide, in part because we have long recognized that events are socially constructed in particular social contexts; in fact, that insight is one of social psychology's distinctive contributions (Asch, 1951) and is reflected in the care we have traditionally devoted to creating coherent contexts in our research. The shift in emphasis away from the context and procedures of data collection to the intricacies of data analysis may put us at risk, however. Some students feel that the insights they gained from running focus groups are totally lost in the regression analyses of the final study, that the questions that they cared about have been translated into questions that they don't care about, and they feel stirrings of mistrust for the quantitative approach.

The true excitement of research is to bring the yin and the yang together, to generate ideas about real people and then to turn them into questions that can be posed with rigor and precision, providing replicable data that embody the human meanings of the original idea. Writing about literature, E.M. Forster said, "There are in the novel two forces: human beings and a bundle of various things not human beings, and . . . it is the novelist's business to adjust these two forces and conciliate their claims" (1927, p. 105). It is our business, too, and the achievement of this synthesis has traditionally been one of the social psychologist's strengths, from Triplett to La Piere to Asch to Festinger to Nisbett and Ross. Our subjects' experiences were meaningful and involving both to themselves and to people who read about them later. Our claims, however, were based on quantitative analyses of their behavior, not on our personal impressions. The experience was authentic, but measurable and testable. Neglecting either the scientific comparison and analysis or the minds of the people we study would impoverish the field and lead to results of dubious validity.

## Demonstration, Falsification, and Honest Comparison

One of the concerns that inspired Bill to write the "Yin and Yang" article, providing the introductory background to the koan themselves, is that we are not really asking questions at all, because we are only prepared to believe the answer we expected in the first place. Our studies, whether they take place in the lab or in the field, "turn out to be more like demonstrations than tests. If the experiment does not come out 'right,' then the researcher does not say that the hypothesis was wrong but that something was wrong with the experiment . . ." (1973, p. 449).

Of course demonstrations *can* contribute to knowledge. Some of the most famous studies in social psychology have been demonstrations—Asch's initial study of conformity (1951) and Milgram's of obedience (1963), which didn't even bother with control groups, for example, and more recently many of Tversky and Kahneman's demonstrations of biases and heuristics (1974). These studies showed that people could behave in ways that were quite unexpected and deeply troubling. They made the world think. They were useful, more useful than many hypothesis-testing studies. Most studies that claim to test hypotheses, however, are really intended to "demonstrate their obvious truth" (McGuire, 1973, p. 448) and do not shake up the beliefs of the world at large but simply show that one particular belief can be made to look true. This is not particularly interesting, and the researcher would have done better to ask a genuine question.

Something like a demonstration is also useful as a first step in a program of research. If I want to know whether culture or status or feedback from the facial muscles affects a person's emotional response to a situation, I might begin with situations in which I think my manipulations or stimuli are most likely to show differences. I will choose situations that I expect will be experienced very differently by people in the cultures I've chosen to study, or I will make sure that my manipulations of power or facial expression are unmistakably clear and unconfounded. If I can't reliably produce the phenomenon, given my most blatant and loaded efforts, I will either rethink or abandon the idea. With a new idea, it is sometimes important to know whether it can be demonstrated at all before worrying about its complexities and limits, which can be addressed in follow-ups. What is appropriate at one stage of the research process may not be at another (Ellsworth, 1977; McGuire, 1999).

Sooner or later, though, whether or not one begins with a demonstration, real hypothesis testing requires putting one's hypothesis in jeopardy, testing it in ways that might bend it out of shape. Popper (1961) argued that empirical research could never confirm but only disconfirm a universal or general hypothesis; therefore, because verification is impossible, our scientific goal should be falsification. McGuire (1999, p. 408) pointed out that philosophically, the strong Popperian argument is both oversimplified and outdated, and I would add that it is also psychologically impossible for most normal researchers in the real world. When we finally think we have a really good idea, a hypothesis we care about, it is too much to ask that we begin by trashing it. Our reputations depend on publication, and publication depends on providing evidence that supports an idea, not evidence that refutes it. The only time we feel committed to the principle of falsification is when it is somebody else's theory, and the only time an article that simply falsifies a theory has a prayer of being published is when the theory is widely believed.

If confirmation is meaningless and falsification is professional suicide, what is left for the researcher who strives for quality? There is at least one good answer. It is not new, but it is still excellent and still largely ignored. It was proposed by Chamberlin (1890/1965), by Platt (1964), and by McGuire himself (1999, p. 420). It is the idea that every research enterprise, even every individual study, should be designed to test "multiple working hypotheses" (Chamberlin, 1890/1965). Ideally, the researcher should actually *entertain* multiple working hypotheses, all of which she considers to be at least somewhat plausible, rather than a single hypothesis to be confirmed or disconfirmed or a favored hypothesis and a bunch of implausible straw man alternatives.

Before conducting a program of research, we should force ourselves to generate several alternative explanations of the results we expect (and, if we are exceptionally clever, of results we don't expect). We should consider other possible influences on our outcome measures and add the most plausible as additional independent variables. We should ask ourselves, "What is the hardest problem for my theory?" None of this is easy to do, but colleagues can be enormously helpful. Tell them that you have already confirmed your hypothesis and suggest your favorite explanation, and they will supply you with alternatives. Your task is then to rephrase these apparently ridiculous alternatives so that at least some of them are actually plausible to *you*.

Having generated multiple working hypotheses, the investigator now must design research that can test two or three (or sometime more) of them at once. Thus rather than asking, "Is this hypothesis true or false?" the researcher asks, "What is the evidence for each of these different hypotheses?" Designing such a study may mean adding experimental conditions or comparison groups. It may mean adding measures of moderator, mediator, or outcome variables that are not central to the original hypothesis. It may mean adding new comparisons in the process of data analysis, comparing various models with each other.

Obviously, designing an experiment to test multiple competing hypotheses involves more effort and more creativity than testing a single hypothesis against the null hypothesis. Generating theoretically interesting alternative hypotheses is hard work, especially if we are very attached to our original idea. Consciously or unconsciously, we may succumb to the temptation to propose stupid, easily falsifiable "alternatives," resulting in a design that may be elegant in form but devoid of real content. Faced with this daunting task, we can turn to Bill McGuire for help. The creative heuristics he proposed for generating an initial hypothesis (McGuire, 1997, 1999; see also the Appendix) are at least as suitable for generating a second, third, and fourth.

Also, our design has to be good enough so that we ourselves would believe the results, whether the evidence supports our own hypothesis, one of the alternatives, some combination, or none at all. If we know in advance that we are going to reject some of the possible outcomes of our study, then the study is not ready to run. There's no point in carrying out a study if we are only prepared to believe one of the possible outcomes.

Although designing such an experiment is mentally taxing and time consuming, there are advantages. Most of all, the experiment is no longer a win/lose proposition producing a (likely spurious) confirmation or a disconfirmation that can't be turned into anything useful. If several different working hypotheses are compared, the study is much more likely to produce interesting information that can be developed and refined in follow-up research. Many *different* patterns of results are possible, each one pointing in new directions.

## Conclusion

Since 1973, when Bill published his article about progress in social psychology, we have made progress on some of his recommendations but lost ground on others. Our data sources are more diverse, including greater use of archival resources (Koan 4), and our analytical techniques are far more sophisticated (Koan 5), allowing us to address more complex questions (Koan 2).

However, we have made little if any progress in creative hypothesis generation (Koan 1), and our increased sophistication in data analysis has been accompanied by diminished attention to research as an interactive process in which we see our subjects as actively interpreting the situation they find themselves in, the questions we ask them, and the people they encounter (Koan 3). It is as though we do not really become interested in the people we study until they become data points or in the methods we use unless they have implications for our statistical choices. If the numbers are the yin of social psychology and the people are the yang, then the two are seriously out of balance. If the imbalance persists and grows, it could lead to a polarizing split of the sort that has occurred in other disciplines and a neglect of many of the most interesting questions.

Bill's introductory argument in the "Yin and Yang" article is that we should emphasize proof less (because it is generally unattainable) and discovery more (because it is always attainable and always more interesting). Most published articles in social psychology still either demonstrate a supposedly new phenomenon, test a hypothesis against the null hypothesis, or show that a hypothesis is robust across minor variations in procedure. Examination of multiple working hypotheses in the same publication is exceedingly rare, and it should not be. As researchers, we should strive to design programs of research that investigate several possibilities at once; as reviewers, we should demand as much attention to conceptual alternatives as we do to analytical ones, and we should count the number of different hypotheses tested rather than the number of studies conducted. We should value reports of the development of the study through pilot work more than additional studies that are no more than minor variations on a theme. A win/lose design stifles discovery and produces boring win/lose emotions like satisfaction and disappointment. A multiple hypothesis design can provide results we never thought of, stimulating perplexity, excitement, engagement, and most of all, a passionate curiosity. These are the appropriate emotions of science.

# References

Agee, J., & Evans, W. (1939). *Let us now praise famous men.* New York: Ballantine.

Aronson, E., & Carlsmith, J. M. (1968). Experimentation in social psychology. In G. Lindzey & E. Aronson (Eds.), *The handbook of social psychology* (2nd ed., Vol. 2, pp 1–79). Reading, MA: Addison-Wesley.

Asch, S. E. (1951). Effects of group pressure upon the modification and distortion of judgments. In H. Guetzkow (Ed.), *Groups, leadership and men* (pp. 177–190). Pittsburgh, PA: Carnegie Press.

Campbell, D. T., and Stanley, J. C. (1966). *Experimental and quasi-experimental designs for research.* Chicago: Rand NcNally.

Campbell, D. T., & Fiske, D. W. (1959). Convergent and discriminant validation by the multitrait-multimethod matrix. *Psychological Bulletin, 56,* 81–105.

Cannell, C. F., & Kahn, R. L. (1968). Interviewing. In G. Lindzey & E. Aronson (Eds.), *The handbook of social psychology* (2nd ed., Vol. 2, pp. 529–595). Reading, MA: Addison-Wesley.

Carlsmith, J. M., Ellsworth, P. C., & Aronson, E. (1976). *Methods of research in social psychology.* Reading, MA: Addison-Wesley.

Chamberlin, T. C. (1965). The method of multiple working hypotheses. *Science, 148,* 754–759. (Reprinted from *Science* [old series], *15,* 92, 1890)

Ellsworth, P. C. (1977). From abstract ideas to concrete instances: Some guidelines for choosing natural research settings. *American Psychologist, 32,* 604–615.

Ellsworth, P. C., & Gross, S. (1994). Hardening of the attitudes: Americans' views on the death penalty. *Journal of Social Issues, 50,* 19–52.

Ellsworth, P. C., & Mauro, R. (1998). Psychology and law. In D. T. Gilbert, S. T. Fiske, & G. Lindzey (Eds.), *The handbook of social psychology* (4th ed., Vol. 2, pp. 684–732). Boston: McGraw-Hill.

Ellsworth, P. C., & Scherer, K. R. (2003). Appraisal processes in emotion. In R. J. Davidson, H. Goldsmith, & K. R. Scherer (Eds.), *Handbook of affective sciences* (pp. 572–595). New York and Oxford: Oxford University Press.

Forster, E. M. (1927). *Aspects of the novel*. New York: Harcourt Brace.

Freedman, J. L. (1969). Role-playing: Psychology by consensus. *Journal of Personality and Social Psychology, 13,* 107–114.

Gross, S. (1998). Update: American public opinion on the death penalty: It's getting personal. *Cornell Law Review, 83,* 1148–1475.

Gross, S. R., & Ellsworth, P. C. (2003). Second thoughts: Americans' views on the death penalty at the turn of the century. In S. P. Garvey (Ed.), *Beyond repair? America's death penalty* (pp. 7–57). Durham, NC: Duke University Press.

Hastie, R., & Stasser, G. (2000). Computer simulation models for social psychology. In H. T. Reis & C. M. Judd (Eds.), *Handbook of research methods in social and personality psychology* (pp. 85–114). Cambridge, UK: Cambridge University Press.

Kashy, D. A., & Kenny, D. A. (2000). The analysis of data from dyads and groups. In H. T. Reis & C. M. Judd (Eds.), *Handbook of research methods in social and personality psychology* (pp. 451–477). Cambridge, UK: Cambridge University Press.

Lindsley, D. B. (1951). Emotion. In S. S. Stevens (Ed.), *Handbook of experimental psychology* (pp. 473–516). New York: Wiley.

McGuire, W. J. (1973). The yin and yang of progress in social psychology: Seven koan. *Journal of Personality and Social Psychology, 26,* 446–456.

McGuire, W. J. (1997). Creative hypothesis generating in psychology: Some useful heuristics. *Annual Review of Psychology, 48,* 1–30.

McGuire, W. J. (1999). *Constructing social psychology: Creative and critical processes*. Cambridge, UK: Cambridge University Press.

Milgram, S. (1963). Behavioral study of obedience. *Journal of Abnormal and Social Psychology, 67,* 371–378.

Nisbett, R. E., & Cohen, D. (1996). *Culture of honor: The psychology of violence in the South*. Denver, CO: Westview Press.

Nisbett, R. E., & Wilson, T. D. (1977). Telling more than we can know: Verbal reports of mental processes. *Psychological Review, 84,* 231–259.

Platt, J. (1964). Strong inference. *Science, 146,* 347–353.

Popper, K. R. (1961). *The logic of scientific discovery*. New York: Science Editions.

Reis, H. T., & Judd, C. M. (Eds.). (2000). *Handbook of research methods in social and personality psychology*. Cambridge, UK: Cambridge University Press.

Salovey, P., Rothman, A. J., & Rodin, J. (1998). Health behavior. In D. T. Gilbert, S. T. Fiske, & G. Lindzey (Eds.), *The handbook of social psychology*. (4th ed., Vol. 2, pp. 633–683). New York: McGraw-Hill.

Schachter, S., & Singer, J. E. (1962). Cognitive, social, and physiological determinants of emotional state. *Psychological Review, 69,* 379–399.

Schwarz, N., Groves, R. M., & Schuman, H. (1998). Survey methods. In D. T. Gilbert, S. T. Fiske, & G. Lindzey, (Eds.), *The handbook of social psychology* (4th ed., Vol. 1, pp. 143–179). New York: McGraw-Hill.

Tversky, A., & Kahneman, D. (1974). Judgment under uncertainty: Heuristics and biases. *Science, 185,* 1124–1131.

Vidmar, N., & Ellsworth, P. C. (1974). Public opinion and the death penalty. *Stanford Law Review, 26,* 1245–1270.

Webb, E. J., Campbell, D. T., Schwartz, R. D., & Sechrest, L. (1966). *Unobtrusive measures*. Skokie, IL: Rand McNally.

# 20

# The Resting Parrot, the Dessert Stomach, and Other Perfectly Defensible Theories

*Anthony G. Greenwald*

Perspectivism calls upon scientists to use empirical work to do delibera-tively the contextual exploration that they now do furtively while pretend-ing to be doing hypothesis testing. (McGuire, 1989, p. 244)

## Prologue

In *Against Method*, Paul Feyerabend (1975) concluded that any attempt to specify bounds of scientific method would be misguided. The specified bound-aries, he argued, would inevitably exclude methods that are valuable in the accumulation of scientific knowledge. Feyerabend's argument drew heavily on an analysis of Galileo's methodological flexibility in advancing Copernicus's heliocentric theory over the dominant geocentric theory.

One reason for my finding Feyerabend's argument compelling is that I have long questioned the wisdom of a principle of proper method in psychol-ogy that is now widely advocated: the belief that empirical research is valuable only to the extent that it advances theory. I see this principle advocated every time that, as editorial reviewer, I receive a copy of an editorial rejection declar-ing that the reported research, even though acknowledged as interesting, did not advance theory.

Fortunately, this principle has not always been used to decide what should and what should not be published. Among the important works that have managed to achieve publication without advancing theory are some of the major works by Asch (conformity), Sherif (norm formation), Milgram (obe-dience), and Zajonc (mere exposure). I take occasional pleasure in managing to get into print an article that contains no theory (e.g., Greenwald, Draine, & Abrams, 1996; Greenwald, McGhee, & Schwartz, 1998).

In a few methodological articles, I have tried to make the point that much time and effort can be wasted in excessive focus on confirming theories or in trying to resolve disagreements among theories. I have discovered that theory is so sacred a cow in our discipline that my methodological articles have led more than a few colleagues to conclude that I am generally an opponent of theory.

My contribution to this Festschrift takes a further tack in describing costs of overemphasis on theory. It will no doubt strengthen the impression that I am against theory. Accordingly, I call attention to a quotation that I strongly endorse: "There is nothing so practical as a good theory" (Lewin, 1951, p. 20). I endorse it because I understand that the only way to relate empirical findings to practical applications is to have a theory that provides the basis for generalizing beyond the laboratory.

* * *

A common property of many long-unresolved theoretical debates in psychology is the flexibility of the competing theories: They are readily modified to accommodate unanticipated findings. Although theory modification is essential to scientific progress, repeated modifications can make contending theories effectively interchangeable, in turn making their competition illusory. Because theory competitions can be either sustained or resolved by voluntary actions of researcher/theorists, there is no way, beyond generalizing from the past, to predict that a specific theory competition will be sustained in illusory fashion. This makes it a challenge to develop strategies that will protect against the waste of research resources on unresolvable theory competitions.

Of those who join here to celebrate Bill McGuire's scientific contributions, I can claim the opportunity to have been influenced by Bill almost as long ago as any. Bill was an instructor of a team-taught course at Yale on Human Culture and Behavior that I took as an undergraduate in 1957–1958. Bill's obviously favorable perspective on the Hovland, Janis, and Kelley (1953) *Communication and Persuasion* volume was no doubt an influence that pointed me toward choosing attitudes as my first area of research specialization. It wasn't until several years later that I began to read Bill's published work, starting with his theoretically ingenious and empirically convincing 1964 chapter on immunization-like processes in resistance to persuasion.

Bill's methodological works, starting with the famous "Yin and Yang" article (McGuire, 1973) and continuing through his several writings on perspectivism, have influenced me so much that I cannot identify which (if any) of the methodological points that I subsequently made in print may have occurred to me prior to my reading them in Bill's work. The ideas in this chapter build on a recurring theme in Bill's series of methodological works: the description of research strategies in terms of their potential to facilitate or hinder progress.

I thank this volume's editors for having obliged relatively short contributions. To cope with this limitation, I ask readers to assume that some of my more contentious points are plausible, after which I proceed as if I had established these points convincingly. If I am allowed to get away with this, I am sure that I will try it again in the future; it is remarkably liberating.

On reading an earlier draft of this chapter, one of this volume's editors commented that it seemed pessimistic concerning the functioning of theory in psychology. I hope not to be read as a pessimist. Some of the challenges that psychologists face in dealing with theory are caused by the youth of psychology as a discipline. By developing an understanding of these challenges, I hope to facilitate progress in dealing with them.

## Competition Among Theories

Competing theoretical accounts of novel findings attract researchers like moths to flame. J. R. Platt (1964) gave the approving label *strong inference* to experiments that are designed to choose between competing theoretical interpretations of a phenomenon. It is easy to conclude that competition between theories is generally desirable.

Is it? If competition among theories is a good way of doing science, we should expect theoretical controversies to have a short life expectancy. When a controversy occurs, we should expect that experiments designed to choose among the theories will resolve the controversy within perhaps a few years. It is therefore informative to examine the life expectancy of theoretical controversies.

My informal review of theoretical controversies reveals that it is easy to identify publications that initiated many well-known controversies, but it is virtually impossible to identify publications that brought any of these to resolution. For example, there has been a long-lasting controversy about the nature of mental representations that underlie the human ability to rotate objects mentally (Shepard & Metzler, 1971). Are these representations propositional (verbal or symbolic) or analog (involving visual features)? More than 30 years later, this debate shows little sign of ending. It is easy to identify other similarly durable controversies pertaining to representations underlying mental categorization (dating from Labov, 1973), serial versus parallel mental processes in memory search (dating from Sternberg, 1966), and bipolar versus orthogonal dimensions of positive and negative affect (dating from Nowlis & Nowlis, 1956). The life expectancy of these controversies is certainly long, and it may be indeterminate. A genuine competition between theories should eventually reach a conclusion. Psychology's well-known theoretical controversies appear to offer only the illusion of competition. Their prevalence calls into question the belief that theory controversy is a useful propellant for the advance of scientific knowledge.

## How to Determine Whether Theory Competitions Are Illusory

Alas, there is no way to determine conclusively whether psychology is plagued with illusory theory competitions. One possible method would be to establish by analytical reasoning that *all* competitions between theories are necessarily unresolvable. This assertion has indeed received careful attention from philosophers of science. Ironically, philosophical analyses of the prospects for using empirical methods to resolve theoretical disputes display their own lengthy, unresolved controversy, which can be found easily in the philosophical literature by searching for articles on the topic of "underdetermination of theory by data." This is the body of literature in which one runs repeatedly into the names of Quine, Duhem, Popper, Kuhn, Lakatos, and Feyerabend, who were the major contributors before about 1980.

Even if philosophy can break its own deadlock to establish that psychology's theoretical controversies are in principle resolvable, it would nevertheless be possible for scientists to pursue such controversies so as to indefinitely avoid resolution. Also, perhaps a bit more surprisingly, even if philosophers could persuade us that some or all such controversies are in principle not resolvable, it would nevertheless be possible for scientists to resolve all such controversies.

As an example, consider a theoretical controversy that has recently occupied the time and attention of astronomers: Is the astronomical object Pluto a planet or is it a large comet? Regardless of any conclusion that philosophy of science might reach about the possibility of resolving this debate, astronomers have it in their power to prolong the debate endlessly, just as it is possible for them to achieve a speedy resolution. More generally, it is always an option for researchers either to prolong or to resolve any competition between theories. As a result, working scientists effectively make the philosophers' analyses irrelevant.[1]

To appreciate researchers' power to control the fate of any theoretical controversy, imagine that, when a research article claims that its findings refute an old theory and establish a new one, advocates of the old theory might say, "Our theory had a long life and is now gone. Long live the new theory." If that does not happen, imagine that advocates of the old theory publish a reply in which they argue that the apparent threat to their theory was entirely misguided. At that point, nothing need stop proponents of the new theory from declaring, "Hallelujah! The venerable old theory has risen. Let our upstart pretender rest in peace." Despite such possibilities for concluding any theoretical debate, psychological researchers generally choose to sustain debate. They choose with apparent uniformity to defend any attacked theory.

## What Are the Consequences of Illusory Competition?

Although illusory theory competitions do not achieve the goal of choosing among the competing theories, they might have other benefits that make them scientifically valuable. As an aid to thinking about costs and benefits of illusory competitions, I offer a fictitious illustration for which we can be sure that the controversy is illusory.

Imagine that you and a friend are 18th-century Yale philosophy professors time-transported to New Haven in the year 2003 as part of a laboratory exercise by electronic beings of the 24th century. (We shall assume that this laboratory exercise has been approved by the local review network for research on carbon-based forms.) Arriving at the Elm–Broadway intersection in 2003, you and your friend immediately notice the noisy vehicles that dominate the street. Your electronic hosts decide to make use of your fascina-

---

[1]At the Festschrift conference, I showed a video recording of Monty Python's "Dead Parrot Sketch" (Chapman, Monty Python, 1969/1989) to illustrate the opportunities that exist for optionally prolonging theoretical debates. In that episode, a customer returns a parrot to the pet shop from which he recently purchased it and presents the pet shop owner with the complaint (theory) that the parrot is now dead and was indeed dead at the time of purchase. The pet shop owner presents and defends several alternative views, especially (and repeatedly) the theory that the parrot is resting (providing part of the title of this chapter). In this inspired and hilarious piece of comedy, the shop owner's persistent and imaginative refutations of the dead parrot theory illustrate the possibility of prolonging a theoretical debate indefinitely by defending alternative interpretations even in the presence of compelling data.

tion with automobiles in order to test your intelligence. They inform you that these vehicles are moved by something that is located under the hood and they challenge you to explain how the movement is produced. They permit you to observe the operation of these vehicles either as a passenger or by watching from the street. (It is significant that you do not have the opportunity to look under the hood—this is crucial to the metaphor for behavioral psychology.)

Taking up the challenge and the position of front-seat passenger, you notice that whenever the driver applies steady foot pressure to a certain pedal, the vehicle steadily gains speed. In addition, you hear a noise that rises in pitch as the vehicle moves faster. Looking out the window, you also notice that there are places at which several vehicles are stopped while their drivers supervise the injection of some unseen substance into the vehicles' bodies. After pondering your observations, you conclude that the injected substance fills a hidden trough from which it is consumed by a powerful beast that runs on a treadmill. This treadmill is the source of both the power for movement and the sound; you theorize that the rising pitch of the sound is produced by the treadmill's increasing speed. In your theory, the pedal acts much like a horse's reins. The foot pressure on the pedal transmits a signal to the unseen beast, causing it to run on the treadmill and thereby to produce the power needed to turn the vehicle's wheels.

Your colleague has made similar observations but, unlike you, has observed that as the vehicle gains speed, the accompanying sound first rises in pitch, then drops, and then rises again. Based on this evidence, your colleague declares your theory to be hopelessly incorrect and proposes in its place a two-beast theory. In the two-beast theory, each beast has its own treadmill. The second beast starts running when the first one is fatigued. The two-beast theory includes an elegant explanation of why the second sound does not rise to a higher pitch than the first even though the vehicle has gained more speed. The explanation appeals to a gearing mechanism that allows the vehicle's wheels to turn faster for the same treadmill movement.

After conducting additional observations while listening more carefully, you conclude that your colleague's observations are valid. Nevertheless, you see no reason to abandon your one-beast theory. To explain all of the data, you need only to add a second treadmill, which you hypothesize to be operated by the one and only beast that resides under the hood. The audible changes occur when the beast steps off the first treadmill, causing it to slow down, and before the second treadmill gets up to speed. You are excited to have identified a well-defined difference between the two theories. You and your colleague immediately begin to discuss possibilities for tests that will decisively determine whether each vehicle houses one or two beasts.

A relatively sophisticated early 21st-century automobile user will, of course, see these developments as unfortunate. You and your colleague are about to waste a good part of your visit to the 21st century on the illusion of a competition between two plausible, but somewhat misdirected, theories. Also, while you are engaged in this competition, you will be ignoring the interesting idea that your two theories share—the idea of a transmission that allows an engine with a limited range of revolution speeds to control wheels that have a much wider range of revolution speeds. This theory, on which the two of you agree, actually explains the sound patterns that were the original source of your disagreement. However, in your eagerness to focus on the disagreement between your theories, you failed to appreciate the value of a theoretical proposition on which you agree.

Let us leave this thought odyssey behind, hoping that its absurdity will not prevent appreciation that the competition it describes may share characteristics with many of psychology's theoretical controversies. Specifically, the one-beast-versus-two-beast controversy has three characteristics: First, the competition is unresolvable in the sense that the competing theories are flexible enough to be empirically indistinguishable. Second, the competition has the potential to generate a progression of ultimately unimportant findings. Third, the competition distracts attention from interesting ideas on which the competitors agree.

Proper evaluation of the proposition "Illusory competitions are likely to generate inconsequential findings and divert attention from more valuable research efforts" requires a more detailed analysis of currently unresolved controversies than can be offered here. Once again, I limit my goal to trying to establish plausibility. Therefore, consider that (a) it seems unlikely that an extended debate over whether Pluto is a planet or a comet will generate important findings, (b) researchers' attempts to decide whether altruism is intrinsically or extrinsically motivated may be diverting effort away from interesting questions about how to influence the frequency of altruistic acts, and (c) for all the journal pages that have been devoted to them, studies designed to test whether mental categories have structures identifiable as features, prototypes, exemplars, or rules have yielded relatively little gain in understanding categories beyond Jerome Bruner's (1957) point that categories go "beyond the information given."

Unresolved controversies may have their most positive impact in encouraging the development of new observational methods. The attempt to propel the controversy puts pressure on researchers to generate observations that go beyond already available evidence. So, in seeking to resolve whether Pluto is a comet or a planet, astronomers may find ways to make observations of previously unobservable characteristics of Pluto. Those new observational methods may prove valuable even though they will not resolve whether Pluto is a planet or a comet. It will not resolve the debate because the debate, insofar as it is an illusory competition, is only about how the words "planet" and "comet" should be used. Similarly, the debate about altruism is largely one about the meanings of the terms "intrinsic motivation" and "extrinsic motivation." Debates about word meanings can be handled much more efficiently by negotiation among those who need to use the words than by gathering new data that allow different groups to modify existing meanings in different fashions.

## Why Are There Illusory Competitions?

The reader is again reminded that I am proceeding as if my superficially illustrated arguments have been established convincingly. On that basis, I have concluded that there is indeed an epidemic of illusory theory competitions in psychology; these competitions are illusory in that they turn out to be debates about the meaning of words rather than about the nature of relationships among observable empirical phenomena. Having established this point, I am now free to ask, "Why do these competitions develop and thrive in psychology?"

I have a simple two-part answer: First, researchers tend to be ego-involved advocates of *their* theories. This point is far from new, and it does not apply uniquely to psychology. The point was made very well by the geologist T. C. Chamberlin (1890/1965) when he wrote the 19th-century predecessor of J. R. Platt's (1964) "strong inference" article. The second reason, because it does apply specifically to psychology, seems the more important reason: Most of psychology's theories concern unobservable mental entities—things such as representations, motives, and traits. It is a constant challenge to psychologists to come up with measures for these unobservable entities. The difficulty of measuring unobservable mental entities makes it relatively easy for well-trained researchers to challenge the validity of any such measure. This explains equally the ease of attacking the empirical evidence for any theory and the ease of defending a theory against empirical attacks.

## A Conflict of Interest

Because researchers tend to be ego-involved advocates of their theories, researchers' self-respect is tied to judgments about the validity of their theories. Most psychological researchers have many occasions to experience a conflict of interest between their self-respect and their scientific objectivity. This conflict can occur whenever they encounter results that appear to refute theories with which they are identified. Perhaps regrettably, it is all too easy for psychologists to resolve the conflict in favor of the preferred theory. I have developed a three-item questionnaire intended to demonstrate the conflict. Readers are invited to answer these questions not for themselves but as descriptions of "other typical researchers." However, the questions are indeed intended to provoke self-questioning. (The italicized answer to each question indicates resolution of a conflict of interest in favor of self-respect.)

1. When conducting multiple parallel tests of a prediction from a preferred theory, the typical researcher will most likely conclude that a test that produced a statistically significant confirmation was more valid than one that produced a statistically nonsignificant result. (*True* or False?)
2. When an experiment fails to produce a result predicted by a preferred theory, the typical researcher will actively seek publication of that theory-refuting result. (True or *False*?)
3. When reviewing a manuscript that bears on a preferred theory, the typical researcher will be more likely to write a favorable review when the manuscript's research supports the theory than when it does not. (*True* or False?)

## Who Cares About This Conflict of Interest?

It is of interest that the American Psychological Association's (2002) *Ethical Principles of Psychologists and Code of Conduct* contains no mention of researchers' conflict of interest when it comes to evaluating their own theories.

The closest reference is one brief statement in Ethical Principle 8.10(a) to the effect that "Psychologists do not fabricate data" (APA, 2002). The Fifth Edition of the APA *Publication Manual* gives a brief elaboration of this principle: "Errors of omission also are prohibited. Psychologists do not omit troublesome observations from their reports so as to present a more convincing story" (APA, 2001, p. 348). This reference to "troublesome observations" is the sum total of the American Psychological Association's ethical advice bearing on the possibility of researcher self-interest influencing the conduct of research.

It is provocative to compare research psychologists with litigators who actively work to construct a one-sided case for their clients. Lawyers' professional ethics allow this unmitigated partiality in the context of an adversarial system in which each contending party has its own advocate. In contrast, in its near silence on the topic of researchers' conflicts between self-interest and scientific objectivity, APA's code neither encourages nor discourages researchers' bias in advocating their own theories.[2]

## Resolving the Conflict of Interest

Solutions to the conflict between self-interest and scientific objectivity can be divided into those that would legislate the conflict out of existence (the first three of the following) and those that recognize and try to manage the conflict of interest (the last two).

1. A MODIFIED CODE OF ETHICS. When researchers make editorial decisions and when they review grant proposals or manuscripts submitted to journals, they act in the role of judge or jury. In the courts, judges or jurors are expected not to participate in cases in which they have a relationship with a contending party. By analogy, researchers could excuse themselves from reviewing manuscripts or grant proposals that concern theories with which they are associated. A serious problem with this suggestion is that it would exclude reviewers and editors from participating in just those reviews for which they are most qualified. An even more severe problem is that this proposal does not touch on the frequently arising conflicts that occur in the process of dealing with one's own research results.

2. SEPARATING THE ROLES OF THEORIST AND DATA COLLECTOR. If theorists played no role in producing the data that test their theories, their partiality would not enter into evaluations of their theories. This proposal draws on the traditional separation of theorist and experimentalist roles in the discipline of physics. However, this otherwise reasonable solution seems impractical for psychology because of the radical shift that it would require in the culture of the discipline.

3. SEPARATING THE ROLES OF RESEARCHER AND GATEKEEPER. Another role-separation solution to conflicts between self-interest and scientific objectivity

---

[2]The American Psychological Association disagrees with the interpretation of the Ethics Code as stated here. This statement should therefore not be interpreted as representing an official position of the American Psychological Association.

is to define separate career paths for potential researchers and potential decision makers (such as editors and grant givers). A model is provided by the legal profession's separation of the career path for judges from that for advocates. Again, however, this change would require a radical change of the culture of scientific psychology and therefore seems quite impractical.

4. CHAMBERLIN'S (1890/1965) METHOD OF "MULTIPLE WORKING HYPOTHESES." Researchers in many disciplines are under pressure from reviewers and editors to establish the theory relevance of results that they report in manuscripts or of the research that they propose in grant applications. This aspect of publication culture encourages one-sided theory advocacy as an expository device in reporting research. An alternative means of emphasizing theory is to stress multiplicity and complementarity among theories. This is a point that Bill McGuire, in his perspectivist approach, has urged repeatedly. It relates to a suggestion that Chamberlin made after he commented on the tendency of scientific theorists to have a parental affection for their theories:

> The moment one has offered an original explanation for a phenomenon which seems satisfactory, that moment affection for his intellectual child springs into existence; and as the explanation grows into a definite theory, his parental affections cluster about his intellectual offspring, and it grows more and more dear to him, so that, while he holds it seemingly tentative, it is still lovingly tentative, and not impartially tentative. . . . There is an unconscious selection and magnifying of the phenomena that fall into harmony with the theory and support it, and an unconscious neglect of those that fail of coincidence. The mind lingers with pleasure upon the facts that fall happily into the embrace of the theory, and feels a natural coldness toward those that seem refractory. Instinctively, there is a special searching-out of phenomena that support it, for the mind is led by its desires. There springs up, also, an unconscious pressing of the theory to make it fit the facts, and a pressing of the facts to make them fit the theory. (1890/1965, p. 755)

Instead of asking researchers to present results that show how theories fare in competition with one another, researchers can be asked to show how theories complement one another—locating the boundaries between domains in which different theories apply. For those familiar with the language of construct validity, this is a suggestion to include evidence for discriminant validity in research designs and reports.

5. COLLABORATIONS INVOLVING THEORETICAL ANTAGONISTS. If proponents of competing theories could work together on the design of research, several desirable consequences, beyond the added resources of combined forces, could be expected. The most important desirable consequence is that debates about meanings of words would be played out in private without flowing into journal pages. Second, the collaborative research would likely be designed to give both (or all) theories their best chances for confirmation, including the possibility that different theories would be demonstrated to be valid under different conditions (again pointing to the desirability of evidence for discriminant validity). An illustration that this is possible, even if difficult, can be found in

the recent "adversarial collaboration" exercise by Mellers, Hertwig, and Kahneman (2001).

# Epilogue

My wife and children still recall the moment of what may have been my most brilliant theoretical creation—never mind that I was later disappointed to discover that others had preceded me in the theory. It was at a hotel in downtown Columbus, Ohio, to which our family had gone for a Sunday buffet. After filling ourselves on various combinations of shrimp, cheese, salads, casseroles, vegetables, fish, turkey, and, in my case, at least one more piece of roast beef than seemed prudent—to the point of being simply unable to eat more—we all discovered that it was still possible to make a trip to the dessert table and to eat at least one dessert. Primed by the title of this chapter, the reader will by now have anticipated my theoretical insight—the dessert stomach. The dessert stomach is an extra digestive organ that functions like the pinch hitter in baseball, resting on the sidelines until it is needed late in the game.

The dessert stomach theory neatly explained the otherwise puzzling all-you-can-eat-buffet data. However, the true test of this theory, like any other, is whether it can be applied successfully. Can the dessert stomach theory be put to use to achieve a result that would not have been thought possible until this theory came along? I reasoned that, if the extra capacity of the dessert stomach indeed existed, then it should be possible to put that capacity to some other use. That was the moment when—already filled to capacity—I got up and approached the dessert table. I hypothesized that an approach to the dessert table would suffice for my unseen internal digestive machinery to switch open the dessert stomach. After arriving at the dessert table, I stopped, changed direction, and walked instead toward the table at which pieces of juicy, rare roast beef were being carved. As those in my family well recall, that was the first observation of a piece of roast beef being tricked into the dessert stomach.

I bring up this accomplishment not merely to impress you with my theoretical skills, but because it may be an illustration that helps point the way to psychology's future. The dessert stomach theory could be perfectly defensible in any journal that obliged researchers to rely only on behavioral data. It is easy to imagine an unending controversy between advocates and critics of the theory. On the basis of nothing but behavioral data, the dessert stomach theory is, as the title of this chapter suggests, "perfectly defensible." However, as soon as any researcher would undertake to look inside the abdomen for the dessert stomach, the theoretical fate of this hypothesized digestive organ would be promptly resolved.

In contemporary psychology, only rarely are we able to look inside, or under the hood, in order to locate and identify our theoretical constructs. When we can do that, we sometimes get answers to questions that would otherwise be candidates for an unending theoretical controversy.[3] With the application of

---

[3]See the articles by Kosslyn, Digirolamo, Thompson, and Alpert, (1998), and Ganis, Keenan, Kosslyn, and Pascual-Leone (2000). These indicate a possible path toward resolution of the previously described debate about representations underlying mental rotation by using evidence obtained from looking under the hood (using positron emission tomography scans) and otherwise tinkering under the hood (administering transcranial magnetic stimulation).

computers to the processing of event-related potentials and the increasing temporal and spatial resolution of brain-imaging devices, we are perhaps at the beginning of an era in which psychology's theorized entities will be increasingly tied to identifiable inside-the-brain structures. In that coming era, we may not see the kinds of prolonged theoretical controversies that are so readily found in today's psychology. This coming era may well arrive during the professional lifetimes of many of those who join in this volume to celebrate Bill McGuire's career. Its arrival may even be hastened if, in the meantime, we can divert less of our collective professional resources to illusory competitions among theories.

# References

American Psychological Association (2001). *Publication manual* (5th ed.). Washington, DC: Author.

American Psychological Association (2002). *Ethical principles of psychologists and code of conduct.* Washington, DC: Author.

Bruner, J. S. (1957). Going beyond the information given. In H. Gruber et al. (Eds.), *Contemporary approaches to cognition* (pp. 41–69). Cambridge, MA: Harvard University Press.

Chamberlin, T. C. (1965). The method of multiple working hypotheses. *Science, 148,* 754–759. (Original work published in 1890)

Chapman, G., & Monty Python (1989). *The complete Monty Python's Flying Circus: All the words* (Vol. 1). New York: Pantheon. (Original work published in 1969)

Feyerabend, P. K. (1975). *Against method: Outline of an anarchistic theory of knowledge.* London: New Left Books.

Ganis, G., Keenan, J. P., Kosslyn, S. M., & Pascual-Leone, A. (2000). *Cerebral Cortex, 10,* 175–180.

Greenwald, A. G., Draine, S. C., & Abrams, R. L. (1996). Three cognitive markers of unconscious semantic activation. *Science, 273,* 1699–1702.

Greenwald, A. G., McGhee, D. E., & Schwartz, J. L. K. (1998). Measuring individual differences in implicit cognition: The implicit association test. *Journal of Personality and Social Psychology, 74,* 1464–1480.

Hovland, C. I., Janis, I. L., & Kelley, H. H. (1953). *Communication and persuasion.* New Haven, CT: Yale University Press.

Kosslyn, S. M., Digirolamo, G. J., Thompson, W. L., & Alpert, N. M. (1998). Mental rotation of objects versus hands: Neural mechanisms revealed by positron emission tomography. *Psychophysiology, 35,* 151–161.

Labov, W. (1973). The boundaries of words and their meanings. In C. J. Bailey & R. Shuy (Eds.), *New ways of analysing variation in English* (pp. 340–373). Washington, DC: Georgetown University Press.

Lewin, K. (1951). *Field theory in social science; selected theoretical papers* (D. Cartwright, Ed.). New York: Harper & Row.

McGuire, W. J. (1964). Inducing resistance to persuasion: Some contemporary approaches. In L. Berkowitz (Ed.), *Advances in experimental social psychology* (Vol. 1, pp. 191–229). New York: Academic Press.

McGuire, W. J. (1973). The yin and yang of progress in social psychology: Seven koan. *Journal of Personality and Social Psychology, 26,* 446–456.

McGuire, W. J. (1989). A perspectivist approach to the strategic planning of programmatic scientific research. In B. Gholson, W. R. Shadish, Jr., R. A. Neimeyer, & A. C. Houts (Eds.), *The psychology of science: Contributions to metascience* (pp. 214–245). New York: Cambridge University Press.

Mellers, B., Hertwig, R., & Kahneman, D. (2001). Do frequency representations eliminate conjunction effects? An exercise in adversarial collaboration. *Psychological Science, 12,* 269–275.

Nowlis, V., & Nowlis, H. H. (1956). The description and analysis of mood. *Annals of the New York Academy of Sciences, 65,* 345–355.

Platt, J. R. (1964). Strong inference. *Science, 146,* 347–353.

Shepard, R. N., & Metzler, J. (1971). Mental rotation of three-dimensional objects. *Science, 171,* 701–703.

Sternberg, S. (1966). High-speed scanning in human memory. *Science, 153,* 652–654.

# 21

# Unified Theory

## Norman H. Anderson

### Prologue

Any quest for unified theory must begin with two axioms: the *Axiom of Purposiveness,* which is almost synonymous with everyday life, and the *Axiom of Integration,* which recognizes that virtually all perception, thought, and action depend on integration of multiple stimulus determinants. Purposiveness confers value on each separate stimulus; these values are tendencies to approach and avoid goals and are prominent in affective sensory systems of pleasure and pain and in the pleasures and pains of everyday life. Integration of the values of multiple stimuli then yields a net goal-oriented, approach–avoidance reaction.

The key to unified theory lies in finding a solution to the twofold problem posed by the two axioms: first, measuring the values of separate stimuli on true psychological scales and second, finding the law that governs integration of these separate values. Unless this twofold problem can be solved, unified theory will not be possible.

By great good fortune, nature has provided a solution: People exhibit general algebraic laws—averaging, adding, and multiplying of stimulus information. These algebraic laws transform the two axioms from plain facts into working scientific realities. They unify because they hold true empirically in virtually every area of psychology.

A bird's-eye view of this development, known as Informaciɔn Integration Theory (IIT), is given in this chapter. Much of the initial development of IIT, which involved some difficult issues solved with contributions from many sterling colleagues, was done in person cognition—a paradigm for psychology of everyday life. This base has been extended throughout the psychological field, as may be seen by glancing over the section headers: Person cognition, Attitudes, Attribution, Marriage, Moral attitudes, Group dynamics, Functional memory, Integration psychophysics, Language, Judgment–decision, and Developmental.

This spectrum of work opens up a new horizon in psychological science, but it is a bare beginning. Information Integration Theory has many limitations, but it provides solidly grounded theoretical concepts and methodological tools that can help with other work.

# Unified Theory[1]

Is unified theory possible in psychological science? It might not seem so. Psychology is fragmented into largely noncommunicating fields, such as social psychology and learning, which are further fragmented into subfields, such as attitudes and attribution, and still further fragmented into specialized issues within each subfield. This fragmentation increases steadily.

Unified theory is possible, however, based on two axioms:

Axiom of Purposiveness

Axiom of Integration

Purposiveness provides priceless simplification: It reduces complex reality to one-dimensional values of approach and avoidance. Goal objects generally induce complex experiences, such as with a date or even a cup of coffee. A good part of such experience, however, can be treated as approach–avoidance value. This one-dimensional value omits much, of course, but it captures a central characteristic of perception, thought, and action.

The Axiom of Integration embodies the fact that all perception, thought, and action depend on multiple determinants. Multiple determinants operate when you eat: Odor, temperature, sweetness, sourness, saltiness, bitterness, and texture all determine food value. Multiple determinants operate similarly in every social interaction: Appearance, speech, compliments, criticisms, and so on all influence our impressions of and reactions to other people and to our selves.

Integration of multiple determinants is a key problem, in some ways *the* problem, in psychology. Until psychologists understand the integration process, their understanding of perception, thought, and action will be limited.

Unified theory requires a solution to the two axioms. Consider a person oriented toward some goal. Each of multiple determinants is *valuated* to assess its value, positive or negative, with respect to the goal. These multiple values are *integrated* to obtain an overall net value, which then governs goal-directed action. An effective solution to these two axioms has been developed in Information Integration Theory.

## Psychological Measurement

The integration problem presents a singular difficulty: True psychological measurement is needed. Consider the simple case of addition of two determinants:

$$\rho = \psi_A + \psi_B \tag{1}$$

Here, $\psi_A$ and $\psi_B$ are the values of the two determinants and $\rho$ is the integrated response. Unless researchers can test this simple rule and prove or disprove it, they can hardly handle more complex integration. To test this addition rule requires measurement of the two stimulus values, as well as the response. This measurement problem is critical.

---

[1]Many able men and women have contributed to development of IIT (see dedication in Anderson, 1996, p. v). Reference citations are minimized here by space limitations, but detailed discussion of studies is given in the six referenced volumes on IIT.

To appreciate this measurement problem, consider a goal with one avoidance tendency greater than either of two approach tendencies. Will the two approach tendencies combine to overcome the avoidance tendency? Will the person move toward the goal? Even the direction of action cannot be predicted without true measurement of the three tendencies.

Psychology has lacked such theory of measurement. As a consequence, psychologists have addressed problems that could be solved with available tools. This standard approach led to remarkable discoveries in many areas, such as child development and visual perception. However, this standard approach is also partly responsible for increasing fragmentation in the field of psychology.

Unified theory must solve the problem of multiple determination; this problem is central in every field of psychology. To do this requires an effective theory of psychological measurement, one that can yield true linear (equal interval) scales (see Anderson, 1981, chap. 5; 1996, chap. 3; 2001, chap. 21).

The measurement problem is so important that it deserves a second illustration. Interpretation of most interactions in analysis of variance depends entirely on whether the response is measured on a true linear (equal interval) scale. If not, the interaction may be mere illusion (Anderson, 2001, chap. 7). Most interactions in published articles thus have doubtful psychological meaning. This measurement problem is critical for the numerous theories aimed at treating statistical interactions as psychological phenomena: person $\times$ situation theories in personality, aptitude $\times$ treatment theories in educational psychology, cognitive consistency theories in social psychology, and a diverse array of contextualist theories.

## Functional Measurement

Solving the measurement problem required a conceptual shift of 180°. Consider the simple addition model of Equation 1. The traditional approach was to measure the three terms to see if they added up. Had they added up, all would have been well—but they didn't. This might mean that the integration was not additive, but it might also mean that the measures were not true linear (equal interval) scales.

A jujitsu strategy is employed by functional measurement theory: *Use the addition rule itself as the base and frame for measurement.* This strategy can be extremely simple. Suppose two variables, *A* and *B*, are thought to have additive effects. Manipulate them in factorial design and plot the factorial graph. Observed parallelism is strong evidence for the addition hypothesis. This is shown next, in a "parallelism theorem."

Let $S_{Aj}$ and $S_{Bk}$ be stimulus levels for two variables, with psychological values $\psi_{Aj}$ and $\psi_{Bk}$. Let $\rho_{jk}$ and $R_{jk}$ be the implicit and observed responses, respectively, to the stimulus combination $\{S_{Aj}, S_{Bk}\}$. Two premises are needed:

$$\rho_{jk} = \psi_{Aj} + \psi_{Bk} \qquad \text{(Premise 1: addition ) (1a)}$$

$$R_{jk} = c_0 + c_1\rho_{jk} \qquad \text{(Premise 2: linear response scale ) (1b)}$$

According to the linearity premise, the observable response, $R_{jk}$ , is a linear function of the implicit response, $\rho_{jk}$ ($c_0$ and $c_1$ are zero and unit constants that may be set at 0 and 1 for simplicity). Two conclusions follow:

Conclusion 1. The factorial graph will be parallel.
Conclusion 2. Row means of the factorial data table will be a linear scale of the $\psi_{Aj}$; similarly, column means of the data table will be a linear scale of the $\psi_{Bk}$.

Observed parallelism strongly supports both premises together. No less important, observed parallelism supports *meaning invariance:* Each stimulus has the same fixed meaning regardless of the other stimuli with which it is combined. If the stimuli did interact to change one another's meanings, parallelism would generally fail.

Note the simplicity of this parallelism analysis: *Just graph the participant's responses and look.* Observed parallelism supports both premises jointly. Also, the stimulus values are measurable as the marginal means of the factorial design (Conclusion 2). These stimulus values are those that were functional in the cognitive processing. This method, accordingly, is called *functional measurement.*

Functional measurement is not a magic wand. It depends on empirical reality of addition rules (Premise 1). As it turned out, adding-type rules (mostly averaging, actually) are common in virtually every area of human psychology, even in 4-year-old children. In fact, a general cognitive algebra has been demonstrated.[2]

## Integration Diagram

The information integration approach is summarized in the Integration Diagram of Figure 21.1. A chain of three operators, V–I–A, leads from observable stimuli, denoted by $S$, to the observable response, $R$. Each operator subserves prevailing goals.

The valuation operator, V, transforms physical stimuli into psychological representations of those stimuli, which are denoted by $\psi$. These $\psi$ are values relative to the goal. For concreteness, consider the basic task of person cogni-

---

[2]A few comments on experimental procedure and model analysis deserve mention. The method of functional rating yields true psychological measures by using experimental procedures to eliminate well-known biases. These are simple enough: testing only one participant at a time, special end anchors to fix the two ends of the rating scale, and preliminary practice to stabilize each participant's frame of reference (Anderson, 1982, chap. 1).

The parallelism theorem applies to adding models but to averaging models only when all stimulus levels of any one design factor have equal weight. To enjoy this easy parallelism analysis, steps to ensure equal weighting may be worthwhile. For example, the biographical president paragraphs discussed later under Experimental Applications of Attitude Integration Theory were constructed to contain roughly equal amounts of information.

Averaging produces predictable deviations from parallelism with unequal weighting. Opposite effects is an extreme example. Unequal weighting allows measurement of the weights, which is not easy but otherwise not generally possible.

Multiplication models may be analyzed with the linear fan theorem.

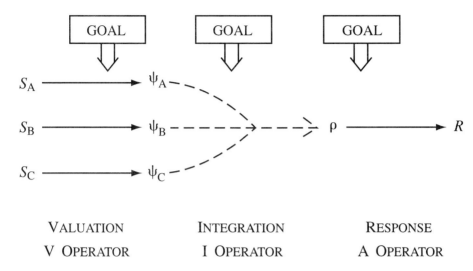

Figure 21.1. Information Integration Diagram. The chain of three operators, V-I-A, leads from observable stimulus field, {S}, to observable response, R. The valuation operator, V, transforms observable stimulus, S, into subjective representation, ψ. The integration operator, I, transforms subjective stimulus field, {ψ}, into implicit response, ρ. The action operator, A, transforms implicit response, ρ, into observable response, R. From *A Functional Theory of Cognition* (p. 6), by Norman H. Anderson, 1996, Mahwah, NJ: Erlbaum. Copyright 1996 by Erlbaum. Reprinted with permission.

tion, in which participants judge persons described by sets of personality trait adjectives. Each adjective is processed to obtain a value along the prescribed goal dimension, which could be to judge likableness, fitness for some occupation, or clinical prognosis. Note that V represents the Axiom of Purposiveness.

The integration operator integrates the psychological stimuli, ψ, to obtain an implicit response, ρ. Thus, I represents the Axiom of Integration.

Finally, the action operator, A, transforms the implicit response ρ into the observable response R. In the personality adjective task, ρ would be your feeling about the likableness of the person, R could be your rating of likableness on a 1–20 scale. The action operator, A, also represents the Axiom of Purposiveness.

In terms of the Integration Diagram, observed parallelism supports a cornucopia of five benefits.

1. The integration rule is additive.
2. The observed response is a true linear (equal interval) scale.
3. The main effects are true linear scales of each variable.
4. Stimuli do not interact but rather have fixed meaning.
5. Valuation and integration are independent processes.

The first two benefits are just the two premises of the theorem; the third is Conclusion 2. These three benefits correspond to I, A, and V, respectively, of the Integration Diagram.

The last two benefits are conceptual and more important. Lack of interaction in this personality adjective task disproved a large class of interactionist and cognitive consistency theories en bloc—an example of the power of mathematical analysis. Meaning invariance has been widely verified, most interestingly in psycholinguistics.

The last benefit, independence of valuation and integration, is fundamental: Valuation–integration independence makes true psychological measurement possible. Valuation is extremely sensitive to the operative goal. In the personality adjective task, *happy-go-lucky* would have positive value in a picnic companion but negative value in a research assistant. In general, stimulus values depend on motivational goals and on situational context.

In the face of such contextual fluidity of values, how can unified theory be attained? Independence of valuation and integration is the answer. The stimulus informers do not interact with each other; rather, they interact with the situational context, especially with the motivational state of the person.

This valuation–integration independence implies that context-dependent values can be measured with an integration rule, fulfilling McGuire's (1983) aim. The parallelism theorem yields true values by virtue of Conclusion 2; these values are just the marginal means of the factorial design. These are functional values—functional for the individual in that context. Integration rules are thus a key for analysis of cognitive functioning.

## Conceptual Implications

Conceptual implications of algebraic integration rules are more important than the rules themselves. These rules are means to greater ends. I wish to illustrate this point before reviewing applications of IIT.

The conceptual implication of meaning invariance holds special interest because it disagrees with phenomenology and with numerous previous theories, not only in social cognition but also in psycholinguistics. Meaning invariance could hardly be established without an algebraic rule, of course, but meaning invariance is a qualitative, conceptual implication about the nature of cognitive processing.

It is a strong conclusion about the structure of cognition that valuation and integration are distinct processes, or modules, to use a current term, with valuation preceding integration. Justification for this conclusion about the structure of cognitive processing lies in the success of the algebraic integration rule.

Meaning invariance and valuation–integration independence are not universal. Stimulus–stimulus interactions violate both. Both are surprisingly robust, however, as my colleagues and I found in an early study that showed small effects of even gross stimulus inconsistency (Anderson, 1981, p. 192).

Stimuli are conceptualized as *informers*. This term reflects the functional perspective embodied in the Integration Diagram. The term *informer* includes *reinforcer* as a special case that applies to learning.

## Information Integration Theory in Social Psychology

Early work on IIT was mainly in social psychology. Some areas are noted here.

## Person Cognition

The foregoing parallelism theorem is basic in person cognition. Most initial work on IIT asked participants to judge likableness of persons described by sets of personality trait adjectives. Asch (1946) used this task to argue that the adjectives interact to change one another's meanings in each description.

A powerful analysis of meaning change is possible with IIT. If meanings really do change, nonparallelism will generally be found with adjectives combined in factorial design. Sharply contrary to meaning change, parallelism was observed in our first experiment (see Anderson, 1981, p. 106, Figure 2.1). Parallelism has been extensively replicated: Many other areas of psychology exhibit meaning invariance.

Detailed evaluation of Asch's experiments led to the conclusions that "The main criticism of Asch's formulation is that it failed to clarify the conceptual issues" and that "When the conceptual structure of the problem is made clear, Asch's evidence is seen largely to reach conclusions that are obvious and uninformative" (Anderson, 1981, pp. 217, 218). This evaluation has been extensively confirmed in subsequent work. Some writers continue to cite Asch's claim, but none, to the best of my knowledge, has accounted even for parallelism, much less for the full network of evidence.

## Attitude Integration Theory

ATTITUDE AS KNOWLEDGE SYSTEM. Attitudes are considered *knowledge systems* in IIT. These knowledge systems act through the valuation operation to determine functional values of informer stimuli—values relative to operative goals.

IIT thus distinguishes between attitude as knowledge system and the diverse attitudinal responses that any attitude knowledge system may subserve. This distinction avoids the common conception of attitudes as one-dimensional, favorable–unfavorable reactions; these are only attitudinal responses, not attitudes in the conceptual sense of knowledge systems.

FUNCTIONAL THEORY. The Axiom of Purposiveness places IIT among the functional theories of attitudes. The early functional theories made useful contributions by calling attention to primary functions of attitudes, including ego-defensive functions. In IIT, these functions constitute motivations and goals that operate in valuation processes.

AVERAGING THEORY OF ATTITUDES. By a blessing of nature, attitudes follow an algebraic law, namely averaging. Averaging may be distinguished from adding with the opposite effects test. Measure the change when the same medium value stimulus informer is added to a high informer and to a low informer. The changes should be in the same direction with additive integration and in opposite directions with averaging. This test has uniformly favored averaging over adding formulations of Abelson, Fishbein, Gollob, and Wyer.

Disintegration is an important capability of integration rules. These rules can help researchers dissect the integrated response to measure the effect of each individual informer. This analytical capability, illustrated with Conclusion 2 of the parallelism theorem, is a key to cognitive analysis.

BASAL–SURFACE STRUCTURE. Attitudes have two components: *basal* and *surface*. Basal attitude is resistant to change; surface attitude is quite labile. The first definite evidence for basal–surface structure was obtained in attitude integration theory, which has also developed methods for experimental analysis. Attitude measures in most experiments may be mainly surface component, with minor significance (Anderson, 1996, p. 147).

EXPERIMENTAL APPLICATIONS OF ATTITUDE INTEGRATION THEORY. Experimental applications include attitudes in marriage, attitudes formed in group discussion, basal–surface structure of attitudes, and functional memory in attitude knowledge systems (see following sections). Of special interest are Martin Kaplan's pioneering integration analyses of mood and personality dispositions, Michael Birnbaum's incisive work on source credibility, and James Jaccard's insightful studies of the neglected issue of attitude decision theory (see Anderson, 1996).

Much of our early work was involved with establishing a solid base for averaging theory. Some of this work relied on our standardized biographical paragraphs on 17 U.S. presidents. These paragraphs allow powerful within-participants design, because each participant can be tested under several conditions with comparable material from different presidents. In one application, between-participants design would have required 510 participants to get the same power as 48 participants using within-participant design. Except for pioneering work by Bill McGuire and some work by Tony Greenwald, attitude researchers mainly use between-participant design, which severely limits the analytical power of the research.

Attitudinal responses derive from integration of multiple determinants. Without understanding of these integration processes, progress on attitude theory is severely constricted. IIT has provided an effective foothold on the integration problem. This foothold can be used to attack the no-less important problems of structure of attitudes as knowledge systems and structure of functional memory (Anderson, 1996, chaps. 5, 11).

## Attribution

People often seek to choose between different causes to explain a person's actions. For such causal attribution, the decision averaging law of IIT has done rather well. For two causes, A and B, the decision averaging law may be written as the relative ratio

$$R = \frac{\text{Cause}_A}{\text{Cause}_A + \text{Cause}_B}, \text{ (decision averaging law)} \qquad (2)$$

where the two "cause" terms represent the weight of information for each cause.

This decision averaging law is a special case of the general averaging law of IIT. It applies when the response dimension is polarized, such as with a decision between two causes. Our first experimental study compared this decision averaging law with a similar relative ratio model from Bayesian statistical theory, which is centrally concerned with just this kind of causal inference (see Anderson, 1996, chap. 10). The Bayesian model did poorly; the decision averaging law did well.

Causal attribution has also been a major topic in social psychology, such as with Kelley's ANOVA cube and its three dimensions of Consensus, Distinctiveness, and Consistency. The ANOVA cube is a clumsy misconception of psychological process. To illustrate, suppose you see a person flee from a snake. Fleeing results from two causal forces: fearfulness of the person and dangerousness of the snake. The decision averaging law is thus:

$$\text{Fleeing} = \frac{\text{Fearfulness}}{\text{Fearfulness} + \text{Dangerousness}}. \tag{3}$$

Kelley's three dimensions are not causal forces but merely information about the two causal forces. This misconception is one reason why causal attribution in the social area has been "stunted," to quote a major proponent (see also Anderson, 1996, pp. 157–168).

## Social Averaging Theorem for Group Dynamics

IIT provides a simple quantitative analysis of group conflict and resolution. Consider a group decision about, say, what proportion of the Inyo National Forest should be open to roads and logging. Each group member, $i$, is assumed to have a preferred position, $\psi_i$, on this decision axis. Any proposed decision, $\psi^*$, will be more or less unsatisfactory to some members, and they will try to change it through persuasion, lobbying, and other means.

The force exerted by member $i$ on the group decision is proportional to the difference between $i$'s preferred position and the proposed decision; the proportionality coefficient is $i$'s social power, $\omega_i$. Thus,

$$\text{Force}_i = \omega_i(\psi_i - \psi^*). \tag{4}$$

The final group decision occurs when the positive forces balance the negative forces. It follows readily that the final decision is the weighted average of the preferred positions of the members,

$$\psi^* = \sum \omega_i \psi_i / \sum \omega_i. \tag{5}$$

This social averaging theorem was supported well in a striking thesis by Cheryl Graesser (reported in full as chapter 1 of Anderson, 1991b). Social power for individuals became measurable, and large individual differences in social power were found. These individual differences alone eliminate most previous models of group compromise.

In two additional experiments, Graesser compared social averaging theory with Davis's social decision schemes, using the same experimental task that formed the backbone of Davis's scheme theory. Social averaging theory again did well. In contrast, Davis's "schemes failed on their own ground, in their own terms" (Anderson, 1991b, pp. 27, 36).

In other studies of group dynamics, IIT has done well with husband–wife interaction on judgments about discipline for children and on social attitudes formed in group discussion (Anderson, 1996, pp. 168–180).

## Marriage and Personal Design

Any theory of marriage must cope with the Axiom of Integration and with individual differences. Given the complexity of marriage and family life, a simple rule could hardly be expected. Yet there may be a simple rule, namely averaging.

Personal design aims to embed experimental tasks within the experiential framework of each individual. Personal design is especially appropriate for studying marriage, a microcosm for all social psychology. We used personal design with divorced persons to avoid ethical problems from asking about negative experiences in existent marriages (see Anderson, 1991c, chap. 6).

Divorced women judged how satisfactory they would consider a week of their marriage characterized by two or three recollected incidents from that marriage. Following this, they judged a similar set of hypothetical incidents graded along dimensions of appreciation, affection, and understanding.

These results supported averaging theory. Of special interest, real and hypothetical incidents about marriage gave very similar results (Anderson, 1991c, chap. 6).

We also studied judgments of marital unfairness in a similar experiment. With women, the data again supported averaging theory and real and hypothetical incidents again yielded similar results.

Men, in sharp contrast, did not furnish us with incidents of unfairness from their marriages. They had no shortage of negative incidents, but these did not have the phenomenal quality of unfairness. This outcome emphasizes the value of integrating phenomenology and experiment, as personal design seeks to do. This outcome is also a sharp comment on gender differences in current social knowledge systems.

I realize that these results are very limited—but they do suggest that personal design is a useful method for experimental analysis of marriage and family life. This area should be of transcendent concern in social psychology. Functional measurement can help because it allows complete, personalized experiments for each individual (Anderson, 2001, pp. 315).

## Moral Attitudes

Attitudes about right and wrong are basic to stability of society. A promising beginning on moral attitudes has been made in IIT.

BLAME SCHEMA. Blame and punishment are primary policing agents to maintain society. The blame schema involves two major determinants of blame for a harmful act. Symbolically,

$$\text{Blame} = \text{Intent} * \text{Damage}, \tag{6}$$

where $*$ is a generalized integration rule.

Psychological measurement theory is vital with the blame schema. The two determinants, Intent and Damage, must be measured in psychological metrics—separately for each individual—as must Blame.

It might seem that the Intent behind a harmful act should amplify the Damage. If so, $*$ would be akin to multiplication, which can be analyzed with the linear fan theorem. Empirically, however, most participants average. Averaging is demonstrated by the opposite effects test, together with parallelism of the Intent $\times$ Damage factorial graphs for individual participants. One interesting result obtained in my work with Wilfried Hommers is that recompense or apology has remarkably large effects in reducing blame, even with children as young as 4 years of age (Anderson 1991b, chap. 3; 1996, chap. 7).

This work showed that some schemas have exact algebraic form. It also showed that the much-vaunted concept of "default value" was erroneous.

SOCIAL COMPARISON. Social comparisons are central to fairness, equity, and justice. Common sense suggests algebraic models for such comparisons, models such as Aristotle's assertion that justice requires equality of two ratios: The ratio of rewards for two persons should equal the ratio of their contributions. Alternative models have been conjectured over the past 40 years, but they remained conjectural capability for psychological measurement.

Excellent results in fairness theory have been obtained with functional measurement. Fairness and unfairness follow the same decision averaging law illustrated with attribution theory in Equation 2. Comparison processes involving multiple outcomes and multiple comparison persons were studied in an impressive thesis by Arthur Farkas (reported in full as chapter 2 in Anderson, 1991b). Here again, the main importance of algebraic models is their conceptual implications, in this case about structure of social comparison. In its comparison structure, Aristotle's model was psychologically superior to its most prominent modern alternative. Social comparison is a long-standing issue, on which algebraic models can provide insight not otherwise available (Anderson, 1996, chap. 7).

STAGE THEORY OF MORAL JUDGMENT. I believe that IIT has strong advantages over Kohlberg's stage theory, which is the dominant position in moral psychology. Kohlberg delineated five successive stages, and each stage was said to be governed by one single moral principle, beginning with obedience and culminating with rational, egalitarian reasoning.

Three objections to Kohlberg's theory need consideration. First, integration of multiple determinants is the essence of resolving a moral dilemma. On this essential issue, however, Kohlberg said nothing besides a handwave at "balancing or weighing of conflicting claims." Second, Kohlberg's interview method cannot be used for those under 10–12 years of age, thereby missing what many would consider the main origin of morality. Third, Kohlberg ignored, or rather denied, social psychology, claiming that morality has unique nature.

IIT allows unification of Kohlberg's approach with social psychology. Kohlberg's five principles are attractive, but his denial of social psychology seems to me bizarre. Applications of IIT to study blame and other moral judgments, by Margaret Armstrong, Manuel Leon, Colleen Surber Moore, and John Verdi in the United States; Wilfried Hommers in Germany; Yuval Wolf in Israel; and Etienne Mullet and his numerous associates in France, have gone far toward unification. This unification has capability for studying moral development across cultures and down to 3–4 years of age (Anderson, 1991b,c; 1996, chaps. 6, 7).

## Functional Memory

Serendipitously, attitude integration theory led to a functional conception of memory, quite different from the traditional conception of memory as reproduction of given material. In a 1963 experiment, we found a memory–attitude dissociation between attitude toward a person described by a set of personality trait adjectives and verbal memory for those adjectives (see Anderson, 1981, pp. 249ff). Verbal memory showed pure recency in the serial curve; person memory showed pure primacy. This memory–attitude dissociation indicated that participants extract goal-relevant information from a given stimulus and, having integrated this information, may forget the stimulus while retaining the integrated resultant. This attitude–memory dissociation was neatly corroborated by Susan Fiske and Reid Hastie (Anderson, 1981, p. 249; 1996, chap. 11).

As a historical note, I did my postdoc at Yale with Carl Hovland, who had the great hope of utilizing the mass of experiments on verbal learning as a base for attitude theory. The idea was that attitudes are determined by those verbal materials retained in memory. Hence Jost's laws and other results from verbal memory could be transposed directly to the social field. This verbal memory conception of attitude memory was once standard, but the memory–attitude dissociation showed that it was a misdirection. This distinction between functional memory and reproductive memory is now popular in social psychology (Anderson, 1991a, p. 17; 1996, chap. 11).

The function of memory is to utilize past experience for present action. Integrated resultants of past valuation–integrations are thus primary content of attitudes as knowledge systems. The strong evaluative component of attitudes comes from informational learning of good–bad, approach–avoidance reactions.

Functional memory is attuned to everyday life. Individual stimuli in present situations are valuated and integrated with respect to present goals. Such integrated resultants, including affect and belief, are primary content of functional memory. The original individual stimuli are often not retained in memory; instead, the integrated resultant may be stored, becoming part of functional memory, that is, part of one's attitude knowledge system. Person memory is a good example of functional memory: We may have strong attitudes toward others with limited, fragmentary reproductive memory for past interactions with them.

Mainstream memory theory, in contrast, continues in monolithic pursuit of reproductive memory, this despite complaints from prominent memory researchers that more than a century of intensive work has produced almost no generalizations of significance.

Social psychology, unlike mainstream memory theory, is focused on memory in everyday life. This work extends early concerns of Carl Hovland, Don Campbell, and Bill McGuire with a fundamental aspect of cognition. Social psychology can help liberate mainstream memory theory from its narrow rut (Anderson, 1996, chap. 11).

## Applications in Other Fields

Extensive applications of IIT have been made in almost every field of psychology.

### Functional Cognition

IIT is a functional theory, one that treats everyday life in something like its own terms. This is illustrated in the preceding discussions of person cognition and functional memory.

COGNITION AND AFFECT. Cognition and affect are unified in IIT, as foreshadowed in the Integration Diagram. Both I and V are cognitive processes. Each may operate to produce both affective and nonaffective values. Cognitive–affective unification is empirically fulfilled with the averaging law, in which y may represent affect, whereas $\Psi$ would typically represent such cognitive concepts as probability and amount of information. Person cognition may thus be a paradigm for unified science.

ANALYTICAL CONSTRUCTIONISM. Constructionism is a fundamental characteristic of IIT: Integration *is* construction. IIT may be considered analytical constructionism through its capability for analysis of processes that do the constructing, specifically valuation and integration. Some form of constructionism has been advocated by numerous writers, but most of their proposals remain hopeful promissory notes. Analytical constructionism is not a promissory note: It has been empirically effective in almost every field of human psychology.

CONSCIOUS AND NONCONSCIOUS. The constructionist character of IIT applies to consciousness. What reaches the level of consciousness is an integrated resultant that often includes nonconscious determinants. IIT thus mandates rejection of the identity assumption—that preconscious and conscious are essentially equivalent—which has characterized fields as far apart as emotion and psychophysics (see index entries for *nonconscious* in Anderson, 1996).

Functional measurement can help in dissecting conscious experience into preconscious components in some cases. Applications include the size–weight illusion and snake phobia (cited on pages 34 and 52, respectively, of Anderson, 1981). True quantification of nonconscious processes thus becomes possible. This same analytical approach may help in the study of nonconscious effects of stereotypes discussed in the chapters by Greenwald and by Banaji (Banaji, 2004; Greenwald, 2004).

MOOD AND EMOTION. The two axioms of IIT are prominent in mood and emotion, which are affective survival tools. Purposiveness appears in affects, which embody good–bad, approach–avoidance valuations of goals. Furthermore, mood and emotion typically result from valuation and integration of multiple determinants. Appraisal is thus built into the integration–theoretical approach to affective phenomena.

Most of the numerous theories of emotion have sought typological frameworks for all emotions, although usually excluding mood and everyday pleasure and pain. Typologies, however useful, are inadequate: General theory can only be attained through solution of the problem of multiple determination. This solution, moreover, must include mood and everyday affect as well as emotion. Integration analysis is feasible and attractive with emotions that are experimentally manipulable, such as disgust or phobias (Anderson, 1989).

## Cognitive Foundation for Judgment–Decision Theory

Cognitive theory of judgment–decision has been well-grounded through many applications of IIT. This cognitive foundation departs from the normative, rationalist framework that has dominated the judgment–decision field. Inadequacy of the normative framework is clear in the explosive reaction of biases and heuristics. Biases and heuristics, however, have not led to unified theory. Instead, they have led into a bewildering maze of minitheories.

Judgment–decision theory is replete with conjectures about algebraic rules, but these rules could not be established without true psychological measurement. Functional measurement provided the first definite evidence for the classic rule, subjective expected value = subjective probability × subjective value (Anderson, 1981, Figure 1.13, p. 47). This integrationist approach has been much extended by cogent contributions from Michael Birnbaum, Richard Bogartz, Jerome Busemeyer, Clyde Hendrick, Samuel Himmelfarb, James Jaccard, Michael Klitzner, Lola Lopes, Jordan Louviere, Barbara Mellers, Colleen Surber Moore, Etienne Mullet, Gregg Oden, Peter Petzold, Anne Schlottmann, James Shanteau, Mingshen Wang, James Zalinski, and Shu-Hong Zhu. Unified cognitive theory of judgment–decision thus seems attainable (Anderson, 1996, chap. 10).

## Developmental Psychology

Integration theory has considerable affinity with Piagetian theory. Nearly all of Piaget's work involved integration tasks, especially tasks of commonsense physics, such as Area = Height × Width and Distance = Speed × Time. The guiding assumption throughout Piaget's theory is that cognitive development consists of internalization of the structure of the physical world, such as with the two cited multiplication rules.

A very different view emerged when IIT was applied to study children. This work revealed striking cognitive capabilities at far earlier ages than found by Piaget. Contrary to Piaget's claim that young, preoperational children cannot integrate, IIT studies revealed algebraic integration laws even in children younger than 4 years of age, and whereas Piaget claimed that children did not develop a proper concept of time until age 10 or 12, IIT showed a proper time concept at the far younger age of 5 years. These and other results by Clifford Butzin, Diane Cuneo, Wilfried Hommers, Manuel Leon, Colleen Surber Moore, Anne Schlottmann, Ramadhar Singh, Friedrich Wilkening, and Yuval Wolf reveal a new direction in development psychology (Anderson, 1991c; 1996, chaps. 6, 8).

## Language

Language, being intensely social, is an important domain for social psychology. In recent decades, some linguists and psycholinguists have recognized that language usage involves person cognition as well as nonlanguage context. Attribution of intention, for example, may be critical to understanding what is spoken. Nonlinguistic informers, such as facial expression or gesture, may also be integrated.

Four results from extensive work on language processing illustrate the potential of IIT. One result is meaning invariance, first established with person cognition. Although meaning invariance has been denied by psycholinguists, it has been verified in several linguistic tasks. A second is Gregg Oden's decision averaging model for resolving ambiguity, a central issue in understanding language, which was extended in his work with Dominic Massaro. A third result is Shu-Hong Zhu's application of averaging theory to demonstrate cognitive reality of prototypes. The fourth is a set of studies of cognitive algebra of language quantifiers. Cognitive algebra may thus be a language universal (Anderson, 1996, chap. 12).

## Integration Psychophysics

The conceptual reorientation that results from focus on integration processes is nicely illustrated with the long-dominant concept of *psychophysical law* initiated by Fechner. This concept of psychophysical law has turned out to be a blind alley. Instead, integration psychophysics has established *psychological laws*. In the Integration Diagram, psychophysical law corresponds to valuation and psychological law to integration.

These psychological laws solved a key problem in psychophysics, namely true measurement of psychological sensation. The long-sought psychophysical law is thus a by-product of more basic psychological law. Integration psychophysics owes much to Danny Algom, Diane Cuneo, Bob McBride, Sergio Masin, David Weiss, and Friedrich Wilkening (see also Anderson, 1996, chap. 9).

## Psychological Measurement Theory

True measurement is essential for progress on the axioms of purposiveness and integration. This need for psychological measurement was emphasized with the parallelism theorem, which also opened the road to a solution. Functional measurement has four distinguishing characteristics.

1. Solid empirical foundation in many diverse areas.
2. Laws of integration as the base and frame for psychological measurement.
3. Idiographic measurement of functional values for individuals.
4. Metric response measures instead of nonmetric choice or ranks.

Nearly all other measurement theories insist on nonmetric choice or rank response. Nonmetric response was emphasized by Thurstone and reemphasized by Coombs, Guttman, Luce, and others. These nonmetric approaches have all completely failed to achieve actual measurement (excepting Thurstone's sociological group scales). They once seemed attractive, even necessary, because they avoided known biases of metric response, and they have been the subject of dedicated study from exceptionally able individuals—but nonmetric approaches were a blind alley; nonmetric data are fundamentally inadequate for psychological measurement theory (Anderson, 1981, chap. 5; 2001, chap. 21).

Functional measurement succeeded because of the development of simple experimental procedures to eliminate the biases that can trouble metric response (see Footnote 2) and by establishing psychological laws. Of prime importance, a validated metric response can be used generally; a linear response measure provides a faithful image of psychological reality. Factorial design is no longer essential, therefore neither is an algebraic model. Hence a linear response measure can be a unique tool for studying interaction, configurality, and general nonalgebraic integration (Anderson, 1996, chap. 3; 2001, chap. 21).

## Toward Unified Theory[3]

IIT represents cumulative science. The concepts and methods are simple, yet they have done well across diverse areas of psychology, as shown in this bird's-eye view. It thus seems fair to say that IIT is a unified, general theory (Anderson, in preparation).

IIT has many limitations; what remains to be done is mountainous compared to what has been done. IIT does, however, provide a new way of thinking that has been effective in many areas.

---

[3]The philosopher Silverberg (2003, p. 299) has affirmed this claim for unified theory in his discussion whether psychology can aspire to true laws like those in natural science. Silverberg included detailed discussion of experimental evidence and concludes

> N. H. Anderson and his colleagues' achievements are relevant . . . to much discussion in philosophy of cognitive science. For example, there has been much controversy whether there can be a science of ordinary psychology, that is of higher cognition and propositional attitudes, that would bear comparison with the sorts of developments that have been achieved in the natural sciences. There has been much controversy as to whether such a psychological science would contain laws. There has also been much controversy as to whether the notions of ordinary "folk" psychology would figure in, would play constitutive roles, in the formulation of such science and its laws. N. H. Anderson's work presents strong grounds for affirmative answers to these questions.

IIT is a functional theory of cognition. Everyday life is its primary concern. One class of theoretical concepts is taken directly from everyday life, as with the blame schema, Blame = Intent + Damage, and the expectancy–value schema, Behavior = Expectancy × Value. This everyday level of theory contrasts with associationist and connectionist theories, which begin with hypothetical "elements," far removed from the goal-directed consciousness of everyday life. It is at this everyday level of cognition that true psychological laws have been found.

Success of an integration rule, such as the blame schema, helps establish scientific reality of the everyday concepts that appear in the schema. This helps put phenomenology on a scientific base. Functional measurement can also go below phenomenology to exact analysis of some nonconscious processes.

Cognition and affect are unified in IIT. The affect-as-information principle of IIT embodies this unification. Affect-as-information follows from the motivation-as-information principle, which conceptualizes motivation as information used in valuating goals and goal-relevant informers. The cited studies of person cognition are empirical demonstrations of this cognitive–affective unification. Cognitive–affective unification appears similarly in attitude integration theory.

Cognitive algebra represents transhistorical laws. Some writers have argued that such laws could not be found in psychology—that human nature changes continually, in line with continual changes in culture and physical environment. However, some algebraic laws do not come from culture. Indeed, even rats and pigeons may follow algebraic laws (Anderson, 2001, chap. 11).

*Conceptual implications, not algebraic laws, are the most important outcome of IIT.* This point deserves reemphasis to dispel the stereotype of mathematical models. Cognitive algebra is mainly important for conceptual clarification. Although algebraic laws are certainly interesting functions of cognition, their main contribution lies in their conceptual implications. Among these implications are functional theory of memory, basal–surface structure of attitudes, structure of social comparisons, some unification of person cognition with language processing, integrationist alternatives to the stage theories popular in developmental psychology, and a cognitive foundation for judgment–decision theory.

Two conceptual implications have central importance. These are meaning invariance and the associated independence of processes of valuation and integration in the Integration Diagram. These provide an Archimedean lever to deal with individual differences and with ever-changing motivations and situational context, which pervade the context–stimulus interaction that constitutes valuation. I realize that the work on IIT is a bare beginning, but I believe it indicates that unified theory is attainable.

To dedicate this chapter to Bill McGuire is a deep pleasure and great honor. His masterful command of vast masses of material in his canonical chapters on attitudes (McGuire, 1969, 1985) has done much to help unify social psychology. Bill has been an inspiration to me since I met him during my postdoctoral fellowship at Yale 40-odd years ago, an inspiration that deepened during the too-brief years we were colleagues at UCSD. His example has encouraged me to "strike up for a new world."

# References

Anderson, N. H. (1981). *Foundations of information integration theory.* New York: Academic Press.

Anderson, N. H. (1982). *Methods of information integration theory.* New York: Academic Press.

Anderson, N. H. (1989). Information integration approach to emotions and their measurement. In R. Plutchik & H. Kellerman (Eds.), *Emotion: Theory, research, and experience* (Vol. 4, pp. 133–186). New York: Academic Press.

Anderson, N. H. (Ed.). (1991a). *Contributions to information integration theory. Vol. I: Cognition.* Hillsdale, NJ: Erlbaum.

Anderson, N. H. (Ed.). (1991b). *Contributions to information integration theory. Vol. II: Social.* Hillsdale, NJ: Erlbaum.

Anderson, N. H. (Ed.). (1991c). *Contributions to information integration theory. Vol. III: Developmental.* Hillsdale, NJ: Erlbaum.

Anderson, N. H. (1996). *A functional theory of cognition.* Mahwah, NJ: Erlbaum.

Anderson, N. H. (2001). *Empirical direction in design and analysis.* Mahwah, NJ: Erlbaum.

Anderson, N. H. (in preparation). Unified social cognition.

Asch, S. E. (1946). Forming impressions of personality. *Journal of Abnormal and Social Psychology, 41,* 258–290.

Banaji, M. (2004). The opposite of a great truth is also true: Homage to koan #7. In J. Jost, M. Banaji, & D. Prentice (Eds.), *Perspectivism in social psychology: The yin and yang of scientific progress.* Washington, DC: American Psychological Association.

Greenwald, A. G. (2004). The resting parrot, the dessert stomach, and other perfectly defensible theories. In J. Jost, M. Banaji, & D. Prentice (Eds.), *Perspectivism in social psychology: The yin and yang of scientific progress.* Washington, DC: American Psychological Association.

McGuire, W. J. (1969). The nature of attitudes and attitude change. In G. Lindzey & E. Aronson (Eds.), *Handbook of social psychology* (2nd ed., Vol. 3, pp. 136–314). Reading, MA: Addison-Wesley.

McGuire, W. J. (1983). A contextualist theory of knowledge: Its implications for innovations and reform in psychology research. In L. Berkowitz (Ed.), *Advances in experimental social psychology* (Vol. 16, pp. 1–47). New York: Academic Press.

McGuire, W. J. (1985). Attitudes and attitude change. In G. Lindzey & E. Aronson (Eds.), *Handbook of social psychology* (3rd ed., Vol. 2, pp. 233–346). New York: Random House.

Silverberg, A. (2003). Psychological laws. *Erkenntnis, 258,* 275–302.

# 22

## The Eighth Koan of Progress in Social Psychology: A Variable Anointed as "Special" Will Demand Special Treatment

*E. Tory Higgins*

I have come to feel that some specific tactical changes should be made in our creative and critical work in social psychology so as to enhance the momentum and the ultimate sweep of this wave of the future, whatever form it may take. (McGuire, 1973, p. 450)

### Prologue

I first met Bill McGuire in the Department of Social Psychology at the London School of Economics and Political Science (LSE). I was getting the proverbial "MA from LSE" after graduating in Sociology and Anthropology from McGill University. It was 1968. LSE was far left and activist. It was also British in intellectual style, as McGill had been. The style of both the times and the training was to hate hypocrites, phonies, and intellectual dilettantes, and we spotted them everywhere. I note all this because it was clear even then that Bill was "serious"—the highest accolade. I did not know it at the time, but Bill had just completed his classic attitudes chapter for the *Handbook of Social Psychology*. As psychologists now know, that chapter is the benchmark for serious scholarship in social psychology. Another kind of seriousness is reflected in his "Yin and Yang" article: a serious concern for how we can make progress in social psychology. As his gracious notes of thanks and congratulations sent to colleagues reveal, Bill is also serious about the social glue that binds this profession together. When I reflect on my experiences with Bill since that first meeting, the phrase that comes to mind is "a scholar and a gentleman."

What has Bill been serious about as a scholar? Is there a common theme running through his disparate areas of research? I believe that there is. Perhaps not surprising, it has to do with people being serious. People are serious about figuring out how the social world works. They want to understand what is distinct about themselves and other objects in the world. This search for meaning is reflected in people's language, attitude and belief formation, and self-representations—and it is not only laypersons who are serious in their everyday lives. Scientists are serious about how they search for meaning. A second theme in Bill's scholarly work is the proposal of ways in which social psychologists can be more critical and creative. By following Bill's dictums or koan, social psychologists will be more serious and thus make even greater progress.

All social psychologists, as scientists and theoreticians, are concerned with both real-world phenomena they find fascinating and with abstract relations among psychology variables that they find compelling as explanations and as generative tools. Nonetheless, social psychologists vary in whether their inspiration derives more from the former "bottom-up" source or the latter "top-down" source. I would characterize myself, and Bill as well, as predominantly a top-downer. I remember once when Stanley Schachter, one of the all-time great bottom-uppers in the history of social psychology, sat in on one of my graduate proseminar lectures and later, shaking his head in wonder, said to me, "You really *do* believe in theory, don't you?"

It is also the case that although all scientists and theoreticians in social psychology need to practice both promotion eagerness and prevention vigilance, they vary in which of these strategic inclinations predominates. I have always taken a promotion eagerness approach to science. I have been willing to make mistakes to increase the opportunity to discover something new. I have always worked on multiple research programs simultaneously because I don't want to miss the chance of finding something exciting in some area that interests me. In this regard, I am also like Bill. In the "Yin and Yang" article, Bill described himself as an "irrepressible optimist" (McGuire, 1973). He believes that social psychology will make progress. Indeed, he believes that social psychology has a unique contribution to make to the scientific study of humans and to tackling social problems. I share his optimism.

Unlike many of the social psychologists in this volume, I was never fortunate enough to have Bill as my advisor, colleague, or close personal friend. However, I was fortunate to have him as a role model. As in his work, the common theme of my research has been people's understanding of their social world, how it works, and how to get along in it. I also have been described as an "irrepressible optimist," and, yes, I have tried to be serious in my scientific and professional life—but not so serious as to miss the fun of being a social psychologist. Once again, Bill is a role model. His wit is as legendary as his wisdom, but of course, as Bill would appreciate, "wit" derives from "to know."

\* \* \*

It is an honor and a joy to participate in this celebration of the scientific and scholarly contributions of Bill McGuire. The final section of this book concerns theory and metatheory in social psychological science. It is fitting to conclude this volume with this section because Bill McGuire is rare, if not unique, in his passionate concern for the future of social psychology and has for decades made profound contributions to social psychologists' understanding of the strengths and weaknesses of their paradigms. In an early and now classic article, "The Yin and Yang of Progress in Social Psychology," Bill McGuire recommended new ways to carry out the mission of social psychology in the form of seven koans, or paradoxes, to yield enlightenment.

In the spirit of Bill McGuire's continuing concern with the construction of social psychology as a scientific discipline (see McGuire, 1999), I propose an addition to his proposed tactical changes for how social psychologists carry out their critical work. Like McGuire's changes (McGuire, 1973), the change I recommend is presented in the form of a koan to mask my own uncertainties about precisely what new paradigm should emerge. To join McGuire's seven koans, I propose Koan 8: *A variable anointed as "special" will demand special treatment.*

I make two basic arguments in this chapter. First, it is natural for people to anoint some variable as "special," and this tendency has drawbacks for an accurate understanding of the social world. Second, like other people, social psychologists have naturally tended to anoint certain variables as "special," and this tendency restricts progress in social psychology's mission of understanding the social world. The meaning of Koan 8 is that there are unintended consequences of treating a particular variable as special. Specifically, selecting a variable as "special" does not simply highlight its significance. It also leads to treating it as unique, thereby limiting understanding of more fundamental and general psychological principles with respect to which it represents just one condition or one source of variability.

## The Natural Tendency to Anoint a Variable as "Special"

People's natural tendency to select a variable as "special" is a basic assumption of what I have called the "aboutness" principle (see Higgins, 1997, 1998). The aboutness principle refers to the following tendency: When people perceive a response (or outcome), whether their own or another person's, they represent it as being about something, and this thing that the response is *about* is inferred to be the *source* of the response.

I propose with the aboutness principle that people generally share three natural assumptions about psychological processes. One assumption is that responses or outcomes do not simply occur by themselves, randomly, with no relation to anything. People ask themselves, "Where did that come from?" and they believe that there is some source of the response. This assumption is adaptive, because perceiving the responses of self or others in the world can only serve its self-regulatory function of facilitating action if the responses are represented as being about something. A second assumption is that a response is about a particular thing. It is natural and economical for people to assign *a* meaning to an event, to represent the response as being about some *thing*. The thing that is represented as what the response is about is singled out. In this sense, it is assigned a "special" status in the representation of the event.

People's third assumption is that whatever thing a response is about is the *source* of the response. Once again, this is not an unreasonable assumption, especially with respect to people's early experiences. Common experiences involve responses to objects that are the source of the experience. When smelling a rose, one perceives the rose as the source of the fragrance one experiences. When a baby girl feels happy while being hugged by her mother, the mother's hug is the source of her happiness. There are problems with this third assumption, however (for a fuller discussion, see Higgins, 1997, 1998). One problem is especially relevant to the theme of this chapter. By assigning a "special" status to the thing that was singled out in the event representation, it is treated as *the* source of the response. It is typical, however, for a response or outcome to have *multiple sources* rather than a single source. Indeed, many of the best known biases in social cognition that have been identified by social psychologists since the 1970s illustrate the problem with people naturally assigning a "special" status to a single variable (for a fuller discussion, see Higgins, 1997, 1998).

The classic "correspondence bias" (Jones, 1979) or "fundamental attribution error" (Ross, 1977) refers to people's tendency to infer that the source of an observed behavior is a disposition in the actor that corresponds to the behavior he or she produced, rather than the situation in which the behavior took place (i.e., either the entity toward which the behavior was directed or the surrounding circumstances). Consider the input in the classic study by Jones and Harris (1967), for example. Each participant in the study was shown an essay that either supported or opposed Fidel Castro and was told either that the author had freely chosen to advocate the position taken in the essay or that the author was a member of a debating team and had been assigned the position by the debating coach. The surprising finding of the study was that even in the "debating team" condition, participants believed that the private attitude of the essayist reflected whatever position that essayist advocated.

This specific tendency may appear to be ubiquitous, because in many studies the participants believe that the study is *about* an individual who has performed a certain behavior, and the procedures of the studies typically promote this perception (see Quattrone, 1982). Thus, the participants are likely to represent the behavior as being about the actor. According to the aboutness principle, then, the participants will emphasize the actor, rather than the situation in which the behavior occurred, as the source of the behavior.

As another example of a social-cognitive bias, consider the "assimilation bias" from construct accessibility. In a study by Higgins, Rholes, and Jones (1977), for example, the participants were incidentally exposed in a "perception" task to one or another set of trait-related constructs, such as priming either the word "stubborn" or the word "persistent." In a subsequent task on "reading comprehension," the participants were asked to characterize the ambiguous behaviors of a target person, including an ambiguous "stubborn"/ "persistent" description. The participants tended to use whichever trait construct had been made more accessible in the "perception" task to categorize the target person's behavior in the "reading comprehension" task—an "assimilation bias." According to the aboutness principle, it would be natural for perceivers to represent their response to the target person's behavior, i.e., their categorization, as being about the behavior. The perceivers would then infer that the source of their categorization was simply that behavior. The problem with this inference is that the increased accessibility of the primed construct is another important source of the perceivers' categorization.

The "correspondence" and "assimilation" biases provide examples of the unintended biasing effects of a variable being assigned "special" status. In each case, people represent their own response or the response of another person as being about one variable and then treat that variable as the source of the response despite the fact that the anointed variable was not the only source of the response and might not have been even the primary source.

These are not the only cases of unintended biasing effects of anointing a variable as "special." Indeed, such cases are pervasive in social cognition (see Higgins, 1997, 1998). Moreover, the problems with such anointment are not restricted to lay psychology. I believe that social psychology as a scientific discipline has suffered from unintended negative consequences of social psychologists anointing some variable as "special." These scientific drawbacks are considered next.

## Social Psychologists' Tendency to Anoint a Variable as "Special"

I should begin by noting that there are reasons beyond the aboutness principle for social psychologists to assign some variable "special" status. Chief among these is social psychologists' traditional concern with social issues. It is both reasonable and admirable for social psychologists to pay special attention to variables that especially affect people's quality of life, such as aggression or prejudice. There is another source of social psychologists' assigning "special" status that is more problematic, however. This is the search for surprising or fascinating phenomena. When such phenomena are discovered, there is a tendency to identify some "special" variable that underlies them. In the next section, I consider some examples of phenomena that were anointed in this way, and I describe the problems with such anointment.

### Anointing Phenomena as "Special"

As one example of a phenomenon being anointed as "special," person memory researchers in the 1970s found that self-related information was remembered better than self-unrelated information (e.g., Kuiper & Rogers, 1979; Markus, 1977). It was suggested that special cognitive–structural properties of self-knowledge were the source of this phenomenon. Person memory researchers in the 1970s also found that information inconsistent with prior knowledge was remembered better than information that was not inconsistent (e.g., Hastie & Kumar, 1979). It was proposed that special properties of processing inconsistent information were the source of this phenomenon. Subsequent research indicated in both these cases that any "specialness" of these variables was contingent on a host of factors and conditions and that general principles, such as knowledge activation principles, underlie these and other phenomena (see Higgins & Bargh, 1987).

The "correspondence" bias described previously provides another example of social psychologists missing the big picture by inferring that the source of the special phenomenon was a special mechanism. Social psychologists represented the special phenomenon as being *about* people underestimating the impact of situational forces and then they inferred a special "fundamental attribution error" or "correspondence bias" as the source of the phenomenon. However, depending on additional qualities of the input (e.g., Quattrone, 1982; Taylor & Fiske, 1975), or even the explanatory predispositions of the perceiver (e.g., Miller, 1984), perceivers will represent an actor's behavior as being about either the actor or the situation and will infer that the source of the behavior was either the actor's disposition or situational forces, respectively (see Higgins & Bargh, 1987). More general principles, such as people's mental models of the sources of behavior and general hypothesis-testing principles, are at work here. These general principles can account for both the initial surprising phenomenon and the less surprising exceptions to it.

There are two additional ways in which assigning "special" status to some variable or phenomenon has restricted progress in social psychology. First, social psychologists have identified phenomena that are "special" in being *about* situational effects and then have inferred special situational variables to account for them, thereby distinguishing social psychological variables from personality variables. Second, social psychologists have discovered phenomena that are "special" in being *about* errors and mistakes that people make and then have inferred special variables to account for such problems, thereby distinguishing costly psychological variables from beneficial psychological variables. How each of these ways of assigning "special' status has restricted progress in social psychology is considered in the next two sections.

## Social Psychological Variables as Unique and "Special"

What is social psychology? Most people, whether they are professional experts on social psychology or not, think of social psychology as the study of how social situations influence people. The phenomena that are "special" to social psychology are represented as being *about* situational effects. It is natural, then, for social psychologists to infer that special situational variables account for these effects. Similarly, personality psychologists infer that special person variables account for special personality effects. Accordingly, a unique set of psychological principles, such as cognitive dissonance (e.g., Festinger, 1957) and obedience to authority (e.g., Milgram, 1974), has developed over time in the area of social psychology. The implicit assumption is that these principles are social psychological principles that provide unique "situation" explanations for people's psychological states. These principles are contrasted with personality principles of psychology that provide unique "person" explanations, such as personal constructs (Kelly, 1955) and achievement motives (McClelland, Atkinson, Clark, & Lowell, 1953), for people's psychological states.

I propose that rather than anointing some explanatory principles as "special" social psychological variables and others as "special" personality variables, psychologists identify a set of general principles for which *both* persons and situations are sources of variability. From this *"general principles"* perspective, "situation" and "person" variables can be understood in terms of the *same* general principles. Social psychological variation across situations would be reconceptualized as simply one source of variability in the functioning of psychological principles that vary across persons as well (see Higgins, 1990, 1999, 2000a).

Let me begin by discussing what I mean by a "source of variability." Imagine that a group of psychologists examined the psychological states of a large sample of Americans engaging in many different activities. Social psychologists would investigate how the psychological states varied across situations, personality psychologists would investigate how the psychological states varied across individuals, cultural psychologists would investigate how the psychological states varied across ethnic groups, and so on. Note that each investigation compares people's psychological states. Moreover, each investigation includes precisely the same sample of psychological states of the same persons. The only difference among the investigations is the choice of comparison. What differs among the areas of psychology is the source of variability in the data that is of *special* interest to them.

Social psychologists are interested in how different situations influence people, and thus they choose to investigate variability across situations. This naturally influences how they describe differences among the psychological states. Each description becomes a special phenomenon of interest to them. They are then tempted to discover the *unique* explanations and related psychological principles that underlie their own *special* phenomena. They can fail to recognize that the same set of principles underlie variability across situations, individuals, cultures, and so on. I believe that it is a mistake for social psychologists and personality psychologists to anoint certain variables and explanatory principles as their own when there are general psychological principles that produce the basic psychological states that vary across both situations and persons. By identifying such general principles, psychologists would improve the economy of principles in psychology, provide a common language of principles across psychological areas that would facilitate examining interrelations among those areas, and enrich understanding of how each principle functions across a broad range of conditions.

For several years, I have investigated two general principles that can vary across situations and across persons: *accessibility* as a general "cognitive" principle of knowledge activation and *regulatory focus* as a general "motivational" principle of self-regulation. In both cases, I have found that these principles have similar effects when either persons or situations are the source of variability. Goal selection, goal striving, and goal monitoring also vary across both situations and persons, and these two sources of variability have been found to have similar effects (see Higgins, 2000a).

Basic social-cognitive and self-regulatory variables are not social psychological or personality variables. They are psychological variables with multiple sources of variability, including situations, persons, age, and culture. An implication of a general principles perspective is that traditional social psychological variables need not be studied only across situations. Variability in states of cognitive dissonance, for example, could be studied across persons as well. Similarly, variability in states of "motive to succeed" or "fear of failure" could be studied across situations and not just across persons (see Higgins, 1990, 1999, 2000a). In this way, the boundaries of both social psychology and personality would be expanded. For social psychology to make progress, we social psychologists need to refrain from anointing certain variables "special" social psychological variables; otherwise, we will overlook the relevance to social psychology of other nonanointed variables, such as those considered to be personality variables, and we will fail to recognize the general principles underlying both the anointed and nonanointed variables. It is by understanding the functioning of general principles that greater progress, including the suggestion of new types of situational variability to explore, will be made in social psychology.

## Beneficial and Costly Phenomena as Deriving From Distinct and "Special" Variables

The costs of social cognition have especially fascinated psychologists since the 1950s. This fascination has derived in part from the psychologists' being surprised to observe social-cognitive errors in rational people and in part from their being concerned with the problems produced by such errors. These special phenomena are represented as being *about* costs, and psychologists have typically inferred that costly psychological variables are the source of them. These costly psychological variables are then distinguished from beneficial psychological variables.

Historically, there have been different perspectives on the nature of the costly psychological variables. The classic psychodynamic perspective is that costs arise from the conflicts among different self-regulatory systems. A rational executive (ego) has to deal with both unconscious pleasure-seeking impulses (id) and societal demands (superego) that can also be unrealistic (e.g., Freud, 1923/1961). The notion that endogenous impulses and exogenous pressures can overwhelm adaptive information processing still exists. From this perspective, benefits and costs derive from *different* variables. For example, the costly conflicts between the id and the superego interfere with the benefits of the ego. Irrational motives interfere with rational information processing. According to this "conflict" perspective, people are intellectually capable of accurate processing and sound reasoning, but motivation produces cognitive failures.

To the extent that the 1970s cognitive revolution in social psychology was a "revolution," it was because it provided a nonmotivational perspective on social-cognitive failures or costs (see, for example, Dawes, 1976). The information processing of people as lay or intuitive scientists is compared with the information processing prescribed by normative models, and people are found lacking. Benefits would derive from people using the normative models, but limitations in their information processing capacities force people to use alternative strategies that are often costly. From this "limited capacity" perspective, the beneficial normative models are different from the often costly nonnormative models that people actually use.

Beginning in the 1980s, social psychologists began developing a new perspective on social-cognitive costs. In contrast to the "limited capacity" perspective, proponents of this new perspective proposed that under the right conditions, people *are* capable of elaborate and systematic processing that basically follows normative prescriptions. Under other conditions, people use alternative heuristics and strategies that produce costs. Rather than people being inherently "faulty," there are momentary conditions that reduce effort allocation (e.g., low personal relevance) or reduce cognitive capacity (e.g., high load from interfering task), which results in people using the more energy-saving but error-prone processes (see Chaiken & Trope, 1999). According to this "dual process" perspective, there are different kinds of processes, and the benefits from one process and the costs from another are distinguished.

These classic "conflict," "limited capacity," and "dual process" perspectives share the assumption that there is one set of "special" variables that produce mostly psychological benefits and there is another set of "special" variables that produce mostly psychological costs. I believe that this distinction between beneficial and costly psychological factors was an unintended consequence of anointing certain psychological costs as "special" because of their significance to social cognition and their often surprising nature. Special and unique variables were then identified as the sources of these "special" costs. They were distinguished from variables that were not related to these "special" costs, such as variables that were the source of psychological benefits. Once again, the problem with this approach was that more fundamental and general principles that were the source of both the costs and the benefits were overlooked. Rather than there being two distinct sets of variables, one set producing costs and one set producing benefits, there is one set of general psychological principles that, because of their inherent functioning, naturally have both costs and benefits (i.e., trade-offs).

I have proposed a "trade-off" perspective on social cognition (see Higgins, 2000b) that differs from these earlier perspectives in highlighting the fact that the *same* social-cognitive principle can have both benefits and costs (see also Kruglanski, 1992; Smith & Mackie, 1995). Historically, there has been a tendency for different researchers to study either the benefits or the costs of these principles and for their research to appear in different social psychological areas—but the trade-offs are inherent to these principles and need to be examined together as part of studying each principle in depth. I believe that more progress would be made in social psychology through examination of the trade-offs of general principles than by separately anointing "special" costly outcomes and "special" beneficial outcomes. Indeed, by basing research on the notion of trade-offs, social psychologists are likely to better understand issues of concern to social psychologists. Let us consider a couple of examples, one from the "cognition of social psychology" and the other from the "social psychology of cognition" (for a fuller discussion, see Higgins, 2000b).


BENEFITS AND COSTS OF ACCESSIBILITY. The historical roots of the cognition of social psychology are found in the Gestalt principles of perception, which emphasized that people's experience is organized (e.g., Lewin, 1951). By connecting one isolated elementary input to other kinds of information, organization provides answers to questions such as, "What is it?" "What's happening?" and "What's going on?" For people to learn from past experiences, knowledge must be stored so that it will be available later to be used in processing. Available knowledge, in turn, varies in its accessibility or activation potential. The accessibility of stored knowledge has been shown to increase when it has been recently or frequently primed (see Higgins, 1996). This is functional because higher accessibility makes it easier to activate stored knowledge, and one would want stored knowledge that is related to a recent or frequent event in one's environment to be easy to reactivate given that a recent or frequent event is more likely to reoccur. Recent or frequent evaluation of objects also increases the accessibility of the association between the object and the evaluation, which is functional because exposure to the object quickly activates the inclination to approach or avoid it (see Fazio, 1986). Stored knowledge that relates to events that are highly valued or are expected to occur also have higher accessibility (e.g., Bruner, 1957). This is functional as well, because one would want stored knowledge to be activated more readily when it relates to things one values in the environment or predicts will occur in the future.

Higher accessibility also has costs, however. Monitoring unwanted thoughts in order to suppress them can itself increase their accessibility, thereby making the thoughts more likely rather than less likely to recur in the future (see, for example, Wegner & Erber, 1992). Simply beginning hypothesis testing or problem solving with a specific hypothesis or anchor as a starting point primes stored knowledge selectively, thereby biasing the process and final conclusion (e.g., Mussweiler & Strack, 1999). In social psychology textbooks, the benefits from attitudes and social learning in general are traditionally treated separately from the costs of biased hypothesis testing and anchoring effects. These benefits and costs, however, can be understood as trade-offs of the same general principle of accessibility.

BENEFITS AND COSTS OF SHARED REALITY. People's reality is mostly social. The reality of our subjective meanings is anchored in the fact that others share the reality. The use of language to communicate, for example, would not be possible if the interactants did not have a shared reality with respect to the lexicon and grammar. In order to survive in the social world, individuals need to become part of a shared reality of norms, roles, identities, and so on that connect them to others and permit mutual understandings and collaborative interactions (Hardin & Higgins, 1996). The reality of our subjective meanings is anchored in the fact that others share the reality (see also Smith & Mackie, 1995).

The fact that social verification transforms subjective experiences into objective realities has costs as well as benefits, however. Brown (1958) suggested that the essential problem with stereotypes was not so much that they were inaccurate generalizations but that they were ethnocentric. Attributes contained in stereotypes, such as "superstitious" or "dirty," are more evaluative than they are descriptive, and as evaluations, they assume that the standards of one's ingroup are objective. Because one's subjective preferences and values have been verified by other ingroup members, one acts as if they have the status of objective truth. Anything different, then, is evaluated negatively. A related cost of shared reality is that by belonging to an ingroup whose members agree with one another and prize their similarity, people's differences with outgroup members are accentuated (Tajfel, Flament, Billig, & Bundy, 1971). Because these differences include perceived values and goals, shared reality within ingroups increases the likelihood of conflict with outgroups. Social psychology textbooks, once again, treat the benefits of shared reality, such as interpersonal communication, separate from the costs of shared reality, such as prejudice and intergroup conflict. These benefits and costs, however, can be understood as trade-offs of the same general principle of shared reality.

## Concluding Remarks

In addition to Bill McGuire's seven koans for the yin and yang of progress in social psychology, I have proposed an eighth koan: A variable anointed as "special" will demand special treatment. Given the pervasiveness of the "about-ness" principle in people's social cognitions, it is not surprising that social psychologists tend to assign special status to a specific explanatory variable when trying to understand a social phenomenon they consider to be "special." I have discussed three different ways in which social psychologists have done this. First, social psychologists have constructed special explanatory variables to account for "special" phenomena they observed when there were more general psychological principles that could account both for the original phenomena and for exceptions to those phenomena. Second, social psychologists have developed unique social psychological explanatory principles to account for what they regard as their own "special" social psychological phenomena when there are general psychological principles that manifest themselves not only in variabil-ity across situations (social psychology) but also in variability across persons (personality). Third, social psychologists have proposed distinct sets of vari-ables to account for special costly phenomena and for special beneficial phe-nomena when the same set of general psychological principles has functional trade-offs that can account for both the costs and the benefits.

If there is a general lesson to be learned from these cases, it is that progress in social psychology would be enhanced if social psychologists reduced the tendency to anoint fascinating or surprising phenomena as "special," which then requires special treatment in theory construction. A "special" phenomenon need not have its own "special" explanatory variable. The fascinating thing that social psychologists represent a phenomenon as being *about* need not be reflected in the source of the phenomenon. The fasci-nating phenomenon of people underestimating the impact of situational forces, for example, need not be caused by a "fundamental attribution error." The same general psychological principle could account for both a surprising phenomenon and the less surprising exceptions to it. The fact that, as social psychologists, we find some phenomena and psychological issues more fasci-nating than others and in this sense consider them "special," should not con-strain us as theoreticians. To make progress in social psychology, we need to examine the nature and functioning of these general principles and investi-gate their implications beyond the social psychological phenomena that ini-tially captured our attention.

My suggestion is that social psychologists reduce our tendency to anoint fascinating or surprising phenomena as "special." I am not suggesting that we eliminate it: Like everything else, this tendency has benefits as well as costs, not the least of which is that "special" phenomena excite and motivate social psychologists to do more research and attract others to study social psychology. By increasing their understanding of the general principles underlying these phenomena, however, social psychologists can more effectively use them to grapple with the issues that so fascinate and concern them. After all, a phe-nomenon should be no less fascinating or surprising simply because the general principle that underlies it also underlies more mundane phenomena.

# References

Brown, R. W. (1958). *Words and things.* New York: Free Press.

Bruner, J. S. (1957). On perceptual readiness. *Psychological Review, 64,* 123–152.

Chaiken, S., & Trope, Y. (1999). *Dual-process theories in social psychology.* New York: Guilford Press.

Dawes, R. M. (1976). Shallow psychology. In J. S. Carroll and J. W. Payne (Eds.), *Cognition and social behavior* (pp. 3–11). Hillsdale, NJ: Erlbaum.

Fazio, R. H. (1986). How do attitudes guide behavior? In R. M. Sorrentino & E. T. Higgins (Eds.), *Handbook of motivation and cognition: Foundations of social behavior* (pp. 204–243). New York: Guilford.

Festinger, L. (1957). *A theory of cognitive dissonance.* Evanston, IL: Row, Peterson.

Freud, S. (1961). The ego and the id. In J. Strachey (Ed. and Trans.), *Standard edition of the complete psychological works of Sigmund Freud* (Vol. 19, pp. 3–66). London: Hogarth Press. (Original work published 1923)

Hardin, C., & Higgins, E. T. (1996). Shared reality: How social verification makes the subjective objective. In R. M. Sorrentino & E. T. Higgins (Eds.), *Handbook of motivation and cognition, Volume 3: The interpersonal context* (pp. 28–84). New York: Guilford Press.

Hastie, R., & Kumar, P. (1979). Person memory: Personality traits as organizing principles in memory for behaviors. *Journal of Personality and Social Psychology, 37,* 25–38.

Higgins, E. T. (1990). Personality, social psychology, and person-situation relations: Standards and knowledge activation as a common language. In L. A. Pervin (Ed.), *Handbook of personality* (pp. 301–338). New York: Guilford Press.

Higgins, E. T. (1996). Knowledge activation: Accessibility, applicability, and salience. In E. T. Higgins & A. W. Kruglanski (Eds.), *Social psychology: Handbook of basic principles* (pp. 133–168). New York: Guilford.

Higgins, E. T. (1997). Biases in social cognition: "Aboutness" as a general principle. In C. McGarty & S. A. Haslam (Eds.), *The message of social psychology* (pp. 182–199). Cambridge, MA: Blackwell.

Higgins, E. T. (1998). The aboutness principle: A pervasive influence on human inference. *Social Cognition, 16,* 173–198.

Higgins, E. T. (1999). Persons and situations: Unique explanatory principles or variability in general principles? In D. Cervone and Y. Shoda (Eds.), *The coherence of personality: Social-cognitive bases of consistency, variability, and organization* (pp. 61–93). New York: Guilford.

Higgins, E. T. (2000a). Does personality provide unique explanations for behavior? Personality as cross-person variability in general principles. *European Journal of Personality, 14,* 391–406.

Higgins, E. T. (2000b). Social cognition: Learning about what matters in the social world. *European Journal of Social Psychology, 30,* 3–39.

Higgins, E. T., & Bargh, J. A. (1987). Social cognition and social perception. *Annual Review of Psychology, 38,* 369–425.

Higgins, E. T., Rholes, W. S., & Jones, C. R. (1977). Category accessibility and impression formation. *Journal of Experimental Social Psychology, 13,* 141–154.

Jones, E. E. (1979). The rocky road from acts to dispositions. *American Psychologist, 34,* 107–117.

Jones, E. E., & Harris, V. A. (1967). The attribution of attitudes. *Journal of Experimental Social Psychology, 3,* 1–24.

Kelly, G. A. (1955). The psychology of personal constructs. New York: W. W. Norton.

Kruglanski, A. W. (1992). On methods of good judgment and good methods of judgment: Political decisions and the art of the possible. *Political Psychology, 13,* 455–475.

Kuiper, N. A., & Rogers, T. B. (1979). Encoding of personal information: Self-other differences. *Journal of Personality and Social Psychology, 37,* 499–512.

Lewin, K. (1951). *Field theory in social science.* New York: Harper.

Markus, H. (1977). Self-schemata and processing information about the self. *Journal of Personality and Social Psychology, 35,* 63–78.

McClelland, D. C., Atkinson, J. W., Clark, R. A., & Lowell, E. L. (1953). *The achievement motive.* New York: Appleton-Century-Crofts.

McGuire, W. J. (1973). The yin and yang of progress in social psychology: Seven koan. *Journal of Personality and Social Psychology, 26,* 446–456.

McGuire, W. J. (1999). *Constructing social psychology: Creative and critical processes.* New York: Cambridge University Press.

Milgram, S. (1974). *Obedience to authority*. New York: Harper & Row.

Miller, J. G. (1984). Culture and the development of everyday social explanation. *Journal of Personality and Social Psychology, 46,* 961–978.

Mussweiler, T., & Strack, F. (1999). Comparing is believing: A selective accessibility model of judgmental anchoring. In W. Stroebe & M. Hewstone (Eds.), *European review of social psychology* (Vol. 10, pp. 135–167). New York: John Wiley & Sons.

Quattrone, G. A. (1982). Overattribution and unit formation: When behavior engulfs the person. *Journal of Personality and Social Psychology, 42,* 593–607.

Ross, L. (1977). The intuitive psychologist and his shortcomings: Distortions in the attribution process. In L. Berkowitz (Ed.), *Advances in Experimental Social Psychology* (Vol. 10, pp. 173–220). New York: Academic Press.

Smith, E. R., & Mackie, D. M. (1995). *Social psychology*. New York: Worth.

Tajfel, H., Flament, C., Billig, M., & Bundy, R. P. (1971). Social categorization and intergroup behavior. *European Journal of Social Psychology, 1,* 149–178.

Taylor, S. E., & Fiske, S. T. (1975). Point of view and perceptions of causality. *Journal of Personality and Social Psychology, 32,* 439–445.

Wegner, D. M., & Erber, R. (1992). The hyperaccessibility of suppressed thoughts. *Journal of Personality and Social Psychology, 63,* 903–912.

# Appendix: Perspectivist Worksheets for Generating a Program of Research

## *William J. McGuire*

### WORKSHEET, page 1

Page 1 (or a photocopy of it) is due, filled out, at Class Meeting 2. It will be returned to you with comments at Meeting 3.

In carrying out the assignments on each page, it will help to read the assigned pages in McGuire, W. J. (1989). A Perspectivist approach to the strategic planning of programmatic scientific research. In B. Gholson, W. R. Shadish, Jr., R. A. Neimeyer, & A.C. Houts (Eds.), *Psychology of Science: contributions to metascience* (pp. 214-245). NY: Cambridge University Press. At the outset read pp. 214-226 on Perspectivism, a psychology of science that lies behind these Worksheet exercises.

### I. Selecting Personality/Social Variables for Your Research Program

A.  The purpose of page 1 of the Worksheet is to get you started thinking about a variety of promising personality/social variables, one of which may serve as the focus of your research program. See McGuire, W.J. (1989), pp. 214-229; especially pp. 226-229.

   1.  A personality/social variable is a dimension of thought, feeling, or action on which people differ.

   2.  This Worksheet will guide your designing a research program, including an initial experiment that explores the theoretical contexts of your initial hypothesis. Your initial hypothesis is a statement that predicts how peoples' positions on your selected personality/social variable *A* will be related to their positions on some other variable *B*. (*B* may or may not be itself a personality/social variable; it may be an antecedent, consequent, or concomitant of the personality/social variable *A* to which you are predicting it will be related.)

B.  Discuss three initial nominees for personality/social variable *A* on which you might focus your research program.

   1.  Describe a variable that might serve as your variable *A* in this study: (a) give several labels for it, underlining the best label; (b) give a (formal) definition of it; (c) give a few self-descriptive questions, responses to which could be used to measure where persons fall on it; and (d) mention some variable *B*s that you hypothesize might be interestingly related to this personality/social variable $A_1$.

(a) _____

(b) _____

(c) _____

(d) _____

   2.  Discuss a, b, c, and d, as above for an alternative variable $A_2$ on which you might focus your individual project.

(a) _____

(b) _____

(c) _____

(d) _____

   3.  Report a, b, c, and d for a third candidate for a promising personality/social variable $A_3$ around which to construct a research program.

(a) _____

(b) _____

(c) _____

(d) _____

Dr. McGuire can be reached at Department of Psychology, Yale University, New Haven, CT, 06520-8205, USA.

# WORKSHEET, page 2

Pages 2 and 3 are due, filled out, at Class Meeting 4. They will be returned to you with comments at Meeting 5.

## II. Proposed Hypothesis on Which You Might Focus Your Research Program
(Read McGuire, 1989, pp. 226-229)

A.  Select a personality/social variable $A$ that interests you. It may be, but need not be, one of the three "$A$" variables that you designated on page 1 of this Worksheet. In choosing, take into account my comments on your page 1 proposals.

1.  What is your tentative label for the personality/social variable you have selected? _____

    a.  Define this variable $A$ in a sentence or two. _____

    _____

    _____

    b.  Give several other variable $A$ labels that are synonymous to the II $A$ 1 label. _____

    _____

    c.  List several other labels that are close to synonymous but not quite what you mean. Indicate for each label how it is less apt than the one you will use. _____

    _____

2.  If it becomes necessary to divide this variable $A$ into two separately measured subvariables, which two are they likely to be? Give each subvariable ($a$ and $b$) a label and a definition.

    Subvariable $a$._____

    Subvariable $b$. _____

3.  Write out three questionnaire self-descriptive statements that could be used to measure your variable $A$.
    a. _____

    b. _____

    c. _____

4.  See McGuire, 1989, pp. 227-228, for additional word games to be played at this point to clarify variable $A$.

5.  Why do you regard this variable $A$ as worthy of your choice as the one on which you will develop a research program?

    _____

    _____

    _____

6.  Give a considered formal definition of this variable $A$._____

    _____

# WORKSHEET, page 3

Pages 2 and 3 are due, filled out, at Class Meeting 4. They will be returned to you with comments at Meeting 5.

B.  Now select a second variable, **B**, that you are hypothesizing will be related interestingly to the variable *A* you designated on page 2.

    1.  What is a label for this variable **B**? Give several synonymous labels for it:_____

        a.  Describe **B** in a sentence._____

          _____

        b.  Give several other labels that are close but not as good as the II **B** 1 labels. How does each fall short?

          _____

          _____

        c.  Describe how you would measure this variable **B** . _____

          _____

C.  For simplicity, start this exercise by hypothesizing a simple monotonic, main effect (see McGuire, 1989, p. 231) relation between variables *A* and *B*, above. (If you judge *A* and *B* variables' relation to be nonmonotonic or to involve an interaction rather than main effect, then go back to pages 1 and 2 and choose another variable *A* or *B* that does so relate.)

    1.  Do you predict variable *A* to be related to variable *B* positively or negatively? Word the hypothesis so that the direction will be clear._____

          _____

    2.  Word the hypothesis to maximize positivity in its three components (the *IV*, the *DV*, and the predicted relation between them), wording each of the three in as affirmative as possible terminology._____

          _____

    3.  Why do you think these variables are related in this way ? That is, give a theory, an explanation that accounts for the relation._____

          _____

    4.  Why do you think this relation is sufficiently uncertain so that it needs testing?_____

          _____

    5.  What context variables do you think might limit, accentuate, or change direction of the hypothesized relation? (See McGuire, 1989, p. 232).

          _____

          _____

    6.  What changes in our abstract thinking or concrete action would be called for, depending on whether this research confirms versus disconfirms your hypothesis?_____

          _____

          _____

## WORKSHEET, page 4

Pages 4 and 5 are due, filled out, at Class Meeting 6. They will be returned to you with comments at Meeting 7.

### III. Expressing Your Hypotheses in Multiple Modalities
(Read McGuire, 1989, pp. 229-232)

At this point, considering your current thinking and what was said on pages 1 to 3, decide on an initial hypothesis on which you want to center your research program.

A. Express your hypothesis (your predicted $IV_1 \rightarrow DV_1$ relation) in words. It should be a simple but interesting hypothesis, predicting a monotonic (unidirectional), main-effect relation between a single independent variable ($IV_1$) and a single dependent variable ($DV_1$). At least one of the variables should be a personality/social variable. Phrase each variable as continuous and affirmative, where possible.

   1. Express the hypothesis verbally._____

_____

   2. In the above verbal expression, put parentheses around the independent variable ($IV_1$) and brackets around the dependent variable [$DV_1$].

B. Below, express this hypothesis verbally, symbolically, pictorially, tabularly, and statistically for each of the three scaling cases indicated. Please write small but legibly.

| Modality of expression \ Scaling Case | (1) *IV*, continuous; *DV*, continuous | (2) *IV*, dichotomous; *DV*, continuous | (3) *IV*, dichotomous; *DV*, dichotomous |
|---|---|---|---|
| a. Verbal (Formalized) | | | |
| b. Symbolic | | | |
| c. Graphical High values up and to the right) | | | |
| d. Tabular High value to the right) | | | |
| e. Statistical, descriptive and inferential | | | |

# WORKSHEET, page 5

Pages 4 and 5 are due, filled out, at Class Meeting 6. They will be returned to you with comments at Meeting 7.

## IV. Informally Stating Theories That Could Account for the Relations Predicted in Your III A Initial Hypotheses and in Its Contrary.
(Read McGuire, 1989, pp. 234-235.)

A.  The task here involves your generating theories from which your III A hypothesis (page 4) can be derived. Most scientific researchers agree that they should postulate a theory from which their initial hypothesis can be inferred. This Worksheet exercise, being based on a Perspectivist psychology of science (McGuire, 1989), goes further in two regards. (1) One theory is not enough—you should propose two-plus quite different theories that can account for your initial hypothesis, and (2) you should have two-plus additional theories that account for the contrary hypothesis. (Contrary hypotheses are those that include the same two variables, $IV_1$ and $DV_1$ but predict the opposite relation between them, e.g., $IV_1 \xrightarrow{+} DV_1$ versus $IV_1 \xrightarrow{-} DV_1$).

1.  Consider the initial hypothesis that you stated in III A on page 4 and describe a broader theory from which this hypothesis can be derived as one of the theory's implications, a theory that accounts for (explains) the initially hypothesized $IV_1 \xrightarrow{+} DV_1$ relation.

    _____

    _____

2.  Now describe a second broad theory, quite different from your IV A 1 theory above, from which that same III A 1 hypothesis can be derived.

    _____

    _____

B.  State a hypotheses that makes the prediction contrary to the one stated in III A1 on page 4, that is, that predicts the contrary relation between the same two variables, $IV_1 \xrightarrow{-} DV_1$._____

    _____

C.  Generating theories from which this contrary IV B hypothesis can be derived:

1.  Describe a broad theory from which this contrary hypothesis, IV B, can be derived.

    _____

    _____

2.  Describe a second theoretical explanation, quite different from the one just described in IV C 1, from which this contrary IV B hypothesis can also be derived._____

    _____

    _____

## WORKSHEET, page 6

Pages 6 and 7 are due, filled out, at Class Meeting 8. They will be returned to you with comments at Meeting 9.

### V. Syllogistically Formalizing (Mediational) Theories
(Read McGuire, 1989, pp. 235-236)

Pages 6 and 7 of this Worksheet are designed to provide practice in restating your theories more formally (page 6) and stating them in multiple modalities (page 7). On page 5 you expressed your theories informally. Here in Section V you are asked to restate theories formally as syllogistic arguments. Such a formalization provides checks on the adequacy of your theory and helps untangle and test alternative theoretical explanations for your initial hypothesis ($IV_1 \rightarrow DV_1$) by creatively generating additional distinctive mediational hypotheses (considered in this Section V) and distinctive interactional hypotheses (considered in Section VII, page 8).

A. Express your initial monotonic main-effect hypothesis in words in the form $IV_1 \xrightarrow{\ r\ } DV_1$. Express each variable as continuous and as affirmative, where feasible. _____

B. Formalize syllogistically one of your explanatory theories on page 5 in mediational form that accounts for your initially hypothesized relation ($IV_1 \rightarrow DV_1$) asserted in V A above in terms of a mediating variable ($MV_1$). The syllogism's conclusion is the hypothesis to be explained; its two premises are the explanation.

1. State the minor premise ($IV_1 \rightarrow MV_1$) _____

   _____

2. State the major premise ($MV_1 \rightarrow DV_1$)_____

   _____

3. State the conclusion (the above Section V A hypothesis, $IV_1 \rightarrow DV_1$). _____

   _____

C. Functions of formalization. Formalization is often disparaged as mere tidying up or even as creativity-stifling but it can satisfy at least a half-dozen needs:

1. It allows determining if the theory is a valid explanation of the hypothesis.
   (a) Variables check: In explanation V B above is $IV_1$ the subject of both the minor premise and of the conclusion_____? Is $DV_1$ the predicate of both the major premise and of the conclusion_____? Is $MV_1$ the subject of the major and predicate of the minor premise_____?

   (b) Relations check: if the directions of relations of the two premises are the same (both affirmative or both negative) is the conclusion's relation affirmative_____? If the two premises have oppositely signed relations, does the conclusion have a negative relation_____?

2. It provides a check for tautology. Is $MV_1$ nonoverlapping with $IV_1$_____? With $DV_1$_____? To the extent that there is overlapping, then the theory merely repeats the hypothesis rather than explaining it.

3. Its formalization allows plausibility checks. How plausible is the minor premise_____? The major premise_____? Insufficient plausibility identifies potential weak points or creative novelties in the theory.

4. It allows clarification of the theory by exploring its $MV_1$'s meaning and label by word games, etc., such as clarified $IV_1$ and $DV_1$ above, in Sections I and II on pages 1 and 2. (See McGuire, 1989, pp. 226-229.)

5. It permits a check of independence of alternative explanations of the hypothesis. Is $MV_1 \neq MV_2$_____?

6. It suggests multiple interaction hypotheses generated by each premise. See Section VII (page 8) and McGuire, 1989, pp. 236-239.

7. It distinguishes two premises that can be separately tested (see McGuire, 1989, pp. 235-236).

# WORKSHEET, page 7

Pages 6 and 7 are due, filled out, at Class Meeting 8. They will be returned to you with comments at Meeting 9.

## VI. Expressing Syllogisticaly Formalized Theories in Multiple Modalities, for Two Common Scaling Cases
(Read McGuire, 1989, pp. 236-238.)

A.  In Section III (page 4) of this Worksheet you expressed your initial *hypothesis* in multiple modalities for each of three common scaling cases. Here you are asked to express one of your *theoretical explanations* of that hypothesis in multiple modalities. Please review the explanation that you have expressed in syllogistic verbal form in Section V B on page 6, and here express it in multiple modalities for each of the two most common scaling cases, *A* and *B*.

1.  For scaling Case A, where: IV, MV, DV are all measured continuously (or on many levels)

    a.  Express this explanation verbally in syllogistic form for scaling case A:

    b.  Express symbolically this mediational explanation for scaling case A.

    c.  Express graphically this mediational explanation for scaling case A.

    d.  Express this explanation tabularly for scaling case A.

    e.  Express this explanation in descriptive and inferential statistical terms.

2.  For scaling Case B, where IV is measured dichotomously and MV and DV continuously (on many levels)

    a.  Express this explanation verbally in syllogistic form for scaling case B:

    b.  Express symbolically this mediational explanation for scaling case B.

    c.  Express graphically this mediational explanation for scaling case B.

    d.  Express this explanation tabularly for scaling case B.

    e.  Express this explanation in descriptive and inferential statistical terms.

B.  You may want to get more experience in formalizing your theories and explaining them in multiple modalities by carrying out Exercise VI (page 7) on still other theories (e.g., Section IV, page 5) accounting for your initial hypothesis or the contrary hypothesis.

## WORKSHEET, page 8

Pages 8, 9, and 10 are due, filled out, at Class Meeting 10. They will be returned to you with comments at Meeting 11.

### VII. Disentangling Theories by Spinning off Distinctive Interaction Hypotheses from the Premises of Each Theory
(Read McGuire, 1989, pp 238-241.)

A.  The purpose of pages 8 and 9 of this Worksheet is to provide you with training in creatively deriving multiple distinctive interaction predictions from each premise of each mediational theory that you generated (e.g., V B on page 6) to explain your initial hypothesis, $IV_1 \rightarrow DV_1$ (e.g., Section V A on page 6).

   1.  An interactional hypothesis is one that identifies an additional independent variable ($_iIV$) that multiplies an initially hypothesized relation ($IV_1 \rightarrow DV_1$). The interaction prediction is usefully expressed symbolically as either $_iIV \times (IV_1 \rightarrow DV)$ or ($_iIV \times IV_1) \rightarrow DV_1$. Note that for $_iIV$ to be an interactional variable, it is not necessary that $_iIV$ itself has a main effect on $DV_1$: What is crucial for its interactional status is whether $IV_1$'s relation to $DV_1$ is affected by the level of $_iIV$.

   2.  You should begin by stating one or more of your theoretical explanations in syllogistic form (i.e., $IV_1 \rightarrow MV_1$; $MV_1 \rightarrow DV_1$; therefore, $IV_1 \rightarrow DV_1$), as you practiced on pages 6 and 7.

   3.  When a given theoretical explanation for the initial hypothesis ($IV_1 \rightarrow DV_1$) is stated as a formal syllogistic argument (i.e., $IV_1 \rightarrow MV_1$; $MV_1 \rightarrow DV_1$; therefore $IV_1 \rightarrow DV_1$) each premise, the minor premise ($IV_1 \rightarrow MV_1$) and the major premise ($MV_1 \rightarrow DV_1$), can be used creatively to generate distinctive interactional hypotheses. Each premise can be used to generate both dispositional and situational interaction hypotheses, whose $_iIV$s multiply that premise's relation and therefore also multiply the conclusion's relation (which is your initial hypothesis, $IV_1 \rightarrow DV_1$). For example, if $_iIV$ interacts with the minor premises, $_iIV \times (IV_1 \rightarrow MV_1)$, it interacts also with the initial hypothesis, the conclusion of the syllogistic explanation, $_iIV \times (IV_1 \rightarrow DV_1)$.

   4.  By generating for each theory one or more distinctive interacting independent variables ($_iIV$) that follow from the given explanatory theory but not from alternative explanatory theories that account for your initial hypothesis, then the distinctive $_iIV$s suggested by each of the alternative explanations can be added to the experimental design to investigate, not only if the initial hypothesis obtains, but also for which theoretical reasons it obtains and in what conditions it especially obtains. That is, the addition of the interacting variable allows testing both the hypothesis itself and the theoretical explanation of it that implies the interaction.

B.  To give you practice on generating and exploiting interaction variables, you are asked here to work with a theory from page 5 other than V B (on page 6) that accounts for your initial hypothesis ($IV_1 \rightarrow DV_1$). Restate here this initial hypothesis from page 5.

_____

C.  Please state in syllogistic form another explanatory theory, different from explanation V B on page 6, that accounts for this hypothesis $IV_1 \rightarrow DV_1$, on the basis of an alternative mediational variable, $MV_2$.

   1.  Minor premise ($IV_1 \rightarrow MV_2$)_____

   _____

   2.  Major premise ($MV_2 \rightarrow DV_1$)_____

   _____

   3.  Conclusion ($IV_1 \rightarrow DV_1$, your initial V A hypothesis)_____

   _____

# WORKSHEET, page 9

Pages 8, 9, and 10 are due, filled out, at Class Meeting 10. They will be returned to you with comments at Meeting 11.

D. Consider this VII C alternative theory (p. 8) that explains your initial hypothesis, $IV_1 \rightarrow DV_1$ and focus on its major premise (VII C 2 on page 8) and please generate an interacting independent variable ($_iIV$) suggested by this major premise that would multiply the major premise's relation, $MV_2 \rightarrow DV_1$, and therefore would also multiply the initially hypothesized relation, $IV_1 \rightarrow DV_1$.

1. To keep it conveniently available, please restate the major premise ($MV_2 \rightarrow DV_1$), VII C 2 on page 8 of this second theory to account for the initial hypothesis._____

_____

2. Now generate an interacting situational variable ($_iIV_s$) that will multiply the relation in this major premise, $MV_2 \rightarrow DV_1$. A "situational" variable, in contrast to a "dispositional" variable, is a dimension on which people's environments (as opposed to the persons themselves) tend to differ.

   a. Label and define this interacting situational variable ($_iIV_s$)._____

   _____

   b. Indicate verbally the direction, positive versus negative, enhancing or reducing, in which this $_iIV_s$ will multiply the major premise, $MV_2 \rightarrow DV_1$, and therefore also will multiply the initially hypothesized relation ($IV_1 \rightarrow DV_1$).

   _____

   _____

   c. Explain why $_iIV_s$ will so interact with $IV_1$ by affecting how $MV_2$ relates to $DV_1$ given that the VII C theory on page 8 is correct._____

   _____

   _____

   d. Express this $_iIV \times (MV_2 \rightarrow DV_1)$ interaction prediction in graphical form (assume dichotomous $IV_1$ and dichotomous $_iIV_s$ and continuous (multi-leveled) measured $DV_1$).

   e. Express this interaction prediction in tabular form. Again, assume that $IV_1$ and $_iIV_s$ is each dichotomously measured and $DV_1$ is measured continuously (multi-leveled).

   f. Express this interaction prediction in statistical form, descriptive and inferential.

   g. Express this interaction prediction in statistical form, descriptive and inferential.

3. You may want to get more experience in identifying and using interaction hypotheses for knowledge generation by carrying out this "D" exercise on other premises of the same theory and on the premises of other theories, and using both situational and dispositional interacting variables.

# WORKSHEET, page 10

Pages 8, 9, and 10 are due, filled out, at Class Meeting 10.  They will be returned to you with comments at Meeting 11.

### VIII. Generating Explanatory Theories ( and Their Implications) for the Contrary Hypothesis

A. State a hypothesis that predicts a relation between your  initial $IV_1$ and $DV_1$ and that is the exact contrary relation to that asserted in your initial hypothesis ,VII B on page 8.  [This contrary hypothesis will have the identical $IV_1$ and $DV_1$ as did your initial hypothesis but will posit the opposite (positive vs. negative) relation between them.]

_____

B. State formally in terms of a minor and a major premise a broader mediational theory from which this contrary hypothesis can be derived.
  1.  Minor premise ($IV_1 \overset{+/-}{\rightarrow} MV_c$):_____

_____

  2.  Major premise ($MV_c \overset{+/-}{\rightarrow} DV_1$):_____

_____

  3.  Describe the mediating variable, $MV_c$, implied by this theory._____

_____

C. Depict by a series of graphs the theorized role of this mediator in accounting for the hypothesized contrary relation.

D. Express in tabular form the theorized role of this mediator in accounting for the hypothesized contrary relation.

E. Generate an interaction hypothesis.
  1.  Describe an additional variable, $_iIV_3$, either a situational or dispositional variable, which the VIII B theory above predicts will interact with the $IV_1$, multiplying the contrary hypothesis: $_iIV_3 \times (IV_1 \rightarrow DV_1)$.

_____

_____

  2.  Depict this predicted interaction graphically and in tabular form.
  a.  Graphical Depiction                                    b.  Tabular Depiction

  3.  Explain how theory VIII B predicts this E 1 interaction effect._____

_____

# WORKSHEET, page 11

Pages 11 and 12 are due, filled out, at Class Meeting 12.   They will be returned to you with comments at Meeting 13.

### IX. Selecting Ten-Plus Variables for the Design of Your First Experiment (and a Review)

The preceding pages 1-10 of this Worksheet guided your use of a Perspectivist (McGuire, 1989) approach through the a priori conceptual phase of sketching out the domain of your research program. Here on page 11 the Worksheet exercises start providing guidance toward the a posteriori empirical phase of your research program by directing you through designing the first experiment in your research program.

Deciding on the experimental design of this first empirical study in your research program calls for your selecting the variables that will enter this first experiment: that is, deciding on the variables on which the units of observation (e.g., the participating persons) are to be measured and between which variables you will be calculating whether the hypothesized relations obtain.

In using a Perspectivist approach to laying out the conceptual phase of your research program on pages 1-10 you evoked, actually or potentially, dozens of variables of at least six logical types. These include at least one independent variable ($IV_1$) and one dependent variable ($DV_1$) that entered into your initial and contrary hypotheses. Mediating variables are a third type ($MV_n$), including at least two for alternative theoretical explanations that account for your initial hypothesis and at least two ($_cMV_n$) for alternative theories accounting for the contrary hypothesis. Fourthly, several interaction variables ($_lIV$) are suggested of the dispositional type and several of the situational type by each premise of each theory that accounts for your initial hypothesis or its contrary. A fifth type of variable includes large numbers of extraneous variables that might be controlled to lessen the ambiguity of the results. Finally, exploratory variables might be included to discover serendipitous relations (e.g., easily measured sex of participant may be introduced by your participant-selection procedures or the rotation of material may introduce order variables).

This initial tour of the horizon reveals in principle, across the six types of variables, several dozen promising variables from among which you can choose approximately 10 for your initial experimental design.   Criteria for choice of the initial set of variables include the variables' entry into crucial relations, how easy it is to measure the participants on the variables, how varied the participants will be on these variables, and so on.

Here pages 11 to 13 of the Worksheet will guide you in selecting a set of 10 variables to be included in your first experiment, a set large enough to be interesting and to promise creative discovery of new relations as well as critical testing of the already hypothesized relations.  The Worksheet proposes that you include at least the independent and dependent variables that make up your initial hypothesis and its contrary, at least two theories ($MV_1$ and $MV_2$) that account for the initial hypothesis, at least two theories ($_cMV_3$ and $_cMV_4$) that account for the contrary hypothesis, and at least one interaction variable implied uniquely by each of these four theories.  Hence, your initial experiment would include at least ten variables as follows.

A.  Regarding your basic hypothesis to be investigated, $IV_1 \rightarrow DV_1$.

1. State a new hypothesis to be investigated ($IV_1 \rightarrow DV_1$)._____

_____

2. What is the dependent variable ($DV_1$), the variable to which you are predicting?_____

_____

3. Describe how you will measure this dependent variable.  Give specific examples._____

_____

_____

_____

4. How will the $DV_1$ measure be scaled (e.g., nominally, two-leveled, continuously, etc.)?_____

## WORKSHEET, page 12

Pages 11 and 12 are due, filled out, at Class Meeting 12.  They will be returned to you with comments at Meeting 13.

B.  To test your initial hypothesis and its contrary, the experimental design of your first study should include also the independent variable, $IV_1$ .

    1. What is the independent variable ($IV_1$) of your hypothesis, the variable from which you are predicting?

_____

    2. Describe how you will measure this $IV_1$.  Give specific examples._____

_____

_____

    3. How will this $IV_1$ measure be scaled (e.g., nominally, dichotomously, continuously, etc.)?_____

C.  Regarding your first explanatory theory for your initial hypothesis:

    1. State in the form of minor and major premises a broader theory from which your initial hypothesis can be derived:

        a.  Minor premise ($IV_1 \rightarrow MV_1$):_____

        b.  Major premise ($MV_1 \rightarrow DV_1$):_____

    2. Label and define the mediating variable ($MV_1$) in this first theory. _____

_____

    3. Depict by a series of graphs and in tabular form the theorized role of this mediator in accounting for the hypothesized $IV_1 \rightarrow DV_1$ relation.

        a.  Graphical depiction of this $MV_1$ theory        b.  Expression of this $MV_1$ theory in tabular (and descriptive statistical) form

    4. Describe an interactional variable, $_iIV_1$ , that your $MV_1$ (C 1) theory predicts will interact with the $IV_1$ of your initial hypothesis in affecting the hypothesis' dependent variable, $DV_1$ .

_____

    5. Depict the interaction relation $_iIV_1 \times (IV_1 \rightarrow DV_1)$ predicted in C 4 in graphical and in tabular forms.

    a.  Graphical form        b.  Tabular (and descriptive statistical) form

6. Explain how your $MV_1$ theory in Section C 1, above, predicts this C 4 interaction effect. ( Indicate which premise implies the interaction and how.)

_____

_____

# WORKSHEET, page 13

Pages 13 and 14 are due, filled out, at Class Meeting 14. They will be returned to you with comments at Meeting 15.

D. A second explanatory theory to account for your new initial hypothesis ($IV_1 \xrightarrow{+} DV_1$).

   1. State in the form of minor and major premises this theory, different from the C 1 theory on page 12, from which your hypothesis can be derived:
      a. Minor premise ($IV_1 \rightarrow MV_2$):_____

      b. Major premise ($MV_2 \rightarrow DV_1$):_____

   2. Describe an additional interactional variable, $_iIV_2$, that your second, D 1 theory predicts will interact with the $IV_1$ of your hypothesis in affecting your hypothesis' dependent variable, $DV_1$.

      _____

E. Regarding a first explanatory theory to account for the hypothesis contrary ($IV_1 \xrightarrow{-} DV_1$) to your initial hypothesis

   1. State this theory formalized as minor and major premise. It should be different from the IX C and IX D theories.
      a. Minor premise ($IV_1 \rightarrow _cMV_3$):_____

      b. Major premise ($_cMV_3 \rightarrow DV_1$):_____

   2. Label and define the mediating variable, $_cMV_3$, introduced by this IX E theory._____

      _____

   3. Depict by a series of graphs this mediational theory ($_cMV_3$) that accounts for the contrary hypothesis.   4. Depict in tabular form this $_cMV_3$ theory that accounts for the contrary hypothesis.

   5. Label and define an interactional variable, $_iIV_3$, suggested by this IX E theory as multiplying the relation in your contrary hypothesis IV$_1$ $\xrightarrow{-}$ DV$_1$._____

      _____

F. Think of a second explanatory theory, quite different from IX E 1 above, that accounts for your contrary hypothesis:

   1. Label and define the mediating variables, $_cMV_4$, implied by this theory._____

      _____

   2. Label and define an interacting variable, $_iIV_4$, implied by this theory._____

      _____

G. Describe three extraneous variables ($CV_1$, $CV_2$, $CV_3$) that especially need controlling, and why and how:

   1. _____

   2. _____

   3. _____

# WORKSHEET, page 14

Pages 13 and 14 are due, filled out, at Class Meeting 14. They will be returned to you with comments at Meeting 15.

### X. Procedures for Collecting and Analyzing the Data and for Writing the Report

Here you are asked to think over and describe when and how you will collect the data (i.e., measure the participants on the variables), analyze these data to measure the relations among the variables, and interpret and report these results.

A. Participants

1. What sources of participants will you use and how will they be recruited?_____

_____

2. About how many participants and why this number?_____

3. What possible stresses on the participants call for special concern and how might these risks be mitigated?

_____

4. What other interests of the participants especially need safeguarding, why and how?

a. _____

b. _____

B. Statistics, descriptive and inferential, needed for estimating the size of various types of predicted relations.

1. Describe the statistics to be used for estimating the size of the relation predicted in the initial hypothesis (or its contrary) $IV_1 \rightarrow DV_1$.

_____

_____

2. Describe the statistics to be used for estimating the extent to which the various theories account for these hypotheses, $IV_1 \rightarrow MV_1 \rightarrow DV_1$. _____

_____

3. Describe the statistics to be used for estimating the size of the interaction effects predicted by explanatory theories, $IV_1 \times (IV_1 \rightarrow DV_1)$. _____

_____

C. Timing

1. Within what dates will you be collecting the data (i.e., measuring participants on the variables)?_____

2. Within what dates will you be analyzing the data (i.e., determining how the participants' scores on one variable are related to their scores on other variables in the design?)_____

3. By what date will you complete a first written draft of the report?_____

4. When will you complete the final draft and submit it?_____

D. What style guide will you use in writing your report?_____

# Index

# About the Editors

**John T. Jost, PhD,** received his doctorate from Yale University (1995) as the last graduate student of William J. McGuire. He taught at Stanford University until 2003 before moving to New York University, where he is currently associate professor of psychology. He has been a visiting scholar at the University of California, Santa Barbara; the University of Bologna, Italy; and the Radcliffe Institute for Advanced Study at Harvard University. Dr. Jost has published dozens of scientific articles and book chapters on such topics as stereotyping, prejudice, political ideology, and system justification. He currently serves on editorial boards for *Personality and Social Psychology Bulletin* and *Group Processes and Intergroup Relations* and is the editor of *Social Justice Research*. His awards include the Gordon Allport Intergroup Relations Prize, sponsored by the Society for the Psychological Study of Social Issues, and the SPSP Theoretical Innovation Prize, sponsored by the Society for Personality and Social Psychology. He is coeditor of *The Psychology of Legitimacy* (2001) and *Political Psychology: Key Readings* (2004).

**Mahzarin R. Banaji, PhD,** received her doctorate from Ohio State University (1986) and taught at Yale University until 2001. In 2002, she moved to Harvard University as Richard Clarke Cabot Professor of Social Ethics in the Department of Psychology and Carol K. Pforzheimer Professor at the Radcliffe Institute for Advanced Study. Dr. Banaji has served as secretary of the American Psychological Society, on the Board of Scientific Affairs of the American Psychological Association, and on the Executive Committee of the Society of Experimental Social Psychology. She has been associate editor of *Psychological Review* and the *Journal of Experimental Social Psychology* and is currently coeditor of *Essays in Social Psychology*. Her awards include Yale's Hixon Prize for Teaching Excellence, a James McKeen Cattell Fund Award, and a fellowship from the Guggenheim Foundation. Her work with R. Bhaskar received the Gordon Allport Intergroup Relations Prize. With Anthony Greenwald and Brian Nosek, she maintains a prize-winning educational Web site measuring automatic attitudes, beliefs, and stereotypes (http://implicit.harvard.edu).

**Deborah A. Prentice, PhD,** received her doctorate from Yale University (1989) and began teaching at Princeton University, where she is currently chair of the Department of Psychology. Her research addresses social influence and intergroup relations, especially the ways in which social norms, beliefs, and values influence people's perceptions and behaviors in social contexts. Much of her work has focused on gender, including the ways in which social beliefs and conventions regarding gender serve to reproduce and sustain gender differences and divisions. Dr. Prentice is currently on the Executive Committee of the International Society for Self and Identity and has served on the Society for the Psychological Study of Social Issues Council. She is on the editorial board of *Group Processes and Intergroup Relations* and has been associate editor of the *Journal of Personality and Social Psychology* and is currently on its editorial board. Her awards at Princeton include a Laurence S. Rockefeller

Preceptorship in the Center for Human Values and the President's Award for Distinguished Teaching. She has also received numerous research grants from funding agencies such as the National Institute of Mental Health, the Russell Sage Foundation, and the Andrew W. Mellon Foundation. Prentice is coeditor of *Cultural Divides: Understanding and Overcoming Group Conflict* (1999).